The Hat That Killed
a Billion Birds

ALSO BY ARTHUR G. SHARP
AND FROM MCFARLAND

The Bear *and the* Northland: *Legendary Coast
Guard Cutters in the Alaskan Ice* (2023)

*Let There Be Baseball: The 60-Year Battle
to Legitimize Sunday Play* (2023)

The Hat That Killed a Billion Birds

The Decimation of World Avian Populations for Women's Fashion

Arthur G. Sharp

McFarland & Company, Inc., Publishers
Jefferson, North Carolina

All photographs and illustrations are from the Library of Congress.

ISBN (print) 978-1-4766-9328-6
ISBN (ebook) 978-1-4766-5170-5

LIBRARY OF CONGRESS AND BRITISH LIBRARY
CATALOGUING DATA ARE AVAILABLE

Library of Congress Control Number 2024002632

© 2024 Arthur G. Sharp. All rights reserved

*No part of this book may be reproduced or transmitted in any form
or by any means, electronic or mechanical, including photocopying
or recording, or by any information storage and retrieval system,
without permission in writing from the publisher.*

Front cover image: "The lady of the Mount," by Frederick S. Isham.
Bobbs-Merrill Co., 1908 (Library of Congress); Birds © Shutterstock

Printed in the United States of America

*McFarland & Company, Inc., Publishers
Box 611, Jefferson, North Carolina 28640
www.mcfarlandpub.com*

To all the people, past and present, who have recognized the value of birds in our world. Thanks for stepping in and working to save them so present and future generations may appreciate their songs and services.

Table of Contents

Introduction	1
1. The Birds Start Slipping Away	7
2. How Did It Happen?	12
3. Follow the Money	17
4. Bird Murder and Women's Hats	22
5. Bicycles, Tricycles, and Fashion Cycles	26
6. But Did the Ladies Listen?	35
7. Which Birds Is It Okay to Kill?	42
8. Who Was to Blame?	48
9. Fashion Writers Play a Key Role	53
10. Another Skirmish in the War Between the Sexes	58
11. Editorial License	64
12. Blow Guns, Knives, and Other Cruel Weapons	68
13. There's an Endless Supply of Birds—Isn't There?	74
14. Save the Birds	79
15. The Audubon Society Picks Up the Cudgel	86
16. "Arbird" Day	90
17. Laws Are Literally for the Birds	98
18. Who Owns the Birds?	102
19. The Turning Point Arrives	111
20. Embarrassment Knows No Boundaries	115
21. Regional Rivalries	119

viii Table of Contents

22. The Audubonists' Antithesis	125
23. Reading the Signs	129
24. Silz Courts the Supremes	133
25. Welcome to Finley's World	138
26. Meet Max Schlemmer	143
27. Looking at the Moon Without Rose-Colored Glasses	147
28. Delaware Thanks the Milliners	152
29. The Law of Fashion Prevails	155
30. From Missouri to Massachusetts	162
31. Milliners and Hats Are on Top	167
32. The Milliners Fight Back	172
33. Two Sides to the Story	179
34. The Business of Business	186
35. Calling All Ladies	191
36. White Herons and Birds of Paradise	197
37. The Ostrich	202
38. Game Wardens	208
39. The Hunters	212
40. Birds Don't Have to Die When They Can Be Dyed	216
41. Those Who Refuse to See the Birds for the Trees	219
42. The Campaign Goes International	223
Epilogue: One Good "Tern" Deserves Another	227
Appendix A: Confusing Bird Protection Laws	231
Appendix B: Expansion of the Migratory Bird Treaty Act of 1918	233
Notes	235
Bibliography	247
Index	254

Introduction

"Is there not something incongruous in that the gentler sex, the sex most given to pity and tenderness toward all weak and helpless things, should become the worst enemy of the birds?"[1]

Imagine a world without birds. It could happen. It almost did, roughly between 1880 and 1920, due to the wanton slaughter of birds for millinery purposes. It was the era of murderous millinery and an emerging conflict between the movements for women's rights and animals' rights, when ladies wore high hats, known alternately as bird or theater hats, because they obstructed the views of patrons at operas, plays, and other public performances. Some bird species did not survive the period.

The bird loss was appalling. When the figures of the millinery slaughterhouses were totaled in 1905 for previous years it was amazing that any species remained. Experts estimated that 10,000,000 birds a year were required to supply the women of the United States with suitable hat trimmings. The numbers included 40,000 terns in a single season on Cape Cod, 1,000,000 bobolinks near Philadelphia in a single month, and 20,000 birds sent to New York dealers in four months from one village on Long Island.[2]

England imported between 25,000,000 and 30,000,000 birds a year. One London dealer received from the East Indies alone 400,000 hummingbirds, 6,000 birds of paradise, and 400,000 miscellaneous birds. Altogether, it was estimated that between 200,000,000 and 300,000,000 birds perished each year to trim the hats of the women of the world.[3]

Women, who were stereotyped by the norms of the time as sympathetic and warm-hearted, grew addicted to millinery adorned by birds. They didn't always show sympathy for the creatures perched atop their hats. It was almost a question of which came first, the hat or the bird. Some hats were so garish people wondered whether they were hats with birds on them or dead birds with a few decorations around them.

There was a period when the use of dead birds in millinery was celebrated in a unique manner: some people had their departed pets stuffed and decorated "in memoriam" bonnets with them. That was carrying the craze to extremes in some people's minds.[4]

Some prescient people realized around the turn of the 20th century that humans could impose a horrible burden on their environment if they did not pay attention to how their actions adversely impacted it. Such was the case with the global bird slaughter that ravaged the world in the closing years of the 19th century. Even today some species of birds are disappearing, but not due to a lack of protection or a need for people to wear them on hats.

The ivory-billed woodpecker was declared officially extinct in September 2021. So were Bachman's warbler, a yellow-breasted songbird that migrated between the southeastern United States and Cuba, the Kauai O'o, a Hawaiian forest bird, and eight other birds. Gone, never to return, like the passenger pigeon, the bird of paradise, and at least six other species of birds that became extinct around the turn of the 20th century.[5]

The loss of any endangered bird species has a devastating effect on civilization. But species come and go because of natural evolution. There are times, however, when humans adversely affect natural evolution. That's why passenger pigeons, herons, birds of paradise, and other species disappeared or became endangered in the early 1900s. They were victims of a high hat fad that generated the wanton slaughter of millions of birds, along with tropical beetles, terrapins, and other creatures.

People engaged in strange millinery fads in the late 1800s. Tropical beetles and terrapins on gold chains dangled from women's clothing, little mink boas encircled women's necks and shoulders, live lightning bugs set off women's charms, brilliant chameleons or assorted lizards warmed themselves on the arms or bosom of Parisiennes, stuffed birds sat atop the millinery of fair damsels…. There was a triangular pattern there, comprising women, fashion, and Paris.

Entertainer Lillian Russell (photographed by W.M. Morrison, ca. 1898) wearing a plumed hat typical of the late 1800s.

For women in particular the late 1880s was a fashion contest to see who could employ the most exotic taxidermic as a means of adornment. The use of live insects and reptiles as ornaments was considered *très chic* for a lady of fashion. Often, the trend was set by fashion designers in Paris and then spread across the globe:

> At one time the feminine portion of the haute ton of Paris went wild over lizards, who seemed to be happy. And doubtless the lizard was, too, or if he wasn't under such circumstances he was a very unreasonable beast. The latest fad in this direction has reached New York en route to Kansas City, possibly. Nice little terrapins, imported from Japan, are made prisoners at the behest of fashion and, attached to slender gold chains, are much in vogue as ornaments.
>
> It is said the terrapin is frequently worn with evening dresses, at swell functions, and often astonishes the guests by crawling over the owner's alabaster neck and shoulders. But the terrapin never shows any signs of astonishment and continues his explorations with a calm and unruffled demeanor.
>
> Consider the felicitous lot of those terrapins. Too young to be made into soup; not a care in the world to cause them worry. Nothing to do but eat flies from the hand of a fair mistress, and from the vantage ground of a snowy shoulder look around with disdain, upon envious bipeds of the genus homo.
>
> The terrapin may be slow, but he is not wanting in appreciation, and doubtless considers that such a situation beats sunning one's self on a log in a stagnant lagoon all hollow.[6]

Bert Green's illustration for the March 29, 1911, cover of *Puck* showing a young woman wearing the Middle Eastern pantsuit style typical of women in a harem, topped off with a feathered hat.

4   **Introduction**

The thrust of the article was humorous. In retrospect, the fads may seem ludicrous. Like most fads, they were quickly consigned to the dustbins of history. In the case of birds adorning millinery, the fad lasted 60 long years, during which millions of birds were wantonly slaughtered and entire species exterminated across the globe in a process labeled "murderous millinery."

The 60 years were not continuous, which was why the fad lasted so long. One line, almost unnoticed, demonstrated that. It began, "There is an enormous demand for plume birds by the millinery trade in years when they are in fashion."[7] The hats were in fashion only when Paris designers decided they were. Therefore, the demand for feathers rose and fell according to their whims and the amount of pushback they received from bird protection crusaders.

The bird-wearing custom was a throwback to the barbarous times when women wore nose rings, one scribe declared. The word "barbarous" appeared often in the literature of the murderous millinery era. So did the accusation that women were almost entirely to blame for the fad, which did not set well with them.

"So merciless has been the slaughter of the innocents to provide millinery adornments that certain species of birds have become almost entirely extinct," the scribe continued. "Is it not enough to revolt tender-hearted women? Thousands of women do not realize what a wholesale bird butchery has been necessary to give them a little pleasure."[8]

The fad began innocuously in the United States and ended almost unnoticed, but before it did, it became one of the most controversial in American history. In its early days hats adorned with feathers were not particularly auspicious, and because there were gaps in the timeline when there was no great demand for dead birds, the slaughter went practically unnoticed. Deputy game warden William H. Armstrong of Washington County, Maryland, highlighted that when people began to realize that bird slaughter was a problem. He decreed that the state's newly passed game and fish laws would be enforced and he appealed to citizens to observe them.

"A momentous crisis has come concerning the decimation of birds, the guardians of fields and orchards," he said, to which he added a significant question: "Are the ways of Providence or of women to win?"

Armstrong offered a history lesson and a warning, both of which were at the heart of the bird slaughter crisis:

> The bonnet of the grandmother was simple, sensible and civilized. Its decorations were composed of a few ribbons and flowers. But the headgear of women today is a grotesque illustration of savagism; its chief element, consisting of feathers, is something so excessive that it represents the whole bird section of a zoological museum.
>
> Entire species of the most useful of the feathered tribe have been nearly exterminated. Weed-seeds and harmful insects have enormously increased and not only the comfort, but the material interests, of man have been seriously affected. There is a veritable revisitation of the plagues of Pharaoh.[9]

Perhaps he was being a bit hyperbolic. Most people prior to 1898 had not had a problem with displaying nature in the form of birds, a few feathers, and game animals on millinery. Legislative bodies, especially at the federal level, were not very concerned. Dr. T.S. Palmer, a government assistant in charge of game preservation and biological survey, made that clear in "Federal Game Protection—A Five Years' Retrospect":

> The opening year of the twentieth century marked the beginning of a new era in game protection in the United States. The first general Federal law for the protection of game went into

Introduction

effect on May 25, 1900, and inaugurated a policy which was in striking contrast with that of the previous century. From colonial days the States had made repeated efforts to protect their game, and some of them had developed their laws to a comparatively high degree of complexity. Disputed points had been carried to the highest courts and in a few cases to the Supreme Court of the United States. The Federal Government, on the other hand, had done comparatively little.[10]

It was amazing how long it took for Americans to recognize the seriousness of the bird slaughter that was taking place and connect it to the millinery items that were the fashions of the day for a half a century. Even more amazing was that it took that long for Americans to finally put an end to it through legislation and the weight of public opinion, both of which came into prominence only when a need for laws against the wearing of high hats at the theater emerged around the turn of the 20th century. Those laws disappeared long before the demand for fancy feathers, quills, birds, and bird parts did. Before they did, they created social upheaval across the country.

Despite repeated assurances during that time from anti–bird slaughter proponents that bird populations were rebounding, the murderous millinery practices continued. That was a double-edged sword. The slaughter was attracting more interest in birds from the public, which encouraged the Audubon Society to pursue every protection that the law and an educated public sentiment could impose. That could only mean trouble for the millinery trade.

There were ebbs and flows, but stopping the fad took decades, despite one reporter's claim, "However, the agitation in this country has about reached the point where fashion will decree a cessation of the savage slaughter, and when fashion frowns the end is come."[11] But fashion had been frowning for years up until then. The question remained: Why did it take so long for the fad to end?

1

The Birds Start Slipping Away

"In recent years ladies in fashionable circles, both at home and abroad, have developed some remarkable zoological tastes."[1]

The first hint that American birds were disappearing appeared just as the American Civil War (1861–65) was ending, when ornithologists observed that the ultimate extinction of America's birds was in progress. People laughed at them. The sky may have been falling according to the ornithologists, but the birds somehow stayed in the air.

In 1865 Americans could look into the trees and skies and see birds of all species in large numbers flitting about. Thirty years later they saw a change in the bird count. The extermination the ornithologists had feared in 1865 was close, they warned, unless people took extraordinary steps to check the slaughter of birds that was caused mostly by a demand for millinery adornments. That alert didn't resonate with people.

Troubling reports surfaced in 1894 about the diminishing numbers of popular

THE WOMAN BEHIND THE GUN.

The irony of it all: a woman, possibly Coco Chanel, flaunting feathers shooting birds (Gordon Ross, artist, *Puck*, May 24, 1911).

7

8   **The Hat That Killed a Billion Birds**

species of birds. They revealed that at least 50 species formerly abundant in all parts of the United States east of the Mississippi River were now seen only rarely. The birds that were being exterminated most rapidly were those whose brilliant markings made them prey of the millinery trade, which had hunters employed everywhere to kill them.

Experts estimated that as many as 8,000,000 birds were being slain annually to satisfy the vanity of the women of America.[2] The allusion to women was significant, since they were the villains in the piece. Women were the primary wearers of "murderous millinery," as bird-adorned products became labeled and grew in popularity.

Bird lovers focused on the number 8,000,000. That sounded like a lot of birds. But no one was sure what the number really meant, since even the experts had no idea how many birds actually lived in the United States—or anywhere else. There had never been a count of birds made in the country to enumerate the most popular non–game birds such as robins, swallows, sparrows, blue jays, and orioles, and there wouldn't be until 1908.[3] Until at least a ballpark estimate was ascertained, the 8,000,000 figure, though large, was meaningless.

Experts offered valid reasons why a bird census should be taken. Members of a biological survey proposed to approach the U.S. Congress to obtain the authority for one and the funds to conduct it. Their plan was to tap into the regular appropriation for the agricultural department, of which the biological survey was a part. They cited the need for a more effective protection of the birds of the country than had been available previously. Moreover, they said, there was no way of knowing what was happening to the birds of different species or whether they were increasing or decreasing in numbers. Finally, they claimed, they wanted to learn whether certain species were numerous enough to make them economically advantageous.

Economists estimated that birds' activities saved more than $100,000,000 annually in the United States for agricultural purposes alone.[4] But the benefit they provided went beyond mere dollars. It affected people's quality of life. Experts claimed that in many sections of the country insect life was so abundant it would make human life almost unendurable without birds. They compared that situation to other sections where the numbers of insects were kept in check by birds, where the quality of life was better.[5]

There was no place where, were this check removed, they estimated, it would not greatly hold the balance of power. Economists claimed that from daylight until dark, all through the summer months, birds waged incessant war on insects, the enemies of man. All anyone needed was a count of the birds to reinforce their claims. They looked to the government to provide the numbers.

Census takers were happy to help. Like the economists, they argued that many birds were of value to farmers and humanity in general and that scientists who studied the subject would be able to estimate how many birds there should be per acre or to any stretch of territory for the purpose of doing the most good and the least injury. If there were to be better protection for birds, they said, it would be worthwhile to know everything possible about the numbers of birds extant in the United States and in their varieties. The question was whether such a study was too little, too late.

There had been a start toward a census of birds in Indiana under the direction of S.A. Forbes, a professor of zoology who was well known in biological circles.[6] He planned to observe bird life across the state. The census takers would see for themselves how many birds existed in the state and in what varieties. And they would gain valuable information by talking to residents to learn about the numbers of birds observed about farmhouses and residences, the number of mating pairs, and so on. That may have not been the most scientific survey, but it was a start, even if it didn't help anyone in 1894, when the problem of bird slaughter was becoming more acute.

According to bird lovers, it was far from an exaggeration at that point to say that one bird out of every four worn as a bit of feathered finery represented a nest full of fledglings doomed to slow starvation by the death of the parent! After all, one of the worst features of the wanton killing of birds for women's hat ornaments was that the hunters employed by the wholesale milliners chose nesting time, when the adult birds were most easily found and approachable, as their most profitable season.

Bird protection proponents cited Chicago, Illinois, as a prime example of bird loss. They noted that only a few years earlier the wooded banks of Lake Michigan north of the city were the breeding grounds of hundreds of scarlet tanagers, which they believed was possibly the most beautiful bird known to American ornithology. By 1894 they were so rare that birders had to search a whole summer day just to find a single specimen.[7]

Concomitantly, the red-winged blackbird was fast disappearing. Baltimore orioles, which had until recently built their nests at the ends of drooping boughs of the elms in the hearts of large eastern cities, were now seen rarely, except in remote country districts. Worse, they were as shy around people as they had once been friendly. The story grew worse.

The numerous and beautiful warblers, whose diminutive size was their protection, were disappearing fast. Many varieties of the warbler family had traditionally nested north of Chicago, but great numbers of the little creatures were being killed during the spring migration. Woodpeckers, too, were decreasing in numbers.

CAUGHT NAPPING.

Even hunters got tired of shooting birds during the slaughter era (Currier & Ives print, 1879).

10 **The Hat That Killed a Billion Birds**

The red-headed woodpecker, which had been a staple in Chicago, had been forced out to the suburbs. A few were still seen occasionally in Kenwood and other southern city districts, but the hunters for the millinery market had all but decimated them. More tragically, small boys with noiseless air guns were fast depleting their numbers. The cumulative effects were devastating to humans, and not just for sentimental reasons.

It had dawned on people by the turn of the 20th century that the economists were right: there was an integral link between birds and the economy. Ornithologists pointed out that nearly all the birds of bright plumage were insectivorous. They said that a statement of the number of noxious insects that a single songbird killed in one day would tax a person's credulity if it could not be proved so easily. That lesson didn't resonate with a lot of people. They did not understand the importance of the role birds played in American life, especially the "good" ones—and, in their opinions, most birds were good.

Ornithologists counted about 800 varieties of American birds. Of this number, the varieties that had no excuse for their existence could be counted on one hand. Even some of those "bad guys" had some saving grace, although it may not have been understood, even by the farmers who were the chief beneficiaries of birds' work. If nothing else, the "bad" birds could replace the "good" birds on hats and benefit humanity in that manner.

"Some could be spared," an editorial writer said. "Considerable outcry has been raised against the practice of wearing the plumage of birds on the millinery creations of the gentler sex. No doubt many songsters suffer in consequence, but the lovers of birds go a little too far sometimes in their desire to protect the feathered tribe from destruction."[8]

He stressed that many varieties of birds deserved to be slaughtered, especially those on which bounties were placed. No one would care if English sparrows or crows were to be annihilated.

"The farmer could get along nicely without either the crow or the hawk," he opined. "And there are other birds which do not add to the peace and welfare of the inhabitants of either town or city. If some woman would only start the fashion of wearing these birdies in their hats a great good would be accomplished and the shafts of criticism would no longer be hurled at the sex."[9]

Experts lectured those farmers about killing birds of any species and stressed that if they would consult their own interests and protect bird life they would reap the benefits. But, as important as their role as protectors of avian life was, they said, the continuance of the birds rested mainly with women. If they would permanently substitute ribbons and flowers for feathers as articles of hat decorations "the trill of the song sparrow and the liquid note of the hermit thrush may be heard in our meadows and woods for the years to come."[10] That wasn't going to happen as long as the tyranny of fashion reigned.

Women were divided on the need to save the birds. Neither science, the law, nor public opinion were going to convince some of them that birds were better off in the wild than they were atop hats.

Despite the efforts of the Audubon societies and lovers of birds generally to arouse public sentiment against it, the sacrifice of bird life on the altar of fashion went on relentlessly as 1900 arrived. Scientists were expressing increasing concerns that the loss of avian life in the United States and elsewhere was a serious problem. A report published by the national museum in Washington, D.C., listed the species of birds that had gone extinct due to the increasingly cruel and useless slaughter.[11]

1. The Birds Start Slipping Away 11

The study also warned that certain other species would soon be exterminated unless vigorous measures were adopted to save them. There was some good news in the publication. Scientific bureaus in Washington were collecting more accurate information in regard to the birds of the country, with a view to their better protection. Some states had made it a misdemeanor to have in one's possession any dead, harmless bird other than game birds, and those only in the season when the law permitted them to be killed. But the laws were mostly ineffective.

The scientists noted that in almost any jurisdiction where such a law existed it would be no trouble for policemen within the space of a block to round up a wagonload of women wearing dead birds on their headgear. But they didn't do it, primarily because public sentiment did not demand the enforcement of the law. "It is a hard thing to antagonize the tyranny of fashion and legislate against the woman's bonnet," critics admitted.[12]

The law did not matter to some people, they lamented. "To the shame of our civilization be it said that legislation alone cannot save the birds," one wrote. "The most effective means for their preservation lies in an awakened and enlightened public sentiment setting itself resolutely against the practice of using birds for millinery purposes."[13]

That happened, albeit slowly. Unfortunately, the women who resolutely refused to give up their murderous millinery did not heed that advice about public sentiment until it was almost too late to save the birds. No one was laughing at the ornithologists then.

2

How Did It Happen?

"In the absence of large game, many who might be called real sportsmen look for small game, and the man who kills the last specimens of rare species of water fowl in his locality not only finds pleasure in doing so, but he is the envy of his fellow sportsmen."[1]

In 1898 William T. Hornaday, director of the New York Zoological Park, sounded an alarm regarding an insidious and devastating loss of birds in the United States. He released a lengthy, depressing report to support his contention that the wanton destruction of bird life would have an adverse impact on the country's economy and social fabric.[2] His findings served as a baseline to give outsiders a picture of how dire the situation was to society and how people responded to it.

W.T. Hornaday, author of *Our Vanishing Wildlife: Its Extermination and Preservation*, in which he told readers that "birds and mammals now are literally dying for your help" (Bain News Service).

Hornaday based his conclusions on the root causes listed in an 1896 U.S. Agricultural Department report and feedback derived from extensive correspondence with naturalists, ornithologists, game wardens, and other experts in positions to speak authoritatively.

He stressed that in compiling its data the zoological society was leery of accepting anything sensational and underrated the percentages of destruction to be on the safe side. His study results were based on answers to several key questions:

Are birds decreasing in number in your locality?
About how many birds are there now in comparison with the number fifteen years ago?
What agency (or class of men) has been the most destructive to birds in your locality?
What species of birds or quadrupeds are becoming extinct in your state?

More than 200 observers, including guides, collectors, sportsmen, and taxidermists from every state and territory in the

Between the hunters and the dogs, prairie birds in the South Dakota fields didn't have a chance (H.C. White Co., Bennington, Vermont, ca. 1906).

union responded. Ninety percent of the answers showed that they had been compiled with great care, and the closeness with which the estimates in different states agreed was surprising and important. The most significant finding was that 80 percent of the correspondents declared that the decrease in bird life was unmistakable.

Other findings included:

> In four-fifths of the area of the United States, exclusive of Alaska, bird life is being annihilated, edible birds are rare and on the point of extinction, and plume birds are practically extinct.
> There is an alarming scarcity of quadrupeds and large birds compared with the number that existed eight years ago.
> The destruction can be attributed to four primary causes, ranked in the order of importance: sportsmen, boys who shoot, the clearing of timber for cities and towns, and feather hunters.
> Secondary causes included market (commercial) hunters, shooters generally, egg collectors, the English sparrow, Italians and others who eat songbirds, cheap firearms, drainage of marshes, hunting contests, and bird collectors, such as taxidermists and ornithologists.
> There are now only 25 percent of the game birds that existed fifteen years ago.
> Without radical changes in the laws for the preservation of game birds in the next fifteen years, we might see the entire annihilation of all 144 species of them.

A new danger threatens many species of birds. In Connecticut, Pennsylvania, Massachusetts, and Wisconsin, on Sundays, hordes of ignorant Italians and some other foreigners throng the woods with cheap guns and kill everything that wears feathers—except women. In California, larks and some kinds of doves are now killed for food.

Egg collecting has become an important factor in bird destruction in the northeastern quarter of New York and many other localities. Bird nesting is a pleasant diversion, and the interests of science furnish for it a ready excuse. The value of most of these collections to science is small, almost nothing, and the egg collecting must stop, at least for five years, if the entire destruction of birds be not speedy.

The side hunts of sportsmen is another cause of prolific bird slaughter. An annual affair in Enosburg, Vermont, is an example. In October, 1896, at the annual side hunt there, 666 head of game were killed.

Plume hunters are destroying birds. After having swept clean entire states and the entire Atlantic coast, they are turning to Mexico, Lower California, Central America and the headwaters of the Amazon in their search for marketable plumes.

In New York State the decrease in bird life in the past fifteen years has been 48 percent.

Florida has suffered the greatest loss, nearly 90 percent. Nebraska has lost only 10 percent, and, were it not for the slaughter of game birds, bird life there would have been balanced for the period.

In only one part of New York State was bird life reported as on the balance.

Hunters in Belhaven, in eastern North Carolina, ca. 1900–1920.

2. How Did It Happen?

This was from a taxidermist of Brockport, but answers from the districts immediately around showed a decided decrease.

In North Carolina, Oregon, and California bird life has suffered no decrease during the last fifteen years. Kansas, Wyoming, Utah, and Washington have shown an increase within the specified time. Excellent game laws have been chief among the influences responsible for this condition.

Hornaday broke the game birds down by general classification: gallinaceous birds, such as pheasants, grouse, partridges, quail, etc., 31 species; pigeons and doves, 12 species; shorebirds, such as snipes and sand pipers, 47 species; ducks and geese, 43 species; cranes, herons, ibises and other birds shot for plumage, 10 species; rails, eight species.

He added to those the gulls, terns and other ocean-goers, birds of prey, perching birds and woodpeckers.

"At one time the game birds represented about one-third the total bird life in the United States," he said. "Beyond all question it was once within the power of the United States to have maintained for the game birds one half the United States as a vast shooting preserve, capable of providing sportsmen and hunters with a continuous large supply."[3]

Significantly, several species were mentioned by respondents as becoming extinct. They included the passenger pigeon, wild turkey, ruffed grouse, bluebird, geese and ducks, pinnated grouse, heath hen, flamingo, Carolina parquet (parakeet), and hawks and owls.

Florida hunters carry five wild turkeys they shot, ca. 1926 (Burgert Brothers, Tampa).

Hornaday specified that extinction was far off for the majority of the species listed, but their almost complete annihilation was imminent. Among them:

the edible birds, about 150 species, are being severely persecuted

song and insectivorous birds are being killed for food purposes

persecution of birds during the nesting season by egg collectors and by boys generally has become so universal as to demand immediate attention

excepting in a few localities, existing measures for the protection of birds, as they are carried into effect, are notoriously inadequate for the maintenance of a proper balance of bird life

destructive agencies are constantly increasing

under present conditions, except in a very few localities, the practical annihilation of all our birds, except the smallest species, and within a comparatively short period, may be regarded as absolutely certain to occur

"It is time to unite and become aggressive in measures designed to save the birds," he concluded.[4]

The question was whether the milliners and conservationists were willing to reach an agreement on those measures.

3

Follow the Money

"Even as late as the 1880s native insectivorous birds, gulls, terns, small owls, etc., were used in numbers and it was not until public sentiment was stirred by the Audubon movement, and existing laws against the destruction of birds were enforced in some states and better laws enacted in others, that the milliners of the United States began to give up the use of the plumage of native wild birds."

—Edward H. Forbush[1]

The primary antagonists in the struggle over the use of birds for millinery were milliners and conservationists. The milliners wanted to protect their livelihoods and earn profits. The conservationists were not averse to that, as long as the milliners left the birds alone. They didn't like the component of the millinery trade that threatened the extinction of numerous species of birds across the globe. That loss was created by the tremendous and unceasing demand from women for millinery items that featured entire birds and large amounts of plumage in grotesque displays on them.

As 1902 approached experts predicted a veritable war between the two antagonists, one which the milliners were favored to win. That was evident in newspaper accounts, as journalists predicted that birds and feathers of every description would be pushed by the trade more than in years past as a reporter speculated with a reference to the ins and outs of popular creatures.

Birds, big birds, bigger every day, are coming to the front. Possibly before the season is over women will appear with nothing on their heads but an enormous bird. It is remarked, however, with a gasp of wonder, that, while green is to remain the color par excellence for fall headgear, the green parrot is nowhere to be seen. After posing as an extreme novelty for one season, this bird seems to have betaken himself to his Amazonian forests.

Then he hit on the crux of the seemingly never-ending fad.

As a matter of fact, extreme things are never permanent among American women. Certain new styles, like, for instance, the made neckwear [custom-made neckwear like ties] introduced a few years ago, they take up and make permanent, adopting it as a constituent part of their wardrobe. The most sanguine dealer did not anticipate more than one season's popularity for the neckwear when it was introduced, but it has become as much an accepted part of his stock as black silk or blue polka dot calico. Other new things have a run of a few weeks, and die out before the season is over. So the women are really the court of last resort as to styles, after all.[2]

But it wasn't just birds that were the problem. There were secondary problems that amounted to a veritable assault on nature: the killing of large animals such as alligators, tortoises, and even elephants to make accoutrements such as combs and pocketbooks to accompany millinery products and bird egg collections. The bird egg collections were the more serious of the two, since each egg gathered meant the loss of at least one baby.³ Fortunately, collecting proved to be a passing craze.

Newspaper stories reporting on the phenomenon were common in the 1880s. Reporters noted that while the war against the extermination of beautiful birds for millinery purposes was going on, the devastating effects of bird egg collections was practically being ignored. As one taxidermist told a reporter, it was becoming fashionable for large numbers of people to have their own private collections of birds' eggs for ornamental purposes.⁴

"You may go into hundreds of wealthy homes in any city and find a box of the eggs displayed in a conspicuous place," one claimed. "The eggs are being taken out of the nests."⁵

The battle line was drawn and the opposing sides dug in with their allies. Wisely, conservationists concentrated on the bird slaughter problem. Events favored the milliners because very few people paid much attention to the shrinking numbers of birds across the globe or correlated them to the hats on which they became prominent parts. That all changed around 1898 when a growing number of conservationists drew more and more supporters to their side.

Among the new class of protectionists were sympathetic newspaper editors, who were almost without exception against killing birds by the millions just to adorn hats. Theirs became a powerful voice. One writer demonstrated the power of the press in publicizing the perils of profligate bird slaughter and highlighted the primary issues in the argument for and against it.⁶

The article introduced several other elements of the story: the cruel nature of the wanton slaughter, people's naiveté about conservation, the economic consequences of the killings, the battle between the sexes, the fraud involved in bird harvesting, the role

Ocean birds weren't safe, either. Hunters shooting them from their blind by the shore (Detroit Publishing Company, ca. 1900–1920).

3. Follow the Money

of and need for public relations and education programs to make everyone aware of the relationship between fashion and nature, the introduction of the blame game to find a scapegoat for the deleterious effects of the attack on wildlife....

The story was reported close to the beginning of the second phase of the high-hat, bird-slaughter era, when bird-adorned hats were still considered just a novelty—a novelty that lasted for another 40 years.

Slaughter of seabirds for millinery and mercantile purposes

During a recent trip with the Orpheus Sailing Club of Baltimore to the well-known Cobb's Island the following facts were ascertained and created a very unpleasant impression. An enterprising woman from New York has contracted with a Paris millinery firm to deliver during this summer 40,000 or more skins of birds at 40 cents apiece. With several taxidermists she was carrying out the contract, having engaged young and old to kill birds of different kinds and paying them ten cents for each specimen not too much mutilated for millinery purposes.

The plumage of most of the birds to be obtained at this island is plain, but with the assistance of a little dye it can be transformed into that of the gaily colored tropical birds. The birds comprised in this wholesale slaughter are mainly the different species of gulls and terns or sea swallows, of which many species in large numbers could formerly be found upon the island. But now only few of these graceful birds remain upon Cobb's Island, and the pot-hunters, or rather skin-hunters, have to go some distance to carry out their cruel scheme.

If we consider that with each old bird killed—and only old birds have a suitable plumage—also, many of the young birds, still unable to take care of themselves, are doomed to starvation, this wholesale slaughter becomes more infamous and criminal. A good deal of dissatisfaction was shown by some of the guests at the hotel about the matter, but they did not do anything about it.

Some contended that no matter how many gulls and terns would be killed now there would be plenty more during the next season. Poor reasoning. Gulls, like all other birds, have certain places to build their nests and rear their young. Furthermore, all gulls go for this purpose only to these places where they were born and consequently, by killing both parents and young in one season, none remain to return to their breeding places the following season.

It is true, there will be plenty of gulls at the island during the late fall and winter. But, these are only visitors of different species that nest further North and which will return to their homes with the return of spring.

The beautiful and peculiar black skimmer, or cut-water, which formerly was found only in large numbers upon this island, will soon be a rare bird in its own home. The black skimmers are more social and move synchronously, which is not the case with any of the other terns. They feed chiefly in the dusk of the evening, gliding and swimming swiftly along just over the water, their bill is opened, the lower or under mandible is in the water, and so they take their food in a manner that is analogous to the feeding of whales.

The practice of wearing stuffed birds as ornaments on the hats of ladies is a very cruel one, inflicting an endless amount of misery and pain upon innocent and beneficial birds, and such a practice should be discontinued. Why not start clubs, the lady members of which agree not to wear any stuffed birds themselves. Such clubs exist in Europe, and American ladies surely have as much feeling as ladies elsewhere.

The roughly 40-year battle accelerated around 1880, when some innovative fashion designers added bird plumes, feathers and parts and entire birds to ladies' millinery, dresses, and accessories. Bird lovers saw a problem with that, since the number of birds required to equip one hat alone was significant. It wasn't the number of feathers that was the issue. It was how they were gathered.

For the most part the only way for hunters to gather the feathers was to kill the adult birds giving them up. They developed heinous methods of killing the adult birds and then left their carcasses to rot. That left the young birds without any means of survival, so they died too. Most of the birds the hunters killed were considered songbirds. The more beautiful the bird was, the more likely it was to die. Soon, entire species were threatened with extinction.

Conservationists recognized that birds were disappearing from the planet in record numbers. They stepped forward to protect their avian friends.

Hunters even used their lunch hours to shoot quail around 1900 (T.W. Ingersoll, Publisher, St. Paul).

The conservationists recognized that birds had more value to humans than just providing occasional songs. They were significant players in the complex world of human and economic survival as well. Birds helped farmers and prevented the spread of diseases to humans by eating insects, for example. So in 1886 the appropriately named George Bird Grinnell, natural history editor of the magazine *Forest and Stream*, formed the Audubon Society to help protect the birds.

Similar organizations joined the "Audubonists." Together they created a formidable anti-millinery force. Their leaders addressed various government lawmaking agencies at all levels, foreign and domestic, to enact laws for the protection of birds and implement public relations programs to educate the public on the threat of avian extinction. Optimists suggested that this was a sign that society could save the birds:

> From present indications it would seem that there is hope of a reaction against the wanton slaughter of song birds for millinery purposes. The "maniac patchwork" in feather ornaments will cause women of taste to abjure them. When the goldfinch is "tricked out" with bird of paradise plumes and hummingbirds have the tails of parrots the incongruity shocks even those women who have no "compunctious visitings of nature" at wearing song birds upon their hats or bonnets.[7]

The optimism was justified, but the battle to win the women over had just begun. It was long and arduous.

Meanwhile, the milliners formed lobbyist groups of their own to countermand the conservationists' influence. They wanted to keep the millinery industry afloat, even if they eliminated the source of their success. Both sides used a variety of logical, ethical, and emotional arguments to win people over to their sides. The ladies who bought their products were caught in the middle, since they composed the milliners' target consumer base.

Millinery fashionistas designed preposterous hats and garments and tried to convince their customer base that wearing products displaying stuffed birds, bird parts, feathers, plumes, and other avian-related components would bring them closer to nature. Unfortunately, it did just the opposite; the new fashions brought nature to people who did not care to see it in certain places, such as theaters.

Some of the hats ladies wore to theaters were monstrosities. They were described as being three to four stories high. It wasn't the wearing of the hats that bothered theatergoers. The fact that the ladies chose to wear them during the performances did. The wearing of the hats upset the people sitting behind them. Soon those theatergoers who paid good money to see performances but who got to see nothing but the backs of ladies' hats began clamoring for protection. They turned to lawmakers to enact anti–theater hat laws.

The wave of new anti–theater hat laws rolling across the United States did not make the ladies happy. They thought they were being singled out. They were, but only because they were the primary purchasers and wearers of the high hats. The age of high hats for men had long since passed.

George Bird Grinnell, American anthropologist, historian, naturalist, writer, and founder of the Audubon Society (Hargrave, New York, ca. 1899).

The ladies sprang into action to fight against the laws, often on principle alone, although many of them complied with the laws or voluntarily removed their hats during performances. Many did not, which exacerbated the problem and sparked calls for more laws. The implementation of the laws began a gender war, but it didn't solve completely the dual problems of high hats in theaters or the impending extinction of birds.

Meanwhile, milliners kept designing garish avian-themed hats and clothes and keeping the bird hunting industry afloat. Conservationists continued pushing for laws domestically and internationally, with a modicum of success. Customers kept purchasing the bird-themed items with a few breaks in the cycle as fashion styles changed back and forth.

The best hope for everyone was that sooner or later the people who bought the hats, gowns, and accessories would recognize that they were driving birds to the point of extinction to satisfy their fashion whims and stop buying them. That is eventually what happened. Eventually can be a long time.

4

Bird Murder and Women's Hats

"Feather brains will insist on wearing feathered hats."[1]

At some point in the mid–19th century, fashion designers thought it would be aesthetically pleasing to adorn women's clothing with bird feathers. The idea caught on and the demand for bird feathers reached epic proportions. No bird was safe as "murderous millinery" took flight; it became a frequently repeated talking point in speeches, writings, and even ads on the subject.

"Long Feathers and the bird is living in millineries this season in all sorts of designs. Natty decorations for turbans and walking hats leaders at 10c, 15c and 25c bunch," one advertisement proclaimed.[2] Using the word "living" in conjunction with birds seemed like an oxymoron. The birds adorning millinery in 1898 were anything but—and they numbered in the millions.

The demand for feathers and other bird parts took on an international aspect as demand outstripped supply. Entrepreneurs in countries all across the globe stepped in to fill the demand. That was less than pleasing to high hat opponents everywhere. Sparrows, mockingbirds, herons … if a bird had a feather it died.

Hunters slaughtered birds wholesale and sold them the same way. As one writer put it, "Fancy runs riot among birds and plumage." There never was a time when single quill feathers were so freely employed, as many as 13 being used on one hat, the writer said. Statements of that type horrified the people who strove to protect birds. They didn't seem to faze milliners, taxidermists, and other people engaged in the gathering of feathers and plumage whence came those 13 quill feathers. The feathers were simply picked and appropriated.

Not infrequently, the writer observed, these feathers have a rough, undressed appearance and seem to have been picked and appropriated without any previous preparation, though on the contrary, there are single quills showing careful elaboration as to dye and otherwise. One reference in the article had to make people wonder why fashion designers had to use real birds. "Wings seem not so popular as entire birds with outstretched pinions and in evidence of such partiality, mention may be made of large imitation birds in jet or spangles, whose outer wings extend a half foot on either side, while the space within is filled with minor simulations."[3]

The answer to the writer's wonder had to be that the buyers of the hats preferred real birds, even though the technology of the time made possible passable pseudo birds in lieu of perishable passenger pigeons. The ladies preferred their exaggerated high hats instead of small bonnets, which led to legislation banning them in theaters.

Exaggerated was no exaggeration. Why did women even want the monstrosities that masqueraded as hats in the high hat era? The answer may have been summed up in two words: jealousy and competition. Cost was an afterthought in some cases, especially for the ladies of the upper classes. And, as wags pointed out, the only people who really paid a cost were the people who made the hats and the ones who plunked down the payment—the men.

"An Ohio girl is suffering from nervous prostration, caused by trimming bonnets with little birds in a millinery shop. The ladies who wear the bonnets are not so sensitive. The men who pay the bills sometimes have nervous spells, however," the jokesters said.[4]

One newspaper reported that "not long ago a London auction room sold a single consignment of nearly 500,000 birds, which had been gathered from different parts of the world. A late fashionable item in a Paris paper announces that birds are worn more than ever and blouses made entirely of feathers are coming into fashion."[5]

American surgeon, explorer and naturalist Samuel Washington Woodhouse holds a stuffed bird specimen (ca. 1847).

A *London Saturday Review* writer explained why the ladies of London needed so many birds executed on their behalf and how their desires sparked an economic uptick:

> A woman in Paris or London may discover that the tail of a bird "sets her off." She walks forth, and lo! Tails are the rage, and millions of birds have been slaughtered for the mere gratification of tender-hearted woman. It is not an exaggeration to say that in whatever part of the world beautiful birds are found there will be found also the agents of the draper and the milliner. The part they play is that of supplying the demand woman wants.[6]

Sales of women's clothing featuring feathers, especially hats, soared while fewer and fewer birds did the same. The drastic decrease in the number of birds caught the eyes of government officials, environmentalists, naturalists, and other stakeholders in the avian world. The next thing women knew, their right to wear huge hats in theaters was banned and they wondered why.

To be fair, men wore hats to the theater too. But, for the most part, they were more of the small cap variety, whereas women's hats were often described as being three or four stories high or as big as bales of hay. And most of the millinery ads in newspapers of the time were aimed at women in particular. Thus, the battle line between the genders over the issue of hats was drawn.

In the 1890s in particular the issue came to the fore. Newspaper columnists began writing profusely about bird decimation and anti–theater hat ordinances. They did not always agree on the need for laws against either. Strangely enough, in general they rarely

24 The Hat That Killed a Billion Birds

connected the two issues. Legislators, too, failed to connect the dots. Since most of the legislators were males, it was easy to see why so many women thought they were being singled out.

An editorial writer suggested the legislators were correct in blaming women:

> Wings no longer suffice, but women carry on their pretty but cruel and thoughtless heads whole charnel houses of beaks and claws and bones and feathers and glass eyes. Fashion never yet demanded a more wicked and absurd sacrifice on its altar, always smoking for fresh prey. All the considerations involved in the question—its wastefulness in the economy of nature, the evil and cruelty involved, the injury done indirectly to the interest of the farmer, the blow struck at the aesthetic enjoyment of country life—have been frequently presented, and yet feather brains will insist on wearing feathered hats.[7]

No matter who was to blame, the killing of birds continued unchecked but not unnoticed. Farmers, who relied on birds for certain services, cited their diminishing numbers. The Massachusetts legislature took note. It passed a law punishing the shooting or trapping of birds other than game birds with a heavy fine. Ironically, the same state was among the first to ban high hats in theaters—but as a separate issue.

William Dutcher, president of the Audubon societies of the United States in 1909, pointed out that birds saved farmers $200,000,000 a year via the destruction of noxious insects and noxious weeds.[8] But, Dutcher declared, milliners, the great destroyers of birds, were interfering with the farmers' and the birds' livelihoods. He allowed that there was a legitimate reason for killing some birds and that birds destroyed for food were restocked by natural processes. He declared sadly that the plume hunters recognized no closed season, so they knocked the natural replenishment process askew.

Millinery interests in America represented $38,000,000 worth of work done by the birds for the farmers, Dutcher explained. The bobwhite was the arch destroyer of the potato bug, the cuckoo of the caterpillar, the woodpecker of the boring grub, the lark of the grasshopper, and the sparrow of the weed seeds. With that in mind, he said, the birds were entitled to fair play from the milliners. They hadn't gotten it for at least 25 years, he averred, and as long as consumers kept buying bird hats, they weren't going to get it anytime soon.

A study by a biological group concluded that in 1907, 38 species of birds in the United States ate boll weevils, insects that feed on cotton buds and flowers. Those insects were cotton farmers' most hated nemeses, since they could do serious economic damage to crops. Of the 38 species, some ate the weevils only sparingly, while others ate them freely. Among the most important birds to feed on the weevil were orioles, nighthawks, and swallows, including the purple martin. The orioles' value to farmers in particular did not save their lives, despite laws to protect them.

Six kinds of orioles lived in Texas, but only two inhabited the southern states generally.[9] Orioles were among the few birds that evinced a preference for weevils. Since they persistently hunted for the insects on the cotton bolls, they filled a place that no other birds did. Consequently they were protected by law in nearly every state in the union. Unfortunately, their economic value to milliners overrode that protection.

Their bright plumage made them among the most salable birds for millinery purposes. Despite the protective laws in place, considerable numbers of orioles were killed for the hat trade. Conservationists pointed out that in light of their importance as insect eaters everywhere, they had to be protected, especially in the cotton belt. Fashion once again prevailed. Orioles were on their own, usefulness be damned, as was the case with other species.

4. Bird Murder and Women's Hats

So in spite of all attempts to lessen the murderous tribute exacted by fashion and feminine vanity, the war against the feathered tribes proceeded more doggedly than ever before, abroad and in America.

The prestigious preacher the Rev. Dr. DeWitt Talmage announced just what bird lovers did not want to hear:

> The French actresses, a precious group, some of them divorced two or three times, and with a system of morals independent of the Ten Commandments, have re-enforced a fashion which it was hoped until this autumn was dying out. I refer to the bird millinery or the adornment of hats with the winged denizens of the sky.
>
> Taxidermists are in the destruction of birds for the purposes of fashion, not only silencing the songs of our forests but surrendering the agriculture of the land to the worst insectile devastation that the world ever saw since the locusts and the flies came down to plague Egypt.[10]

In short, the world's birds were under attack again, and a cycle that would not be broken reappeared. There was some good news, though. One thing that contributed to the durability of the craze was changing fashions, which saved some species of birds from extinction or vastly reduced numbers as the favored birds of the day kept changing with the new designs.

One year it would be terns, the next year owls, the next roosters. The species changed, but the fad kept going. The cycles were interrupted by assurances that the high hat era was over, but they never panned out. Cycles ruled the world of fashion and determined which birds lived and which birds died.

5

Bicycles, Tricycles, and Fashion Cycles

"In the future, everyone will be world-famous for 15 minutes."[1]

A giddy journalist declared erroneously in 1887 that the murderous millinery movement was in decline:

Pride goeth before destruction and a compliant woman beneath a big bonnet. There is no desire to give occasion for premature rejoicing, but the indications are unmistakable that there are serious defections in the ranks of elevated millinery, and perceptible wavering along the line gives promise of a general stampede. The glad tidings may be safely proclaimed that the colossal hats and bonnets of the theater are in a state of incipient collapse.[2]

Just a year earlier fashion experts said that the destruction of birds for millinery purposes continued and ladies would wear birds and wings of all sorts and descriptions on their winter hats.[3] And bonnet strings were being tied directly under the ladies' chins, not to one side. That allowed hats to grow higher and higher as the season progressed. The conflicting statements epitomized the cyclical nature of the murderous millinery movement.

A salient example of the cycles appeared in an article written in the early stages of the movement. The journalist revealed that the hats of the women would be decorated with eagles, owls, and blue jays and predicted what would become popular in coming years. The story disclosed details about the types of birds used for millinery purposes, the processes used to prepare them, the insensitivity of the people who performed the work, the laissez-faire attitude people had about animals at the time, the role of taxidermists in what was for them a "golden age," a harbinger of things to come as the bird slaughter era evolved … in short, it provided a valuable inside look at the bird slaughter problem as it was then and what it would become.

The reporter visited a wholesale millinery store on Broadway, one of many of its kind in the area. The store was filled from the boxes in the rear to the show windows in the front with specimens of birds prepared for millinery purposes. Since the store was near the shopping district there were crowds of women in front of it all day long.

The prevailing style of hat which was formed on one model, and which varied in regard to size only, called for something more ornate than a monotonous ball fringe and ostrich tips or the decoration found on a scarf or other piece of clothing. Birds were chosen as the proper ornaments for these hats.

Myriad bird and fowl species were represented in the store's window. Among them were common chickens, Spanish roosters, Poland fowl, Brahmas, Russian cocks, and pelicans, all without their broods and the signs of the wounds inflicted upon them when they were killed; sea gulls, with their black-tipped wings; pretty blue jays, crows, staring

5. Bicycles, Tricycles, and Fashion Cycles

Even America's national symbol, the eagle, was not safe from hunters (M.W. Baldwin, artist, November 1898).

owls…. The birds came from virtually all parts of Europe and America. The proprietor told the reporter that the fall outlook for the trade in birds for hats was very promising:

> I never saw women running after birds for their hats as they are doing this season. Last year a few small rare birds were worn, but now there is no telling where the demand will stop. You never can tell what a woman wants, anyway; and when it comes to hats, well, white pigeons and sea gulls are favorites. It doesn't make any difference whether the hat, the bird, or both or either is becoming; they've got to have what some other woman, or every woman or any woman has— you know what I mean; some woman wears something that some other woman wants, and the whole thing is so complicated that I am astonished at myself for getting up this stock I have.
>
> White pigeons have been leading by far, but I think blue jays will soon be ahead. The birds are divided into two parts, when it is intended that the ornament shall make a graceful curve in the hat. In many cases, however, the whole bird is stuffed and one side is flattened down a little. Young ladies like to have the bird in its entirety, but married women prefer to have the divided article. You have no idea of the number of persons who are engaged in the business of furnishing birds to us from different parts of North and South America, and besides we import birds from Paris.
>
> You can have a bird of some kind at any price you choose to fix. Here is a pretty blue jay for $10; you've shot them often for fun, I've no doubt, and here is a domestic male barn-yard fowl, commonly called a rooster, which is worth $20, because his tail was imported and entered on the ship's manifest.

I can sell you a bird for a hat as low as 50 cents; but women "size up" the value of everything so quickly that no woman with any self-respect will buy a low-priced article. If you want to find out anything about the preparation of birds, go down to North William Street. There are people in this city who not only stuff dead birds for their grief-stricken owners, but for the prospective owners of umbrella hats.

The reporter then visited a taxidermist's store on North William Street. It was like a zoo for dead animals. It had a deceased tiger much the worse for wear and an orangutan grinning in a manner that would have been impossible for him during his lifetime. "Monkeys hung from the ceiling as carelessly as spider webs in a deserted house, and feeble bears as hollow as the little girl's doll that was stuffed with sawdust tried to stand erect with the aid of stout poles," he wrote. Lions, dogs, cats and a man sitting behind a screen as if to protect himself were also in the store. He was mounting a delicate canary.

Before the reporter had an opportunity to ask the proprietor any questions, a young lady accompanied by a gentleman entered the store. The gentleman produced the body of a parrot from within a number of paper wrappings and asked the taxidermist whether he could fix up the bird.

No duck was safe from hunters (Universal View Co., Philadelphia, ca. 1906).

5. Bicycles, Tricycles, and Fashion Cycles

The taxidermist examined the parrot, then jabbed a needle into it. There was a half smothered sob from under the young lady's veil, and then the gentleman suggested that any further jabbing of the pet bird might be done in private.

"Oh, that's nothing to what I'll have to do with it," the insensitive taxidermist said.

The taxidermist admitted that he was doing a big business for millinery houses. "Nearly all the birds I get for sale come from South America, Russia, Austria and New Jersey," he said. "I don't know what connection there is between the birds of a foreign country abroad and a foreign country in this country, so to speak, so far as birds are concerned. Talking of hats, my own opinion is that American eagles, six feet from tip to tip of the wings, will be the favorites this winter."[4]

That was a hard prediction to swallow for bird lovers. Small birds were bad enough. The use of an eagle on a woman's hat was inconceivable. People were still grappling with the sight of the generic birds that were all the rage at the time.

A fashion writer who apparently assumed that all bird adornment devotees were masters of the French language wrote eloquently that "ceil blue with old red straps is now a favorite mixture for full dress and sleeves, which are made for evening wear tres epaulees."[5] She followed that innocuous statement with news that would be repeated all too often in the next 50 years. "The fashion for wearing birds a tete rasee [a tall, elaborately-ornamented style of woman's hair dress or wig] is not confined to millinery alone, but birds are now placed on the shoulder of a low dress, and a chaperon of very tiny ones called a nichee is not unfrequently ordered under a tulle overdress."

Birds was a generic term, but specific birds took turns as featured hat decorations. Chickens ruled the roost in the early stages of the murderous millinery era.[6] In 1882 feathers—and plenty of them—were the most popular idea in millinery. Downy chicks appeared among the infinite variety of birds used in millinery. The variety of birds increased quickly as new favorites emerged and then faded in popularity. Reports that year showed that stuffed birds were again in request in almost numberless varieties.[7] These embraced not only the small birds of the American forests and the highly-colored South American and East Indian birds, appropriated for millinery purposes, but also many aquatic birds such as sea gulls and ducks.

Birds for millinery trimmings were stuffed softly, providing job opportunities for taxidermists. When the birds were added to ladies' hats they hugged them very closely. Certain large birds, as they were stuffed, were sufficient alone for the garniture of a hat. Another bird frequently completed the ornamentation, with drapery of velvet as the objective trimming.

In 1892 the black parrot assumed its perch as the latest thing in millinery bird, rivaling the favorite blackbird in popularity.[8] A new trend emerged about that time, which could not have been good news for animal rights champions. Although birds of any hue were used as hat ornaments, cute little animals' heads which peeked out from among the velvet and ribbons atop hats grew in popularity.[9] Two years later the birds were back in fashion. "After all the talk about the cruelty of killing the birds, and in the face of the society formed for the suppression of bird slaying, the millinery shows a greater number of wings and birds used than for a long time."[10]

Another two years passed and the messages from designers became more mixed than ever, which was an ongoing state of affairs throughout the bird slaughter era. One account was headlined "The Reign of Birds' Wings Succeeded by a Passion for Ribbon.... Flowers are so clearly in ascendancy that some of the milliners even make no use of feathers, unless ordered."[11] Not everywhere, apparently.

30   The Hat That Killed a Billion Birds

Birds and feathers have disappeared entirely, a report said in August 1886.[12] They were only gone for a month. Three weeks later large felt hats featuring borders of velvet in contrasting colors were the rage. But the crowning triumphs of millinery were felt hats splashed with dots in velvet or satin. Quills, too, were ring-streaked and spotted, and millinery birds were ornithological curiosities with four or even six wings. It was hard for anyone to keep track of fashion changes as they came and went.

It was impossible for anyone to say who was responsible for the revival of the bird and feather fashion in 1886. Millinery buyers claimed it began in Paris and London and New York followed. Whoever started it, shop windows in virtually every city were filled with headgear and ornithological exhibits that would do credit to a museum of natural history.

The fad grew larger. So did the birds. Fashion writers were determined to push their products despite the cries of despair from conservationists. Bigger was better in the fashion writers' minds, especially as 1899 arrived. Imagine sitting behind a hat like this at a theater.

A prominent feature of late midsummer millinery is the whole bird, which now crowns a tulle or straw headdress. Formerly we were content with quills, pinions, a pair of wings or perhaps the breast feathers; but now nothing less than the entire bird will suffice. If you cast to the winds all prejudice of the "Audubonnets" you will admit that the new decoration is extremely showy. A little straw toque is modestly trimmed with brown velvet, sparingly applied. On the left side, toward the front, is perched the stuffed figure of a tiny brown sparrow, his little head cocked to one side in a wonderfully natural manner.

An entire gull is poised on the side of a hat intended for mornings on the beach or driving about the neighborhood in a village cart.

Even dress hats for visiting or concert going are supplied with the whole bird. Some of these are surprisingly large in size. Their plumage is also astonishing of hue, and difficult of identification by an experienced ornithologist. It is an open secret that these birds are artificially colored in delicate or brilliant hues, made up to order by minute directions of the "French" dressmaker, to match the latest and loveliest toilet ordered by the all-conquering American belle. A whole bird does not look well on a bonnet. It requires some brim to carry it off. The toque, round hat, shade hat and walking hat are favorite perches for the whole bird.[13]

The anti–theater hat laws being passed in various places did not have much of an impact on the production of high hats. A fashion prediction for 1903 suggested that "in millinery for fall and winter wear the high-crowned hat in the big shape and the turban in the small shape are the favorites." Bird feathers and birds would still be in vogue too, but bird lovers did not have to be concerned.

In garnitures, shaded effects will be much used for the expensive hats. Long ostrich plumes are now dyed in patches showing in one plume perhaps five tones of the same color.... Birds are to be worn more than ever in millinery, but the bird lovers need not despair, for these trimming birds are made in Paris, and never sang a song. Had the good designers in the "City of Light" seen the light?

Stuffed birds have come to be regarded as tasteless by French milliners, as they cannot be bandied with at all the same ease and effect that the made bird can. The wings of the stuffed bird are stiff; those of the made bird are pliable and easily bent to follow a crown or bend around a hat rim. The feathers of common birds killed for food or because they are nuisances are used to make these birds.[14]

No matter how bird lovers looked at it, birds were still being killed to make hats. But the herons would no longer be victims—if anyone could trust the milliners.

5. Bicycles, Tricycles, and Fashion Cycles 31

"The much criticized heron's aigrette will not be seen in millinery after the first of the year," the report announced. That was because the Milliners' Association had reached an agreement with the Audubon Society to that effect. But just because herons' aigrettes would no longer be used in hat making didn't mean aigrettes in general would disappear. Other birds' plumes would take their place. If that was a message to placate bird lovers, it was confusing.

"Aigrettes will be seen whose use will not violate this agreement," the writer continued. "It is found that peacock and other common feathers can be chemically treated to duplicate almost perfectly the egret. Coque plumes are to be very much used. Beautiful specimens are shown rivaling in exquisite finish the best ostrich plumes."[15]

If there was any good news it was that many feathers would not be accessible to all buyers due to their cost. Marabou (a large dark gray African stork) feathers were said to be popular and beautiful, and costly feather capes of this and other varieties would be worn only by people who could afford them. That was of small consolation to bird lovers who were clamoring for legislation stopping the slaughter of all birds, regardless of how valuable their feathers were. The sales of high hats displaying birds and bird parts continued unabated.

A new favorite emerged in 1910, the chanticleer. The craze tremendously increased the amount of bird trimming in millinery. "We Americans are the only people making a fuss about the rooster," a fashion writer noted. Still, that put roosters on the bird slaughter chopping block.[16]

Whereas some birds, such as herons and birds of paradise, were hunted relentlessly, others enjoyed their "15 minutes of fame" and then ceded their popularity to different species as fashion gurus decided. That gave the out-of-favor species such as the bird of paradise time to repopulate. The birds of paradise were unique in the bird world.

Probably no famous bird had a smaller habitat than the bird of paradise. Birds of paradise were restricted to Papua New Guinea and eastern Australia. No one knew why that was the case, since there were many other islands not far away where conditions seemed to be equally favorable to their existence. Most of the more popular birds killed for their plumes and feathers were spread out over more than one continent, e.g., North and South America. They might have been spared, but public opinion in England against bird slaughter there forced hunters to seek alternatives to native birds. That meant birds of paradise.

From a business standpoint that was a boon for milliners but a drawback for consumers. Because the numbers of birds of paradise were limited in availability and they lived in a remote region of the world, their feathers were among the costliest of all. That allowed fashion designers to introduce them into the mix as part of the ever-changing cycle.

There was such a universal outcry in England in 1896 at the wholesale slaughter of birds that ladies were afraid to wear their beautiful aigrettes. Milliners sought other devices to replace them. They consigned hunters to kill birds of paradise, whose plumage was an excellent substitute. That was a mixed blessing as far as bird slaughter opponents were concerned.

They hoped that since the plumes of the bird of paradise were so costly, and not becoming to every wearer, their popularity would not last very long. And they counted on public opinion against the slaughter of the birds of paradise to curtail it. They knew that wasn't going to happen. They were right. As late as 1910, due to the high prices offered for the plumes of birds of paradise, along with white herons, hummingbirds, albatrosses, and similar species in the European markets, they were still being slaughtered and were reaching the point of extinction.[17] Such warnings were not new: "The murder of the innocent will begin once more, unless, perhaps, public opinion makes it impossible. Shame be it said, but there is not one woman in a thousand, when purchasing her hats, who gives a thought to the feathers introduced into its chic trimming. The effect pleases her. And if she is able to pay the price, that is the end of it."[18]

It wasn't until 1922 that the bird of paradise plumage was scheduled to make its last appearance in New York millinery shops.[19] The expectation was that by the following year it would disappear completely, because selling it was going to be dangerous. Laws had finally made that possible, after 26 years. It was a miracle that the bird of paradise species hadn't become extinct during that time. The crusade to stop its wanton slaughter had moved at a glacial pace, but at least it had moved—as was the case with the fight against bird slaughter in general.

Ethel Reed wearing a plumed hat (Frances Benjamin Johnston, photographer, ca. 1895).

Despite the ongoing popularity of the birds of paradise plumage between 1897 and 1923, designers' tastes continued to run in cycles, as consumers waited with bated breath to see what Paris had in mind for them. One year the designers featured certain parts of birds on hats. The next year they concentrated on feathers and plumes. The following cycle highlighted entire birds on hats. Then they combined feathers, parts, and plumes. And so it went. There were times when fashionistas simply could not make up their own minds whether birds on hats were in or out.

If members of the millinery trade could not keep track of what was in and what was out, how were consumers expected to know? That confusion summed up the entire bird slaughter era.[20] There were some off years when designers lost interest in birds and daintily arranged buttons, bows, and beads to the exclusion of birds and bird parts. Those were the years that gave bird slaughter opponents hope that birds had lost their popularity as millinery adornments. Their hopes were always dashed.

Every bird, large or small, except for the ostrich, got its turn. Ostriches did not have to be killed for their feathers. They gave them up voluntarily, although reluctantly, and

5. Bicycles, Tricycles, and Fashion Cycles

went back to grow some more. Meanwhile, the other birds were trapped in what resembled an offshoot of the Chinese Zodiac, a classification scheme based on the lunar calendar that assigns an animal and its reputed attributes to each year in a repeating 12-year cycle. In this case birds were substituted for animals. Eighteen ninety-eight became the "Year of the Owl."

Owls became the trimming du jour for women's hats.[21] The owl had always been known as the bird of night, shrinking from the glare of sunshine and finding the greatest comfort in dark caves and the hollows of old trees. It emerged only at night, until fashion designers recognized its value as a hat adornment. Thus, in 1898, owls were displayed on the side of virtually every woman's hat. That generated a howl of protest across the United States. The designers did not seem to care, as a journalist suggested:

> In spite of the society formed to prevent the killing of birds for ornamenting millinery and the thousands of signatures annexed to the numerous petitions sent broadcast all over the country, in which women pledge themselves not to wear birds or feathers of any kind on their hats, this is essentially a bird year, and the favorite of all the feathered tribe is the owl. To be strictly fashionable the head, wings, and tail feathers of the birds must all be used on one hat, and sometimes these hats are very expensive.[22]

Owl hats dominated the millinery stores for a while. The "wise" bird's brooding, flat face, small eyes, and hooked beak surmounted fresh, rosy, youthful faces and formed by contrast a strange frame for the female faces they adorned. During the summer that year ultra-fashionable women sported two or three great owl heads crushed in among the wings and ribbons on their traveling hats. Critics noted that from the very oddity of the idea the hats were striking and stylish. But the designers were not satisfied with just heads. They decreed that the whole bird would adorn the fall and winter sailors and toques.

Three years later ostrich feathers took the spotlight. They were conspicuous in autumn millinery, and plumage of all sorts, dyed in all sorts of colors, was made up into breasts, wings and birds, as real as the genuine songsters, for winter hat ornaments. Sea gulls and pigeons became conspicuous in hats for seaside wear. The gulls in particular were dyed in hues never seen in the gull family before.[23]

It didn't take long before owls returned to the top of the list. Their heads were hidden among a plethora of plumes and feathers that resembled the pages of an Audubon catalog.

Fashion writers had their usual field day describing the new designs and spoke about the feathers as if they were grains of sand taken from a remote Saharan desert that would never run out. There was a limit to the number of grains of sand that deserts could hold, however. The writers never seemed to think that was true of feathers and plumes as well as they penned their seemingly endless flow of descriptions.

In just two paragraphs a *Millinery Trade Review* writer could cite more birds and bird parts than an ornithologist could name out loud in the time it took to read them.[24] One revealed in 1905 that the ostrich feathers garnishing the new French models were used demi-long, mostly in couples, and swept around the left side of the crowns of hats. Bird of paradise plumes displayed in the same manner trimmed some of the more elegant of the new imported hats, and marabou plumes, taken from a large, dark gray African stork, retained their regained favor for dainty garnishing effects.

The writer dropped in the news that "owls' heads have been again brought forward by the dictum of the mode for headwear adornment." They'd been out of fashion for seven years and had time to regenerate the species.

The writer added that the plume of the aigrette continued to be the requirement of the arbiters of styles in millinery for the trimming of small bonnets. Apparently he was unaware—or did not care—that the herons from which the aigrettes were plucked were almost extinct. Unless someone devised a way to create aigrettes out of grains of sand they were bound to become less of a requirement soon. Once a species became extinct so did its feathers and parts. That may not have occurred to millinery designers as their fashion cycles came and went.

It was no wonder, then, that a journalist maintained in 1902 that it was a rather striking circumstance that after all the agitation against the use of birds and feathers on women's swagger millinery that bird decorations were still the rage with no end in sight.[25] "It is a fact, nevertheless, and the fad is bound to grow in popularity while these pretty multi-hued denizens of the air, the forest, and the fields may be used in ways that flatter the feminine vanity for gay plumage. Even for young girls, birds are the most popular trimmings."[26]

Young girls had never been left out of the fashion picture. They were introduced at early ages to current trends. An 1885 ad noted that:

> English Hats of Felt are chosen for misses; these are in the high-crowned shape, or else they are lower turbans with the brim turned up all around.
> The trimming of velvet or plush is in high loops in front, with a very narrow band around the crown. Wings, quills, or small birds are set in the front trimming. The pointed poke bonnets are used for very dressy occasions, and are becoming to most young girls. Very large Scotch caps of plush or velvet with a button in the center of the crown are also worn.

The fashion world was bound to capture females as customers at an early age. The birds were in trouble as a result. And they would continue to be for the unforeseeable future.

6

But Did the Ladies Listen?

"Fashion issued her decree for sea birds' feathers with which to decorate women's hats. Swiftly the New York millinery dealers dispatched their gunners to the breeding place of the gulls and terns and all summer the roar of their guns answered loudly the roar of the ocean. A few seasons of this and the vast flock had disappeared."[1]

If only birds were cats and had nine lives. That was wishful thinking. Birds had one life apiece. Fashion designers apparently thought certain species had more than one, at least in their world of cycles. The problem of their recurring moments in the spotlight would not go away.

Bird protectors were trapped in a hall of mirrors. They looked one way and saw hunters chasing herons. The protectors went to save the herons and the herons transformed into gulls. Off the protectors went to help the gulls and the gulls morphed into eagles. The protectors could not keep up with the fashion cycles of featured birds, even though they had advance notice of coming attractions.

While the protectors tried every way possible to save all the birds, women kept buying murderous millinery. That was the most frustrating part of the bird slaughter era for the bird protection crusaders. So part of their program was to conduct a public relations campaign to convince women they were killing birds vicariously just by wearing hats.

Realists recognized that many women refused to wear birds on their hats for the sake of humanity. Pessimists believed they were comparatively few in number and not a great deal could be expected from individuals in changing fashion dictates. Concerted action was needed. Crusaders fanned out across the land to convince women to abandon their murderous millinery.

Speakers and journalists, male and female alike, lectured, flattered, cajoled, pleaded, scolded, shamed … they did everything they could to teach women how their actions were killing birds. The ladies, especially those considered leaders, did not always respond favorably. When the Audubon Society of New York City held a meeting to voice their objection to the use of murderous millinery, several "eminent" gentlemen took part in the protest but no women of equal prominence were present.

Critics did not make a big deal out of that protest. They noted that nothing would result from one meeting and that the ladies' input would not have been helpful anyway. They speculated that the women would have argued that a bird on a bonnet had as much to do with the promotion of human happiness as a bird in a glass case in a museum—to whose massacre nobody objected.[2]

In a like vein a silky-tongued journalist made fun of some women's opposition to criticizing their "sisters" for wearing bird hats: "The *Davenport Times* imagines that 'the

36   **The Hat That Killed a Billion Birds**

stuffed birds on the hats of the delegates to the National Federation of Women's Clubs probably looked pleased when it was decided by the members that the killing of birds for millinery ornaments is to be deplored."[3]

That satirical comment was unfair, since not all women treated the issue that way. But it was not uncommon to think they were all of a similar mind in their support of bird hats. Even if women were not inclined to join the protests, one newspaper warned, the public relations blitz was necessary as yet another wave of murderous millinery approached America's shores:

> Once more the rage for decorating hats with birds has taken possession of womankind. Every other woman met in the streets of New York has a bird pressed against the crown or perched on the brim of her hat. The women who have such a decoration use wings, aigrettes, or feathers. Instead, every bird lover hoped and sincerely believed that the crusade against this custom several years ago had sent it out of vogue forever. But here it is again, and there is nothing for bird lovers to do but to go to work with renewed zeal and create a sentiment against the slaughtering of myriads of innocent songsters.[4]

George O. Shields, president of the League of American Sportsmen, took the warning to heart. He appealed to women's common sense. In a lecture before a prominent woman's club in the west, he said:

> There is abundant reason to congratulate the women of this country on their good sense. When their attention was called to the needless and heartless destruction of bird life which was being perpetrated in order to gratify their love of beautiful raiment, thousands of them stopped wearing birds on their hats.
>
> It is safe to say that five per cent of the twenty thousand women who belong to the Audubon Societies today were formerly patrons of the bird millinery traffic. They had not before stopped to think of the wrong that was being done as a result of their patronage, but when their attention was called to it they were as ready to discard the sinful ornaments as they always are to join in any good movement.[5]

He may have been preaching to the choir. If flattery didn't work, maybe dazzling women with numbers would:

> Ladies who patronize the use of birds' feathers in millinery may be interested to know that certain species of birds are threatened with extinction by the prevailing fashion. A French paper reports that in one market recently and at one sale there were disposed of 12,000 humming-birds, 28,000 paroquets, 15,000 king-fishers, 121,400 aigrettes and many thousand other birds of gorgeous plumage.
>
> Germany sends to London every year 20,000,000 feathers to be worked up into trimmings. The one hope for the poor birds is that the day may soon arrive when to wear the feathers of wild birds will be deemed bad form. Nothing else can save them. The greater their beauty the worse their impending fate.[6]

Similar numbers were available in myriad articles in newspapers and magazines. But the only numbers some women were interested in were the ones on the price tags or the bird counts on their hats. The former seemed less important since, as so many people said, they didn't actually pay for the headgear. So the problem was not theirs. It was men's.

One observer said that if women couldn't be reached on the bird millinery question on moral or esthetic grounds, and if they refused to see the cruelty or the ugliness of museum millinery, maybe they could understand a financial argument.[7] He conceded that this would mean putting the matter into the hands of men, who no doubt paid the majority of the millinery bills. Their attitude was simple: let him refuse to pay for the bird hat or to be seen in company with its wearer. That would draw women's attention to the problem and spur them to action. They were certainly capable of taking up a cause.

The observer pointed out that societies of women had banded together to boycott smokers. Why shouldn't men protect themselves against a worse evil, save money in the bargain, and teach women the value of a dollar while saving birds? He added facetiously that some women believe that four-and-twenty blackbirds gathered into a pie for masculine consumption is as great a sin against bird nature as the placing of this same feathered tribe upon a hat for the gratification of female vanity. If that were the case, the money argument might work.

One of the more outspoken critics of women was American poet and writer Ella Wheeler Wilcox. "Laugh, and the world laughs with you; weep, and you weep alone," she wrote in one of her poems. She did not laugh at the sight of birds on women's hats, however incongruous the sight may have been to her. Nor did she weep alone at the loss of bird life. Laughing or weeping, she offered a plan to women on how to wean themselves off the bird craze.

"There is no more grotesque sight than a woman's club luncheon, where women wearing every known manner of birds on their heads meet together to discuss the best ways of bringing kindness into the world and lessening cruelty," she said. She cited statistics concerning bird deaths and sales to highlight why it was so wrong to wear such headgear, addressed the issue of birds' rights, and presented her plan.

To her, the statistics she reeled off meant that the women of Europe and America had given an order for the ruthless extermination of birds while ignoring the creatures' rights. She chided:

> The cause of this failure must undoubtedly be sought in the general lack of any clear conviction that animals have rights, and the evil will never be thoroughly remedied until not only this particular abuse, but all such abuses, and the prime source from which such abuses originate, have been subjected to an impartial criticism. In saying this I do not, of course, mean to imply that special efforts should not be directed against special cruelties.

Wilcox made no bones about who was at fault in the murderous millinery movement. It was women.

> I have already remarked that the main responsibility for the daily murders which fashionable millinery is instigating must lie at the door of those who demand, rather than those who supply, these hideous and funeral ornaments. Unfortunately, the process, like that of slaughtering cattle, is throughout delegated to other hands than those of the ultimate purchaser, so that it is exceedingly difficult to bring home a due sense of blood-guiltiness to the right person.

She appealed to every woman who claimed to be more than a mere skeleton upon which fine apparel is hung, who believes she has a heart and a mind, to pause and consider the enormity of the crime against the feathered creatures of earth which fashionable millinery waged. She implored them to use their feminine ingenuity and taste to create hats and bonnets for their own use which did not require the corpses of or feathers of dead birds to make them beautiful.

Wilcox had a lot to say in addition as she outlined her plan for them:

> Besides the cruel aspect of this subject, there is the appalling FACT that the decrease of birds means the increase of insects and moths, and the consequent destruction of grains, vegetables and trees.

> From an industrial, as well as a humane point of view, women should organize a no-bird millinery movement. Beautiful creations in headgear are fashioned out of ribbons, lace, ferns, flowers, and jet.
>
> Analyzed, the idea of carrying a dead bird, or anything which means the destruction of life, on the head is monstrous, inartistic and senseless.

Strangely enough, she justified the use of dead animals by saying that the wearing of furs can be defended by the argument that wild animals would soon own the earth if not destroyed and that human beings need their skins to keep them from the cold. But, she admonished, no such argument could be offered in excuse by the women who cause birds to be slaughtered by the millions for their use in head decorations.

Wilcox implored women to engage in conversations with their milliners to tell them to create the most exquisite hats possible out of nature's and art's most inanimate articles. Suggest ideas to her, she said, and try to produce something which is so beautiful that it puts to shame the miniature butcher shops that other women sport.

Get on the bandwagon, she urged ladies. Talk to your friends and to your enemies and familiarize them with the details of bird slaughter. Refuse to belong to a club that does not consider this question one of importance to the progress of woman. Make the women who attend your church ashamed of wearing dead birds. Refuse to believe in their religion until they cease to aid the cause of murderous millinery.[8]

Nothing that she asked of women or suggested was radical. Examples abounded of women who were working alone or in tandem to eliminate the bird slaughter problem. And they had been doing so for years. Mrs. Julius I. Brown of Atlanta, Georgia, was a prime example.

Mrs. Brown was an enthusiastic bird lover. She alone had secured pledges from more than 3,000 of the best women of her state that they would not in the future use the plumage of wild birds as millinery ornaments. The signers pledged not to kill or hurt

Five hunters, somewhere in the Dakotas around 1890, with their dogs and the game they shot (Farr, artist).

6. But Did the Ladies Listen?

any living creature needlessly or destroy any beautiful thing but to strive to comfort all gentle life and guard and perfect all natural beauty on earth. In addition, through her efforts more than 2,500 of the school children of Atlanta were subscribers to a pledge not to harm or annoy wild birds. Such activists made Ms. Wilcox proud.[9]

Fifteen years before Wilcox offered her ideas there was word of a meeting of the New England Woman's Club at which the attendees adopted a resolution to place themselves on record as entirely opposed to the wearing of the plumage of bodies of wild birds for ornamental purposes and to discountenance the practice, both in themselves and others.[10]

A storeowner in Los Angeles was heralded for her "no bird" products.

Mrs. Wood likes medium-sized hats. She sits in her pretty shop at 346 South Broadway and frowns at the ultra in millinery. The three-story mountains of bird, beast and fish that our friends are wont to attach to their coiffures are not to be found in this artistic establishment. Beautiful models—hats that will appeal to all ages and complexions—are to be found here in harmonious combinations and unusually attractive numbers.[11]

There were still people who derided the "do-gooders" who were trying to save the birds. When the ladies in Fond Du Lac, Wisconsin, railed against murderous millinery the Scrooge in a nearby town sneered:

Now the federated club women in convention at Fond du Lac would abolish the old-time Christmas tree because it devastates the forests. We'll have to go barefoot next for fear of denuding the sheep, or use chalk milk out of kindness to the poor little calves.

Dear, good women, you may cut down millinery bills by tabooing bird ornaments, save dressmaker's expenses by wearing Mother Hubbards, but do leave us the good old times of Christmas trees, stockings to hang up and occasional sprigs of mistletoe to practice under.[12]

Religious appeals were part of the attempt to persuade women to leave the birds in peace. At times Christians sounded less than Christian in their diatribes against women who wore the high hats. One man railed:

There was a time when we could attribute the wearing of birds to the thoughtlessness of women. After all that has been said and written in condemnation there is no longer room for charity. There should be no hesitancy in denouncing every woman who appears in public adorned with dead birds as heartless, shameless and a disgrace to her country. A vile woman in the city of Paris set the hideous fashion, and women considering themselves cultivated and Christian are following it; professing to worship God, yet ruthlessly sharing in the destruction of one of his most beautiful creatures.

He prevailed on the people to demand the enactment of a law which would make the killing, selling or wearing of songbirds a punishable crime. After all, he said, referring to the recent presidential election in 1896, winner William McKinley has saved the honor and manhood of our nation: "Now let something be done to save the womanhood, and we may stand approved of God and angels."[13]

Poet/writer Ella Antoinette Hotchkiss was a bit more charitable. She wrote:

The more beautiful the bird the worse is the cruelty practiced upon it, such as stripping it of its wings and throwing it down to die and the handsome wings to be flaunted on a milliner's hat. Too anguishing to hear have some women deemed the cruelties to the bird race. And still they wear the plumage without the least compunction. It is a relief to remember other women, who at a lecture, upon hearing for the first time the dreadful ravages, took off their hats, removing wings and aigrettes.

40   The Hat That Killed a Billion Birds

Stories of women who took off their hats and swore off murderous millinery were rife. In Hotchkiss's mind all Christian women should follow suit lest God smite them. Even the vaunted British army had grown ashamed of decorating itself with this murderous millinery, which military authorities had discarded.

And warnings of sad eternities like this were issued to make women aware that their fates hung in the balance if they persisted in wearing birds atop their hats. "Ponder this pitiful picture, you Christian women, who flaunt these martyr plumes in the face of heaven, Sunday after Sunday, from out of your consecrated pews."

Hotchkiss was not one to withhold her Christian bearings in the matter of headgear. One passage in her writings said:

> No truly Christ-like mind will shrink from knowing, for sake of active interest required. The hideous crime should be abolished that brands the name of womankind. If any are so ignorant as not to believe the extent of the wickedness perpetrated by the other sex for the demand of women, let them learn in due season, thus deserving the name of disciples of the pure Jesus, who scorned not one of the dumb creatures in his heavenly Father's creation. He it was who said, "Not a sparrow falleth, etc.," and do you think that the Father's "notice" is without reproof to the human heart?[14]

The answer to that question would fall as silently as a bird shot with a blow gun. The lack of responses did not dissuade crusaders from their efforts to convert women from bird adornments to flowers, ribbons, and lace. But were enough of them listening? Probably not, if this reproach was any indication. Ironically, it involved Massachusetts, where it was allegedly rare around 1900 to see a hat trimmed with the body or feathers of any native songbird.[15] That marked an amazing turnaround based on a report from only three years earlier, after the state had passed a law against the use of birds as millinery trimming.

Boston's city authorities vowed to have the police enforce the recently enacted law against killing birds indiscriminately. Officials of the Museum of Natural History in the city ran an impromptu test to see how that was going. They compiled a list of birds observers saw used in adorning headgear. There were 40 species represented, ranging from sparrows to woodpeckers. In all they saw 173 wild birds, or parts of them, on hats. Of these birds at least 32 varieties were protected by law during all or a major portion of the year.

So much for women listening to the crusaders or adhering to laws against murderous millinery. The attraction of the most popular hat adornment of all time, the aigrette, was apparently too much for fashion-conscious women to ignore. It had disappeared for a while, but its turn for the spotlight arrived again two years later.[16]

An editorial writer with a flair for the dramatic wrote:

> There is, however, in spite of these encouraging features of the contest between vanity and ignorance on the one hand, and broader sympathies and enlightenment, one stronghold in which the powers of darkness threaten to make a desperate stand. It is announced that the aigrette, which has never ceased to be more or less fashionable, will come into greater demand than ever during the coming winter.

Those words gave him a chance to admonish women for their inability to eschew the aigrette. He said that the delicate plumes, beautiful as they seem to anyone ignorant of the method by which they must have been obtained, rightly stamp the wearer absolutely ill-informed in these times of many books and many lectures. Either that or

6. But Did the Ladies Listen?

they were utterly lacking in sympathy for humans' most charming and most defenseless friends, the birds. He concluded:

> We must hope that if the fashion is setting in in the threatened direction, Massachusetts, at any rate, will be found strong enough to resist the demand to return to more heartless and ignorant conditions. The truth was that Massachusetts was no different than any other state. The women there were as adept at virtue signaling as their counterparts anywhere. They may have talked a good game about giving up aigrettes and other feathered fineries, but many ladies in the Bay State were still wearing them.

Nineteen hundred three was predicted to be another glory year for aigrettes. Fashionistas forecast that consumers would see more of them than had ever been worn before. "It does not seem possible that after the peculiar cruelty that attaches to the getting of these beautiful plumes is known, even the most careless-minded woman could ever bring herself to wear them again," the editor lamented.[17]

They could—and they did. The crusaders continued their efforts to wean the women off the murderous millinery, with limited success. The years went by and the dates changed, but the fashions did not. Aigrettes were as much in vogue 10 years later as they were in 1903, and even then people had to wonder if they would ever lose their place in the cycle of popularity.

The only question left to answer was which species was next on the hit list.

7

Which Birds Is It Okay to Kill?

"There's more to a blue-jay than any other creature. He has got more moods, and more different kinds of feelings than other creature; and mind you, whatever a blue-jay feels, he can put into language. And no mere commonplace language, either, but rattling, out-and-out book-talk—and bristling with metaphor, too—just bristling! And as for command of language—why you never see a blue-jay get stuck for a word. No man ever did."[1]

People did not understand the importance of blue jays—or of any other birds. That was part of the reason the bird slaughter went on unabated for so long. When folks finally began giving serious thought to the need for bird protection they still had mixed feelings about slaughtering birds strictly for millinery purposes. Some believed that all birds should be protected. Others said none were worth saving.

Birds are birds, the latter group maintained. There are so many flying around that we can't possibly kill them all. That philosophy was put to a test as one species after another disappeared. In truth, based on repopulation rates, people could kill them all eventually. One Vermont farmer estimated that for every 100 birds killed only 60 were born. At that rate, they would all disappear, although no one could pinpoint a certain date.[2]

Opinions about which birds it was okay to kill were almost as numerous as the number of species extant. Sportsmen, ornithologists, farmers, fruit growers, legislators, ordinary folks … everyone had an opinion. There was no consensus in sight. People and lawmakers divided species into villains and "good guys." That did not help lawmakers as they struggled to protect the birds.

Some maintained that only insectivorous birds should be protected. Everything else was fair game—especially game birds that were pests. How "pest" was defined was in the eye of the beholder. Of course, what was left protected or unprotected depended on which birds' feathers and parts women preferred on their hats. Kingfishers were an excellent example.[3]

Officials in Louisiana and Mississippi in particular labeled kingfishers as pests. Paradoxically, Louisiana was relentless when it came to protecting seabirds but not kingfishers. Too many people in those two states contended that their destruction was a public blessing, so the world was welcome to all the kingfisher plumes it could use. That was evident in almost every list of birds released by dealers. The numbers of kingfishers made available were huge.

The kingfishers' crime against humanity was their penchant for destroying planters' land along both banks of the Mississippi River. For generations, in tandem with

7. Which Birds Is It Okay to Kill?

Hunters shooting, probably for birds, as indicated by upward trajectory (Detroit Publishing Co., ca. 1895–1915).

minks and muskrats, they had cost the states of Louisiana and Mississippi millions of dollars by causing cracks in the levees and overflows at the time of the spring floods.

Kingfishers made their nests in tunnels. The nests were about three inches in diameter and about 12 feet deep. The birds drove them into the river bank. During the spring, when the river rose, the water reached the tunnels and enlarged them. The sides caved in, which opened crevasses that allowed the water to flow through into the cultivated lands, so the birds had to be eradicated to stop the damage.

It was practically impossible for anyone to locate the kingfisher nests, because the birds skillfully concealed them. The alternative was to shoot the birds. For years, levee commissioners in Louisiana and Mississippi encouraged people to hunt them by offering a reward of a dollar a head. In some places along the Mississippi and its tributaries men made it a business to hunt kingfishers the year round. They made more money doing so than by raising either cotton or corn. Decimating kingfishers may have paid off for the hunters but not for the birds.

The arguments about pest classification went back and forth as they had for decades. Meanwhile, birds continued to die, and protection, where it was afforded, was inconsistent from city to city, state to state, and country to country. The latter difference was important, since bird slaughter was a truly international problem.

There was a stark difference between American and English law, for instance. The two countries differed noticeably in their approaches. In England all birds were treated alike and all were protected, but only during the five-month breeding season. In the United States it was customary to divide birds into two or more categories.

Each set of laws had its advantages and disadvantages. The English laws were more comprehensive than most U.S. statutes, but the principle of establishing protection only during the breeding season opened serious objection in many states because of their legislators' tendency to class a number of insectivorous birds as game. As a result, such birds would be killed for market in large numbers during the winter months.

U.S. game birds were protected only during the breeding season. The other species were protected at all times—if they were protected at all. A few states, notably Georgia, North Carolina, and Tennessee, treated all birds alike. But they did not protect many species. There was a selective process in those states which extended to the entire country.

Birds of prey were generally unpopular everywhere, so they had limited protection. Some states tried to exterminate hawks and owls via bounties. Pennsylvania alone awarded bounties of more than $100,000 for hawks and owls in the late 1890s. People did not understand the role these birds—or birds in general—played in the nature cycle. Even when they got curious birds died.

A farmer near Bangor, Maine, typified that quirk of human nature reminiscent of a Vietnam War officer who promised, "We'll save that village even if we have to destroy it to do so."[4] The farmer noticed that wheat was being picked from the heads of standing grain. When he spied flocks of yellow birds flying about the wheat, the farmer shot some of them. He opened the dead birds' crops and found only three grains of wheat, and, by actual count, 350 weevils. They hadn't been eating the wheat after all.

The lesson was clear: it was better that farmers knew whether they killed friends or foes. This particular farmer had saved the birds' reputations as friends—but they were destroyed in the process. That was true with the hawks and owls as well. Eventually the states withdrew the bounties, but they still withheld protection for such raptors.

One look at the stomachs of hawks and owls might have changed some minds, as it did for the Maine farmer. They were eating machines, as Dr. C. Hart Merriam, chief of the division of ornithology of the U.S. Agricultural Department, observed in his 1895 paper, "The Relation of Birds to Crops."

Merriam studied the contents of the stomachs of hawks, crows, owls, blackbirds, meadow larks, and other North American birds for years prior to releasing his findings. He concentrated on birds that were considered either significantly beneficial or injurious to farm crops. He wrote:

> The stomachs of over 7,000 birds, taken at different seasons of the year, have been analyzed and the contents determined, while some 12,000 are still unexamined. The results in some cases have been remarkable, showing in several notable instances that popular ideas regarding the injurious effects of certain birds were wholly mistaken and that they have been the victims of an unjust persecution.[5]

That persecution was due in large part to the general population's ignorance about birds and their feeding habits, like the Maine farmer. One way to resolve that dearth was to educate people at an early age. Consequently, there was a movement in the late 1800s and early 1900s to add ornithology to school curriculums. The idea was that teaching children about birds would turn them into protectors of their feathered friends. Strangely enough, the folks who really needed the education in many instances were the farmers and fruit growers who worked most closely with the birds. It turned out that they had a lot to learn about their unpaid "helpers."

7. Which Birds Is It Okay to Kill?   45

Studies similar to Merriam's helped them learn. People had some idea of birds' value in farming. They did not understand just how necessary they were on farms—and not just the ones perceived as good. Farmers had misconceptions about a variety of birds that helped out around their crops, such as crows, robins, woodpeckers, blue jays, and Kingbirds. Scientific studies helped them lose their misconceptions.[6]

Farmers disliked crows because at certain times of the year they pulled up corn plants in order to eat the sprouted kernels—or so it appeared—and consumed large amounts of grain.[7] Observers learned that when a crow was digging up the corn, where it started to uncover the seed it was actually after a farmer's true enemy, the dreaded cut worm, not the corn. But how much of either corn or grain did crows actually eat?

Studies proved that thousands of crows had been killed in the name of research by scientists and their stomachs examined. The researchers showed that in the majority of instances crows ate very little grain and a great many insects. The findings suggested that crows, like so many other birds branded as pests, were greatly maligned and that in reality they were the friend of the farmer.

Fruit growers frequently shot robins because they ate a few berries. In reality, the robins worked throughout the spring and early summer to destroy the insects that would have ruined the crop. The growers should not have begrudged the robins the few berries they ate in the process. Rather, they should have considered the losses as full compensation for such a valuable service.

Farmers resented woodpeckers because they pecked holes in the bark of trees and allegedly killed the trees. As ornithologists pointed out, the woodpeckers were after grubs and insects. The holes they made were just deep enough to dislodge their food but did not have a lasting impact on the trees.

Likewise, Kingbirds were said to be fond of honey bees, which had an adverse impact on the cross-pollination process that helped crops grow or abetted "at-home" honey-making. But when the birds were killed and the contents of their stomachs were analyzed, few honey bees were found—even when the birds were killed working directly among the bees. Ninety percent of their food consisted of injurious insects. Contrary to popular belief, the Kingbirds provided significant protection to farmers.

In a similar vein, people commonly perceived the blue jay as a corn-eating, nest-robbing thief. That may have been true to some extent, though there was scant direct evidence to prove the allegation. Blue jays actually ate corn only when nuts and acorns were out of season. Researchers found that 20 percent of a blue jay's food comprised injurious insects.

Knowledge such as that explained why ornithologists and other scientists urged farmers—and everyone else—to learn about birds before they killed them and pressed for the passage and enforcement of bird protection laws. They especially pushed for milliners and the ladies who bought their hats to learn more about the lives of birds. Their message was simple: people can learn more about birds when they are alive than when they are dead. Above all, all birds should be protected.

Merriam's findings regarding hawks and owls were particularly enlightening. Examinations of the stomachs of the birds he studied proved conclusively that 95 percent of their food comprised field mice, grasshoppers, crickets, and the like, which were more injurious to farm crops than the birds supposedly were. He found that only five kinds of hawks and owls ever touched poultry, and then only to a very limited extent.

A study by the Biological Survey of the United States Department of Agriculture disclosed that many hawks were valuable to nature.[8] Some owls were found to be among the most useful of all birds. The researchers concluded that these birds destroyed not only many noxious insects which moved about mainly by night and so were not susceptible to the attacks of day birds but that they also formed a chief check to rodent pests which otherwise would be quite as destructive as the insects. What milliners inferred from the report was that owls deserved a spot of prominence atop ladies' hats. Who would miss them? The answer was simple: everyone.

George O. Shields made that clear in an address he gave to a high school gathering in Caldwell, Idaho.

> Scientific men have figured that if all the birds were destroyed, the country would become totally uninhabitable in three years, by reason of the ravages of the insects on which the birds now feed and exist.... The whole social, political and business structure of this country is based on agriculture.
>
> Without husbandry, the country could not survive five years. How vastly important it is therefore that we should all think and act seriously in the interest of bird protection. Time will not permit me to enumerate the various species of birds which should be saved and conserved, but nearly all of them claim our consideration.[9]

Even Shields was unclear as to which ones deserved consideration and which ones didn't. That was completely unfair to the birds and to the sportsmen he represented. With no proper guidance neither they nor anyone else had a clear idea which birds were protected. It was a mystery as to why some, such as hummingbirds and canaries, were killed at all—and why the milliners denied outright or tried to hide the fact that they were being slaughtered.

Proponents of murderous millinery suggested that a great deal of unnecessary agitation had been created among a specific group of wealthy women over the barbarity of wearing birds, their wings, and other parts on their hats. It appeared to them reports of the large numbers of birds used for millinery purposes were made up. They admitted that a few real hummingbirds and other small ones were being killed for the purpose, but they were exceptions to the general rule and very expensive.

The implication was that only a "certain class of women," supposedly those in the affluent tier, could afford hummingbirds and canaries. No mention was made of canaries anywhere. But one letter writer assured readers that they were being killed:

> To affirm that the domestic canary is never used for millinery purposes is untrue. The writer saw a hat only a short time since with five canaries upon it, arranged in such fantastic attitudes as to suggest the idea that the wearer was a fit subject for the lunatic asylum. Either we must believe what the feather dealers tell us, and distrust the evidence of our own senses, or we must believe what the leading ornithologists of the country tell us, and for my part I prefer to believe the latter.[10]

For everyone else the manufactured and dyed feathers would have to do, and even they weren't cheap. Hardly anyone could tell the difference between them and real feathers. The feathers of the ordinary fowl were dyed with tedious workmanship in order to blend the various tints in a harmonious reproduction of the real bird. Each feather was stuck on separately by skilled and clever workers.

The work was so exacting that many of the strange, fantastic, winged creatures seen on hats were made and imported from Paris, but the most expensive and natural came from a manufacturer in Berlin.[11] But when small whole birds were needed, canaries and hummingbirds fit the bill—or their bills fit the hat—so they made the "okay to kill" list.

Another factor influencing the establishment of bird protection laws was the varying delineations between sportsmen, who had a lot of input into legislation affecting birds, and lawmakers. To sportsmen, birds were either game birds or non-game birds. Legislators identified three groups: species which should be protected at all times, species which may be killed in certain seasons for food or sport, or species considered injurious and should therefore be excluded from protection.

Legislators broke down the groups further: insectivorous or songbirds, game birds, and injurious birds. No matter how they were classified the groups were necessarily arbitrary, considering that there were about 1,125 species and subspecies of birds living in North America north of Mexico at the time. Of those, only about 200 (18 percent) were considered game. The breakdowns led to a patchwork of bird protection laws that often defied logic and complicated conservationists' efforts to preserve any species.

A graphic mid-slaughter–era report card explained the confusion regarding bird protection around the turn of the 20th century. (See Appendix A.) It was a good thing birds could not read. They would have been scratching their heads wondering if they were or were not protected. Certainly, some humans were unsure. The members of the millinery trade were as well. But, for them, the uncertainty was a good thing. They could continue to buy, sell, and mount birds until someone told them they couldn't. Just who that someone would be was unclear. The enigma continued, but it did not stop some people from trying to put an end to murderous millinery.

8

Who Was to Blame?

"Extermination Threatened by the Prevailing Fashions.... IF THE WOMEN ONLY REALIZED.... Craze of women for feathered hats makes American water fowl scarce...."[1]

Headlines like the above were not uncommon during the bird slaughter era. The writers made it clear that if it weren't for women's predilections for aigrettes and other fine feathers, plumes, and bird parts, there would be no murderous millinery problem. But was that charge fair? They were not acting alone to keep the movement going.

It is difficult to single out the chief villain among the supporters of the murderous millinery era. There were many candidates. The long-lasting bird slaughter fad could not have endured if it did not have designers, fashion writers, milliners, hunters, taxidermists, advertisers, manufacturers, cold store specialists ... anyone who had an economic interest in the production and sales of the merchandise—and that was just about everybody. Finding the most culpable party was like trying to identify the snowflake that started a blizzard.

History proves that if there is a problem someone is to blame for it. That is human nature. Sometimes people spend more time trying to find a scapegoat than they do trying to solve the problem. That was true during the world's murderous millinery phase.

Why was the bird craze so popular? And who was to blame for it? Those were questions people were asking during every stage of the bird slaughter era. The answers were not forthcoming, but people thought they knew. Many agreed with the headline writers: the women were at fault.

Punsters had a field day with blaming the ladies for the world's ills. "It is calculated that if the finger of opprobrium can be thus directed in public against each bird-wearing lady bird ornaments will soon become very unpopular," one suggested.[2]

Another said, "Feather-wearing will surely cease to be fashionable among women when the hunters can no longer find any birds to kill."[3]

In truth, there was enough blame to go around. And not everybody blamed women.

A naturalist reported that in Norfolk, Virginia, in the spring of 1886 hundreds of woodpeckers and songbirds were exposed for sale. Those birds, he cautioned, could not be attributed to anything women did. They and the game birds whose destruction had been so improvident that extinction was only a matter of a little time were killed by males. The women were practically innocent, he emphasized.

He admitted that ladies occasionally ate a reed bird or bobolink on toast at some fashionable restaurant or private table. But, he observed, they were not the ones who traveled to Long Island in the hunting season where a sportsman supplied his table for weeks at a time with the eggs of the birds that bred numerously in his vicinity just

8. Who Was to Blame?

because he liked the wild flavor of those delicacies. Nor were they responsible for the small boys who killed a bird on sight just for sport if he could hit it with a stone or pea-shooter. "Not until women destroy bird or animal life for mere sport can they be held to be guilty as are the men of the present threatened [sic] destruction of bird life on this continent," he opined.[4]

That defender of women was not alone in thinking the phenomena of bird hats would be of short duration. He was simply echoing the words of newspaper correspondent Annette Givry: "Whatever naturalists and tender hearted women feel, I cannot help expatiating on the smartness of wings and birds in millinery, though at the same time this fashion creates too much righteous indignation to remain, I think, long in vogue."[5]

She wrote those words long after the fad began and long before it ended. Perhaps she underestimated women's influence in continuing it. That was the one thing that will stop the killing, people supposedly in the know declared—that is, women's influence. "She has but to allow disapprobation of the fashion and millions of bird lives will be preserved every year," they believed.[6] If they could all see the light like a fashionable milliner in New York had done, the birds could take to the air again, sing to their hearts' contents, and gorge on insects until they fell from the sky.

The woman to whom they referred had been in the habit of going to Boston each season with a large supply of bird-adorned hats. But she learned a hard lesson in 1895 when she visited the city to display her wares. As usual, she set up a table at an elegant hotel in town. That year her usual female clients arrived and looked at her creations but refused to buy them. They'd had an epiphany, thanks to the Audubon Society's influence.

The milliner became interested in the society and joined it. From that day forward she would not sell a hat with birds or aigrettes on it. She went to Boston the following year with hats decorated otherwise and did a thriving business.

There was a similar story about a young lady in New Haven, Connecticut, who spoke to Ella Antoinette Hotchkiss about her conversion. The young lady said that when she was formerly working in a milliner's establishment her articles of sale were the dead birds. One day a lady customer took her greatly to task for the cruelty. She had never before heard about it. It was not exactly the way to touch a heart to tenderness.

But the customer had "sat, every Sunday, behind so many dead birds that she could not close her eyes in prayer nor worship properly!" That conversation alone changed the salesperson's heart. She changed careers and went to work in a bookstore.

According to Hotchkiss, among the books that young lady sold was one named *Beautiful Joe*, a charming story for children. "Dear Joe has influenced many a heart among humanity." In it the protagonists says: "I love human beings. I love to have them talk to me." Hotchkiss noted that Joe spoke for the birds as well.

"The girl or woman that wears a circlet of birds about the crown of her hat resembles the masculine plunderer with the birds hooked to the belt around his waist, himself a brigand in appearance," she charged. "One masculine writer has likened the woman's bird-beset hat to a 'walking graveyard.'" Hotchkiss apparently favored plain adornments on millinery. She had another story to relate in that respect.

One recent day a young girl of sweet countenance and pleasing manner entered a street car. Her hat was particularly noticeable. The dainty head gear was becoming to the fresh complexion, the glow of honor in the dark, brown eyes. No wing nor aigrette, nor dead body of bird rested upon it. It was of brown that corresponded to the eves in shade. Very simple were the trimmings, so simple that they are not now remembered. But the face of the lovable girl is not forgotten. Perhaps she was not setting an example (consciously) by means of her pretty hat.[7]

Leastways, Hotchkiss said, it was an example, even if expressing only the personal liking of its owner of simple adornments. It was pleasant to believe that she had excluded birds and plumage from her decorations for a moral purpose. The car was full of feathers and of birds—not one of which was alive to tell the story!

Hotchkiss may have used poetic license in her writing, but there were a lot of converts to plain adornments who vowed that they would not wear hats or bonnets decorated with any kind of plumage except that from the domesticated birds and the ostrich. They wondered if women realized that if they stopped wearing murderous millinery they would live longer or become magically prettier. And if they stopped wearing high hats men would benefit as well.

An unnamed eminent scientist attributed the remarkable longevity of a woman who died at the age of 109 to the fact that she never wore a high bonnet in a theater.[8] Conversely, the vigorous health of a Philadelphia man in his 99th year was attributed to the fact that he never went out between the acts of a performance to make astronomical observations through a glass, that is, gulp down an adult beverage.

Newspaperman Charles Dudley Warner tied theater hats to women's attractiveness.[9] He told *Forest and Stream Magazine* that a dead bird does not help the appearance of an ugly woman and a pretty woman needs no such adornment. If you can get the women to recognize these two things, he said, a great deal will be done for the protection of our songbirds.

Observations such as those notwithstanding, no one wanted to take the blame for the inclusion of bird plumes and parts on millinery. The most logical source of blame was the millinery trade and its members. The designers concocted the hats and other garniture that featured bird-related components. Yet fashion writers described the hats designed by the Paris milliners in such flowery language that women felt they couldn't do without birds on their hats.

They and milliners spoke in nebulous terms of far-off arbiters of styles and the ubiquitous dictum of the mode. That way they could downplay the fact that birds were the victims of some invisible group of people whose job was to design and sell the millinery without worrying about the origination or fate of the adornments.

Wholesalers stockpiled feathers, plumes, whole birds and parts and hired hunters to collect them. Retailers stocked their shelves with the resulting products and featured them in their store windows. Women bought them in profuse numbers and sales of bird headgear continued to flourish. They became scapegoats for the other stakeholders in murderous millinery.

The rationale was straightforward: if they didn't buy the products then the millinery trade would either go out of business or be forced to redesign everything to the exclusion of birds. Of course, since it was an era when men paid for almost everything, they could not be held blameless. The vast majority of hunters were males whose greed knew no bounds. Professional plume hunters found it worthwhile to violate the law, and the law did not reach many parts of the world where the destruction of bird life was greatest.

The boys were killers, too, with their peashooters and air guns. But it was ultimately men who controlled the finances in their homes, so they had to be chiefly responsible for the ongoing sakes of bird hats. The industry's fate was in their hands.

8. Who Was to Blame?

Theoretically, if the men refused to pay for the hats, sales would go down. Demand and the pressure on the millinery trade to kill birds would lessen. Or, if men refused to be seen in public with the women who wore the monstrosities on their heads, they would shame the ladies into wearing less garish headgear.

Practically, if men wanted to keep the peace between the two genders they were not about to do anything of the sort. But was it up to men alone to keep the peace? Didn't women bear some responsibility for that too? As Hotchkiss said:

> Woman, it may be said, is not the chief sinner, since man need not heed her foolishness with such indulgence as to hunt or slay for her pitiless passion. At whatever door we lay the origin of the sin, and sin it surely is, and one in which men, women and children have been all too long participating.
> Children are the least in blame. Few children are there without natural tenderness of feeling. They are quickly influenced by their elders. Indeed, some of them have set the righteous example for their elders; an example not always encouraged.

She admitted there was a connection between women's hats and their vanity.

> Here, there, everywhere, turn which way one will, is seen the display of woman's petty vanity. It has gained ludicrous favor, a meaningless parade of feathers, feathers of even artificial hues (would that all were of artificial composition!) and the more colors that are combined, it would appear, the greater the vanity.[10]

Could that vanity spark a war between the genders when the blame game was being played? Lawmakers shared some blame. They were too slow to enact laws at times. When they did it was often too late and they were ineffective. That was especially true at the federal level. Moreover, law enforcement authorities were lax in their enforcement. So the blame game persisted for decades without making an appreciable dent in ending the wanton slaughter of birds. In most people's eyes, the women remained the chief culprits, but there was simply no way to lay the blame on one group or factor, as one astute writer opined:

> It is impossible to say who is responsible for the revival of the bird and feather fashion. Millinery buyers say that it began in Paris, and that London and New York followed. One thing is certain, though, and that is that every shop window in the city filled with hats, bonnets and turbans has behind the glass an ornithological exhibit which would do credit to a museum of natural history.
> Tender-hearted, sympathetic woman goes into ecstasies over these exhibits and decides that she must own a bonnet with a bird on it. She never stops to think of the millions of lives that have been destroyed to gratify her vanity and that of her sisters; nor does she realize, it is to be hoped, that in seven cases out of ten the extinction of each life meant either the loss of several eggs or the starving of a number of fledglings in the nest. But it is a fact that professional plume hunters find their business more profitable in nesting time than in any other.[11]

That was a slap at women. Supposedly they as a group had a nesting instinct. It was ironic, therefore, that they wore the aigrettes that could only be harvested when birds were nesting. "How could women tolerate that?" critics asked.

Slaps at women as scapegoats were not uncommon, but they were taken to new heights by one journalist who took advantage of the opportunity to comment on the cycle aspect as well in an article titled "Of Lovely Woman and the Fashions."

> For the immediate moment, by way of example, the high priestess inclines to selection from among the domestic weaponry of the kitchen for her headgear. What prompting turned her

52 The Hat That Killed a Billion Birds

lovely eyes to cast their beams on this neglected field it is not for mere man to say, and we submit to the decree with such grace as we can muster. What the conquering heroine, goddess, queen, says goes in the kingdom of fashion. Stet pro ratione voluntas (let good will stand for reason).

The natural reluctance of the unprotected male to venture on this shifting and uncertain ground impels him to call out the feminine reserves, and so one has recourse without more apology to marshal the embattled words of that accomplished woman writer, Mrs. Josephine Clifford McCracken, who would protect the harmless, necessary birds of the air from the raids of her sex.

That might have been said any time in the last ten years without producing a ripple of consciousness, but now one learns from an authoritative source that the millinery bird of the coming season is to be tailor made, a thing of shreds and patches, a monster bereft of sense or sensibilities, and when one says monster the connotation applies merely to bulk and not to disposition. The tailor-made bird is kind and gentle. He sings not, neither does he claw.

Indeed, the immediate preference is for the vegetable kingdom.

The dazzling creation that contemporary woman wears on her bewitching head is mostly Lenten fare and lacks only a piece of the brisket to complete the similitude of a New England boiled dinner. In the words of a noted poet, now deceased, and therefore out of harm's way, it may be said that the modern woman and trimmings is a creature not too bright or good for human nature's daily food.[12]

There was no doubt where that writer stood on the issue: women were to blame for the bird slaughter. Truthfully, the blame was sharable. Surprisingly, fashion writers may have been at the top of the list.

9

Fashion Writers Play a Key Role

"Trendy is the last stage before tacky."[1]

None of the candidates for blame would have stayed in business without the patronage of the ladies who bought the products, which someone had to make "must-haves." Perhaps no one was more influential in that respect than fashion writers, whose jobs were to sell the products, no matter how tacky they might be, and teach the ladies who could not afford to buy expensive headwear to make their own by producing "how-to" instructions. They were the sales force for the designers and milliners, and their role was as critical as if they were printing dress patterns for homemakers.

Fashion writers did everything from provide instructions on how to create hats at home to solicit and publish tips on their upkeep to save money. "Care should be exercised in packing away winter millinery, since carpet bugs delight in feasting on birds' wings and other millinery ornaments," one advised. "It should be put into perfect boxes sealed air tight by pasting strips of newspaper about the cover."[2] Another wrote, "Make your own: Ladies could make their own hats if they so desired."[3]

Milliners advertised "'a most captivating line of Feathers, Plumes, Tips, Birds, Fur trimmings, Jet ornaments...' anything to simplifying do-it-at home customizing hat projects."[4] The answers to "do-it-yourselfers'" questions were readily available.

"Please let me know as soon as possible, through the Question Box, how to treat wings of a bird for millinery purposes," one interested reader implored the columnist, who answered quickly. "Place the wings with only the flesh immersed in a strong salt solution and allow to remain over twenty-four hours. Then dry thoroughly and they are ready for use."[5]

Other pieces of advice were more detailed:

Some charming and inexpensive evening hats that can be made at home and worn with evening or formal afternoon gowns are of tulle, velvet and plumage or flowers. By changing the band it will match any gown, if one does not care to wear black and white. It is made by swathing a fine wire frame in write or ecru tulle, doing the brim first, beginning at left side and winding around until it overlaps in front like an Arab's turban, the end disappearing beneath the cabachon, which holds the aigrette in place. The crown is then swathed and a wide band of velvet pinned loosely about it, and the cabochon and aigrette added.

If made of white brown velvet with black, aigrette would be exceedingly smart, while one could use certain shades of blue, cherry or wine color for the band. In which case, instead of the aigrette, a huge cluster of grapes, cherries or large white field daisies with black centers would be quite handsome....[6]

Writers seldom explained what an aigrette was, how it was acquired, or the effect it had on herons. Mabel Herbert Urner explained it for her readers in an article titled "On

54 The Hat That Killed a Billion Birds

the Crime of Wearing an Aigrette." But, like so many meaningful articles, it came years after the bird slaughter began, which was too late to save many of the herons.

Urner was addressing New York State's Shea Law, which was about to go into effect on July 1, 1911. "I think every woman, if she knew at what cost the aigrette was obtained, would gladly welcome this law," she wrote. "It is not only that it costs the life of the bird from which these feathers are taken; the cruelty is far greater than that. For every aigrette means the slow starvation of a nest full of baby birds."

Her description of how the aigrettes were obtained was straightforward. "The aigrette is the nuptial plumage of the breeding season. This plumage does not form the tail as is ordinarily supposed, but grows between the wings and must be torn from the back with the skin attached in order to be of value." That is why anti–bird slaughter advocates dubbed the aigrette the "White Badge of Cruelty."

As Urner explained, before the breeding season the feathers were short and of no value. After that season they were worn, ragged, and unmarketable. So it was only when birds were raising their young that the aigrettes were long, graceful, and coveted for the millinery trade.

She could not have been more explicit in her emotional coverage: "The parent bird must be killed in order to obtain these plumes. And after their death the young birds in the nest must slowly starve. But most pitiful of all is the way the parent birds are slaughtered. It is because of their love for their young that they will not leave the nest and so fall an easy victim to this heartless butchery."

She pleaded with women to set aside their vanity and choose millinery that did not require the slaughter of birds. "Many other birds adorn our hats, which, of course, means the cost of that bird's life. This in itself seems a big price to pay for a few months' adornment when a flower of any of the many beautiful millinery ornaments would serve as well."

Her conclusion was tear-jerking. "But no bird's head, or breast, or wing represents quite the cruelty of the aigrette," Urner wrote. "Because, in every case, it means the betrayal and outraging of the most beautiful instinct in nature: the mother-love. And yet it is for the vanity of women that this sacrilege is made."[7]

Urner was not unsympathetic to the birds' plight, but she had a job to do. She was not alone in her mixed feelings. One of her fellow fashion writers started a piece with sympathetic words as well in her segment titled "Birds Form a Popular Trimming on Most Hats."

> I regret to observe that birds form a very popular trimming on much of the millinery, the entire bird being most generally used, and one of the most striking examples of the latest fashion in hats is made of pale blue silken beaver, with the brim slightly turning up all the way round, the sole decoration being a huge pale blue bird on one side of the crown on the top, and another beneath the brim at the back. And many of the white flat-crowned beaver hats show large white birds upon them. And again have I seen a flower crown of faded-looking chrysanthemums resting upon a brim made entirely of tiny birds....[8]

She may have regretted what she observed, but that did not prevent her from describing the products she was pushing. That was a dichotomy women faced: whether they should place the welfare of the birds above their adherence to fashion or vice versa. That was the crux of the high-hat dilemma for many women during the bird slaughter era. No wonder fashion writers sugar-coated their attempts to convince women that birds would have enjoyed being the centerpieces of their hats. The prize for that approach went to an unnamed writer who stated that milliners were simply playing tricks on the birds in co-opting their feathers.

9. Fashion Writers Play a Key Role

"It's a wise birdlet that knows its own parent," she began. "Likewise it's a wise old bird that knows its own chick these days. Never in the history of plumage have so many odd tricks been played on birds with millinery tendencies."

She envisioned how a peacock would react if it saw its own feathers on a hat:

> Fancy the proud peacock seeing its gorgeous tail feathers all plucked and beshorn of their pristine colors—their eyes literally plucked out and dyed black, to make a fan-shaped ornament for milady's hat! Juno [an ancient Roman goddess who was the protector and special counsellor of the state] would weep to see her favorite bird so despoiled. Yet the result is one of the very "chicest" effects in fall and winter millinery.

The writer did not even guess at what the peacock or its fellow bird the ostrich would have thought. "The black hatter's plush turban bears another odd feather ornament—the edges of the ostrich tip being capriciously caught in a jet border," as she described one hat. "Many privileges are taken with the poor ostrich who might well hide his head for shame if the results were not so striking and stylish."

If she whetted readers' appetites for feathers she knew where to direct them. "Think of the glycerined ostrich tip—but we have it with us and you don't buy it at the drug counter, either," she concluded.[9]

That writer was a master of descriptive tricks designed to match women and feathers. She failed to mention, however, that the tricks she talked about playing on birds to obtain their feathers cost millions of those creatures their lives. But she had a job to do and she did it.

There was no telling how many readers were affected by the mixed prose of writers like Urner and her sympathetic colleagues. Their reservations were heartfelt, to be sure, but too many fashion writers were extolling the attractions of bird millinery without looking at the damage it was doing to the bird world. They did everything but tell people how to shoot and stuff their own birds and pluck their own feathers. But they didn't have to. There were hunters who would do that for them as an integral part of the process, which began with the designers who decided that real birds, plumes, feathers, and parts would look appealing on women's hats and garments.

It was the designers who created the demand for dead birds. Professional and amateur hunters by the thousands showed a willingness to slaughter the global avian population. Fashion writers stirred up interest in the products with their enticing and cleverly worded descriptions of headgear that customers could not resist. That generated a competition among buyers to see who could buy the most garish products. Rarely did anyone mention the sources of the birds that adorned them.

Fashion writers promoted the bird hats and portrayed them as attractive while downplaying the fact that birds had to die by the millions to make them so. They could turn the simplest design change into something that was being done for the first time, such as a designer's brilliant innovation of slanting wing tips down and setting them back more. Women who liked the change would no longer look like the female warlike characters Brunhilde, from Germanic heroic legend, or Britomart, a young, beautiful, and fearless knight who served the fairy queen Gloriana in Edmund Spenser's 1590 work *The Faerie Queen*, "with helmet-like applications of feathered millinery on their head." That appealed to women's vanity—and sold more hats.

"The appearance of such millinery is no longer martial or imposing," the writer explained. "The wings droop down gently, with nothing aggressive about them. The arrangement known as 'Mercury Wings' is in abeyance."[10]

56   **The Hat That Killed a Billion Birds**

Fashion writers' columns appeared in newspapers from small communities to large cities, which broadened the appeal of the bird products. The writers' descriptions retained a commonality as the years progressed. Not even the "Great War" on Europe stopped the marketing programs.

One mid-continent fashion writer defended the use of birds in millinery while scoffing at the folks trying to save them:

> SHORT plumes tipped with pearls are revived for millinery purposes. THE plum shades find great favor in Paris, but are sparingly imported. WHITE feathers and white pompons are shown in the greatest abundance.
>
> OSTRICH plumes and tips are the leading garniture of imported bonnets and hats.
>
> BIRDS' wings and feathers will be in great demand for fall millinery, despite Audubon societies.[11]

That writer stressed ostrich plumes, which did not require the killing of birds. They could be plucked and regenerated. Ostrich plumes retained their popularity for that reason alone. But as the years passed, designers added the feathers, plumes, and parts of more species. The expansion of the species required to satisfy the demand for dead birds accelerated as the 19th century gave way to the 20th. Despite the Audubonists' attempts to eliminate the bird slaughter, sales continued and stories about the practice filled newspaper pages.

News broke in 1909 that the last white heron had been seen in Oregon.[12] One reporter wrote that should "bring the blush of shame to those who persist in adorning themselves at the expense of bird life, which has been made precarious if not impossible by the persistent onslaughts of the feather and plume hunter, and this speaks of the last survivor of a beautiful species." It didn't.

Imagine! There was only one survivor of thousands of a species in Oregon. But it was not the only species that had been nearly exterminated. The flightless great auk had met a similar fate in the mid–19th century because "the demons of fashion have brought about such butchery that biological historians will in future works record the fact that in 1908 the white heron followed the great auk over the dismal trail that stretches backward to the ages that are gone."[13]

The disappearance of the heron and the auk should have been a harbinger of things to come for the denizens of the fashion world. But it was largely ignored. After all, slaughter proponents theorized, if there was one white heron left in Oregon, then technically the species was not extinct. How one bird was going to mate with itself and resurrect the species was not their problem. There were plenty other species left to wipe out. They did not count on a war. Ironically, the most adversely affected market was one of the rare renewable sources, ostrich feathers.

In March 1916 about a dozen large ostrich feather dealers in New York City, known as the Ostrich Feather Manufacturers' Association (OFMA), met to discuss the general situation in the ostrich feather industry and to find ways to carry them over what portended to be a critical situation in this branch of the millinery trade. They foresaw an unprecedented demand for ostrich feathers in the near future, as evidenced by rising prices for them.[14]

Ostrich plumes which sold in 1914 for $72 a dozen, wholesale, and which, after the war started, sold for $18 and $24 a dozen, were now selling for as much as $54 to $60 a dozen. That suggested that the popularity of birds as parts of millinery had not abated over the long haul despite attempts by conservationists to prevent the practice. The strange thing was that there was no shortage of ostrich feathers in the United States, because when the war started the usual markets in Germany, London, and Constantinople for the South African ostrich output were closed. As a result, the United States became a general dumping ground for the entire output, which lacked quality.

Prices dropped for a short while as indicated above. It was estimated that before World War I started there were 850,000 ostriches on farms in South Africa. When the farmers learned at the outbreak of the war that they would be unable to support these birds, they cut their barbed wire fences. The birds were left to fend for themselves. As a result, only about 150,000 birds survived. They were poorly fed and became unhealthy. Consequently, their plumes became scraggly. That was the problem facing the New York City feather merchants as the war progressed.

American styles at the time showed a large demand for ruchings (pleated, fluted, or gathered strips of fabric used for trimming, boas, edgings, etc.) and French plumes. The high demand and the short supply created a quandary for American manufacturers. They urged everyone to conserve the available supply as best they could. That was good news for conservationists, but it was only temporary. That was made clear in a news release from the OFMA:

> Owing to the dislocated trade conditions in Europe, London has lost one gem out of her crown as mistress of international mercantile trade. We have witnessed the transfer of the world's market in furs from London to New York. The arrival of the *Chinese Prince* from Port Elizabeth, South Africa, due to reach New York on Monday, may make a similar epochal change in the world's ostrich feather trade. The *Chinese Prince* is the second steamer to bring merchandise direct from South Africa to New York instead of to London, as has heretofore been the custom. She has on board what is believed to be the largest consignment of ostrich feathers out of South Africa for some time to come.[15]

Another dire warning followed:

> One of the unexpected results of the present European war is the fact that the ostrich is rapidly becoming extinct, so much so that it will be doubtful whether women can wear ostrich plumes, tips or feathers, unless something is done by the government to relieve the situation in South Africa where the farmers have been so reduced in financial circumstances because of war conditions that they were unable to buy "mealies" [corn] for the birds.[16]

The war did little to reduce women's interests in bird millinery. Shortly after it ended the millinery industry tried to gin up interest in the bird fashions again. One article noted:

> NEW YORK Birds again! Many a season has it been since we've seen such an array of beautiful feathered folk on our millinery! Small birds of various materials are quite the smartest of trimmings for spring hats. Very swagger is this large, swerving brimmed Idaire hat with its black taffeta top accented with royal blue birds. These particular birds are feathered and have saucy, shiny little black beaks and eyes.
>
> The combining of royal blue black is something new in the world and exceedingly effective. One finds the combination on the cleverest of this season's hats and gowns. The hat is faced with tagel straw, which has the advantage of being light of weight as well as beautiful to look upon.[17]

By 1922, when that piece was published, the public was beginning to lose interest in high hats and birds resting upon them. The conservationists were finally convincing consumers that the price of avian species extinction was too high. Men and women still differed about that, though, as they had for decades.

10

Another Skirmish in the War Between the Sexes

> "Truly the dress reformer is always with us, and just as truly is it the case that inconsequential fashion proceeds calmly upon its way pronouncing its dicta with full assurance that both men and women will bow to its edict."[1]

The "murderous millinery" slogan started another battle between males and females that turned into a blame game. The ladies resented the inference that the female gender was totally at fault for the killing of birds and construed criticism of their millinery choices. Actually, it was more than an inference. It was an outright accusation, to which some ladies reacted adversely.

The Cooper Ornithological Club of California epitomized the direct attacks on women as the culprits behind the wholesale slaughter of birds for millinery purposes when it adopted a resolution condemning the custom of women wearing plumage, which "in this enlightened age is held by people of culture to be a relic of barbarism and a vulgar taste."

The club was considered the leading organization in its special field of science in California, so its action was important. The resolution began with a bang:

> [We] deplore and condemn the perverted taste and cruelty of the fair sex in fostering the slaughter of thousands of egrets and countless numbers of other birds of song ... and we view with alarm the appalling fact that more birds are destroyed annually in the United States for each large millinery firm than are contained in the combined collections of bird students in this country—the accumulation of generations.

The resolution ended with an emotional plea to legislators and the press to get involved:

> Resolved ... that every means be put forth to influence legislation for the protection of birds, and to discourage the wearing of birds, resulting in such shameful annihilation of the beautiful creatures of the air, the common inalienable heritage of all who love nature and her children, of hill and valley, wood and shore, and ... that a copy of these resolutions be sent to the intelligent and generous press, who may assist in the elimination of this execrable evil of fashion.[2]

The members of the club didn't have crystal balls, but it wasn't only women who succumbed to the allure of murderous millinery. Eventually men did too. That became clear a few years later when a dress reform advocate in New York called for a uniform dress for women "in view of the present tax upon husbands' pocket-books to meet the vagaries of fashion."[3]

10. Another Skirmish in the War Between the Sexes   59

"As yet there is no indication on Fifth Avenue that the slaughter of birds for millinery needs has ceased, nor is there indication that the various and expensive adornment have fallen before the vigor of appeal of the advocate of a dress of common style for the feminine sex," an editorial writer declared.[4] And then came the shocker.

> Now there comes the word that men's overcoats are going to be radically changed and the roll collar is to be slaughtered and in other important respects the attire of man is to undergo such a metamorphosis as has not been its portion for centuries. It is now in order for somebody to arise in favor of the re-enactment of the old sumptuary laws of England, by which pains and penalties were imposed upon those in various classes of society who went outside the line marked for them in the quality, the style and cost of their attire.

Men embracing murderous millinery too? And a reversion to sumptuary laws that dated back to Elizabethan England in the late 1500s? Such laws were designed to regulate and reinforce social hierarchies and morals through restrictions on clothing, food, and luxury expenditures. They often depended on a person's social rank. Openly shaming women became part of the anti–bird slaughter factions.[5]

An unnamed group, most likely the Audubon Society, promoted a plan to shame women. The purported goal was to persuade women not to wear dead birds in their bonnets. The attackers' tactics were a bit controversial. The organization proposed to place advertisements in street cars, so when passengers read about the wickedness of using birds as millinery they would naturally look around at the bonnets of the women present. As a result, any lady wearing a bird in her bonnet would become accused and convicted on the spot. Such tactics did little more than attract the opprobrium of women.

The street car advertising scheme was harmless compared to a proposed bill floated by an overzealous enthusiast in New York. He announced that the city's aldermen were considering a measure that was reminiscent of Nathaniel Hawthorne's "scarlet letter." The plan was to register women of the town, a polite name for prostitutes, and compel them to wear stuffed birds or feathered millinery as a badge of their calling.[6] The folks who developed the bill hoped to pass and extend it to other cities. That plan feel flat.

A newspaper editor stated the opposition to it in a most direct fashion:

> A great many people who have been thoroughly in sympathy with a movement of the Audubon Society to persuade feminine humanity to relinquish its plumed headgear because of the incentive the fashion offers to the destruction of feathered birds will certainly be disposed to draw the line against the latest device for furthering that end.

The primary reason for rejecting the bill was obvious.

> The scheme, however, would operate so as to brand every woman who, in ignorance, should appear in public with feathered trimmings in their hats and thus to inflict the innocent, while the guilty would be wise enough to don the garb of respectability. The whole proposition is despicable in its plan and scope. If the slaughter of birds can be stopped only by resorting to such means the general public would prefer to let the birds be slaughtered.[7]

Fortunately, that never became a choice.

Popular Boston author Hattie Tyng Griswold flatly rejected the charge that women were to blame for the slaughter. She attributed causes to egg collectors, unregenerate men with guns, and depraved small boys with slingshots and peashooters in her strong rebuke to men. She wrote:

> The women here lately had a great many sermons preached to them about the destruction of bird life. The homilies, all excellent, and true, and admirable, being almost exclusively

60 The Hat That Killed a Billion Birds

addressed to them, as if they alone were to blame for the slaughter of the innocents. Now, while I agree with every word that has been said about the immense, unnecessary, and really fiendish slaughter of the birds for millinery purposes, I have discovered that even in this war of extermination the poor women are not alone to blame.

She snorted:

Egging is a regular business in the spring in many places along the coast, being carried to the greatest extent, perhaps, on the coast of Texas.... It is mere wanton destruction, as the value of the eggs for food is scarcely appreciable, and as barrels of them are always crushed in trying to transport them after they are gathered. For this business the women are surely not to blame.

And she didn't want to hear about pelican oil either.

One other thing: Some enterprising men conceived the idea of making "pelican" oil, and established large trying-works near an island in Corpus Christi Bay, known as Pelican Island from the immense number of these birds raised there.... They exterminated the bird in that vicinity, and the oil proved utterly worthless.... As women cannot be said to have established a market for pelican oil yet, they are to be acquitted of complicity in this crime, as well as that of the "egging."

She was on a roll in defense of women.

One more practice for which women are not responsible is the killing of birds in mere wantonness, which is a very extensive practice, taking the country through.... Boys and even men go out to shoot swallows, robins, and larks.... The small boy with his slingshot destroys many and all for the desire to murder, as not a single person saves the skins for gain; the birds are thrown away or left where they fall.

Griswold allowed that women might share a bit of the blame when it came to food. "The killing of birds for food cannot be only laid to the women of the land, and this is one very large item in the destruction of bird-life. Women undoubtedly take part of these delicacies as well as men, but the women do not shoot them nor demand them as edibles."

She had a similar response to a report from that Norfolk, Virginia, naturalist who reported that in his area in the recent spring hundreds of woodpeckers and songbirds were exposed for sale, in addition to the game birds whose destruction had been so improvident that extinction was considered only a matter of a little time. That slaughter made a fearful showing against the men of the country. Again, she concluded that in this women were practically (but not entirely) innocent.

Finally, Ms. Griswold avowed:

Neither are the women or the little girls responsible for the small boy who, the country over, kills a bird on sight, if by any possibility he can hit it with some stone or peashooter. Not until women destroy bird or animal life for mere sport can they be held to be guilty as are the men of the present threatened destruction of bird life on this continent.

She delivered one more salvo, à la the aforementioned gentleman from Norfolk:

That women have been thoughtlessly guilty of a large share of the unusual destruction of birds the last three or four years I shall not pretend to deny. I only protest against hearing all

Opposite: **Children such as Ma-za-oo-nie, "the Little Bird Hunter," hunted birds for legitimate reasons such as food and skins (carte-de-visite by Joel E. Whitney, Whitney's Gallery, St. Paul, 1862).**

10. Another Skirmish in the War Between the Sexes

MA-ZA-OO-NIE,
(THE LITTLE BIRD HUNTER.)

Entered according to Act of Congress, by J. E. Whitney, in the year 1862, in the Clerk's Office of the U. S. District Court for Minnesota.
WHITNEY'S GALLERY, ST. PAUL.

the sermons and songs aimed at them for what is a mere temporary caprice, when the steady and uniform destruction of the birds and their skins from year to year is clearly traceable to man and to him alone.[8]

Her point was clear. Members of the sisterhood concurred.

Like Griswold, British feminist and writer Madame Sarah Grand said in no uncertain terms that men were responsible for murderous millinery. It was the commercial aspect of the movement run by men that was the cause of the fad. She appealed to women to emancipate themselves from the tyranny of being dictated to by men as to what they should wear. She added that men had one goal: the exploitation of the bird creation for their own selfish profit.

Grand had a point. But men objected to use that profit or parts thereof to pay for the costly bird hats that women wore with little or no regard to how much they cost. They couldn't have it both ways according to William Earl Dodge Scott, curator of ornithology at Princeton University, who sided with the women regarding who was at fault.[9] If men wanted their ladies to be attractive, he averred, they had to be willing to pay the price.

Not the women, but the men, are responsible for the destruction of birds for millinery decoration, Scott said in an address before a conference of Eastern public education associations held in Newark, New Jersey. He argued that every woman who had ever worn a feather in her hat did so to please some man and not herself. He predicted that the destruction of birds would cease when men no longer admired the slaughtered ornaments women wore, and he recommended his argument to the Audubon Society. He did not say whether his wife of 24 years, Marion Johonot, agreed.

Some critics, including W.H. Roberts of Salt Lake City, Utah, were more direct than others. He maintained an air of civility in his plea to save the birds, but he did not hold back on what he really thought. In a "Letter to the Editor" Roberts said:

> When one thinks of woman it should be in line with his loftiest ideals of what God has wrought. But can one do this and be true to his ideal conception of all that is tender, sympathetic, humane in woman, when he meets with an animated "fashion-plate" walking down the street with a hat bedecked, not only with the feathers of little songbirds, but with the bodies of those little silver-throated warblers themselves? I hold that he cannot.
>
> The apparel of either a man or woman is as much an indication of character to the student of human nature as is any division on the phrenological chart. Then how can one reconcile the sacred emotion of maternal love as finding an abiding place in the breast of a woman whose vanity can only be appeased at the cost of a wanton and criminal butchery of our birds? It is, in my opinion, time to call attention to this outrageous cruelty, and stringent and drastic measures should be adopted to put an end to what will result, in a comparatively short time in the total extinction of these birds.

Roberts called for penalties on the women who bought the hats. He said that there should be an extreme penalty for either exposing to sale any article of apparel adorned with the bodies or parts of bodies of birds or for wearing such articles of apparel. If there were no demand for such finery, he reasoned, there would be no supply.

He admitted that some people might consider him an extremist, but there was "no intermediate course to be pleaded in palliation of this wanton brutality, and a wearer of this bird-bedecked millinery not only lends a tacit indorsement to the slaughter, but actually encourages the commission of the crime."[10] It is criminal, he concluded, and no other word so aptly covered the ground.

10. Another Skirmish in the War Between the Sexes 63

Countercharges assessing blame flew back and forth between the genders as the slaughter ebbed and waned. The males had one significant ally in the "war." The majority of the newspaper editors in the country were male and most of them were more than willing to blame the ladies for the carnage. It's no wonder many of the pro–bird millinery thought their editorial license should have been revoked.

11

Editorial License

> "What a newspaper needs in its news, in its headlines, and on its editorial page is terseness, humor, descriptive power, satire, originality, good literary style, clever condensation, and accuracy, accuracy, accuracy!"
> —Joseph Pulitzer[1]

Newspapers and a few magazines were *the* media during the bird slaughter era. Virtually every community, large, small, or in between, had at least one newspaper, and they frequently reprinted one another's editorials so each one received wide local and national coverage. The writers were blunt and somewhat biased—but they got their points across clearly and concisely. They did not, however, always give women the credit they deserved for protesting against high hats and bird slaughter.

Editors' comments carried a lot of weight with the public. Without them and the usual news stories people had limited sources to learn about what was going on locally, nationally, or globally. That was true when it came to anti-hat laws and bird slaughter, and editors did everything in their power to spread the news, good and bad.

Editors were mainly for the anti-hat laws and against bird slaughter. Their viewpoints ran the gamut. Some were lighthearted, some were logical, and some were mean, perhaps none more so than a journalist who labeled the ladies who wore bird hats as criminals:

> The woman who does not gain possession of these facts and order her millinery in accordance with them, when such facts are so easily obtained, is worse than silly. She is criminal. She is not a woman to wear the title of humaneness for which her sex should stand preeminently. If she does wear these ornaments after having gained knowledge of the cruelty that makes them possible, she must surely be branded as a woman devoid of some of the finest and purest traits of her sex: gentleness, sympathy and thoughtfulness.[2]

For readers, it was often difficult to distinguish between news and opinion during the height of the slaughter. It was not a usual practice for reporters or editors to sign their articles in the late 1800s, so it was often a challenge for readers to determine who was doing the writing. It was easier to figure it out in small-town newspapers, because editors and reporters were often one and the same. That was not the case with the large-city publications.

Thus, writers made liberal use of the editorial "we" and let readers figure it out. Editorial license or not, newspaper writers usually made their publications' stances on the bird slaughter issue perfectly clear, even if their readers did not always appreciate them. More often than not the writers let their anti-female biases show through as well, which was a prime contributor to the "war between the sexes" when it came to high hats, bird slaughter, and laws against both.

11. Editorial License   65

A tongue-in-cheek editor typified the biased, shared approach after a W.C.T.U. (Women's Christian Temperance Union) meeting in Minneapolis:

The debate by the ladies of the W.C.T.U. over the question of despoiling the birds for millinery purposes was extremely interesting, but we are pained to see that Rev. Anna Shaw sought to retard a good work by sneering at men for making laws on what women shall wear on their bonnets. The reverend lady forgets that these laws are applicable to men as well as women, and that if a man presumes to decorate his headgear with feathers of a proscribed nature he will be held to strict account.

It was very gratifying to read that the chairman, after a moment's reflection, ruled that "it is distressing to the ostrich to lose its feathers." We believe the ornithologists have decided "that the loss of feathers is more or less distressing to any bird, that it wounds his pride, violates his most sacred feelings, and puts him to the most serious annoyance and inconvenience, to say nothing of bodily anguish."

During the late acrimonious discussion in this city the Audubon Society ruled that all feathers should come under the ban of the society's disapproval, save the plumage of the dodo and the tail feathers of the looloo bird, which seem to be largely in evidence this fall.

To return to our friends of the W.C.T.U. we are agreeably impressed by the remarks of Mrs. Cain, who seems to be doing what she can in a humane way to remove the deep-rooted prejudice against her name. The lady contended that it pains an ostrich extremely to separate him from his feathers, and she compared the suffering with the anguish caused by the extraction of a lady's tooth, whereat the ladies present shivered visibly and immediately passed the resolution imploring the intervention of congress.

The ladies are much to be commended for their humane action, and we trust that they will pray for and labor with the Rev. Anna Shaw, who seems to have it in for men and ostriches.[3]

It is understandable, based on that editorial, which downplayed the seriousness of the issue, why women sometimes construed journalists' comments as attacks on their gender in general, even though many of them were on their side. The attacks continued, no matter how well couched the writers' words were. Women were the villains in this drama and that was that:

In spite of recent triumphs of the Audubons, the glass eyes of dead parrots are seen gazing reproachfully over the brims of some fall hats, and millinery shops reveal that morgue-like appearance that is given them by glass cases filled with the remains of "winged gems." Of course these may be the "made birds," the kind that owe their creation to the manufacturer of millinery goods rather than to that greatest of all manufacturers, nature; but they wear the hues of life, and are proof of the fact that women still look upon birds from the millinery standpoint.

It is said that women dress to please men, yet few men can be found who admire these millinery monstrosities, and some go so far as to say that not only does vanity bear the name of woman, but that cruelty also stalks about under the same sobriquet. And what profiteth a woman, it is asked, to know that there is a parrot in her hat if she be accused of harboring cruelty in her heart?

Of course few bird buyers are conscious of any intentional sanctioning of cruelty, and they buy a stuffed owl with as few ethical scruples as they give to the selection of muslin roses. But the warning voice of the Audubons has so long been heard in the land that ignorance in this matter is no longer looked upon in the light of innocence, and the woman who puts a dead bird in her hat takes her moral life in her hand.[4]

Some editors enjoyed chastising women on their op-ed pages while lauding them elsewhere in their newspapers for their efforts in addressing the bird slaughter problem. Editorials like those above might be juxtaposed with brief stories like this:

The Woman's league, an outgrowth of the Woman's Sound Money league, held its regular meeting yesterday afternoon in the Friday Morning club rooms. Mrs. Carpenter read a paper on "Bird Life." She spoke very earnestly against the killing of birds for the trimming of women's hats and the repulsive practice of wearing the bodies and heads of songbirds. Mrs. Carpenter's paper showed her to be an enthusiastic lover of the feathered creation and an intelligent observer of their habits.

Mrs. Norris followed in a sprightly paper taking the opposite side of the argument. The bright plumaged birds used in millinery, she said, come from Australia and South America, where they are so numerous the quantity imported makes no appreciable difference in the number. A general discussion followed the papers.[5]

Sadly, women were not always kind to one another when offered the opportunity to expound in newspapers. The murderous millinery era coincided with another significant women's movement in the United States: the struggle to attain the right to vote. Yet not all women, aka the "suffragettes," were convinced they needed it.

The British novelist Maria Louise Ramé, whose pen name was Ouida, took the opportunity to scold her "sisters" on two levels: voting and murderous millinery. Ramé, the author of the acclaimed novel *Strathmore*, who was described as being very much ahead of her time when that book appeared, was considered to be very much behind the times a few years later. She not only decried the idea of women being privileged to vote, but she loathed the women who were fighting for it, one editor said. Whether she was ahead of or behind the times, she did not hold back when it came to making her feelings known on both issues.

Ouida wrote:

So long as woman wears dead birds as millinery and dead seals as coats, so long as she invades literature without culture and art without talent, so long as she shows herself without scruple at every debasing spectacle which is considered fashionable, so long as she is unable to keep her sons out of the shambles of modern sport and her daughters out of the miasma of modern society, she has no title or capacity to demand the privilege or the place of man.[6]

That was deep condemnation indeed for murderous millinery. It was the antithesis of sense and sensibility, the title of a Jane Austen coming-of-age novel that had been published almost a century earlier. Ramé's statement was more akin to senseless and sensibility, which a male editor hinted at when writing about how women chose their hats:

There are few women of normal sensibility who could be induced wantonly to take the life of any creature. That the mass of women should be willing to wear upon their heads the cruel trophy of massacre committed in their name is an anomaly for which no adequate explanation has been suggested....

Nature supplies from her copious fountains vegetable dyes, myriad in number and endless in variety. Flower making, in addition to the contribution of dyes and colors, has carried millinery to high perfection, which can be maintained indefinitely without resort to slaughter of the beautiful little creatures whose life is brief at the best and whose presence in the world adds to its animation and its loveliness.

A woman who cannot dress herself becomingly without wearing dead birds on her person is lacking in intellect, in taste and in humanity. The tiny tenant of the trees and sailor of the sky has the same right to its life as woman to her own.[7]

Another writer labeled the role of women in the proliferation of bird slaughter as a contest between vanity and ignorance on the one hand and broader sympathies and

11. Editorial License

enlightenment on the other. The charge was made out of frustration, since it had just been predicted by fashion experts that "the aigrette, which has never ceased to be more or less fashionable, will come into greater demand than ever during the coming winter." That was bad news for bird protectionists, who were in the early stages of their fight to end the bird slaughter that had been in vogue for about three decades by that point.

There was no mistaking the target of "vanity and ignorance," no matter how subtly it was phrased. It was the women who bought the millinery that fueled the demand for feathers and plumes. The writer added that they were the "one stronghold in which the powers of darkness threaten to make a desperate stand.... It is proved extremely difficult to influence the wearers of these heron's [sic] plumes, and the consequent slaughter of the beautiful birds has gone on at an appalling rate."[8] Again, the writer did not attack women directly. Other editors were more forthright in their condemnation.

One did not mince words in a piece titled "BLOODY EASTER BONNETS: Scalps Torn from Backs of Butchered Birds Adorn Latest Millinery":

> With Easter bonnets just peeping out from bandboxes and show windows, the women of Gotham are ready to begin their annual millinery parade that always tells how much humanity really lies in the heart beneath the hat. This year some of the scalps torn from the backs of butchered mother birds are already showing that the gentle sex have not altogether refused to patronize the bloody work of murdering the aigrette and leaving her young to starve.

The writer admitted that not all the feathers were taken from wild birds and that not all women were guilty of wearing such bonnets. The article gave credit where credit was due: "Much of the budding millinery display is, however, built on the barnyard variety of feather to which the hat makers admit they have ready resort [and] thousands of the women who have no taste for bird blood on their bonnets are joining the Audubon workers in opposing these commercial interests."[9]

That last point was significant. Not all women were enthralled with the murderous millinery. Many of them fought hard to obliterate it.[10] In the interest of fairness more than one editor made that point. Others spread the culpability around to spare blaming women for the entire mess.

On the eve of a welcome deal between milliners and Audubonists one editor noted happily that the use of gulls, terns, grebes, humming birds and songbirds for millinery purposes was likely to be checked materially by an agreement between merchants and the Audubon Society in New York. More important, he wrote, effective January 1, 1904, the plumage of egrets or herons and Americans pelicans would be added to the list.

"Bird lovers will welcome such restrictions," he declared. "The slaughter of song birds for women's hats is one of the most shocking manifestations of mercantile heartlessness and of feminine vanity."[11]

There was enough blame to go around, in his opinion, which was shared by many of his colleagues. In the main, though, newspaper editors were somewhat unfair to women in placing fault. They exalted the men like Hornaday, Pearson, and Dutcher who fought tirelessly to end the slaughter, forgetting or overlooking the fact that they had more access to lawmakers than did most women. That made the women's job in addressing the issue doubly hard. But they played a significant role in getting it done despite the obstacles—and the editors who derided them. At least they weren't as vicious as the hunters who killed the birds.

12

Blow Guns, Knives, and Other Cruel Weapons

"A garden without flowers, childhood without laughter, an orchard without blossoms, a sky without color, roses without perfume, are the analogues of a country without song birds. And the United States are going straight into that desert condition."[1]

A committee of the London, England, Society for the Protection of Birds released an ominous report to let people know that the bird population was in for a rough time. "It is with sorrow and shame," it reported, "that we have to confess that the fashion of using the plumage of birds for millinery purposes continues unabated, that, in fact, it has in 1897, assumed greater proportions than ever."

Society representatives had studied the catalogues of the firms which sold the freshly imported birds' skins and feathers at public auctions. They noted that 1897 had been a record year of pillage, devastation, and unmerciful destruction for the bird kingdom—and it was only going to get worse. The society declared:

> The recuperative powers which birds possess are of no avail against this excessive drain on their numbers. If birds and their allies prove incapable of resisting such remorseless foes, the present generation of mankind will have to bear the everlasting odium of having blotted out of existence some of the loveliest of created beings. And not this only, but of having done so often by barbarously cruel means....[2]

The society's generation didn't seem to care. Nor did the next one, despite the proliferation of stories revealing the cruel methods hunters used to dispatch their victims. They were often uncovered to the public via heart-wrenching stories opponents of the practice told to convince people that it had to stop. Their emotional appeals were largely ineffective.

For the most part women ignored the stories of the mini-armies killing and skinning birds, factory workers processing the parts, taxidermists mounting them, and milliners selling them. Bird hats were fine with the ladies as long as they didn't have to see the process from nest to store in person. Comments like these were common among journalists:

> Perhaps some of our tender hearted women may not be aware that many of these birds' skins are taken from living birds.... Some of our most delightful songsters are being skinned alive in. order that our fair countrywomen may be fitted out with "a perfectly lovely hat." The rapacity of the brutes who hunt these feathered beauties is so great that they cannot give the birds time to die, but denude them of feathers while the fluttering victims languish and die under the torments of vivisection.[3]

12. Blow Guns, Knives, and Other Cruel Weapons

The media in those days comprised newspapers, magazines, and word of mouth. Most of what was passed by word of mouth was gathered from newspapers and magazines and was subject to misinterpretation as it was transferred from mouth to ear. The saying "May the words I am about to speak and the words you are about to hear" suggested that people did not always hear what was actually said. They heard what they wanted to hear and passed it on in a slightly distorted context to others who did the same.

Admittedly, stories of cruelty to birds may have been exaggerated at times, often intentionally, to play on people's emotions and heighten awareness of the wanton slaughter of birds. The tactic was effective. One fact remained, though: millions of birds were dying needlessly and violently and the practice had to be stopped, whether the chief villains in the story, the purchasers of the murderous millinery products, wanted to hear about it or not.

Accounts like this were not uncommon among journalists who opposed the bird slaughter: "Most women would recoil in horror if they were accused of torturing birds and dooming young birds to perish from want of food. But no woman can wear these plumes and be quite innocent of this charge." They would go on to detail killings in chilling, graphic terms that placed the blame for them on women: "Egrets can only be shot at their breeding places, when they are building their nests or rearing their young. At this time they hover round their nests, so that their capture is easy. The plume-hunters shoot them down without mercy, and the young birds, unable to look after themselves, are left to die of hunger in their nests—all to adorn a woman's hat!"[4]

Some people excused wearing feathers by claiming the wings were made from barnyard feathers and they used milliners as a source for their claim. But milliners were on shaky ground when they denied using real birds for their products. They could not discount the facts that demonstrated the sacrifice of bird life and branded their claim about not using real birds as false: the feathers of 150,000 herons and egrets and 40,000 birds of paradise were sold in one city alone in 1907—all for a gratification of vanity.[5]

Fashion writers revealed secrets of the trade inadvertently with articles like this that appeared in the *Millinery Trade Review* regarding late summer millinery in 1903: "Birds and wings, which are going to play a very conspicuous part in the trimming of late summer and autumn hats and toques, were not used to any great extent in the adornment of Grand Prix millinery."

The writers did not define "any great extent," as they admitted there were some notable exceptions. "One, for instance, that courted and attracted much attention, was a round, flat hat of white straw, bordered somewhat deeply with velvet, embossed in an Egyptian pattern, and curiously variegated in color. A lace scarf, arranged in a big flat bow, almost covered the rest of the plateau, and on this bow lay a pale-pink Ibis, its wings each side of its flattened body."

Whether that Ibis was real or manufactured was not clarified.

Birds mounted flat in this way must be reckoned among the most fashionable trimmings for the fall. All sorts are provided, large and of medium size. In bright and dark colors, as well as light; same as the case with the Ibis just mentioned in their own natural colors, others artificially tinted. They are as much used for decorating the sides of toques and the rolled brims of hats as the centers of the plateaux.

The acknowledgment that there were artificially tinted feathers used in the millinery was refreshing, but real birds seemed to be at the center of the article. "Small birds

70 The Hat That Killed a Billion Birds

stuffed so as to retain their real form are also among the trimmings extended on provided. Wings are likewise made both to open out flat and hinged so as to assume any position in which the milliner may choose to place them. The new quill feathers are wide and generally rounded off at the tip."[6]

That excerpt did not make it sound as if real birds were going out of style any time soon. Yet experts continued to claim that the slaughter could be stopped in one year if only the tender-hearted, sympathetic women would say the word. But, they said, it seemed they would not. That disheartening statement came in 1908, long after the concern of bird slaughter rose to the fore.[7]

An editor tried to make readers feel the pain the birds felt:

Women do not see the flutter of the bird or hear the cry of pain. No. All that is in the depth of the forest. But can we not carry you, in imagination at least, to the deserted little ones left in the nest to starve? Can we not picture to you the gruesome stillness of the forest made so by the death of these beautiful songsters? Can we not help you to see orchard and meadow made alike desolate, and not only that, but see the fruit and grain ruined by insects which are the food of the bird?[8]

By no means were all the birds killed in gruesome ways "beautiful songsters." Even those who were not likely to win avian beauty contests contributed their parts. Turkey buzzards, for example, were prized for their quills, even though there were laws in place in the United States that prohibited the killing of these scavengers.[9] Hunters trapped them, pulled out their quills, and turned them loose to starve. Even turkey buzzards deserved some pity.

Emotional appeals of that time were poignant, if not always effective. Eyewitnesses complemented such appeals with their tales about bird slaughter methods. Again, some fell on deaf ears.

One eyewitness who had seen the slaughter of the gulls in breeding time said:

I have watched, day by day, a flotilla of boats procuring plumes for the market, one gang of men shooting and changing their guns when too hot; another set picking up the birds and often cutting their wings off and flinging their victims into the sea to struggle with feet and head until death slowly came to their relief. Every plume of an egret, gull, or bird of paradise means a tragedy such as this—the slaughter of the mother bird and the starvation of the young.[10]

Today, there would be photos galore and endless looped clips on cable and network TV and the internet to document the killings. Then, stories in print had to suffice since most of the killing was done out of people's sight and therefore out of mind and photographs were not commonplace. Reporters worked with the tools they had during the bird slaughter era.

Journalists, environmentalists, clerics, and assorted critics did everything they could to spread the word about the heinous practices used to kill birds. They did quite well under the circumstances. Reporters described the methods of slaughter in vivid terms in articles that were common in local newspapers. They depicted the slaughter of birds in foreign countries as particularly appalling. Relatively speaking, the birds that were simply shot died merciful deaths, which was of little comfort to bird protectors.

The slaying of the bird of paradise in New Guinea was particularly brutal. When the male birds of paradise assembled to woo the females by displaying their beautiful plumage the native hunters built a screen in the lower branches and shot the males with

12. Blow Guns, Knives, and Other Cruel Weapons

blunt arrows so as not to draw blood. The shooting only stunned the victim. To prevent the feathers from molting after the bird's skin was dried, the bird was skinned alive. It was left to regain consciousness and then die a tortuous death.

The feet, wings, and skull were then removed and the skin was smoked over a slow fire. Hummingbirds were killed in a similar manner. They were usually shot with a blow tube loaded with fine sand, skinned alive, and thrown on the ground to die. The skins were smoked and packed in crates for transport. Strong efforts were made in New Guinea, India and elsewhere to put a stop to such heinous practices.

The birds of paradise epitomized the damage that the murderous millinery craze did to some species of birds. The males of the species in particular were known for their elaborate plumage, which comprised long elaborate feathers that extended from the beak, wings, tail or head.

Natives had long been "harvesting" the birds in their dense rainforest habitats in Papua New Guinea and eastern Australia, where most of their 42 species lived, for use in their own local dress and rituals. But the murderous millinery fad gave them an opportunity to expand their trade into Europe and the United States and improve their economies. That spelled doom for the birds of paradise and countless other avian species, many of which verged on extinction. Their feathers may have been pretty, but their deaths were not.

Fortunately, there were still birds in New Guinea and India to protect. President David Starr Jordan of Stanford University revealed that the songbirds of Japan had been practically exterminated by the demand among "white women" for birds for millinery.[11] Japanese hunters took advantage of the fact that Japan did not have any bird laws, so they devised a savage method to trap the avians. They smeared bird lime, a sticky substance usually made from the bark of hollies, on twigs to snare small birds in the trees. They practically annihilated the bird life in Japan in the process.

Japanese nightingales were subjected to savagery as well. Hunters blinded decoys by putting their eyes out and then hanging the birds in cages. Their mournful cries attracted hundreds of other nightingales that fluttered around the decoys' cages. In the process they caught their wings in the pitch on the trees and were trapped. The cycle continued.

Hunters devised as many ways of killing birds as there were birds to kill. One of the most devious traps that contributed to the wholesale destruction of bird life was the roccolo used in Italy.[12] It resembled a watch tower standing among a ring of trees on high or rising ground. The tower was surrounded by fine nets that contained hundreds of pockets into which the birds fell. They were attracted to the roccolo by hundreds of decoys of various species.

English bird authority Hubert D. Astley claimed that one roccolo would account for the capture of 600 birds in a week. The victims comprised numerous species of migratory birds. There were reportedly hundreds of roccoli throughout Italy. And that was 20 years after the alarm about bird slaughter had been sounded in Astley's home country of England.

Even the ostrich, a rare bird that sacrificed its feathers without sacrificing its life, was treated harshly.[13] The birds in South Africa were enclosed in pens. When it was plucking time a half dozen men entered their pens. The older birds knew what was about to happen. They recoiled in panic and fear and ran off, which did not faze the pluckers. They concentrated on the younger creatures first, because they did not know what was coming. Had they known they too would have bolted for the fences.

These herons by a lotus pond in Japan may not have been safe from slaughter in 1906 (H.C. White Co., Chicago).

The plucking process was cruel and noisy and involved a lot of hard work for the harvesters. The process caused so much pain for the birds that their screams and shrieks were heard all over the farm. The "hunters" wrestled a bird to the ground and yanked the desired feathers from its body. Sometimes it took as many as six men to accomplish the job, after which the feathers were often stained with blood.

Once the feathers were yanked the pluckers tore off the birds' down, the layer of fine feathers found under the tougher exterior feathers. The question often arose as to why the farmers couldn't simply cut off the feathers. The answer was simple: dealers would not buy anything other than the complete feather. Sadly for the ostriches, the roots of their feathers were embedded so deeply in their flesh that the only way to harvest them was to pull them out.

It was unfortunate that the wearers of the hats weren't required to be in attendance during the process or to participate. That might have cut down on the number of hats purchased so they could display their prize feathers. The only pain they felt was the cost of the hats.

12. Blow Guns, Knives, and Other Cruel Weapons

The mistreatment of birds didn't end with their captures. Even the carcasses were not treated with dignity before they were transported to a factory for processing. Some varieties of birds had skins that were very tender and their removal had to be accomplished with great care. Normally, after the hunters shot the birds they removed the skins without disturbing the feathers, turned them inside out, and sprinkled them with a preparation to keep them fresh. They were then packed in sea grass and shipped to the factory.

After the skins were treated at their destination they were put in a barrel filled with a preparation like dry plaster of Paris. The barrel was spun until the skins became perfectly coated with the preparation. Then they were removed, turned right side out, and turned over to the taxidermists. These specialists stuffed the bodies so as to resemble the live bird.

Birds that were shot near the factory were sent there intact. The carcasses were packed in ice and sold to hotels and restaurants. No matter where they were killed the birds were treated harshly. At least the ones perched atop hats got one last chance to show the world their beauty.

Oddly enough, the wearers could not appreciate that beauty since the birds were out of their sight. To them, that was the beauty of the whole process from nest to hat. The birds were always out of sight, so their deaths were immaterial. There was nothing beautiful in that. Besides, it was common knowledge that the world could never run out of birds. Or could it?

13

There's an Endless Supply of Birds—Isn't There?

"A bird in the hand is worth what it will bring."
—Ambrose Bierce

As early as 1893 the annual report of the Society for the Protection of Birds of Great Britain stated that the goldfinch was threatened with extinction because of the demand for feathers due to murderous millinery. Some people did not understand the concept of extinction. The consensus was that there were so many birds on Earth they could never be eliminated entirely. This rampant belief prevailed while the non-discriminate killing of birds by plume hunters in search of the snowy egret in the United States contributed to the extinction of the Carolina parakeet and the almost complete disappearance of the passenger pigeon.

The demise of the passenger pigeons epitomized the overkilling of birds and its harmful effects.[1] Passenger pigeons abounded in the United States in the mid–1800s. Flocks were so large it took them hours to fly over a single spot. Supposedly, passenger pigeons once constituted 25 to 40 percent of the total bird population of the United States. There were as many as three to five billion of them living when the Europeans arrived in America.

Naturalist A.W. Schorger estimated that in 1871 in Wisconsin alone their great communal nesting sites covered 850 square miles of the state's sandy oak barrens. Schorger estimated that the flocks numbered 136 million breeding adults. That such numbers could disappear was unfathomable to most people, especially since they were valued more for their meat than their feathers.

By the mid–1890s wild flock sizes numbered in the dozens, way below the billions that had existed only a quarter century earlier. At the beginning of the 20th century those numbers were reduced to three captive breeding flocks spread across the Midwest. Around September 1, 1914, the last known captive passenger pigeon, a female named Martha, died at the Cincinnati Zoo.[2] Martha was about 29 years old, with a palsy that made her tremble. She had never laid a fertile egg. Millions of other birds of assorted species didn't either—and many of them died needless and gruesome deaths before they even had a chance to.

(Strangely enough, in February 1918, the last captive Carolina parakeet died, alone in a cage in the Cincinnati Zoo. The last "official" wild Carolina parakeet was spotted in Florida just two years later.)

"Gruesome" was an apt word to describe a story one letter writer recounted in a tale told to him by a friend who had heard it in church. That in in itself was unusual. High

13. There's an Endless Supply of Birds—Isn't There? 75

hats, bird slaughter, and churches were not usually mentioned in the same breath. A newspaper passage noted, "It's very curious that fellows who kick about high bonnets in theaters haven't a word to say about them in churches. Why is that? Those kind of fellows don't go to church as a general thing."[3]

The "I heard it from a friend who heard it from a friend" frequently evoked a bit of skepticism in listeners and made them wonder if perhaps stories about bird slaughter were apocryphal. It was a possibility that in this case the stories were designed to scare large hat wearers or at least make them think about their millinery. However, people familiar with the rocculo method of killing birds in Italy knew the story was most likely true.

The pastor explained that when he was in Florence, Italy, a lady invited him to listen to some birds sing. "Oh, so mournful," she said. He accepted her invitation and found himself in a room full of birds in very small cages. All the birds had been blinded.

The woman explained that the owners took them outside the city and hung the cages in trees. The trees were then smeared with tar. The birds kept up their pitiful singing, which attracted other birds to the cages. The new arrivals became stuck on the tar. Trappers caught them and put their eyes out. The birds' parts were sent to America for ladies to wear on their bonnets.

The storyteller said, "I looked around the congregation to see what ladies had birds on their bonnets and I was glad there were none on mine, and I don't think I can ever wear a bird again."[4] That was one convert, but there were millions more to win over. The conversion process was beginning as the extinction effort continued.

Early in 1898 the news began to circulate about a social crusade in the United States against the killing of birds for their feathers. Americans were allying themselves with the people of England. The question was whether opponents of murderous millinery were too late to save certain species, such as the osprey.

By 1889 these birds, especially those in Egypt, India, and South America, had all but disappeared from their habitats because their feathers were highly prized. True ospreys were driven to extinction in most of the United Kingdom in the late 19th century.[5] A few survived in Scotland until 1916—the same year ospreys were considered extinct in Britain as a breeding bird. There were a few migrating birds seen there, but it was 40 years before any successful breeding resumed.

Not all the ospreys, egrets, or other birds died for their feathers. Some were killed for specimen collecting and taxidermy. Egg collecting greatly reduced breeding success. That was a double whammy for the birds whose feathers were also in demand. That was of no concern to the hunters who slaughtered them. Their goal was to gather and sell feathers, not to worry about maintaining a species.

No species, no matter how large, could survive the cruelty inflicted on them by insensitive hunters. That spurred Ella Wheeler Wilcox to choose her millinery more carefully and encourage her sisters to follow her example. Wilcox pleaded with them to use their good taste and ask milliners to show some original ideas in creating their hats.

"Remember the osprey and aigrette mean the death and torture of the mother birds, and the slow starvation of their young as a rule," she said. "Any refined woman should be ashamed to be seen wearing an aigrette."[6] She suggested that spun glass and preserved grasses and ferns were suitable alternatives that produced significant artistic effects.

Such suggestions were not unusual—nor were they always serious. As a substitute for birds one dealer offered fish on millinery as "the latest Parisian creation."[7] Even if someone had taken such an idea seriously a creature—or a million—would have to die to satisfy the demand. It was bad enough that birds were disappearing in huge numbers. There was no need to decimate another form of life.

Around 1910 ornithologists noticed that water fowl were beginning to disappear.[8] The decrease had been going on practically unnoticed for at least a decade. It was attributed to two primary reasons: greedy hunters fancied killing water fowl for their feathers to supply the millinery trade and improvements in modern technology were making it easier for them to do so. There were also new man-made environmental threats contributing to the decrease.

The new guns and fancy decoys available to hunters were more effective and easier to use, which made more ducks targets. The harmful effects of navigation and the effluence produced by industries were taking away the birds' natural habitats. Added to that were the poisonous oil-polluted waters that posed a danger to them. The picture was growing bleaker for the future of water fowl.

Experts warned that if the slaughter was allowed to go unchecked, the American wild duck would be a thing of the past within a generation, and the only place people would be able to see one was in a museum of natural history. That message was met with a collective "ho hum," even as farmers, the backbone of America, began to feel the pinch.

The slaughter of wild geese and other water fowl that relied on worms and insects for food was costing U.S. farmers hundreds of millions of dollars. They had to devise alternate ways of protecting their crops from pests, since the birds were being depleted. Farmers started caring for wild game in severe winter weather, which incurred additional costs for them. Naturally, they had to pass the new costs on to consumers. Subsequently, they joined the chorus demanding new laws to protect water fowl and wildlife in general. There was a new awakening in progress, which was a blessing in disguise for all classes of water fowl.

There were two classes of ducks, divers and non-divers. The imperiled divers went to the bottom of the water for food and were more likely to come within the range of the hunter through the use of decoys. Life wasn't any easier for the non-divers.

The numbers of ducks being shipped for human use were growing quickly. In November 1910, 5,000 wild ducks were shipped to processors from Georgetown, South Carolina, in one day.[9] That was unusual, and a one-time event, but it was a salient example of the rate at which American water fowl was being slaughtered. There was one significant benefit to the mayhem: sportsmen started clamoring for the passage and strict enforcement of hunting laws.

Lawmakers in almost every state initiated laws to protect the water fowl. New York State, as was often the case, took the lead. It enacted legislation that made it unlawful for any firm in the state to have on sale any part of the skin, head or wing or any plumage of a gull, eagle, tern, vulture, albatross or any plume-bearing heron. That was a major step forward in bird protection. More important, it established a model for other states to follow. Sportsmen's groups united to push for them to do so.

The Water Fowl Club of America held its annual meeting in New York in late December 1910 to generate nationwide interest in the protection of the water birds. The organization wielded significant influence in that regard, since it had played a major role in the passage of the New York State legislation regarding the sale of bird plumage for millinery purposes. The bill, which was approved by Governor Hughes, went into effect July 1, 1911, but not before the milliners made one last attempt to block it.

13. There's an Endless Supply of Birds—Isn't There?

Two hunters with about 30 dead geese at Buffalo Lake, Alberta, Canada, around the turn of the 20th century.

New York State legislators introduced the Long-Sheide and Levy bills to derail the tough new act scheduled to take effect in July. Long-Sheide was designed to extend the duck shooting season on Long Island, New York, to April 1 each year. Levy was aimed at lessening bird protection in the state in general. T. Gilbert Pearson, secretary of the Audubon Society, lashed out at the sponsors.

"Powerful moneyed interests, with high salaried lobbyists to break down bird protection," were behind the bills, he charged.[10] He included domestic and foreign milliners, game dealers, and cold storage dealers as the leading opponents. Pearson said they were sparing no expense to carry the bills through. He noted that a French milliner had asked the Audubon Society not to oppose the Levy bill in particular, because three quarters of the millinery trade in France had fallen away since the passage of the law which it sought to repeal. The lobbyists' attempts failed, as other states acted to step up their own bird protection programs.

More states implemented hunting license systems from which the fees collected were used to pay for the employment of wardens and the enforcement of the laws. By 1910 the system was in operation in all but one or two states. The federal government jumped in to help.

There were so many ducks and geese being killed across America the Department of Agriculture started importing birds and stocking government preserves with

A 1902 stereograph card depicting the return of the duck hunters (International View Co., Decatur, Illinois).

pheasants, partridges, and wild duck. Nearly 30,000 Hungarian partridges were brought from Europe in 1909 and set free in different parts of the United States.[11] The department also took action to save the sea gulls.

There had been so much destruction of seabirds for millinery purposes before Congress finally acted that some varieties were almost exterminated. On the little islands along the Gulf Coast the gulls had been so thick people had to kick them out of the way while walking along the beach. The gulls laid their eggs in the sand to let the warm rays of the sun hatch them. Sadly, the demand for their wings as hat trimming grew so high hunters killed them by the millions. Some experts estimated that the numbers were in the trillions.[12] Numbers aside, the government took it upon itself to restock the islands where they had been the most plentiful by bringing birds and eggs from other places. Its action was literally a species saver.

Overall there was a renewed push to get pending laws passed. In September 1912 the National Association of Game Commissioners passed a vote urging every state to adopt the New York Audubon law prohibiting the sale of wild birds' feathers for millinery. The "fashionable" women who had always come to the fore and routinely refused to wear feathers as decorations for hats and bonnets jumped in to push such statutes as reminders to their thoughtless sisters who did not join the pledge.

An editor reminded the ladies who were loath to join the crusade, "Feathers are savage adornments, and we are emerging from savagery in all its forms as fast as we can."[13] Whether such accusatory wording helped them change their sisters' minds was debatable. Saving the birds was the real issue.

14

Save the Birds

"The saddest cat in Maine is that Presque Isle feline which pounced upon an artificial bird in a millinery store, and ate it, glass eyes and all, before discovering its mistake."[1]

The principles of conservation and preservation were not closely adhered to during the early years of the murderous millinery era. Local and state governments and organizations ranging from large to small, such as the Audubon Society and the Tulare, Nevada, grange, tried to control the destruction of their bird populations. Their efforts took a long time to set in motion.

It took almost a quarter century before some government leaders realized that the ongoing bird slaughter was a problem and that the need for laws against it was immediate. The patchwork legislation that changed at state lines was an invitation for the federal government to get involved, for better or worse. It turned out to be a little of both.

The Audubon Society, which took the lead in the fight to save the birds, was formed in 1886 to fight for the protection of birds. The Tulare Grange issued a plea in 1900 for the end of the march to songbird extermination.

As a farmer's organization, trying to do good, we recognize the song birds of our State as among our best friends in our agricultural and horticultural pursuits…. Their feeding habits show them to be great destroyers of insect pests. We depreciate their wanton destruction for millinery uses. We plead with women and girls of our State to aid the Tulare Grange in this matter of protecting song birds, and ask our lady friends in cities and rural districts to abstain from using dead song birds for millinery purposes or otherwise.

The Audubonists and the grangers were well ahead of the curve. Government bodies, especially at the federal level, were slow on the uptake. Historically, by nature, government authorities are reactive and generally don't take up significant societal problems until it is almost too late to offer any meaningful solutions. When they act it is usually by passing ineffectual laws filled with holes that don't have enforcement teeth, such as the New York State law passed in 1906 that banned the sale or possession for sale of plumage or parts of birds' bodies but did not prohibit women from wearing them.[2] Laws of that ilk were common in conjunction with millinery murder.

A few states passed laws designed to protect game and birds, but the federal government remained on the sideline. By 1906, according to news reports, government officials around the world realized suddenly that certain species of birds would soon be gone. That was the clarion call for the U.S. government to get fully involved.

Newspapers presented dire headlines warning that the terrible slaughter of birds for millinery uses was rapidly exterminating the feathered flocks of the planet. Reporters

80   **The Hat That Killed a Billion Birds**

advised the world to bid a sad farewell to its birds as hunters continued their slaughter. In true doomsday fashion, they predicted that the date of extermination for some species was imminent.

They cited statistics that proved the crisis was truly international—and based on the lust for money.

> In one market alone lately were sold at one time 12,000 humming birds, 28,000 parakeets, 15,000 kingfishers, 20,000 aigrettes and thousands of other gorgeous southern birds of different kinds, as well as doves and even sparrows. France receives every year from America, Tonkin and India millions of birds which are exchanged for millions of dollars. The number of small birds annually imported into England and France may be computed at 1,500,000.
>
> Germany exports nearly 20,000,000 feathers, which are worked up in England into hat trimmings. In London there are every month sales of birds' skins and feathers, India supplying some 30,000,000 feathers alone.[3]

Even though the numbers didn't bear it out, the dove was the most popular bird seen in millinery in 1899, and white satin poppies with light and dark green centers were favored.[4] Political leaders were less interested in which bird was popular at any given time than they were in the destruction of all birds. At least some countries were paying attention.

Reporters informed readers that South American republics were awakening to the danger of extermination of their most ornamental birds and had passed laws regulating their slaughter. A league had been formed in America whose members foreswore the wearing of feathers. No doubt that was a reference to the Audubon Society, which had organized 20 years before that news appeared in print in some places.

Significantly, the reporter who cited that "new" society 20 years late omitted the fact that the U.S. government had taken a major step forward with the Lacey Act, which prohibited interstate trade in wildlife, fish, and plants illegally taken, possessed, transported, or sold. The act wasn't always observed, even though it was viewed as a model act for states to copy. It wasn't the panacea some people perceived it to be. Legitimate bird dealers saw fault with it and claimed that they were going to suffer business annihilation through its application. If their claim was true, that result would be an unintended consequence of the law.[5]

The aim of the act was to protect species of birds that, because of the demand for their plumage, were in danger of extinction. The dealers commended the law as applied to that purpose but claimed it prevented them from dealing in native songbirds kept in cages. That hurt their businesses.

In a petition to Congress the dealers emphasized that they were not averse to any measure that maintained the natural supply of the birds that composed the basis of their stock in trade. But they protested against the provisions of the law that prohibited the capture and sale of songbirds. That may or may not have been the author's intent.

The dealers noted that there had been a large trade in mockingbirds from Texas for years. The easily-trapped birds were common there and kept in large cages, which sometimes held thousands of then. They were well cared for.

An expert attendant watched them with a small syringe in one hand. The syringe was loaded with red ink. Whenever the attendant noticed a songbird he squirted a stream of the ink on it to mark it for shipment as a songster. Unfortunately, the Lacey Act had shut down this industry entirely. The dealers did not expect to restore it immediately. They just wanted to bring their plight to the attention of Congress and would try later to have the law amended.

14. Save the Birds

81

Their dilemma did not upset Henry Beeman, who gushed over the Lacey Act, acknowledging it was doing good service in protecting birds. He noted accurately that it strengthened state bird laws and prohibited the shipment of birds killed in violation of them. But it couldn't accomplish everything the lawmakers claimed it could. He predicted:

> Before another generation begins ladies will be as much horrified at seeing a bird carcass on a hat as they were once indifferent at the sight. There are many lovely women now who would no more wear a dead songster than a dead baby. Both bird and baby are children of heaven and demand equal protection. This happy change in the sentiment of the people that is passing over the country is due largely to the Audubon and humane societies.
>
> Only a few churches and ministers are abreast of the times in this reform movement. But they will pull in lively later; they are never long wanting good word and work.[6]

That was a safe prognostication. Not everyone shared it. The Lacey Act included the usual loopholes inherent in many well-intended bird protection laws, and it wasn't universally observed. As the old saying goes, there is no such thing as a perfect law—especially if people ignore or modify it, as they did in Florida.

The Audubon societies convinced the Florida legislature to adopt the act in 1901.[7] However, hunters applied pressure to the legislators to modify it. They did, by failing to provide any penalties for violations. That rendered the act toothless in the state.

A major motivation for the Lacey Act was the overhunting of birds for millinery work. The law, promoted vigorously by the 3,000-member League of American Sportsmen, was introduced into Congress by Representative John F. Lacey (R–IA) and signed into law by President William McKinley on May 25, 1900. It had two chief components: to be effective where state authority failed and to make sure that shipments of all packages containing dead animals, birds, or parts thereof sent by interstate commerce were plainly and clearly marked. That was designed to eliminate a ruse used by shippers who were mismarking such packages deliberately.

Some shippers sending wild game or bird game products to large markets like New York and Chicago did so illegally. They labeled prairie chickens "poultry," venison as "veal" or "mutton," and quails as "eggs." Cases of bird plumage shipped to millinery establishments went under all sorts of labels. That was highlighted in a 1903 book named *Birds in their Relation to Man* by Clarence M. Weed, professor of zoology and entomology at the New Hampshire College of Agriculture, and Ned Dearborn of the Field Columbian Museum, Chicago.

The authors condemned the pot hunters, also known as poachers, who destroyed birds for millinery purposes and disclosed that many songbirds were being slaughtered and brought to market under the generic name of reedbirds.[8] They revealed that a consignment of 2,700 robins in one lot was received by a Washington dealer as game in the spring of 1897. That "open secret" was exactly the type of chicanery the Lacey Act was designed to stop.

To make sure such mislabeling was checked, the League of American Sportsmen hired detectives in New York, Chicago, Philadelphia, and Boston to check packages of game shipped from other states to those cities and the affixed labels. Fines for such violations were hefty. The law levied a $200 fine on any railway or express company which knowingly received any such plunder killed or offered for shipment in violation of the law.

The law enlarged the duties and powers of the Department of Agriculture and authorized it to purchase game and wild birds or their eggs and to propagate and distribute them over depleted areas. As a result the League of American Sportsmen expected to see the numbers of game of all kinds and song and insectivorous birds to increase rapidly. That happened, but slowly. The act was beneficial in the long run. Local and state governments piggy-backed on it and some law enforcement officials cited it to arrest and prosecute violators.

The Lacey Act remains in effect today, albeit in a different context. It prevents the importation or spread of potentially dangerous non-native species and makes it unlawful to import, export, transport, sell, receive, acquire, or purchase in interstate or foreign commerce any plant in violation of the laws of the United States, a state, or a Native American tribe or in violation of any foreign law that protects plants.

Additionally, it authorizes the secretary of the interior to aid in restoring game and birds in parts of the United States where they have become extinct or rare and regulates the introduction of birds and other animals to places where they have never existed before. Game wardens in different states such as Illinois and Ohio took their cue from it.

An 1898 test case in Illinois gave conservationists hope that the courts would help them save the birds. Game Warden H.W. Loveday coordinated with members of the Audubon Society to put an end to the trapping of native songbirds in the Chicago suburbs and throughout the state for the purpose of selling them to the big millinery and bird stores in Chicago.[9]

Loveday proposed to seize all the native birds in one store to determine if convictions for trapping could be obtained even if the person possessing the birds was not caught in the act of capturing them. He and Audubon Society director Edward B. Clark visited the bird store of Louis Grebasch, where Clark pointed out the birds that came under the trapping laws.

Loveday seized all the Illinois birds in the collection and presented them to Justice George W. Underwood. When the case came up in court, nearly every live bird dealer in Chicago was represented. They understood justifiably that if the people won the case the thousands of native Illinois birds they kept in stock would be liable to seizure by the game warden and set free. The birds had many friends in court.

President M.R. Bortree of the National Game and Bird Protective Association represented his organization. One witness for the defense turned out to be a friend, albeit inadvertently, when N. Slotkin, president of the Atlantic and Pacific Bird Company, testified that none of the kinds of birds in the case ever bred in captivity. This made it apparent to the court that the birds had been trapped.

The defense claimed that the birds Loveday seized had been captured in Mexico and California and in other states and transported to Illinois. Plaintiff attorney Baird refuted that argument by citing two Supreme Court decisions. The defense countered by claiming that some of the allegedly trapped birds were not indigenous to Illinois. An Audubon Society member testified that the contrary was true. The evidence seemed overwhelming in the plaintiffs' favor.

Justice Underwood decided in favor of the trapped songbirds and turned them over to Loveday to be disposed of according to law. That enabled the game wardens in Illinois to initiate a series of cases against dealers in birds and milliners who were violating the state's laws. The trappers did not have to worry about penalties, since Illinois game law did not provide a penalty for them except for the forfeiture of the birds. The birds were set free to sing in freedom.

Another classic case in Cincinnati, Ohio, brought the Lacey Act into play.[10] There, game wardens began a virtual war on milliners who used birds in their practice. Ohio's chief game warden, J.C. Porterfield, took a page out of the Illinois handbook when he began a statewide crusade by filing charges against six leading Columbus millinery firms for selling the plumage of game birds in violation of the state's bird laws.

A year earlier members of the Illinois Audubon Society, led by Edward B. Clark, buoyed by his earlier success in securing the freedom of trapped birds, acted to do the same with plumage. Clark visited the leading wholesale milliners of Chicago and inspected the stocks of plumage on hand. The milliners had not learned much in four years. Clark designated several cases of plumage protected by both state and federal laws for destruction. His raids were effective.

The majority of the wholesalers he visited announced their intention of complying with the laws. Many of them cabled European dealers to cancel their pending orders. The Chicago milliners made a show of saying they preferred to obey the law rather than fight the society. For them, seeing was believing. Porterfield was less successful than Clark.

He announced that he had hundreds of cases against millinery dealers which he proposed to push. Yet only one milliner actually paid a fine. That was easily explained. In general, courts were not interested in prosecuting milliners and often let them off on technicalities, which encouraged them to keep selling their wares. Milliners often treated arrests as a joke.

In Spokane, Washington, a dozen milliners were arrested for having in their possession and offering for sale plumage which was alleged to have come from non-game birds.[11] The action was instituted by game warden Uhlig and Professor Merrill of the State Protective Bird Association. The two men paid particular attention to the milliners who were offering aigrettes for sale.

Ultimately, only two milliners appeared in court to answer to the charge. Due to legal maneuverings, the time of the trial was set and reset. It didn't appear that anyone was anxious to try the case. When the trials were held the cases were dismissed because the prosecution could not prove that the heron was a native bird. Decisions of that type made it plain to prosecutors that they were fighting an uphill battle in their attempts to protect birds. That was Porterfield's situation.

The Ohio milliners announced they would test the validity of the state's statute preventing bird slaughter on the basis that it was unconstitutional.[12] The wholesale houses notified their customers of a meeting which all the milliners concerned attended. Each one agreed to contribute the amount of the fine of $25 to let the case come to trial. They vowed, if necessary, to carry their case to the U.S. Supreme Court.

The dealers remained united. They agreed to bear their share of the expense pro rata. Their collaboration explained why, on January 12, 1903, the game wardens involved in the statewide crackdown were so surprised when they only received the one fine.

"The ladies, bless 'em, needn't be downcast because the game warden is confiscating all the pretty birds in the millinery shops," a journalist taunted. "There are other ornaments for the hat that don't necessitate the slaughter of innocent songbirds: a chunk of coal, for instance, or a load of hay. Cheer up, girls; the world isn't going to the damnation bow-wows just because the game warden is busy."[13]

Porterfield authorized deputy warden Charles I. Ryan in Cincinnati to initiate the action. Ryan engaged allies outside law enforcement to help him promote the public relations side of his campaign. Such alliances became a common practice in the conservation movement. That, Audubonists hoped, would mean that in the future fewer birds would adorn the headgear of the women of Ohio. Deputies throughout the state were instructed to pursue the work begun by the chief warden. They were on their own as to how they enforced the law.

Deputy game warden Charles Truelock implemented a unique ruse in Hamilton.[14] He visited a half dozen millinery stores and appropriated birds. Truelock was accompanied by his sister-in-law, who requested to be shown the birds. The constable seized them once they were produced. Despite their clever approach, they did not issue any warrants immediately. Ryan had a bit more luck.

He joined forces with Alex Starbuck, president of the local Cuvier Press Club, which numbered among its members attorneys, journalists, government officials, and other influential professionals. After Ryan was assured of their support he seized birds held illegally at six millinery shops to be used as evidence against the dealers. The following day he and Starbuck swore out warrants for the arrests of the dealers at whose establishments the birds were seized. Their intent was to introduce test cases against the dealers. The alliance was a major step forward for both law enforcement and social organizations engaged in curbing murderous millinery.

Starbuck acknowledged that the Cuvier Club had been railing against the practice but with no success. The members had conducted a campaign against the indiscriminate slaughter of birds through education and moral programs which generally fell on deaf ears. The alliance with the game wardens strengthened their influence in fighting the trend not only locally but also outside Ohio, where the anti–bird slaughter movement was gaining steam.

Starbuck cited Chicago in particular, where the increasingly active Audubon Society was exercising its influence. Due to the society's reform efforts there thousands of birds' lives had been saved. Significantly, he said, other cities, particularly in the eastern part of the United States, were taking notice and initiating similar reforms. Those successes encouraged his alliance to push for the abolishment of the interstate traffic of birds for commercial purposes, as mandated by the Lacey Act. The act was only three years old, and its effects were taking hold.

Starbuck announced one more step as he and Ryan pushed test cases through the courts in the hopes of favorable outcomes. He solicited the aid of the women of the community in his crusade. Starbuck asked them to stop wearing the high hats that were adorned with birds and avian-related trimmings and encouraged them to spread the word to their peers that such coverings were taboo.

Optimism reigned in Cincinnati and other places where leaders anticipated success in their battle to end murderous millinery. It was rewarded eventually. Until then, legal and public relations efforts to end the practice accelerated domestically and internationally.

Perhaps the first international environmental agreement related to wildlife conservation was the Convention for the Protection of Birds Related to Agriculture, signed by 11 European nations in 1902 to prohibit the capture, killing, or sale of certain species during breeding and migration seasons. Trade-restrictive measures were explicit in the Migratory Bird Treaty, negotiated between the United States and Great Britain in 1916 to protect birds migrating between the United States and Canada. This treaty prohibited or regulated trade in many bird species at the time of active commerce in birds and their feathers.

14. Save the Birds

Similar conventions with other countries followed. Another early example of international cooperation on conservation was the Convention on Nature Protection and Wildlife Preservation in the Western Hemisphere, adopted in 1940 and entered into force in 1942, which included controls on international trade in protected fauna and flora. The effort to protect the birds was gaining steam, but it was slow. Regardless of its speed, the Audubon Society was historically in the forefront.

15

The Audubon Society Picks Up the Cudgel

> There is a story of a day-school teacher who remonstrated with one of the boys in her class whom she had discovered in the act of taking the eggs from a bird's nest. "Think how the poor mother-bird will feel!" she said. "Huh!" replied the boy. "You've got the mother-bird on your hat! I guess she won't feel very bad." The moral of the story need not be pointed out.[1]

The world could do without bird-adorned millinery, but it could not do without birds. Luckily for civilization a group of bird protectors recognized that and came to the birds' rescue. There was joy among bird lovers in 1886 when this announcement appeared in newspapers: "A society taking its name after the great American naturalist and artist, John James Audubon (1785–1851), has been established for the purpose of fostering an interest for the protection of wild birds from destruction for millinery and other commercial purposes. It invites the cooperation of persons in every part of the country."[2]

That same year the American Ornithologists Union drew up a model law for non-game birds, which was passed in New York and later in many other states. That began a significant movement.[3]

The notice meant that influential people were taking a serious interest in the plight of birds in the United States. It also raised the hackles of the millinery trade, which recognized the association as a threat to its operations. In milliners' views organizations such as the Audubon Society were a larger danger to its business than were the splinter groups and individuals operating independently. They were right.

The organization was seeking cooperation with like-minded groups and individuals. It was a welcome invitation which many people believed was too long in coming. But it was timely nonetheless, since 1886 was a pivotal year in the bird slaughter era and vituperative editorial attacks warning against it were again on the rise. Editors had been forewarned about the crisis—and not by people in the world's renowned fashion centers.

An impassioned woman in Seattle, Washington, Helen DeVoe, alerted anyone who would listen that the avian nation needed protection as the popularity of birds as hat ornaments was once again imminent. She told readers in her letter to the editor that the displays of new fall and winter fashions in millinery showed numbers of little birds to be worn on the hats and bonnets of ladies.

Some hats were decorated with four birds. In one showcase she saw a longer line of small blackbirds, all presumably to be worn by ladies of the city before the winter was over. Until women declined to wear such hats there would be no hope of stopping

15. The Audubon Society Picks Up the Cudgel
87

this barbarous fashion, she warned. Campaigns to end it had been useless up to that point in the face of the numberless stuffed birds offered as ornaments that fall. She wrote plaintively:

> Can it be that women, judged to be more gentle than their brothers, will knowingly display upon their heads little dead birds ruthlessly torn from their nests in the wildwood? Is there no protest against a fashion that bids them wear as an ornament that which speaks of the suffering and annihilation of little birds? Birds, while instinct with life, are more than ornaments, and gladden and bless the world with plumes and song. Alas, evil is wrought by want of thought, as well as by want of heart.

Ms. DeVoe waxed poetic on behalf of the birds, before reverting to a presentation of facts. "Who, with the least moiety of poetry in the soul, but would rather see and hear in wood or field the bobolink and skylark of Bryant's and Shelley's song than wear its dead body or to partake of its dainty flesh?" she asked.

She pointed out that the forests of Europe and America were losing their feathered denizens. In England alone one-half of the species had become extinct. "The real meaning of the word comes to us when we try to realize what it would be like to live in a world without birds, with no possibility of bringing them back, of witnessing their marvelous flight, or of listening to their wondrous song," she said.

Finally, DeVoe touched on the economic damage that people could expect if they wiped out the birds. It would be a loss "which entailed upon humanity physical want and suffering, for most birds are among man's best friends, destroying by the millions [of] enemies that he might never be able to cope with alone."

She closed by telling people that if they didn't stop killing the birds the loss of the birds would kill them. "May not this fact, which foretells a possible starvation to mankind, or something akin to it, move those to whom a higher taste and feeling does not yet appeal, so that we may all prefer to neither eat nor wear the little birds of forest and field," she wrote.[4] Her passionate message fell on deaf ears.

The next year New Yorkers noted that stuffed birds in abundance were again exhibited in the windows of the city's fashionable millinery shops. They observed further that birds were to be in fashion for the season's headgear. Critics were amazed. They found it incredible, considering the widespread distaste against the fashion. *Harper's Weekly* magazine attacked women and milliners in particular for the sordid state of affairs:

> The agitation has turned public attention to the subject, and the woman who wears a dead bird for ornament is in danger of being regarded by intelligent persons as they regard a fantastic barbarian. Savages wear the scalps of their enemies, but the birds have done the young women no harm that they all decorate their heads triumphantly with the dead birds' bodies. The lady who wears a dead bird need not effect contempt of her fellow savage who wears a nose ring.[5]

One thing was certain in the writer's opinion. Milliners who offered for sale or the women who wore dead birds after all that had been said on the subject showed a callousness to public sentiment, or a defiance of it, which was by no means a womanly or an admirable quality. By that time comments of that ilk rolled off women and milliners like the proverbial water off a duck's back—if there were any ducks left in the water. They were becoming inured to such attacks, and the more critics harped on the subject the more resolved some of them would be in ignoring them. That was due in part to society's tepid attempts to stop the trade in murderous millinery.

88   **The Hat That Killed a Billion Birds**

Bird protectors' responses to the bird slaughter had been diverse and uncoordinated. They ranged from the formation of organizations such as the Audubon Society and the American Ornithologists Union to social clubs, individuals, and legislative bodies. The problem, as it is so often with crusades against a threat to society, was the lack of a central leadership. There were well-intentioned individuals and organizations galore tilting against windmills, but many of them were acting independently without specific game plans and creating problems for one another.

One group that fell into the latter category was a society of young men in Berlin, Germany, that adopted a unique plan for its crusade against the practice of women wearing birds on their hats.[6] The group's intentions were honorable, but its tactics drew criticism from other crusaders.

If a group member identified a woman who used bird plumage on her headwear, the organization sent a "cease and desist" pamphlet to her address warning her that if she did not voluntarily stop wearing the item a member of the society would stop her on the street and, if need be, remove the bird by force. That plan drew a rebuke from other crusaders.

"It is easy to see the finish of that society," a reporter for the Atlanta *Journal* said. "Some of the zealous crusaders will go to the police court and others will receive invitations signed by husbands, brothers or lovers to a trial of swords at sun up, after the German style. The young men evidently believe the maxim that the end justifies the means. The end is a good one."[7] It was not going to work for the Audubon societies if they expected to succeed. They were viewed by bird slaughter opponents as the saviors of the avian world, although their immediate impact was hard to gauge—unless Henry Beeman was doing the gauging.

Beeman was one of the eternal optimists who believed the societies could perform magic and make the bird slaughter problem disappear altogether, and quickly. He implied that could happen in his article proclaiming that the spring birds had come. Soon, he exalted, "the trees will be vocal with heavenly choirs. Joy to birds, men and angels."

More important, Beeman observed, "The best spring styles in millinery show no dead birds on the ladies' head gear. What a happy contrast. Now the sweetest hats that adorn the heads of the most charming ladies are without birds."[8]

That was not true. Nor was his claim based on a change that had occurred since roughly a dozen years earlier, when nearly all ladies wore birds. He recounted a time when Frank M. Chapman, ornithologist and editor of "*Bird-Lore*," said that one 1885 afternoon in the shopping district of New York he had counted 20 species of native song and insectivorous birds on women's hats. Beeman declared that such a bizarre sight could not be seen in any of the great cities of today. Beeman didn't travel much. Audubon members did.

The leaders of the Audubon Society envisioned building a large coalition, which involved a variety of smaller associations, government bodies, civic organizations, and individuals. Yet, early in the era not a lot of people believed even the strongest coalition would prevail over the powerful millinery trade. The doubters were wrong.

Initially, there was some confusion among the leaders of the society regarding their battle plan. Some believed their mission was solely to pursue educational programs to make sure the public was aware of the threat to the bird kingdom. Others agitated for stronger laws, hiring their own game wardens, apprehending and punishing violators …

15. The Audubon Society Picks Up the Cudgel 89

in short, taking a very active role in supporting governmental authorities. It turned out to be a mix.

The Audubon Society originally was a solo association with a limited leadership. There was no plan to remain in existence once the slaughter of birds ended. To members' chagrin it didn't end quickly, and the organization morphed into a group of societies, not all of which were on the same page when it came to a single defined role or the strategies and tactics they would employ. The mixed messages reduced the overall organization's efficacy, and complacency set in quickly.

Initial results of the society's intervention were encouraging. Only four years after its inception a letter writer noted that "if song birds are not used so much now on hats as formerly, it is owing to the restraining influence of the Audubon Society. This society is an outgrowth of the committee on bird protection of the American Ornithologists' union, and has members today in every state in the union and in Canada."[9] The growth was significant, but complacency set in within four years.

Reports at the end of 1896 indicated that the influence of the Audubon Society and the Ornithologists Union was such that birds and feathers of all kinds except ostrich plumes became drags on the market. Unfortunately, the Audubon Society thought that meant its mission had been fulfilled, since it was no longer the fashion for women to perch swallows or terns on their hats. The society was premature in its judgement, so it gradually fell apart, at least on the national stage.

The Ornithologists' Union, which, unlike the Audubon Society, had work to do besides interfering with the wearing of birds, continued to flourish, with a membership of about 600. When a member of the union was asked if any action would be taken to challenge the revived bird hat fashion, he answered, "Yes, a successful attempt is being made now to reorganize the Audubon Society which did such effective work along this line several years ago, and the union always gives its hearty cooperation to all persons or societies who may be interested in the protection of birds."[10]

The society made a successful comeback. This time it would not be in such a hurry to disband. It returned in an invigorated fashion with a variety of strategies and tactics to employ. Its impact was immediate.

16

"Arbird" Day

"With the return of spring the call of the wild comes to many city-bound men and women, but few respond energetically to the call. They do not know how to take up the quest of nature."[1]

Some people believed that one of the major reasons American women favored hats adorned with birds was their lack of knowledge about nature in general and birds in particular. Americans were too busy living their hectic lives and had little or no desire to learn about either, which explained in part their callous attitudes about the slaughter of birds.

One of the goals of the Audubon clubs was to educate people about the subject, particularly women and children.[2] They chose the women because they were the primary wearers of bird-adorned millinery. They believed convincing children at the earliest ages possible about the deleterious effects of slaughtering birds would pay dividends in the future. That proved to be a wise approach.[3]

One writer explained it bluntly:

The present revival of bird study is doing much to bring into favor that particular sort of outdoor enjoyment which the English people used to call an excursion. Americans are not very fond of walking simply because they do not know how to walk intelligently and enjoyably. They do not always know enough about their surroundings to take an interest in them, and they lack training in the observing of the things that they really see.[4]

Amateur Audubonists and trained ornithologists tried to teach American children and adults to enjoy quiet strolls during which they learned to observe and distinguish common birds by using their eyes effectively to find the birds and their homes and feeding places. The Audubonists' goal was to acquaint the amateur explorers with a few birds and encourage them to make independent discoveries and learn more about the creatures.

Various groups were helpful in that respect. They produced illuminated bird charts, descriptive pamphlets, and bird buttons to help birdwatchers identify what they saw and sponsored illustrated lectures. They placed bird charts in schoolrooms and nurseries, which were efficient teaching tools. The effort was an attempt to increase people's interest in birds, their enemies, and their lifestyles to encourage them to protect their new-found avian friends.

The literature was helpful—and readily available. Macmillan, one of the largest publishers in New York, dedicated a division called Bird Lore as the official organ of the Audubon societies.[5] Its importance became obvious when millinery trade journals announced that the dealers were going to make feathers an extraordinary part of the coming season's millinery.

16. "Arbird" Day

Teacher and grade school children studying caged birds in Washington, D.C. (Frances Benjamin Johnston, photographer, ca. 1899).

The societies' publications provided an effective weapon against the announcements in the millinery trade journals and the propaganda they generated. Moreover, they demonstrated that the efforts of bird lovers were influential when directed toward the traffic of feathers. They eventually helped stop the cruel slaughter of birds for millinery uses. But they were far from the only arrow in the Audubon quiver. Audubonists also employed nature walks led by ornithologists and other avian experts, lectures, literature describing birds and their lifestyles, classroom modules ... whatever worked. Children were slow to realize the importance of birds, however. Education reformers determined to find out why.

Besides the vitally important three Rs, they said, the children study botany and geology. They dig deep into the earth and learn some wonderful things about rocks and strata and the long-gone days of prehistoric man. Yet, they learn nothing about the birds that built nests in their yards and sang in their gardens.

Their reasoning for pushing bird life in schools was sound, albeit a bit specious. "A rock tells a story that is past and done with; the birds sing a song of the present, which to us is the all-important era. We cannot make friends of stones, but with the birds we can be friends, and next to human ties the friendship of animals is the most softening influence that comes to us."

Even the flowers were drawn into the argument: "Not even the culture of flowers is so humanizing, because the flowers can in no way respond to our attentions but bloom spontaneously. And as this heart culture is a vital part of education, why should not it be begun with a study of the birds whose coming and going mark the waxing or the waning of the seasons?"

What did the students need to know, and how would it help them? "To be able to tell one bird call from another, and to distinguish between eggs and nests and colors would be a source of delight to many a child who learns by rote and without interest the peculiarities of rocks of the Paleozoic age. To the average child birds are glowing realities, while shells and clay strata are abstract conceptions of the man who wrote the geology."

The argument fell apart at the end. "Ornithology, cleverly taught, would enhance the interest in the schoolroom and cultivate in the child the virtues of tenderness and pity and love."[6] But would tenderness and pity save the birds? That was not part of the argument for teaching about birds.

Charles R. Skinner, New York's State superintendent of public instruction, raised the level of the argument a notch. He suggested that teaching children about birds was more important than teaching history or foreign languages. He told the New York State Audubon Society in an address on "The Educational Value of Bird Study" that the closer the children are brought to nature, the more the love of the beautiful is appealed to and strengthened, the finer and nobler their characters will become.

"It is more essential to their real happiness," he declared, "to teach children about trees and birds and things about them in daily life, than to teach them stories in Latin and Greek, about things that happened two thousand years ago." He wrapped his message in a biblical reference. "In Eden the birds were not afraid of Adam and Eve, because Adam carried no gun and Eve wore no birds on her bonnet," he said.[7]

Apparently the peace and serenity that reigned in Eden carried over to Yellowstone Park in Wyoming and Montana where, according to the hyperbolic journalist Henry Beeman, "guns are not allowed; animals are tame; bears may be approached and petted like an English mastiff. Friendship and fellowship with birds and beasts ought to be cultivated. No one is a vicious criminal who is a lover of birds and animals and who worships at nature's shrine."[8]

Ornithologist Frank W. Chapman, chairman of the Audubon Society's executive committee in 1898, explained the reason for reaching children early:

> Many women have been told that aigrettes are grasses, or that they are picked up after the herons have shed them, and they believe those stories. The Audubon Society does not propose to let the school children grow up in such ignorance. We are preparing material which Charles R. Skinner will publish in the annual Arbor Day Manual, a portion of which will be entirely devoted to birds. It will be shown how birds protect the trees. In other words, there will be considerable space devoted to the relation of birds to forestry.[9]

The goal was to inculcate in children at the earliest ages possible the story of the birds' crucial role in the ecology. That was something the milliners had a hard time countermanding. They did not have enough influence to gain access to schools to present their side of the story or organize education programs through bird clubs to convince kids that slaughtering birds was acceptable. Their public relations and literature distribution chains were limited mostly to business circles. The bird protectionist organizations had an edge when it came to reaching children with their message, and they took full advantage of it.

Arbor Day and Bird Day, which were often observed separately, provided great opportunities for educators to present their bird programs. Eventually the two were combined into one day in many places, a hybrid "Arbird Day," to let educators combine activities to teach the synergy between birds and the environment in general. The Oil City, Pennsylvania, school system was a pioneer in that respect.

C.H. Babcock arranged a course of bird study for a local school in 1894 in connection with another module, "Nature Study." It became a model for schools near and far. He received letters from superintendents or teachers from Russell, Kansas; New Castle, Titusville, and Bryn Mawr, Pennsylvania; Jefferson, Ohio; and other places in the United States and Europe, saying they were going to adopt the day or had done so.

Babcock's program began in the winter, when students studied the winter birds' names, their ways of living, and their haunts, habits, and language. The work varied in the different grades, but students were engaged from the primary to high school levels. Two periods of 20 minutes each were taken in school every week in which to compare observations, exchange knowledge of bird haunts, and receive directions from the teacher for further work.

Students recounted what they learned in written essays as a part of the regular language work. Many essays were enhanced with original drawings. The work extended through the spring and summer months until schools closed. Students from each school in the district made bird calendars. The teachers were pleased with the results of the program. Babcock said that "by noting the arrival of each kind of bird and afterward keeping track of its movement, it is surprising how much fifty pairs of keen young eyes can see."

Babcock got the idea of "Bird Day" in the spring of 1894.[10] He thought it would be a fitting summary of the students' work, intuiting correctly that it would add interest to the curriculum, since young people were fond of special occasions and days which they could call their very own. They became very involved.

He recalled the first "Bird Day" with fondness. Exercises were held in every schoolroom and lasted during the afternoon session. They consisted of original essays which included the observations of the pupils, of songs, recitations, and readings from prose writers and poets, and of impersonations of birds. The enthusiasm the students developed by this first celebration was catching.

"It is a gala day for the children," Babcock wrote. "They decorate the schoolrooms with flowers and bunting and birds in cages. The people fill the limited space of the rooms, and are as much interested as the children. One gentleman thought so much of the occasion that he gave over 3,000 hothouse roses to the pupils to assist the celebration."

The results were the best part of the day, and they were repeated in school districts across the country. The majority of the schoolchildren learned the names of most of the bird species and yearned to know more about them. The thirst for knowledge extended to adults as well, as did protection for the "new friends." Happily, the number of birds increased noticeably, although that may have been a bit of wishful thinking.

Babcock noted that some birds began nesting near houses, which they had not done previously. Songbirds became more common in Oil City. Most important, the bird studies did not detract from the children's other schoolwork.

"On the contrary, there has been a marked improvement," Babcock noted. "It also tends to the establishment of happy relations between the pupils and teachers. It brings them together upon a subject in which they are deeply interested. A teacher need not be a bird enthusiast to start with; she will soon become one."[11]

The results encouraged similar projects in other cities. Announcements and reports such as the following became commonplace.

94   The Hat That Killed a Billion Birds

On Friday evening, March 2, 1906, Professor Lange, supervisor of nature study of the St. Paul, Minnesota, schools, gave a lecture on birds at the Kenwood School at the request of the Kenwood Bird club.[12] One of the topics he covered was the terrible slaughter of the egret or great snowy heron for millinery purposes.

He told the large audience that these birds used to roam the marshes of Florida by the hundreds of thousands but now they were almost extinct. He highlighted the oft-repeated story of how the bird's only affront to society was that it wore the plumes for which it is killed only in the nesting season. Lange explained that it was shot, the plumes were rudely torn off, and the bird was left to rot. He added that the younger birds, unable to feed themselves, perished from hunger as a result. The message was not lost on the bird hat wearers in the audience—or the children.

One newspaper writer had revealed 21 years earlier that young boys' penchant for killing birds with guns and peashooters was a problem. He wrote that the destruction of the feathered choir by the hunt for sport was growing larger yearly, which was probably not a surprise to many people. But it may have shocked some of them to know that young boys were responsible for much of the killing.

The ownership of guns had ceased to be rare, the reporter noted. By 1885 most young men and nearly all the boys of well-to-do parents possessed them. Worse, there was no effective restraint on the murderous use of these weapons. As bad as shotguns were, peashooters were more dangerous, especially when it came to killing birds, he opined.

> Before nesting time, and during incubation, as well as after, the uneradicated Saxon impulse to kill something that flies or runs has full vent. And, very unfortunately, somebody has devised for boys' amusement a weapon more deadly among birds than a shotgun. The peashooter gives no sound, and can be carried in the vest pocket, but so deadly is it in the hands of a skillful child that the legislatures of some of the western states were obliged to pass laws making the sale of the thing a misdemeanor, and punishing the possession or use of it.[13]

William Dutcher supported the idea that peashooters were as dangerous as shotguns. "Men who claim to be sportsmen, but who are not, kill thousands each year, simply for practice in wing shooting, and boys with their armament of air guns and peashooters kill a far greater number than is realized by the public," he said.[14] Adults suggested that the peashooters in particular were lethal weapons in the hands of children. One example stood out.

There stood in Bridgehampton, on Long Island, New York, a liberty pole 110 feet high, topped by a copper gilt eagle six feet high. According to witnesses, more than one 10-year-old child in that village had fired small pistol balls into the eagle with a peashooter which could be hidden in the hand. Two 10-year-old local boys had confessed that they had used peashooters to kill 50 robins and other birds in gardens, orchards, and the village's cemetery.

Some people charged that such boys existed all over the United States and made war on birds as things made to be killed. One solution to avert this disaster was to invoke legislation and regulate social morality. But, Dutcher stressed, the strongest influence to save the songbirds from extermination was for local societies to organize specifically to protect them from molestation and slaughter. That idea was implemented all across the United States, especially for the benefit of schoolchildren.

Children reacted strongly to the need for bird protection. In one case 850 girls of the Eastern Female High School in Baltimore, Maryland, opted to be "Humane, Not Vain." Never again would they wear feathers on their hats, they vowed.[15]

They were prompted by a graphic and convincing lecture on Arbor Day by J. Hamilton Brown, executive manager of the Maryland Wild Life Protective Association, who explained to them at their Arbor Day exercises the cruelty and sacrifices necessary to supply the bird feathers for the millinery trade. The young ladies inferred that females were killing birds by proxy, thereby encouraging the hunters in their work of cruelty and destruction by creating a market for the plumage of slaughtered birds.

Buoyed by his success, Brown said that this event was merely the opening salvo of a campaign his association would conduct against the slaughter of the beautifully plumaged birds of Maryland. He had just learned a lesson that many other bird protectionists had inculcated decades earlier. Arbor Day, Bird Day, the two combined, and similar events were great opportunities for converting skeptics, especially young ones, into conservationists.

Federal government authorities had suggested in 1896 that Arbor Day and Bird Day be combined. The Agricultural Department in Washington, D.C., issued a circular saying that a day set apart in the schools, known as Bird Day, would increase children's knowledge of birds, and for them to know birds better would mean to love them better. Moreover, it would be better if Bird Day was combined with Arbor Day.[16]

According to the Department of Agriculture, the general observance of Bird Day in schools would probably do more to open thousands of young minds to the reception of bird lore than anything else that could be devised. It noted that several states had published lists of the birds endemic to them individually. That was fine, the department said, but it suggested that the knowledge of birds should come to children through observation rather than through books.

Children should learn through watching how to recognize different species and learn something of their habits. Doing so would make the life of a bird sacred to children and encourage them to work for avian protection. That, in their optimistic outlook, would generate popular interest among people of all ages that "in the near future would result in our forests again re-echoing to the songs of the birds as in former years."[17] That was the hoped-for outcome of the combined Bird Day and Arbor Day.

The purpose of involving children in the educational process was made clear in an Illinois newspaper editorial:

Bird Day and Arbor Day [in Moline] are to be celebrated jointly this spring in the several schools of this city, and the kindergartens will also celebrate the doubly significant day, which might almost be called nature day, or "out-of-door" day, to express the significance that it will bring to the children, whose thoughts can scarcely fail to be drawn outward by the lessons of the day, making them to better see what is about them indoors and out.[18]

Members of the newly formed Audubon Society in Connecticut held their first meeting on January 28, 1898.[19] One of the first items on the agenda was to discuss observing Bird Day in conjunction with Arbor Day in the public schools to stimulate the general study of natural history as a means of preserving the beauties of the country. They were capitalizing on an idea that had been tried in many places before and would be tried again afterward with beneficial results, which was following the advice of Professor Lawrence Bruner in his "Notes on the Birds of Nebraska," published in May 1890: "It might be well to suggest that the subject [of ornithology] is of sufficient importance to call for its being taught in our public schools, to a limited extent at least. We should have a 'Bird Day' just as we have an 'Arbor Day' and a 'Flag Day,' when suitable exercises should be held commemorative of the occasion."[20]

96   **The Hat That Killed a Billion Birds**

As one journalist phrased it: "In some parts of the country they have what they call Bird Day, which is celebrated by the schoolchildren at least. Why keep any other bird day than Arbor Day? He who plants a tree plants also a bird, or rather an endless succession of birds. Wherever there are trees there will be birds."[21]

That same journalist included in his article a bit of good news: "No one can doubt that the bird population of the west has increased enormously in the last half-century; at least as rapidly as has the human population." There may not have been a connection between his two statements, but there was good news in them. Getting children involved in conservation was a wise practice. After all, they had played a part in helping the tern rebound in New Jersey.

Terns and laughing gulls, which had once been plentiful along the Atlantic coast, were in danger of extermination at the beginning of the 20th century. The effort to save them aroused the interest of the American public, especially in New Jersey, where one of the last breeding colonies was located at a small place called Marsh Island. That set off a chain reaction.[22]

After New Jersey passed the first effective bill in 1885 to protect the gulls, several other states implemented laws prohibiting the killing of gulls at any time of the year and the sale of their plumage. Shortly, there were 40 states that protected gulls all year round. Louisiana protected them during the breeding season only. That left five states that offered them no protection at any time of the year. That was a sure sign that progress was slow, but it was making headway.[23]

In 1910 the New Jersey Audubon Society provided safe harbors and breeding places for the birds. It got the school children of the state involved in the project. The children raised $500 for the preservation of Marsh Island as a home for the terns and laughing gulls and learned a valuable lesson in the process. Projects such as that had a significant impact on the environment.

The Audubonists pecked away at the bird slaughter problem. They were active anywhere they could gain an audience, young or old. Katharine H. Stuart, the representative of the Audubon Society of Virginia, under the auspices of the Federation of Women's Clubs of the State, spoke to audiences of both age groups separately.[24]

Stuart visited Bedford City to speak about bird conservation, where she talked to the children of the public schools in the afternoon and the adults in the evening. At the afternoon session Stuart illustrated her remarks with facsimiles of the birds and real nests. In the evening she showed the adults slide projector views that enhanced their interest. Bedfordites promised to organize a local chapter as a result of her visit, which ensured future interest in saving the birds. Stuart's mission had been accomplished, and more school children were educated about the problem of bird slaughter, which was a country-wide goal for conservationists.

Not every state was on board immediately. It wasn't until 1910 that West Virginia became involved.[25] Superintendent of State Schools M.P. Shawkey announced that he was designating April 7 as Bird and Arbor Day in the state's public schools and that his department would be sending a pamphlet to educators in the near future. The "better late than never" aspect was significant for West Virginia school children, just as it was for the birds.

Kentucky changed the dates of its Arbor and Bird Day celebrations to reach more school children and provide additional literature regarding its observation.[26] Until 1911 the day had been observed in the spring. Officials changed the date to October, when the rural schools were in session. The State Department of Education also introduced a 140-page publication scheduled to be sent to every school library in the state.

The book comprised beautiful illustrations, suggestions for the observance of Bird and Arbor Day, lists of the native trees and birds, and a variety of special articles dealing with birds, flowers, and forestry. The purpose was to make sure that Kentucky's present and future generations would be impressed with the importance of the conservation of forestry and bird life at a time when such knowledge was badly needed.

Programs promoting bird appreciation grew in popularity in the early 1900s, especially for urban children. Apparently they were helpful. Iowans noted that children, especially those living in rural areas, already appreciated birds' value. April 26, 1902, was a typical Arbor/Bird Day in Iowa's schools, although it was established by custom rather than law, as it was in most states.[27] Generally, the governor issued a proclamation, the superintendent of schools set the agenda, the education department printed relevant pamphlets, and the children had the fun.

The goal in Iowa was the same as anywhere else: combining the two days generated greater interest in nature among school children, many of whom were bird lovers. They were told that birds were disappearing from Iowa in noticeable numbers, but there was hope for their survival. As the adults taught the kids, there were still many varieties of birds around the state's fields and streams. All the children had to do was learn as much as they could about the birds and work with the adults to protect them. Therein lay the rub.

Connecticut, Kentucky, West Virginia, Iowa … no matter which state, they all shared one thing in common. The adults were finding it difficult to reach agreement with one another on how best to protect the birds. Until they could it did not matter what the children learned, since they were not the ones making the laws to carry out that mission. That was the adults' job.

It did matter, however, what the adults at the Audubon Society were learning. One lesson was that there were never too many laws in place to protect the birds, despite what some of their leaders thought. They quickly took that lesson to heart.

17

Laws Are Literally for the Birds

"The law is a ass—an idiot."

So said Mr. Bumble, a character in Charles Dickens' novel *Oliver Twist*. Milliners during the murderous millinery era agreed. Even one law that interfered with their business was too many for them. Conversely, bird protectors lobbied for all the laws they could get passed to help their cause. The differing opinions set up a classic struggle to win over legislators as the 20th century began.

Frank Chapman of the Audubon Society believed there were enough bird protection laws in place to make a difference. He was an exception among his peers. He declared it was not the society's aim to get any more passed, despite the fact that some people believed that's what they were in business for. One woman proposed to form an Anti-Audubon Society in 1897 because she perceived there were too many bird protection laws in place.

Chapman explained that the woman mistakenly believed that the society carried its good intent and work to such an extreme that many reasonable women who were inclined to aid its cause were prohibited from getting involved. He noted that she, like many women, were woefully ignorant concerning the declaration of principles of the Audubon Society.

Chapman contended that the Audubon Society was not a coercive body: its work was entirely educational. The society did not try to secure legislation for the protection of birds. He made a shocking claim that the country already had excellent laws for the protection of songbirds and many birds of economic value.

"What we aim to do is to create a public sentiment that will enforce the existing laws," he said. "A law is a dead letter unless there is sentiment to uphold it, and 10,000 laws favoring the protection of birds will do no good as long as women demand [murderous millinery] for their personal adornment."[1]

The goal of creating public sentiment was working, at least in Pennsylvania, which was a microcosm of Audubon societies across the country. The third annual report of the Pennsylvania Audubon Society, released in 1900, revealed that its membership had increased 50 percent during 1899.[2] Significantly, it noted that the doctrine of protecting the birds had spread to such an extent in the United States that few birds were being killed in the country for millinery purposes. The great majority of feathers being used in the United States were imported, perhaps due to the influence of the Audubon Society's advocacy for the increased use of the feathers of domestic fowl.

There was some confusion about what laws existed and who they affected. Charles Farmer, editor of the *Millinery Trade Review*, spread doubt when he said that what some

17. Laws Are Literally for the Birds

people thought were laws were not really laws. In his continuing efforts to counter the society's operations he claimed that the Audubonists' interpretations of a New York State law were misleading, if not flat out wrong:

[The society] quotes a recent law enacted by the Legislature and signed by the Governor regarding the handling of wild birds within the limits of this State. The impression has gone forth from that article, which the society has in all probability no intention or desire to convey to the public, that the wearing of such birds is contrary to or in violation of such law.

A bill was introduced in the last Legislature by Representative Abell of Brooklyn, which passed both houses but failed to become a law for want of the Governor's signature, and which would, if enacted, prevent the sale of birds, bird skins and bird plumage as articles of millinery ornament within the domain of the State; but as such a law does not exist there is nothing whatever to prevent the sale of the above articles anywhere within the limits of the State of New York.

Kindly publish the above information, as many of our readers who are engaged either in the wholesale or retail millinery business may be advised of the fact that it is not unlawful for them either to have in their possession birds, bird skins, and bird plumage, or to effect the sale thereof, nor is it unlawful to wear such birds, bird skins and bird plumage.[3]

Farmer's clarification came at a bad time for the Audubonists. The society confessed that it was not having the influence with women that it had hoped for. It was, however, making progress with the young people against bird millinery. That would pay off over time, since it was the young folks who would govern the fashions in a few years. If the society could shape the sentiment of the youngsters so they would remain opposed to the slaughter of birds for hat decorations, the trimmings of the future would not include the plumage of the wild birds. All in all, the Pennsylvania report was encouraging.

Yet, the writers maintained, the use of feathers still included too many wild birds. Beyond the part that sympathy played, universal good should prompt people to encourage the society, for the wild bird was one of the creatures most essential to human welfare. That message reverberated across all Audubon societies. Consequently, their visionary leaders thought it would be more effective if they joined forces.

The organization's leaders opened an active campaign against the illegal traffic in birds and their plumage. William Dutcher presented a speech in October that year on "The Present Demand for Birds for Millinery Purposes and What the Audubon Society Proposes to Do About It."[4] He included a statement aimed at dealers in birds and their plumage in which he defined state and federal laws relating to the protection of non-game birds.

Dutcher warned dealers of the society's intention to prosecute all violators of the law. He distributed 3,000 copies of the statement, which was signed by Morris K. Jessup, president; Frank M. Chapman, chairman of the executive committee, and Adam Dutcher, chairman of the committee on laws to be, to all dealers, Audubon societies, and people and organizations interested in ornithology. That was an indication that the Audubon Society was stepping away from its "nice guy" role and its reliance on education programs to take on more active responsibilities in the statutory and enforcement realms. That was a call to action for the millinery industry as well.

Six years after Dutcher's speech critics addressed its mixed results. One stated:

The Audubon people have been making such a flurry and such a stir in polite society both here and abroad that it is rather surprising to note the fact that plumage is still fashionable. The Audubon ladies set about banishing bird wings from millinery this year with a force and gusto quite unknown in the history of their society. With great worldly wisdom they set about getting the patronage of royalty and the success of their judgment is shown by the fact that there were actually fewer gulls shot this year than ever before.[5]

That fact was encouraging. But it was offset by the limited worldview American women had of the society's mission. Their counterparts in the United Kingdom were engaged in their own anti–bird slaughter campaign led by royalty. The Princess Louise, the Duchess of Fife, and the Princess of Wales endorsed the movement there, and "it looked for a short time as if birds' wings were to adorn members of the feathered tribe only."[6]

But that did not impress American women, who lost a chance to work with their foreign sisters. They laughed at the idea of giving up birds' wings just because the Duchess of Fife approved of it and they asked impertinently what Princess Louise had to say about the propriety of the wearing of murdered blackbirds upon other women's hats. Critics charged that their unwillingness to work together was one of the reasons birds' wings, birds' feathers, birds' heads, and birds' plumage of all kinds were almost as plentiful in 1892 as they were in 1886. The implication was that the women of all countries had to cooperate if they hoped to end the murderous millinery movement.

The societies had an immediate impact in some places, but it waxed and waned. It was years before its influence was felt in different states. Game wardens in some states tried valiantly to turn the public's attention to birds' plight with no success. Once the two started working hand in hand they succeeded. Witness Savannah, Georgia—17 years after the formation of the original Audubon Society and the same year the Audubon societies provided support for Theodore Roosevelt as he set aside the first national wildlife refuge for the protection of birds and other wildlife in 1903. The fact that it took so long to start a society in Savannah was surprising, since the Georgia coast was a magnet for heron hunters.[7]

The Savannah meeting was relevant to what was going on around the United States. Change the date, the city and the people involved, and the species of birds mentioned and Savannah became a microcosm of the country. It showed how important and far reaching the Audubon societies' influence had become across the United States.

Organizers formed an association for the protection of bird life in Savannah which was widely endorsed. Game wardens in particular expressed their appreciation, even though they wondered why the organization was so late. The answer was simple: government and non-government agencies were always reactive when it came to dealing with crises. Time was not of the essence no matter how severe they were.

Game Warden O'Connor focused on that point when he commented, "It is high time that such a society was being formed. It is surprising to me that the matter has not been taken up long ago. The people have allowed it to rock along, until the result is the tribe of beautiful, serviceable and valuable birds which once inhabited the coast has become almost extinct."

O'Connor attributed the lack of action to local people's ignorance of the slaughter that was going on a mere 17 miles down the river from their city. "There are few who know of the inroads which the gunners from the Northern millinery houses have made upon these birds," he noted. "But those who follow the sea or live along the coast can testify that in the last five or six years millions of birds have been shot to supply the trade with feathers."

He took the opportunity to illustrate his point about people's "head in the sand"

17. Laws Are Literally for the Birds

approach to the slaughter. "Why, I saw one lady today on Broughton Street, who, if she had one feather in her hat, she had a dozen different kinds. And she had one, all right. The matter is a serious one. A ladies' hat [sic] is not the most serviceable place for a bird, not by a long shot."[8]

His fellow warden, A. Vestcott, said he would work with the organizers and do all in his power to enroll members. He promised that if the women would take up the program with the schools, kindergartens and ladies' societies, he would try to increase the enrollment of males in the organization and do all in his power to induce legislation to prevent the destruction of the birds.

"There's a game law now pending in the legislature, relative to the summer duck," Vestcott noted. "The way in which the birds have been killed here in the summer months is nothing short of a sin. Unless the practice is abated by law, the summer duck will become as scarce as the snowy herons, which once inhabited the coast in thousands, but which now are as scarce as hen's teeth."

He was right, as the numbers of water fowl in general began to decline a few years later, not only in Georgia but all across the country.

"The hunters kill them when they are breeding," he explained, referring to the herons. "Some of the little ones are so young that the dogs actually catch them. What sort of hunting do you call that?"

Vestcott stated with assurance that the law would not be just window dressing.

And you can just say this, that when that law is passed it is going to be vigorously prosecuted. The law is full and comprehensive, and any person caught with a summer duck in his possession during the months not allowed by law, it matters not where he got the duck, will be prosecuted. It will be useless for him to plead that he killed it in South Carolina. Such a subterfuge is provided for in the law.

I have no doubt that legislation similar to that in other states can be passed. No one is opposed to the movement, because any one who studies the conditions cannot help but see the virtue in the position of the Audubonists. The only trouble is that not enough realize the seriousness of the situation. I heartily favor the formation of a society. It is coming sooner or later and I think it is high time.[9]

That seemed to be the consensus elsewhere, which encouraged the federal government to enter the game. First, one vexing question had to be answered: who owned the birds?

18

Who Owns the Birds?

"Not alone the banishing from the land the beautiful birds of song, the cheery messengers of life that have their rights as well as have human beings theirs, but the shameless manner of hurting and killing is a flagrant sin at the door of every human family—which does not take thought and part in the matter when cognizant."
—Ella Antoinette Hotchkiss[1]

Until U.S. Senator George Frisbie Hoar (R–Massachusetts) introduced his bird protection bill in the U.S. Senate in 1898 the federal government had shown little interest in regulating the slaughter of birds. Federal involvement had been restricted to studies by scientists and occasional lip service regarding the practice for public consumption. The time arrived when the federal authorities could no longer ignore the problem. When it acted the steps it took did not work well at first.[2]

The federal government had different responsibilities than did the states, such as interstate transportation, cooperation with foreign governments, and tariff applications. That created occasional problems regarding jurisdiction, classifications for importation purposes, the establishment of wildlife preserves, etc. The federal government's classification systems were bewildering at times and created unforeseen problems.

An 1894 tariff bill regulating the importation of game bird eggs was particularly confusing. It may have done more harm than good. Worse, it was based on a false premise. Toward the end of the 20th century a story began

Left: U.S. Senator George Frisbie Hoar, who worked with Representative John Lacy to pass the first national law to protect wild birds (B.M. Clinedinst, photographer, ca. 1904).

18. Who Owns the Birds?

Ten hunters with their dogs and the game birds they shot, probably in Webster, Dakota Territory; many birds are attached to a Chicago, Milwaukee, and Saint Paul railroad car, and a pile of dead birds lies behind one hunter (Farr, artist).

circulating that entrepreneurs in Alaska and western Canada were gathering millions of eggs of game birds such as wild ducks, geese, and swans. They were allegedly shipping the eggs east via the Canadian Pacific Railroad and were manufactured into egg albumen for use by bakers and confectioners, in photography, and for other purposes.

Reportedly, eggs from the birds' breeding grounds in the region were shipped in enormous quantities. Single shipments, mostly wild duck and wild goose eggs, purportedly amounted to between 1,000 and 1,800 barrels. Large numbers of the eggs hatched partially during shipping, so they were destroyed. Critics charged that this "industry" did more to diminish the numbers of wild fowl in Oregon, Washington, Idaho, Montana, and California than did all the guns and dogs of sportsmen combined in that vast region. No such industry existed.

Researchers proved that not a single shipment of eggs of ducks or other wild fowl had been shipped over the Canadian Pacific Railroad. The story was fabricated for unknown reasons. Yet people believed it, and the government did not disprove it. Consequently, to prevent the threatened extermination of game birds, the tariff act of 1894 banned the importation of game bird eggs into the United States.

The ban lasted for at least 20 years, with one change. In 1901 Congress passed an amendment that allowed the importation of game birds for propagating purposes only. In the interim, large amounts of eggs imported for propagation purposes had been dumped into New York Harbor. The federal government's attempt to protect game birds had done more harm than good.

At least the federal government recognized the game birds in the west as birds. Ironically, in the infinite wisdom of some officials, not all birds were birds, especially not for tariff purposes. The decision as to which was which was left up to the secretary of the treasury. The results were puzzling.

The central question was simple: was a hen a bird? The secretary decided it was not. The same ruling applied to ducks. Again, the reasoning had to do with eggs and revenue. The fate of birds seemed to be of secondary importance.

If the hens and ducks were declared birds, their eggs, which were imported by the millions annually from China and elsewhere, would enter duty free. If they were not, their eggs were subject to a tariff of five cents a dozen. That made a significant difference in customs receipts. The inference was that federal laws were not always passed in the best interests of birds. They were based on government revenues.

The government applied a perplexing classification called "by similitude." Geese were declared "poultry" and subject to duty as such. Swans were classified as "water fowl." Little chicks and ducklings killed when two weeks old, stuffed with cotton, wired to keep their shape, and imported from Japan by millions for the Eastern market had formerly been labeled "toys." Importers had to pay 35 percent ad valorem. Under the new regulations they were designated as "stuffed birds, not for millinery use" and entered the country free.

Live frogs became "fowls" under the new customs rules, so they were taxed at three cents a pound. Remarkably, frogs' legs were labeled as "dressed poultry" and subjected to a tariff of five cents a pound. Since they were fried like chicken and tasted like chicken, they were classified by the treasury as chicken.

There were cases where birds were actually birds and that meant some would be protected, again for tariff purposes. Even in those cases the rules were sometimes convoluted. Anyone importing five or fewer birds was actually bringing in "baggage," as such small amounts were considered. They could be imported without a special permit. But anyone importing more than five birds had to deal with the Department of Agriculture.

Complications arose for importers when one or more federal agencies engaged in a turf war. They had to know which agency was in charge of what birds. Therefore, importers had to obtain a permit from the Department of Agriculture for the importation of live feathered creatures in large numbers, except for canaries and parrots, which were admitted without restriction. Significantly, 345,210 canaries were imported in 1911. Regardless of how they were classified, the numbers of birds entering the country was high.

In 1911 alone permits were issued for 13,398 pheasants, 36,507 European partridges, 5,394 miscellaneous game birds, and 49,837 miscellaneous nongame birds. In addition to the canaries, there were 24,318 birds brought in that did not require any permits. Most of them were parrots.

Many of the birds imported were admitted on conservation grounds. Of the pheasants, 12,326 were English "ring necks," which were imported to stock game preserves. The other pheasants, including two of the rare Argus species from Java, were headed for aviaries, as were five "greater" birds of paradise. They were the first living individuals of this species ever brought to America.

Another new fad that was emerging among the country's millionaires would help conservation efforts, although that was a secondary purpose. It became fashionable in the first decade of the 20th century for wealthy people to maintain aviaries filled with rare and beautiful birds collected from all parts of the globe, especially fancy water fowl such as the Mandarin duck, which lent attractive ornament and life to small lakes and artificial ponds. The collections may have been small in nature, but they protected birds.

Every little step helped. Even the sometimes uneven patchwork of state and federal laws worked well, despite the various government agencies' lack of agreement at times on which birds were the "good guys" and which were not. Making that distinction was one of Hoar's goals when he ushered in the age of federal intervention in an attempt to protect birds.

Hoar introduced his legislation, called "A bill for the protection of songbirds," on March 14, 1898. He proposed to restrict the traffic in birds or feathers, particularly those used for millinery purposes. It marked a major step forward in the federal government's involvement in legislation designed to address the bird slaughter and excited the Audubonists. Conversely, it opened people's eyes to the fact that there were two sides to the question of bird protection. One side, the milliners, were still not enthralled with legal intervention in their activities, whether it came from local, state, or federal sources.

B.S. Bowdish highlighted that, although he did not castigate all milliners:

> But the fact that the foreign birds of very great value to the human race, living, are freely utilized by the milliners demonstrates how little they are in sympathy with the spirit of protective laws. When I say milliners I refer to the great majority of those who determine the policies of the wholesale trade.
>
> I am fully aware that there are individual milliners who are in absolute sympathy with the spirit of bird protection and who in the course of their business live up to such principles, and I wish that we might see the time before further inroads are made upon wild bird life in this country or elsewhere, when all milliners would eschew the use of bird plumage entirely with the exception of the ostrich, and confine themselves to other millinery ornamentation, of which there is certainly a great abundance.[3]

Hoar's bill would have impacted the millinery trade in a significant way. Specifically, he proposed to prohibit the importation, shipment from one state to another, and sale in the territories or the District of Columbia of birds or feathers for ornamental purposes. Predictably, the bill drew a strong protest from milliners in New York once it reached the House of Representatives.[4]

The manufacturers, importers, and dealers argued that they invested millions of dollars annually in the importation of birds and parts of birds for millinery purposes and that the passage of such a measure would entail great hardship and loss for those merchants who had already placed large orders abroad for the coming fall. In addition, they said, it would deprive from 15,000 to 20,000 men, women and girls in the city of New York of their means of livelihood. These were the workers engaged in coloring, mounting, and preparing the birds and feathers that Hoar's bill would ban from importation.

They also claimed that the measure was sumptuary legislation and interfered unjustifiably with the freedom of interstate commerce. The milliners added that while they endorsed all efforts to prevent the slaughter of native songbirds, they protested placing all birds of every nation in the songbird category, as the bill seemed to do.

The *Millinery Trade Review* asserted that not 10 percent of the birds or parts of birds used in millinery were songbirds or parts of songbirds. It noted that 75 percent of them were imported from China. Their arguments carried the day. Even though Hoar's bill passed the Senate twice, it failed in the House. That was a setback for the federal government but not a fatal blow.

Government officials did not give up. In 1900 the House and Senate passed the Lacey Act, the first federal law to protect wildlife. It met with limited success and was loosely enforced. Its true impact had little to do with the requirements. Rather, it heightened optimism among bird protectors that federal intervention and involvement meant more states would follow Congress' lead and organizations like the Audubon societies

The Hat That Killed a Billion Birds

would gain a little more clout. That happened, although the impact of the increased activity was slow to materialize.

Government researchers delved deeper into the lives of birds and the legislation in place to help them. Dr. Palmer led the way when he published a bulletin on "Legislation for the Protection of Birds." The department was spending thousands of dollars in its work, which was performed by first-tier experts. Extracts from the bulletin provided data on topics ranging from information about birds' contributions to the economy, historical references, and interesting and worth knowing facts regarding legal opinions, all written in clear, concise formats:

> Who owns the birds of the air? Says the Bulletin: "The Supreme Court of the United States has declared that the power of the state to control and regulate the taking of game cannot be questioned."
>
> The necessity of restricting the slaughter of useful birds began to be recognized in the last century, if not before. In 1791 New York enacted a law protecting the heath hen, partridge, quail, and woodcock, from April 1 to October 5, on Long Island and in the city and county of New York.
>
> The legislation of 1901 marks a notable advance in birds' protection over that of any previous year. Systematic, and in most cases successful, efforts were made by the Audubon societies, the Committee on Bird Protection of the American Ornithologists' Union, and bird lovers in many states, to secure adequate protection for the birds which do not properly belong in the category of game.
>
> In all, twelve states and territories (including the District of Columbia) enacted comprehensive new laws during the year. In spite of all that has been accomplished in recent years in the way of enacting statutes for the protection of birds, much still remains to be done before the degree of uniformity essential for the preservation of our migratory birds will be attained throughout the United States.
>
> We must protect our little visitors in winter, if their own states take care of them in summer.
>
> Under some circumstances enormous quantities of weed seed are devoured, as shown by the crop of a dove killed in a rye field at Warner, Tenn., which contained 7,500 seeds of yellow sorrel (Oxalis stricta). As a weed destroyer, the dove much more than compensates for the grain which it occasionally consumes, and the value of its services is certainly greater than the few cents which its body brings in market.

The fact that government agencies were distributing such information in early versions of public service announcements marked a major step forward in attracting citizens' attention to a problem and put the millinery trade on the defensive.

> Flickers are more terrestrial than other woodpeckers, and a large part of their animal food consists of ants, which constitute nearly half the food of the year. Several stomachs contained little else, and at least two contained more than 3,000 each of the insects. Beetles stand next to ants in importance, forming about 10 per cent of the food, and including chiefly May-beetles, a few snapping-beetles, and carabids or predaceous ground-beetles.
>
> Grasshoppers also are eaten at certain times, as shown by several stomachs collected in June, 1865, in Dixon County, Nebr., which contained from 15 to 48 grasshoppers each. A bird with such a record is far too valuable to be killed for food, and is entitled to all the protection ordinarily accorded insectivorous species.[5]

Private organizations participated in a similar vein. The Carnegie Institution dispatched avian experts to the Tortugas Keys reservation opposite the Florida coast to investigate the habits and history of sea birds, the problems of migration, the homing instincts, and other phenomena of bird life. The institution shared its results with members of the public to keep them in the loop. That was a key element in putting a squeeze on the millinery industry as the federal government stepped up its involvement.

There was a lull in legislation after the Lacey Act became law, but there was none in federal activity. The lull did not mean legislators were ignoring the bird slaughter problem. Congressman George Shiras III, an Independent Republican from Pennsylvania and a nature photographer who pioneered the use of nighttime flash photography, introduced a bill in the House that mandated federal control over the protection of migratory birds.[6] He said that since the birds were in one state one day and another the next there was no uniformity in laws that would protect them. Rightly, then, the federal government was best suited to provide that protection. The bill was referred to a committee and forgotten.

The Blue Heron sculpture by Megan Parker outside the Biedenharn Museum & Gardens, Monroe, Louisiana (Carol M. Highsmith, photographer, 2020).

The Hat That Killed a Billion Birds

President Theodore Roosevelt, an avid bird protector, did not wait for Congress to act. Under his guidance the government established a series of bird preserves around the country, mostly west of the Mississippi River. By 1910 there were 57 bird preserves located along the seacoast and inland freshwater lakes. The majority were on government land that had little or no agricultural value.

Among the southern and Gulf states devoted to bird preservation were Pelican Island, off Florida, which was the home of the snowy heron, and the Battledore Islands, off the coast of Louisiana, where the royal tern lived. In addition, a group of small, salt grass islets or shoals known as the Mosquito Islets along the Gulf Coast were included.

There were limitations to the federal government's reach. It could only establish reserves in states where there were public lands, which were scarce in the eastern part of the country. Several states stepped in and established their own reservations. The preserves were established as sanctuaries where colonies of birds could take refuge during the migration and breeding seasons. They demonstrated quickly the efficiency of the plan as a way of saving bird life and increasing their numbers. Several of them included areas of marshland that had never been the breeding grounds of wild fowl.

One of the most significant preserves covered several of the western islands of the Hawaiian group. It contained one of the largest breeding colonies of sea birds in the world. Others consisted of reservoir sites of reclamation projects, where the artificial lakes attracted numerous birds. Members of Congress who were encouraged by the results of the preserve implementation created a new law to complement that plan.

Representative John W. Weeks (R–Massachusetts) and Senator George P. McLean (R–Connecticut) introduced a law that prohibited the spring hunting and marketing of migratory birds and the importation of wild bird feathers for women's fashion. Ostensibly, the Weeks-McLean law would end "millinery murder" by giving the secretary of agriculture the power to set hunting seasons nationwide. That did not happen.

The milliners and manufacturers were not enthralled with the law, which they alleged was influenced by T. Gilbert Pearson. They tried to convince consumers that it would drive up the costs of ladies' hats and create massive job losses and claimed that the rigid enforcement of laws advocated by Mr. Pearson would throw 20,000 persons out of employment. And they labeled Pearson as "the man who sent up the cost of feathers for hats."[7]

The milliners insisted that if the women who persisted in wearing wings and plumage of birds on their heads wanted to fix the blame for the additional cost of feathers that spring they would find a willing victim in Pearson. That was actually a tribute; he had been fighting milliners and manufacturers so long that by the time McLean-Weeks was passed Pearson didn't care particularly who blamed him.

It was no secret that Pearson had been the driving force behind the act and similar laws passed by many state legislatures to prevent the slaughter of birds for ornamentation of millinery. It was no wonder that milliners and manufacturers increased their attacks on him after Weeks-McLean became law. Pearson reveled in them, especially when he boasted that he had done all his work with the expenditure of not more than $200,000.

Weeks-McLean, which became effective March 4, 1913, was the first U.S. law ever passed to regulate the shooting of migratory birds. But it was flawed by a constitutional weakness and became a political football after one federal judge declared it

18. Who Owns the Birds?

Left: George P. McLean, the author of the Migratory Bird Treaty Act of 1918, which still applies today (Bain News Service, CA. 1920–1925). *Right:* John W. Weeks, whose 1911 law made it possible for the national forest system to expand into the eastern United States and provide protection for birds (Bain News Service, November 9, 1926).

constitutional but two others overturned that ruling. Ultimately, it was declared neither constitutional nor unconstitutional due to confusing political wrangling and the passage of a replacement.

It wasn't until 1919 that the American Game Protective Association announced that there had been an erroneous press dispatch released to the effect that the U.S. Supreme Court had declared Weeks-McLean unconstitutional.[8] In fact, the so-called federal migratory bird law had been repealed on July 3, 1917, when President Wilson signed the Canadian treaty enabling act. That made the constitutional vs. unconstitutional argument moot—but a new law surfaced.

The Migratory Bird Treaty Act of 1918 was one of the most significant bird protection bills ever passed. It was first enacted in 1916 to implement the convention for the protection of migratory birds between the United States and Great Britain, which acted on behalf of Canada. The act was wide in its scope from the outset—and grew as the years passed. (See Appendix B.)

The explanation as to what happened ultimately with Weeks-McLean was baffling. According to press reports, what happened in Washington was that the solicitor general had failed to dismiss his own motion before the Supreme Court, which was to test the constitutionality of the original migratory bird law. By that time there was no use in arguing the case anyway, because there was no longer any Weeks-McLean law. Nevertheless, some folks were sure the problem had been settled—as they had been predicting hopefully for years—with the focus on new federal laws. It wasn't.

110 The Hat That Killed a Billion Birds

Do you know that after the first of July it will be against the law to sell an aigrette in the state of New York? And do you know that is why the milliners' windows are filled with aigrette-trimmed hats, marked very low? They are anxious to get rid of their stock before this law goes into effect. For, after July first, all the aigrettes they then have on hand will be a dead loss, as they cannot sell them or ship them out of the state to be sold.[9]

Despite their optimism, aigrettes were still in demand. But progress was ongoing. New federal regulations which protected the birds in the United States were in effect and the Department of Justice protected vigorously any violations of their provisions. But the legislative consternation and confusion continued with the Underwood Tariff Bill of 1913 that was sandwiched in between the Weeks-McLean and Migratory Bird Treaty acts.

19

The Turning Point Arrives

"The only time I ever used the Ford organization to influence legislation
was on behalf of the birds, and I think the end justified the means."
—Henry Ford[1]

It took 33 years from the recognition of the bird slaughter problem in 1880 for the
U.S. Congress to finally do something meaningful to stop the trafficking of bird plumage and feathers into the country. The Lacey Act and the Weeks-McLean bill, while significant, dealt with domestic protection. The Underwood Tariff Act of 1913, which was
pushed forward by an expanded public relations campaign conducted by protectionists,
was the federal government's first attempt to address the issue internationally.

Late in 1913, Congress included an amendment in a tariff bill that prohibited the
importation of many bird products. Like Lacey and Weeks-McLean, it had limitations
and critics. The opposition was more strident, since it affected a wider domestic and foreign audience.

The battle to include any legislation in the 1913 bill banning the absolute importation of bird plumage, as the House of Representatives proposed in a one-paragraph
amendment, was far from easy. If it weren't for the tenacity of Oregon's two Democrat
senators, George E. Chamberlain and Harry Lane, who defied their party's position, and
a spirited public relations campaign, the importation practice might not have been limited at all.[2] The drama extended for five hours on September 5, 1913, as Democrat senators wrangled over the question.

William T. Hornaday was one of the most outspoken supporters of the Underwood
Tariff bill.[3] He appeared in Washington, D.C., before a Senate committee to ask that
Congress stop the extermination of birds for millinery purposes. He requested that a
clause be inserted in the bill prohibiting the importation into the United States of wild
birds for millinery purposes.

Hornaday told the committee and the press that the time had come when the Christian nations of Europe and America had to stop the slaughter for commercial purposes
or suffer the consequences. "The New York Zoological society challenges the right of
the feather trade to exterminate the most beautiful birds of the world," he averred, as
he revealed that 100 species were being exterminated to meet the demands for plumes,
feathers, and skins to use on millinery.

He offered salient facts to back up his contention:

The number of wild birds annually consumed by the feather trade is so enormous as to challenge the imagination. The whole world is under tribute.
No species is spared for sentimental reasons.

112   The Hat That Killed a Billion Birds

The most beautiful and most curious species are the ones in the greatest danger of extermination.

The exquisite birds of paradise are being exterminated literally before our eyes, and the extermination of a species is a crime.

The greater and lesser birds of paradise and the Jobi bird of paradise are now nearly extinct.

The beautiful quetzal of Guatemala cannot be obtained alive at any price.

The scarlet ibis, roseate spoonbill, Carolina parakeet and flamingo are now forever gone from the bird fauna of the United States thanks to the feather hunters.

He cited a case of bird destruction that had been reported a few weeks earlier by his friend T. Gilbert Pearson, who had found in Florida an annihilated egret rookery and 28 dead birds on the ground.[4] The adults had been stripped of their plumage and the young birds lay dead in the nest above.

Hornaday cautioned the committee that despite his remarks people engaged in the importation of feathers and birds were still opposing the incorporation in the tariff bill of any measure to stop the practice. Yet he remained confident that a clause would be inserted in the Underwood bill prohibiting the importation into this country of wild birds for millinery purposes. Hornaday didn't leave anything to chance.

He continued to solicit support from fellow conservationists, such as a group in New Mexico, where a game and fish warden was sending out pamphlets to arouse the public to protect and save the birds under the New York Zoological Society's aegis. The pamphlet, titled "What to Do," appealed to bird lovers in simple terms:

The present is a remarkably auspicious moment for striking a blow against the slaughter of wild birds for millinery purposes. A new tariff bill is rapidly being framed by the house committee on ways and means, for early presentation at the extra session of congress. If the ways and means committee, and the House of Representatives can be sufficiently encouraged to take the decisive step that has been proposed by the New York Zoological Society and the National Association of Audubon societies, the result will be a victory that will completely reform our attitude toward the birds of the world. Think what it would mean to stop, at one stroke, all slaughter of "plumage" birds for the hats of American women, and at the same time wash our hands clean of the odium of this traffic.

This appeal is addressed particularly to the women of America, because we believe that if any considerable bodies of them can be reached and fully informed of the situation, the result will be an overwhelming demand for the entire prohibition of the importation of plumage of wild birds for millinery purposes. The need of the hour is that congress should be informed of the wishes of the American people regarding the matter.

We do not wish anyone to act merely at our request. It is a matter of conscience with each individual.

If you desire to stop the traffic in the plumage of wild birds throughout the United States, the thing to do is to express your wish in writing to each member of congress from your state, and the committee of ways and means of the House of Representatives, Hon. Oscar W. Underwood, chairman. Express your views and your desires entirely in your own way, and leave the rest to congress.[5]

Lane and Chamberlain were of like mind and they defied their party leaders. They had made their positions known when Congress began its deliberations over the issue of bird plumage millinery. The Senate Finance committee used the issue as a football for several weeks, during which they made it clear they wanted to protect the birds. The odds did not seem to be in their favor as the debate began.

Opposition to the importation of feathers came from an unexpected source: fly fishermen.[6] Their concern was that without the appropriate feathers to create flies they would have to resort to bait fishing. They contended that would deplete the stock of freshwater fish and said that an angler using bait might catch ten trout for every one he could take with a fly. That was costly to the government and counterproductive.

G.M.L. LaBranche, the former president of the New York Anglers Club, said that the government, the states, and the clubs were spending large sums for the stocking of streams with trout. He explained that the expenditure would scarcely be justified if there were to be bait fishing in these streams. They would soon be fished out. He emphasized that only a small amount of feathers was used for making flies. LaBranche ended his argument by pointing out that England had a law prohibiting the importation of certain plumage, but it made an exception for materials used in fly manufacturing. He asked why the United States couldn't do the same.

Hornaday dismissed LaBranche's argument with a salient point: "The position of the manufacturer of the flies made from foreign birds' plumage is of course easily understood. He does not wish to be disturbed in the least. Each clause in the new tariff bill is annoying to someone." That was not only the case with the tariff bill, but it also was representative of the arguments from all sides regarding the morality, legality, and practicality of murderous millinery that lasted for six decades.

Perhaps Hornaday was getting ahead of himself. "If any delegation of anglers is actually considering an attempt to convince Congress that to prohibit the importation of the plumage of foreign birds is going to work serious injury to their sport, they may well realize right now that they will get themselves well laughed at for their pains, and I think that is all they will get," he said. That was not accurate. Proponents of the millinery trade still had some fight in them.

Hornaday argued the fly fishermen would no doubt find a way around the ban, but they could find an alternate supply of feathers at home, since there was an adequate number of domestic feathers available. "But," he declared, "if anglers wish to make a fight over such an ignoble issue we surely will meet them in the ring." Opponents accepted that challenge.

A Senate committee rejected the House's proposal as written, suggesting that it was too drastic. The committee suggested a modification, which the Audubon Society and other lovers of birds denounced. They said it would make the House provision absolutely ineffective. Lane and Chamberlain stepped in to support the House version of the inclusion.

The battle over the Senate's modification went to a caucus. After a prolonged debate the caucus decided to stand by the committee's modification. Lane and Chamberlain refused to go along with the decision and convinced several of their colleagues that it was wrong. They drew so much support that party leaders gave up the fight and adopted the House paragraph that absolutely prohibited the importation of the plumage of wild birds, except for scientific and educational purposes. One representative tried to throw a wrench into the deal.

Edwin Y. Webb (D–North Carolina) quietly introduced a bill that would have created a significant loophole in the plumage ban.[7] That prompted officers of the National Association of Audubon Societies to issue a call to fight the bill they said would serve the interests of the professional "bird-butchers" of the millinery market. They had a point.

Webb's amendment would amend the tariff law to admit plumage held in the United States before its passage and taken overseas by Americans. The proposal created a great deal of optimism among milliners that their sources of feathers might not dry up after all. If adopted, it would have given feather hunters an easy way to defy the federal ban that so many Americans had demanded from Congress.

Opponents of Webb's bill speculated that the millinery industry would dispatch scores of scouts overseas with bundles of old aigrettes which they would register with customs agents upon departure and then bring new ones back to the United States along with thousands more. After all, no one could tell where the shipments originated or whether the aigrettes were new or old. According to the wording of the bill, the feathers imported by the milliners' agents would be admitted "upon their identity being established under appropriate rules and regulations to be prescribed by the Secretary of the Treasury."[8]

The opponents of the bill maintained that the idea that feathers could be identified adequately was absurd. Ornithologists they consulted said it was impossible. They could only conclude that Webb's proposed bill would make future enforcement a farce. The enactment of the Webb bill would reverse the success of the original tariff bill, which was working not only in the United States but also internationally.

As proof, the Audubon Society spokespeople revealed that their agents in London had just learned that, in anticipation of the passage of a similar law pending in the British parliament, the English milliners were already designing new styles that excluded wild bird plumage.[9] They regretted the inconvenience caused to the ladies in the process of the necessary customs house enforcement of the new law, but because of the thousand seizures of plumes that had already been made, millions of birds had been spared from hunters.

In the protectionists' view the amendment would make customs agents helpless to prevent it. Worse, it would legitimatize a wholesale smuggling of plumage that would soon restore their old market to the hunters who slaughtered the birds across the globe to supply the costly millinery plumes.

A defiant Pearson responded:

> While the successful carrying out of the provisions of the new American feather law marks a milestone in bird protection among the peoples of the whole world, its amendment according to the Webb bill would surely destroy much of its beneficial effect. Backed by the same sentiment that supported our efforts that resulted in barring imported plumage by the tariff, we shall fight any attempt such as this to nullify any of its provisions, since we know that the American people are squarely behind the law as it stands.[10]

Their adamant support in favor of the House amendment was a victory for bird lovers everywhere. Hornaday said, "It is the first real victory ever won for the birds of the world that rises clear and above and beyond all local issues." It will place our country in a class by itself, on a plane clear above all other nations. It places us in a position to demand of all Europe "go thou and do likewise!" He was careful to point out diplomatically that Lane and Chamberlain did not deserve all the credit. The women who lent their support deserved some too.

"The women of America have redeemed themselves," he declared. "This contest was their one great chance to square themselves on the subject of bird millinery, and they rushed to improve it. It was the women of our land who made this victory possible."[11]

He and his fellow bird aficionados may have been a little too excited.

They expected that the passage of the tariff bill would end forever all importations of wild birds' plumage for millinery purposes. In their view, the stock available at the time of passage would soon be depleted, which would end the need to slaughter birds. Just the opposite happened.

20

Embarrassment Knows
No Boundaries

"When Congress passed the tariff bill with the amendment which prohibited the importation of aigrettes, egret plumes, or so-called osprey
feathers, the general public was given to understand that the practice
of slaughtering wild birds to provide millinery decorations had been
stopped for all time, because of the loss of the heavy American trade."[1]

The Underwood bill contained two glaring omissions: it did not place restrictions
on the sale of feathers and plumage in general, so they continued to appear on millinery
items, and it left the government to prove the origin of any feathers and plumage that
managed to reach America, which was impractical. Anyone trying to sneak them into
the country could feel safe that they would not be held culpable for circumventing the
tariff restrictions.

Almost the only way the federal authorities could obtain a conviction was to catch
a smuggler in the act of bringing bird of paradise feathers into the country. Once the
feathers were in the country, they were as safe as if they had been formally passed by
the customs officials. That led to a new problem: smuggling. Nevertheless, the bill was a
good start at addressing the bird slaughter problem.

Some of the suspected smugglers were women who could not bear to give up their
gaudy hats. The U.S. Customs people were not making it easy for them to buy the hats,
even in Europe. If they did and wore them on the voyages back to the United States they
were likely to lose them and suffer embarrassment in the process. Starting in February
1914 customs agents boarded trans–Atlantic ocean liners and confronted bird hat wearers. The agents did one of two things.

In some situations they cut the showy aigrettes and other plumes from the wearers' hats, which had cost them as much as $200 in Paris, which was equal to $5,209 a hat
in contemporary value. The hefty price tag explained why milliners were not eager to
give up their trade. In other situations the kindhearted agents gave them the option to
ship their hats back where they got them. If they were lucky they could get their money
back. In either case the agents had a stern warning for the ladies. The United States had
in place a new law that protected birds from being martyred for their feathers, and they
intended to uphold that law, which they did, albeit sporadically.

Women who reached American shores without encountering customs agents
aboard ships were still not safe from having their hats clipped. In their defense, they did
not always know that there was a ban in place on feathered hats. That made no difference in most cases, but enforcement at customs houses was up to the whim of an officer.

115

116   **The Hat That Killed a Billion Birds**

Sometimes they cut the adornments off the hats. Other times they let the ladies pass through with a warning and declared the hat as "apparel in use."

Some milliners and their customers were not ready to give up their hats cold turkey. Meanwhile, the supply of banned plumes and feathers in the United States was not diminishing despite the ban. That was hard to explain. Enter the smugglers who acted purely to enrich themselves even at the risk of being arrested.

"Since the prohibition of wild plumage in America, I am informed, there has been no imitation of aigrettes and paradises. Yet, in the five years, when purchase and sale have been illegal, there have been twenty times as much sold as remained in America at the time of prohibition," reporter Sterling Heilig wrote.[2]

Charles Kurzman, who represented the Millinery Chamber of Commerce of the United States and the Eastern Millinery Association in Paris, told Heilig that the practice of using birds on millinery was still common, which surprised him. "It is surprising that reputable concerns in America still handle an article that is so illegal [and] the sale is prohibited. But the government and Audubon Society expect to go after these people, because it puts Americans who come and go from Europe in a bad light," he explained.[3]

The fact that the government and Audubon Society had been trying to shut down these milliners for five years with only a modicum of success suggested that those Americans did not worry about being put in a bad light as long as they could still access plumage, feathers, and parts. Some folks suspected that women who traveled back and forth from Europe were smuggling the contraband in, as were sailors, who were not subtle about their activities. They saw the opportunity to make a few extra dollars and ran their own illegal export businesses, much to the amusement of customs agents at times.

The smuggling of illegal feathers into this country was brisk until 1922, when the omissions in the original law were repaired. During that time the millinery market was barely affected by any shortage. The demand for feathers was as steady as that for diamonds. That was good news for smugglers, who were usually able to dispose of their goods promptly for a sizable profit.

They easily sold the feathers to a jobber who in turn sold them to department stores or milliners. Along with the feathers the jobber provided certificates and other data designed to show that the merchandise had been in the United States the required number of years. The law did not question the good faith of dealers who bought feathers on the strength of these shaky certificates. Neither did the federal district attorneys.

Most of the smuggling was done by seamen and officers of merchant ships from the Mediterranean. Their standard modus operandi was simple: they concealed the feathers under their clothing. "Lean seamen," one customs official noted, "have waddled off their ships swollen and puffed like Falstaffs by layers upon layers of plumes strapped to their limbs and trunks."[4]

"On some lines," he explained, "U.S. customs inspectors first take a glimpse at the neck and then at the waist of the seamen. If they observe a No. 14 neck springing out of a 60-inch torso they make an arrest and usually recover a few thousand dollars' worth of feathers." That was good news for the bird protection advocates.

All the confiscated plumes specified in the 1913 law were turned over to the National Association of Audubon Societies, which formed them into exhibits and distributed them among 60 different museums throughout the country. About $20,000 worth of plumes were found in these collections. That in itself was a teaching tool for the American public, which benefited from the education about bird slaughter provided by protectionists.

20. Embarrassment Knows No Boundaries

The protectionists' battle was uphill all the way, but individuals like Hornaday, Pearson, Lane, and Chamberlain and the societies they represented were equal to the challenge. So were the women who were on their side. Together they created a formidable force as World War I approached and victory seemed like a possibility. That was a false hope.

Even though the intent of the Underwood tariff bill was laudable, its provisions led proponents to believe that the federal government was finally putting an end to the ongoing bird slaughter and that the bill would stop the importation and sales of plumage and feathers completely. They were ultimately disappointed. Realists suspected that Underwood was not a panacea: "It must have been a happy moment for bird lovers and those active in Audubon Society circles when they noted in the press dispatches that under the new federal Underwood tariff law aigrettes and other bird plumage are forbidden from importation," an editor said. "Finally, after a decade and a half of persistent effort, legislation has been secured. It must do the bird lover's heart good."

The heart, maybe, but not the head? The editor knew it was a stopgap measure:

> If the Underwood tariff law has no other commendable feature it will at least have done one great good in prohibiting the further importation of aigrettes or any other bird plumage for millinery purposes. Together with the schedule of the Underwood tariff law and the provision of the McLean migratory bird law prohibiting the destruction of insectivorous birds in this country, much good has been accomplished by the present and last congresses for the protection of American wild bird life.[5]

But was it enough?

The milliners' lobby continued to fight the prohibitory amendment for months after Hornaday had gone home believing he had won the day. Its representatives launched attacks from Washington, D.C., and other localities to exert their influence on congressmen in an attempt to obtain amendments to the tariff bill. Their goal was to modify and perhaps render ineffective the provision prohibiting the importation of plumage birds and their feathers. The congressmen were reluctant to do either.

Since the passage of the tariff act public opinion against the slaughter of birds for plumage had become so crystallized that congressmen had steadfastly refused to introduce proposed amendments that would nullify the plumage import provisions. They were not eager to run afoul of their constituents. Someone was trying to undermine them.

There had been one bill introduced mysteriously in Congress providing for an amendment which, at first glance, was innocuous and well-intended. It was designed to relieve traveling American women wearing aigrettes purchased originally in the United States of the embarrassment and loss caused by customs officers snipping their plumes on their return to this country from a trip abroad. The Audubonists were not fooled.

The amendment would, if passed, open the way to the extensive smuggling of aigrettes and the probable enrichment of unscrupulous millinery jobbers engaging in such an illegal business. Milliners would be able to conduct extensive smuggling operations over the borders between Canada and the United States, or between the United States and Mexico, where customs inspection was not as thorough as at the large ports.

Alternative smuggling ruses existed. Milliners could hire women to travel to Europe or Canada wearing cheap aigrette plumes worth only a few dollars and return with one worth many times that amount. Or, to cut back on travel and time, they could go to Canada wearing a hat containing a small egret plume and return with one with

5 or 10 times as many feathers in it worth upward of $100 to $400. In either case, it was hoped, custom officials would be none the wiser.

The Audubonists had a simple plan for preventing the extinction of the white herons or egrets that supplied the plumes the milliners wanted to exchange in their smuggling operations. They believed that American women could be relieved of any embarrassment caused on returning to the United States from foreign trips if they simply refrained from wearing the plumes abroad. They also pointed out that since the tariff law had been implemented only six months earlier law-abiding American milliners had devised other hat decorations that did not feature aigrettes.

The new aigrette-free decorations were beautiful and far less expensive, they insisted. Therefore, the proposed amendment was unnecessary. And it wouldn't relieve them completely of embarrassment. They could be embarrassed at home as easily as abroad.

Women who insisted on wearing aigrettes and who had acquired them at home were being embarrassed while traveling in some of the states that had strict anti-aigrette laws in place and vigorously enforced them. One case in particular proved that embarrassment was not restricted to overseas locations.

A state game warden in Portland, Oregon, seized an actress' headgear that featured 46 dozen aigrettes.[6] The circumstances were amusing to bird protectors because the warden took possession of the hat while she was wearing it on stage in the middle of a performance. That was embarrassing. Reports suggested the hat was valued at about $412 at the time of purchase.

The actress protested the confiscation of her hat. Undeterred, state authorities kept it despite her claims that it was simply part of her stage costume. The law against aigrettes in Oregon was clear: it prohibited not only the sale of aigrette plumes but made it unlawful for any person to have aigrettes in his or her possession except for scientific purposes. The actress failed to convince the authorities that her costly headgear was for scientific purposes.

The cat-and-mouse games among milliners, Audubonists, and government authorities continued as time passed. Slowly, ever so slowly, the milliners lost the battle. It wasn't for lack of trying. It was because the "good guys" grew better at coordinating their public relations and legislative activities. In the long run the milliners did not have the resources to overcome that factor. Attrition, education, and better, more effective laws were their downfall.

21

Regional Rivalries

"Even as late as the 80s native insectivorous birds, gulls, terns, small owls, etc., were used in numbers and it was not until public sentiment was stirred by the Audubon movement, and existing laws against the destruction of birds were enforced in some states and better laws enacted in others, that the milliners of the United States began to give up the use of the plumage of native wild birds."

—Edward Howe Forbush[1]

The American Civil War ended in 1865. The states were once again united. All it took to separate them again was a dispute as to who was killing more birds, southerners, northerners, or people elsewhere. According to anti–bird slaughter leaders there was no question: it was the southerners.

The American Society for the Prevention of Cruelty to Animals magazine labeled certain sections of the southern states "the black belt of cruelty" and placed the blame for the bird slaughter on the usual suspects:

The strict bird laws of the North can never count for much if our feathered neighbors have to face an ordeal of shot and unmerciful cruelty in their winter abodes. In Georgia and the Carolinas the wholesale shooting of some birds, protected in the North, is widely practiced. It is an ordinary sight to see boys coming into the towns in the early morning carrying long strings of dead robins. Some of our cherished songbirds are netted at their roosting grounds and thousands are sometimes secured in a night, only the choice birds being used and the other thrown away.

Mourning doves which in Northern States are preserved by common consent by sportsmen and repay the courtesy by diligent work against insects, are trapped by thousands in the South. Florida has been for years the scene of the barbaric slaughter of the snowy herons and egrets, until the beautiful birds are now on the verge of extinction.[2]

If there was one saving grace, the robins were the most numerous birds in the United Sates according to a 1915 census conducted by the Department of Agriculture.[3] The English sparrow was a close second, with an average of 60 pairs per square mile. In the northeast robins averaged six pairs to each farm of 58 acres, while English sparrows averaged five pairs per farm. As for density of population on each acre of farm land there was an average of one pair of birds. Thirty-four species of birds were represented.

The census takers cautioned that the bird population was still much less than it should have been. They claimed that if birds were given more protection there would be an increase in numbers. Nevertheless, there was some good news to report.

Anyone who was paying attention recognized that the white heron population was rebounding in the south due to the protection afforded to it by Louisiana, as were gulls,

120   **The Hat That Killed a Billion Birds**

terns, and other species. Louisiana and Alabama had passed laws several years earlier to protect their birds, and they were working well.

Reportedly, Louisiana, in conjunction with the Audubon Society in the north, had done more for the protection of bird life than any other state. The Louisiana legislature created a state commission with full jurisdiction over all game and fish within its territory and with the authority to regulate hunting and fishing. The law required hunters to pay fees running from $2 to $25 a year for licenses. To everyone's surprise there was little protest and an immediate compliance with the statute.

More than 150,000 amateurs and professionals took out licenses for hunting and fishing. The revenue was sufficient to support a warden in every county and township. The law allowed state officials to keep a running census of how many birds and wild animals were killed for food during a given the year. That was a novel idea for its time.

Headlines like "LOUISIANA GAME LAW HOLDS GOOD, Birds in Millinery Stores Confiscated by Wardens" and "ALABAMA GETTING IN LINE" were commonplace in the two states' newspapers. Legislators were defending their laws prohibiting the use of birds as millinery, despite opposition from the ladies who bought it, most of which came from Alabama. The folks in the north could not have missed that state of events.

A flowery caution in one newspaper heralded the impending disappearance of birds as part of millinery in the two states:

> While the song bird and the innocent little insectivorous fowls are beginning to shuffle their stuffed bodies out toward the rims of the Alabama ladies' hats, preparatory to taking flight, there comes the fluttering of wings and the inharmonious squeaking of sawdust voices from the rejuvenated birds of Louisiana. In that wonderful state the game wardens have already begun to give wings to the dusty birds that have for so many years added beauty and individuality to the artificial landscape gardens of that fair southern state.

The writer chastised the ladies in Alabama for challenging its new law:

> The ladies who have been gathering up their skirts and collecting their pitchforks for an attack upon the legislature of Alabama would do well to throw away such ancient weapons of warfare, buckle swords around their waists and ride down upon the state capitol firing shotguns, and pistols, for instead of a crowd of hen pecked husbands behind those barracks they are apt to discover a phalanx of stubborn lighters, armed themselves for a bloody fray.[4]

Commentators claimed that the section of Alabama's game law prohibiting the sale or having in possession any part of birds other than game birds was not slipped in by mistake. The state's legislators were serious about enforcing it. So, they said, when the lady lobbyists reached the state capitol at Montgomery they would find real sentiment among the legislators against their "cruel and heartless practice of wearing murdered birds on their hats, while they themselves faint away when a bug is killed in their presence."

That same sentiment prevailed in Louisiana. One aspect of its law that caught people's attention was the fact that the state had not only passed its game law through both legislative houses but also the game wardens were strictly enforcing it. To them the haphazard style of enforcement in sway in many states was not at play in Louisiana. If their state was going to pass a law to protect game birds, it was going to enforce it.

With their statute in one hand and commission in the other, the game wardens "liberated the imprisoned birds and left the hats of the poor women populated with

21. Regional Rivalries

mere seagulls and chicken feathers."[5] The word "mere" did not apply to sea gulls. They had contributed more than their fair share of feathers to the bird millinery movement and their numbers had sunk to the dangerously low side.

As soon as the protestors and milliners in Louisiana realized that the birds were actually receiving protection under the game wardens and the state was serious about enforcing its laws, they exercised their legal rights as their colleagues in Ohio had done. When a zealous game warden ransacked a millinery store and confiscated every hat with a songbird on it, the enraged milliner brought suit.

The case wound through three levels of the court system. The warden's action was judged constitutional at each level. Despite that, and the fact that Alabama and Louisiana had successfully passed and enforced bird protection laws, people like T. Gilbert Pearson continued to take pot shots at them—even after choosing southern venues to pursue breeding operations.[6]

In 1909 the Audubon Society acquired 25 islands on the Gulf coast east of the mouth of the Mississippi River to maintain as breeding grounds for ducks, wild turkeys, wild geese, gulls and other game and sea birds. The society procured eggs by the thousands in the spring, many of which hatched in the sun during the summer. It brought large numbers of native hens and cocks over from the Florida coast, where they quickly became plentiful. Yet Pearson was still accusing southerners of wanton slaughter four years later.

> Millions of small birds in migration are destroyed yearly by the people of the southern states and used as food. This destruction, now increasing, is having serious effects on the number of songbirds in the North. [Hunters] are armed with guns, and many are proficient in other means of destruction. In the north, also, large numbers of foreign laborers, coming from Europe, kill small birds for food. It is only recently that little birds were sold in large quantities In New York City, and they are still sold by thousands in the south.[7]

Ironically, among the leading proponents of the bird protection laws in Louisiana were the much maligned Italians, who government and Audubon officials had singled out in years past for their role in killing birds.[8] Public opinion in Louisiana in general sustained the bird protection legislation enthusiastically, and diverse opinions were unwelcome. When a few dissatisfied hunters and fishermen threatened litigation to prevent the enforcement of the new game laws they discovered quickly that they would not get any sympathy from their neighbors, especially in New Orleans.

The city had always been famous for its restaurants in which feathered delicacies such as quail, snipe, duck, partridge, and wild turkey were popular. New Orleans was also noted as a fish market, and any legislation passed to regulate and protect fishing was met with hearty approval. The fishermen in the lower Mississippi and along the gulf coast were primarily Italians. They lived in the bayous, where they parceled out the fishing grounds and protected their monopoly fiercely. They understood the advantages of proper regulation and protection and gave their hearty support and assistance to the game and fish wardens.

For all the negative talk about what was happening in the southern states, they were light years ahead of some others. Oklahoma did not join the states which prohibited possession for sale of aigrettes until 1917. At the same time California made the sale of aigrettes, birds of paradise, goura pigeons, and certain other birds used in millinery illegal.[9] The criticisms of the southern states and their enforcement efforts seemed like a smokescreen.

122 The Hat That Killed a Billion Birds

Pearson may not have been aware of it, but he was highlighting the failure of the Audubon societies to do their job uniformly. The Audubon Society was 29 years old at this point and the original problem for which it was formed still existed. That was nothing new, in the east, at least.

Reporters claimed that the big New York millinery houses were still handling songbirds, despite the Audubon societies' efforts to stop them.[10] Conversely, their counterparts in the Midwest had been successful in influencing store owners to stop selling bird-adorned millinery, and one big firm advertised that it would no longer sell plumage other than that obtained from game birds and fowls. Just the opposite situation persisted in New York City, where all the millinery stores still sold the birds—and the managers claimed that the demand for them was on the increase. That opened the door for critics and millinery salespeople to once again blame their favorite scapegoats for the problem: women.

New York City women insisted on having feathers on their hats, the milliners emphasized. Paradoxically, the ladies declined absolutely to be a party to the murder of the songbirds. That explained why the millinery producers were searching diligently to find some substitute. They discovered a way of manufacturing plumage but kept it a trade secret while acknowledging that they could now transform the despised barn yard fowl into a millinery rainbow.[11]

That was not good enough for the average woman of the time, though, referred to as "Miss Knickerbocker." She wanted the real thing, and the sneak previews of the millinery to be released in the fall of 1897 were not calculated to cheer the hearts of the Audubonists because of their emphasis on birds. That remained true two decades later.

Pearson was still saying in 1915 that the prevention of the slaughter of songbirds was a stupendous task that had to be accomplished by educating the public through the schools, the press, and the clergy so better laws and better enforcement of them could be implemented. All it required was more money. The Audubonists had been saying that for 30 years, and they still hadn't eradicated the bird slaughter problem entirely. That was partly because they couldn't do it alone, and some of the groups that were supposedly their allies were pulling in opposite directions at times.

Three years before the "black belt of cruelty" label was levied on southern states, New Jersey, a northern state, was experiencing differences of opinion between its legislature and sportsmen. There was a breach between the state's new fish and game commission and the New Jersey sportsmen's spring game hunting concerning the enactment of new laws regulating the killing of game.[12] The sportsmen objected to a spring game hunting season. The commission favored it.

The sportsmen's associations were in favor of conserving the wild game and making the state's laws conform to the spirit of good laws in vogue in other states. They made it clear that spring shooting was barbarous and destructive, and every true sportsman and lover of nature was opposed to it. The Audubon Society was actively defending the wild birds and had procured laws in all of the seaboard states against the killing of bright plumaged sea birds for millinery use. The Audubonists asked why New Jersey was being obtuse.

The sportsmen wanted to save all species of wild birds from ruthless destruction. Moreover, they wanted to stop another odious practice: the sale of game birds in the markets. Their message was clear: New Jersey could not afford the reproach of indiscriminate slaughter of its wild birds. Neither could any other state, regardless of its geographical location.

21. Regional Rivalries

Out west the Audubonists were carrying their battle to the milliners. The Washington State Audubon Society sent letters to milliners advising them that the state's game laws would be enforced.[13] The letters warned the recipients specifically against selling or having in their possession for purpose of sale any part of the plumage of the American egret or snowy heron (plumes commonly known as aigrettes) or any wings, plumes or other parts of grebes, pelicans, terns, gulls, ibis or other native or migrant birds. These were all protected by Washington State law, which prohibited the sale or possession for purpose of sale of any wild bird or part of a wild bird, other than game bird.

The milliners inferred that the society's members were on the lookout for violations. The letters were of interest to wearers of hats as well as to sellers. They might start wondering if they were sporting hats with illegal birds atop them and become leery about wearing them in public or buying more, lest they be subject to penalties as well. The letters had a psychological effect on milliners and consumers alike. Again, optimists said that Audubon societies of other states were as active as the Washington association and predicted that within a few years the feathers of wild birds would rarely be seen on women's hats. Hope sprang eternal.

Perhaps it was Iowa that set the standard for all states to follow.[14] The state assumed ownership of all wild birds, whether resident or migratory. Iowa's 1906 bird protection act declared that hereafter they were all the property of the state, which aroused the curiosity of state residents. They wanted to know whether a woman could wear any part of a bird on her hat according to the new law. The short answer was that it was doubtful.

The lawmakers made a concession to the ladies. They allowed them to wear the plumage and other portions of dead birds on their hats on Easter and July 4. After that, they could no longer wear the plumage, skin, or body of any nongame bird, native to Iowa or not, on their hats.

Lest anyone was confused about what constituted a game or nongame bird, the law laid it out clearly. Game birds included swans, geese, brant, river and sea ducks, rails, coots, mud-hens, gallinules, shore birds, plover, surf birds, snipes, woodcocks, sandpipers, tattlers, curlews, wild turkeys, grouse, prairie chickens, pheasants, partridges and quails. All other species of wild birds, either resident or migratory, except the ones exempted, were declared to be nongame birds and the property of the state, and their destruction was prohibited under this new law.

Specifically, the law provided that

> no person shall within the state of Iowa kill or catch or have in his or her possession, living or dead, any wild bird other than a game bird, or purchase, order, or expose for sale, transport or ship within or without the state, any such wild bird after it has been killed or caught, except that ordinary cage birds for pets, such as parrots, canaries, etc., are not included in the inhibitions of the act so far as it relates to shipment, sale, etc.

The well-thought-out law also protected the nests of the specified birds and prohibited railroads from carrying the nongame birds. Egg collecting was addressed too. Scientists could be given certificates by fish and game wardens that would entitle them to make collections of eggs and nests and to kill nongame birds but not in breeding seasons. The certificates were not transferable.

The act especially exempted the English sparrow, great horned owl, sharp-skinned hawk, blackbird, and crow from protection of the law. Penalties were reasonable. Violations were punishable by a fine of $5 for each offense, and an additional $5 fine for each extra bird, or imprisonment for 30 days in jail. Moreover, it was provided that "no part of the plumage, skin or body of any bird protected by this section shall be sold or had in possession for sale, irrespective of whether said bird was captured or killed within or without the state."

The language was designed to stop the millinery business, but only so far as birds were concerned. Otherwise, the milliners were free to decorate ladies' hats with anything they thought would look attractive. The law was specific. But there was no rush across the nation to emulate it.

Individual states operated at their own pace when it came to passing bird protection laws. There was no doubt that the longer a state took to act, the longer it took for the country as a whole to save the birds from being slaughtered. That was bad for the birds and the country. But it opened the door for milliners to protect their turf.

22

The Audubonists' Antithesis

"Plumage is going to be a very prominent feature in the summer millinery. Whole birds with long tapering tail feathers, two heads with long crooked beaks, crossed together, and other equally weird-looking 'made' pieces used on the higher-priced hats with other slaughterous trimmings are causing much consternation to the Audubonists."[1]

While the Audubon Society was working to protect the birds and convince women that buying theater hats was wrong, the editors of the *Millinery Trade Review* were doing just the opposite. The two entities caught the ladies in between, which prolonged the fight against the bird slaughter. The duplicitous milliners pretended they were in league with the Audubonists in seeking legislation to regulate the plume industry. Often, they were working behind the scenes to circumvent whatever laws were passed. It was a dangerous game.

There was a breakthrough in the conflict among the Audubon Society of New York, the Ornithologists Union, and the New York Millinery Merchants Protective Association (MMPA) in 1903 when they signed a temporary agreement which included significant concessions in the eastern part of the United States. The MMPA agreed to an absolute withdrawal from the trade and in the trimming of hats of certain species of birds that the Audubon societies and the American Ornithologist's Union had identified. The agreement was slated to remain in force for three years. Notices went out to notify members what plumage could be legally used:

On and after January 1, 1904, the importation, manufacture, purchase or sale of the plumage of egrets or herons and American pelicans of any species is to cease, and these birds are to be added to the list of prohibited species just mentioned.

The restrictions as to gulls, terns, grebes, herons and hummingbirds apply to the birds irrespective of the country in which they might have been killed and captured.

The Audubon Society of New York State agreed to

endeavor to prevent all illegal interference on the part of game wardens with the millinery trade; to refrain from aiding the passage of any legislation that has for its object restrictions against importation, manufacture or sale of fancy feathers obtained from domesticated fowls, or of the plumage of foreign birds other than those specifically mentioned above.[2]

The agreement was more of a concession for the milliners than for the Audubonists, who were gaining the upper hand in the public relations battle. The milliners said for public consumption that they were glad to reach a truce with the society and the Ornithologists' Union. The truth was that the wholesale millinery dealers had found that the constant agitation of their two antagonists threatened to make vast inroads into curbing their bird and feather trade.

The Hat That Killed a Billion Birds

There were two main reasons the milliners accepted the truce: they were preparing to become more involved in the fancy feather trade, for which the feathers were obtained from domesticated fowls, ducks, pigeons, and barnyard roosters, and they hoped to stem the tide of feminine fancy which had turned strongly against birds and feathers because of the alleged inhumanity in wearing these decorations.

Their reasoning was sound. The milliners believed that active support for the boycott of all birds and feathers would cease when consumers learned that the plumage and the trimmings offered in the shops were not the rare birds consumers had always supposed them to be but were the processed pluckings from domestic hens, whose lives had been taken for generally accepted legitimate purposes. And their concession was altruistic: it would open for the American farmer a vast field of wealth which had been hitherto unexplored in this country.

The milliners envisioned that the raising of domestic fowls with their plumage would become a regular profitable industry in the United States, as it had in Germany. The poultry industry would still be devoted primarily to food products, but the use of the feathers as a side business would be a significant addition to the farmers' finances. It was the proverbial "win, win" for everybody, although the milliners claimed that the agreement would cost them great sums of money. But they acknowledged that they were prepared to make that sacrifice to garner favor with the public because of their new-found humane approach to the birds they had been exploiting for years—at least the birds people thought they had been exploiting.

"If the women who are so afraid of wearing a rare bird could only see where we make them up they would not feel so badly about it," one milliner declared. "Often a particularly rare bird will have the breast of a pigeon and the plumage of some other equally domesticated birds. The birds are painted and dyed with aniline dyes so that they resemble the real bird for which they are made."[3]

As proof of their goodwill, milliners said they were making an effort to defeat Dame Fashion in her effort to bring the hummingbird to the front. It wouldn't be easy, they confessed, since the hummingbird was becoming fashionable in Paris, and it wouldn't take long before the craze would reach America. But the Millinery Association promised to nip the fad in the bud if possible, because its members were sure that if it became the rage the trade would be in constant trouble with the Audubon Society.

There was some question as to whether the millinery industry could be trusted to live up to the terms of the agreement for the three years of its existence.[4] There was talk of a separate agreement in the west. In order to extend similar agreements throughout the United States a request would be placed before the Millinery Jobbers' Association at its upcoming convention in Milwaukee. That association controlled all the trade west of Pittsburgh, Pennsylvania.

Only time would tell how the agreements would work out. Skeptics felt that the two sides might as well have agreed to work together to stop Jell-O from shimmering in a dessert dish for all the good their pact would do. If they both lived up to their agreement the millinery industry would have shut down and there would have been no new laws to regulate it if it didn't. The agreement looked good on paper, though. Fast forward six years as the squabbling resumed in newspapers.

By mid–1909 the Boston and New York milliners were allegedly cooperating to check any more legislation attempts by the Audubon Society to prohibit the killing of birds other than songbirds for millinery purposes. Naturalist Edward Forbush came immediately to the society's defense. He accused certain Boston milliners of promulgating false and misleading statements in newspaper articles by ridiculing the Audubon societies and portraying them to the public as an organization of zealots and fanatics who acted on impulse without using reason or judgment.

> It seems, if we are to believe certain of the milliners that they are intending to test the law exempting from use the plumage of the heron and the barnyard fowl, it may be unnecessary for me to remark that no law ever was urged or proposed by the Audubon Societies to exempt from commercial use the plumage of the barn yard fowl. There is no such law in existence. It would be quite as reasonable to legislate to prohibit the shoemakers from using the hides of slaughtered cattle.

He set out to disprove the charge by Boston milliner J. Engle that the societies had included in their list barnyard fowl, pheasants, and grouse. Forbush denied that they had ever tried to prohibit the wearing of the feathers of pheasants, grouse, or other game birds which could be legally killed during the open season. He stressed that such ridiculous statements as Engle's would not help the cause of the milliners.

Forbush looked back at the millinery trade's claim in 1903 that its concessions would cost it millions of dollars when a ban was placed on the use of the plumage of songbirds—which turned out to be true. But, he said, the loss only showed that the milliners had been using great quantities of songbirds and only stopped using them because of the activity of the Audubon societies in influencing public sentiment and in securing and enforcing legislation prohibiting such use.

"We may infer that otherwise the milliners would still continue to sell vast quantities of the plumage song birds at a good profit," he concluded.

Forbush admitted that the Audubon societies were trying to prevent hunters from exterminating non-game water birds that congregated at breeding places to care for their young. That was when hunters killed the parent birds by the thousands and left the helpless young ones to starve in the nests. That, he said, was one of the inhumane atrocities of the millinery business that the Audubon societies were trying to stop.

"The societies have succeeded in preserving many of these species by making the killing of the birds illegal and maintaining forces of wardens on the breeding grounds to enforce the law," he observed. That was a winning emotional argument for the societies.

Forbush did not let up. He employed economic arguments to further destroy the milliners' claims. He declared that there were significant economic reasons for protecting gulls, terns, and certain water fowl. Forbush noted that the tremendous interests of agriculture exceeded enormously those of the millinery business. The choice was clear for society, he intimated: food or millinery?

> Mankind depends upon agriculture for subsistence. Certain species of gulls and terns which feed on injurious insects are very beneficial to the farmer. When the Mormons first settled in Utah their crops were saved from the attacks of hordes of black crickets by gulls which came in thousands to devour the crickets.
>
> Dr. Gaumer tells us that since the destruction of the herons, egrets and other littoral birds for millinery purposes along the coasts of Mexico, disease has increased among the inhabitants of that region. Many of these birds are useful as scavengers.

Forbush scoffed at Engel for ridiculing the idea of protecting these birds. He promised that the Audubon societies would continue to do everything possible to protect threatened useful species from wanton slaughter for commercial purposes, despite the

128 **The Hat That Killed a Billion Birds**

milliners' interference. Forbush highlighted as an example the fact that the millinery trade had opposed a 1908 bill the Audubon Society had introduced in the New York assembly aimed at the use or manufacture of the plumage of birds of paradise to close a loophole in the state's law.[5]

At the time, under the laws of New York State, the plumage of birds of all kinds could be sold with impunity unless it could be proved that it was taken within the state. Proving that in regard to millinery ornaments was usually impossible, Forbush acknowledged. That kept the market open for all kinds of feathers, not only those of birds native to New York State but also from all other states or from any other country.

Accordingly, birds from other states, although killed in defiance of the law of those states, could be shipped to New York and sold by the wholesalers not only in New York, where their sale was questionably legal, but also in other states where it was illegal. That was the kind of law that the wholesalers and importers wanted, since they could circumvent it with relative ease, and they were banding together to keep it on the statute books. The bill introduced by the Audubon societies was intended to repeal the law.

Forbush left his rebuttal to Engle there. He had defined the Audubon societies' views on the debate. It was up to the readers to decide which side had the best arguments as to the legal and moral aspects of the bird slaughter. As had been the case for about 30 years, they were in no hurry to make up their minds. Neither was anybody else.

23

Reading the Signs

"Great things are not accomplished by those who yield to trends and fads and popular opinion."

—Jack Kerouac

Fads generally don't last long. Normally, once they are gone they don't come back. Sadly, that was not the case with bird-themed millinery. It peaked in 1868, disappeared, and then returned 20 or so years later. There were signs during the interim and after the fad's reemergence that bird populations were being threatened, but few people paid attention.

An 1874 *Harper's Bazaar* item reported:

Birds, above everything else, are used on stylish Parisian hats. The whole bird, with even its feet perfect, is perched on the side of the hat, or appears to be flying down its front. Blackbirds, with red-tipped wings and red breast, are evidently most popular. The taxidermist's aid has been called in to designate the starling, the lophophore, and the maroon tanager, which are found among fashionable millinery.

There are also many hummingbirds, some with sapphire, some with emerald, and others with topaz throats. Two tiny "hummers," with their long bills and spread wings, nestle in the diadem wreathes of gray leaves. Sometimes half a dozen sharp, slender wings are stuck in a single wreath.[1]

That was an early—and accurate—warning to conservationists that ladies' hats were gaudy and that if the practice continued it would take millions of birds to meet the demand to decorate them.

Edward Forbush remembered birds being killed en masse a year after the *Harper's* article appeared. "Going back to 1875 when my experience with the millinery business began, the milliners were using insectivorous birds in large numbers. Millinery drummers carried tanagers, orioles, bluebirds, cedar birds, thrushes, etc., which were sold, as were foreign insectivorous birds, in such quantities as they could be obtained," he recalled.[2] So the phenomenon was nothing new by the late years of the 19th century.

Joseph M. Wade, a writer for *Scientific American*, tried to warn readers that the wanton killing of songbirds was going to harm society if it didn't cease. He noted that 20 to 30 years earlier it was not unusual to see songbirds such as scarlet tanagers and Baltimore orioles in abundance in the nation's cities. But, he said, they were killed off and driven back to the woods long before the advent of bird millinery as a fashion. Everybody wanted a specimen—or thought they did. By 1886 they were rarely seen because they were doing their "duty in ornamenting thousands of ladies' bonnets within the past five years."

"These birds have been shot so ruthlessly, both while here and at the South, and during the migration, that hardly a pair could be found during the breeding season of 1886," Wade said. About all that remained to remind citizens of their disappearance was their ragged nests, "belonging to years gone by, as it sometimes takes the storms of many winters to beat them to the ground."[3] Wade prophesied that if the different societies organized to protect native birds accomplished their goals, those beautifully plumaged insectivorous birds would soon become common again. They did, but their recovery was slow.

One of Wade's key points was that the disappearance of the tanagers and orioles seemed to take place slowly. After all, 20 to 30 years is a long time in individuals' lives, and the disappearance of animal species is insidious. One species disappears and hardly anyone notices except for wildlife experts. Two go away and a few more people may take notice. Three ... that may cause alarm. That was the case with the disappearance of the great auk around 1847.

Great auks, prized for their close, rich plumage, were found along the Atlantic coast from Labrador to northern New Jersey.[4] They were about the size of a goose and were noted for their short wings, which they used as paddles for swimming. The last recorded sighting of these birds in the wild in any great number was on an island off the coast of Maine in 1847, when some fishermen slaughtered a large flock. Nobody seemed to notice.

It wasn't for another 60 years that naturalists realized their value. Around 1910 a single skin of an auk was sold at an ornithological sale in London for $800. There were only about 40 specimens in existence at that time, including those in museums and private ownership. Anyone else who wanted one was out of luck, since the great auk was extinct.

A salient example of people's failure to read the signs was the case of the disappearing hummingbird in the early 1900s, when one of the most wanton uses of birds became popular. Both the United States and South America exported 400,000 hummingbird skins annually for use in hat trimmings.[5] Even more were needed for ladies' knee-length automobile coats. Ironically, their creation came at the same time U.S. government officials began their first serious push to stop the bird slaughter.

The coats were gauche and extremely expensive. They cost about $25,000 apiece, about $673,000 in today's terms.[6] Fortunately, very few people could afford them. Nonetheless, each coat sold required the use of thousands of hummingbird skins. By 1913 there were signs that the numbers of hummingbirds in North America were dwindling, and for no discernible reason. The coats were only for show.

Hummingbird skins generated a brilliant beauty in the sunshine. Rene Bache gushed, "A woman clad in such a garment is an animated rainbow; she literally scintillates."[7] So did the hummingbirds when they were alive. But human vanity made sure they didn't. Plus, the coats fairly screamed, "I'm rich!" That was the essence of the story Bache told set in Paris of a real-life Cinderella and a fashionable slipper maker who was always seeking new ways to shock the fashion world. She was pointing out the ludicrous heights the fashion world was reaching and what it was costing wildlife.

The slipper maker fashioned a tiny pair of slippers made from the breasts of hummingbirds. He had no plans to sell them, especially since they were so small no human could wear them. He made them simply as an item of curiosity. But an American millionaire from Louisiana seeking a new way to squander his money to please his brand-new trophy wife changed the creator's plans.

The slippers were soft, glistening things, shading from emerald to gold, and from

23. Reading the Signs

ruby to emerald, as the light fell upon them from different angles. The millionaire's wife had to have them. So he asked the creator how much the slippers would cost.

"Twenty-five hundred dollars," the creator said. That was a pittance to the millionaire, but worth $68,000 in today's terms. The deal was done.

But the slippers were at least a size too small for any grown woman's foot. The wife was not the average grown woman. Legend had it that she had the smallest foot in the world, so the slippers fit her. And the moral of Bache's story fit the times.

Small feet, small birds—and smaller numbers of them. All the hummingbird hunters had to do was kill a few more birds and milliners could create more automobile coats, slippers, or any other product that consumers desired. But even the supply of hummingbirds was finite.

No matter how small hummingbirds were they couldn't hide forever. Not too many years before the turn of the 20th century hummingbirds were among the most numerous species. By 1913 they were threatened with extinction because the business of killing them had been conducted on an almost incredible scale for so short a time. There was one report of 8,000 ruby and topaz hummingbird skins being shipped from a Brazilian port in a single consignment. Another report stated that in just one week 350,000 hummingbird skins were sold at an auction in London!

South America was a major supplier of those skins for the millinery trade.[8] Many Brazilian residents employed their slaves in collecting and preparing them for European markets. Huge numbers of the skins were shipped annually from Rio de Janeiro, Bahia, and Pernambuco. Brazil had plenty of competition, though.

Ecuador was the center of the South American feather trade. That country had more than 100 species of hummingbirds to slaughter. Colombia, too, was a lucrative hunting ground for hummingbirds, which dealers bought in huge quantities at Santa Fe de Bogota and other central points for export.

By 1913 hunting them had been going on for so many years on such a large scale that they were becoming harder and harder to find. Hunters had taken hundreds of millions with blow-guns, nets, and other methods to supply the demands of the millinery trade. Consequently, many of the most exquisite species were nearing extinction.

As Bache warned, "Unless something is done to protect them, indeed, the time is likely to arrive before very long when there will no more hummingbirds anywhere or at all events, only a few, seeking refuge from remorseless man in the densest forests and on the most inaccessible mountain heights of tropical America."[9] Similar warnings had been appearing for years—and had been ignored for just as long.

The paucity of birds predated the anti–theater hat legislation wave by a quarter of a century. That is evidenced by a story that pointed to the low numbers and the cavalier attitude people had about shooting birds in Nashville, Tennessee, as early as 1871. A Boston fashion writer echoed the observation a few years later.[10]

The Boston writer suggested that the blackbird used in millinery was dispensable—and it really wasn't a blackbird as a rule.[11] Rather, it "is any and every kind of fowl, sable died, and there is no use worrying about his silenced wood notes wild, for it is more than likely that he never had any worth mentioning." The scribe added that the millinery fad presented an opportunity for people to get rid of birds they didn't like.

"Here is a use for the English sparrow and if the work of depopulating the Brazilian forest has been so easy why not clear the common and the parks of a few hundred thousand sparrows?" he asked facetiously. But the underlying message was that killing certain species of birds was acceptable as long as they were disliked by the public. That same message came through in Nashville.

The reporter noted that local hunters were complaining about a scarcity of birds that was common in the fall, at least near the city. He attributed the shortage to the frequency and extent of bird hunting expeditions within short distances from town.

The writer presented a paradox that demonstrated the nonchalant attitudes people had about shooting birds in a belief that they would be present forever. He said that one of the best shots and most successful and experienced bird hunters in Tennessee had traveled the country 16 miles outside Nashville within the past few days. He saw only seven birds worth shooting at—so he shot them. His reason was that he wanted to show that he had not overlooked his hand.

When he cannot find and kill birds, the writer declared, it is hardly worthwhile for anybody else to try. Then he asked, "Who can suggest some remedy which will give the birds a chance to recuperate and again become plentiful?" The answer to that question was simple: stop shooting birds for little or no reason. That certainly occurred to the numerous groups of bird protection organizations that started springing up around the United States—and the world in general—only a few years later.

A South Carolina hunter proficient in shooting wild turkeys sounded a warning in 1892 that the wild turkey was in danger of disappearing.[12] He suggested that overhunting was one of the reasons, not only for the food but also for the feathers. "The turkey is the noblest of game birds," he declared. "His magnificent size, beautiful plumage and exquisite flavor as a table delicacy render him an object sought after with the greatest eagerness by every class, from the school-boy to the epicure, who never sees him except on the table."

He noted that the peculiar luster of the bird's feathers makes them preferable to those of the domestic bird for millinery purposes. But, he cautioned, turkeys were quickly becoming scarce in the wild. "As each year passes their traces are less and less apparent, and it is only a matter of time until they will have become a portion of tradition east of the Mississippi." That was simply another warning to be ignored. Fortunately, some people were paying attention as the signs became too obvious to ignore.

A report surfaced in 1886 that 40,000 terns had been killed in one season by a single agent of the hat trade at Cape Cod.[13] Coincidentally, that was the year that the Audubon Society was formed with a goal of ending such slaughter. Its members could not then envision a longtime need for their existence. If they had possessed a crystal ball they would have thought otherwise. The society needed help as the struggle continued. It came from the U.S. Supreme Court just when the Audubonists needed it most.

24

Silz Courts the Supremes

> "If the milliner is to be prevented from selling aigrettes, why is the furrier not interfered with for selling Persian lamb coats or the merchant for dealing in calfskin boots? There is no more cruelty associated with the aigrette than with the Persian lamb coat. Yet a woman who would not wear an aigrette will wear Persian lamb without a qualm."
> —Charles W. Farmer[1]

The U.S. Supreme Court provided the Audubonists with a significant victory in their battle against the milliner trade with its November 2, 1908, Silz decision. The verdict gave them added impetus in their cause but led to a common mistake among crusaders. They almost went too far with their tactics.

August Silz, a New York State poultry dealer known across the United States, had been a thorn in the Audubonists' side for years. He and his cronies were seeking a way to circumvent state laws against the importation of game birds during closed seasons with an eye toward selling them to restaurants and providing the feathers to milliners.

Silz and his associates argued that the state had no jurisdiction over when the birds were imported or where they came from. After setbacks in the New York State judicial system they tried a legislative end run in 1906 that raised the ire of bird protectors across the state and put milliners on the defensive once again. There was a lot riding on the outcome of the attempt and the ensuing legal action for both sides.

The legal merry-go-round began in June 1905 when John Hill, the owner of the Clarendon Hotel in New York City, was arrested and charged with having in his possession game birds out of season, which was a violation of New York State law. He admitted to having the game in his possession but claimed that was not illegal because it was imported. The court ruled that made no difference.

The "out of season" part was important. If possessing imported game birds out of season was illegal, diners in all the restaurants in the city would have one less item to order. Just for good measure, Judge Thomas Maddox of the Brooklyn supreme court ordered the arrest of August Silz, the importer who had sold Hill 48 birds, which he had imported from Russia, Scotland, England and Egypt. He, too, was charged with violating the law.

Hill and Silz filed a writ of habeas corpus, requiring a person under arrest to be brought before a judge or into court, especially to secure the person's release unless lawful grounds are shown for their detention. Maddox squashed the writ and held them in court for what amounted to a test case. Maddox found them guilty. Hill and Maddox filed an appeal and the saga continued.

The next court venue was the state supreme court, Part II. There, Justice Samuel

133

Greenbaum decided in favor of the state when he ruled that having in possession game from abroad in the closed season is unlawful.[2] Again, the defendants argued that all the birds in question were of foreign origin and were not identical to American species. Therefore, Silz's counsel contended that the law did not take cognizance of such species but was intended to apply only to native game. That argument still begged the question: identical or not, were they subject to New York State laws on importing game birds out of season?

The judge left that question of fact with the jury, which found that they were entirely different. That issue would arise again when Silz and his confederates tried to sneak a law through the state legislature. Greenbaum took under advisement the true legal consideration involved. He ruled that, according to the way the law was written, it plainly forbid the possession of foreign game in the closed season for domestic birds.

Silz's attorneys were puzzled by Greenbaum's interpretation of the statute. They maintained that the opinion of the bar was practically unanimous that the game laws were framed to protect the birds of the State of New York and the United States and did not apply to the birds that were lawfully taken in Europe and elsewhere abroad. That was not accurate, a journalist explained:

> As a matter of fact, there is no such unanimous opinion of the bar; there are well-known lawyers of New York City who have for years been contending strenuously for the principle that the law forbidding the possession of game in closed time to all game without reference to its origin; and until recent years the statute was so worded as to leave no ground for uncertainty that view prevailed. There can be no question as to the intent of the framers of the law.[3]

Once again the Silz/Hill team declined to accept a judicial decision. They filed an appeal with the state court's appellate division and vowed to go as high as the U.S. Supreme Court if necessary to get the final decision they hoped for. They almost got their wish.

The five-member appellate court ruled in their favor. It handed down a 3–2 verdict declaring that possessing game birds out of season, lawfully imported from a foreign country where they were killed legally, was not a crime. Moreover, they said, the section of the forest, fish and game law making it one was unconstitutional and void. The victory was short lived. This time their opponents appealed. Six months after their victory Silz and Hill were back in court. This time the court of appeals decided that the legislature had the power to prohibit the possession or sale of game birds in New York during the local closed season.

Chief Judge Cullen, in the opinion of the court of appeals, discussed the constitutionality of the law as it applied to the case. He averred that the New York courts had decided the state had the right to enact legislation to keep out game birds from other jurisdictions, domestic or foreign, during the closed season. Cullen also declared that the provisions of the Lacey Act backed up his conclusion. The state-federal partnership was taking root.

Cullen, who was not happy that the case had even reached his level, wrote:

> To the argument that the exclusion of foreign game in no way tends to the preservation of domestic game, it is sufficient to say that substantially the uniform belief of legislators and people is to the contrary, on the ground that without such inhibition or restriction, any law for the protection of domestic game could be successfully evaded.

Every consideration that led Congress to think it wise to confer on New York State, as well

24. Silz Courts the Supremes

135

as other States, a power over the importation of partridges from New Jersey, Pennsylvania, or Connecticut, is equally applicable to the importation of such birds from Canada.[4]

He expressed his displeasure in another statement:

Concerning the Silz case the opinion makes this comment. The affidavit on which the warrant in this case was issued creates a strong suspicion that the prosecution was instituted by collusion. It states not only that the defendant had in his possession the prohibited game, but also almost every fact by which the defendant's counsel hoped to relieve his client from the penalties of the law: facts which it is difficult, if not impossible, to see how they could have been within the affiant's knowledge. For that reason we should be inclined to refuse to entertain the cause had not the Attorney General intervened and prosecuted the appeal.[5]

That ended Silz and Hill's quest for a judicial remedy in New York State to establish the legal importation of game birds out of season. Silz then tried to inveigle the New York State Legislature into passing a new bill that would accomplish his goal. That failed miserably too.

William Hornaday recognized what the "Silzites" were doing with their proposed legislation and initiated a newspaper campaign to derail their plan. He warned: "The New York Poultry and Game Trade Association has caused to be introduced at Albany a most dangerous and reprehensible bill. The measure provides that certain birds may be imported from abroad and sold all the year round."

Hornaday realized that Silz's only legal hope should his legislative endeavor fail was the U.S. Supreme Court. Hornaday was sure Silz and his associates were loath to take their case there. He underestimated them. Nothing ventured, nothing gained, as far as the Silz gang was concerned. They gave their legislative plan a serious shot before they made that bold step.

"The Silz crowd are endeavoring partly by false representation in the public press, to sneak a bill through the Legislature at Albany which is intended to throw wide open the business of selling and serving game out of season throughout the State of New York," Hornaday wrote. The petitioners were not forthcoming when they listed their supporters.

The bill, which ultimately failed, allegedly had been introduced according to Silz et al. as the result of a conference and agreement between the New York Poultry and Game Trade Association, the attorney general, the State Fish and Game Commission, and the Audubon and Sportsmen's societies. It was a surprise to the latter two groups which, Hornaday announced, would refute the claim. He concentrated on debunking the Silz plan.

Hornaday saw through the ruse. The birds the Silz crowd wanted to import had American equivalents which would be indistinguishable from those respective species when plucked and served. Shades of the trial emerged.

Hornaday wrote:

Anyone who knows even the rudiments of ornithology, or of the tricks that are possible in serving birds under false names, will know full well that if the game dealers' bill becomes a law the door is wide open for the slaughter and sale of American birds out of season. The people of New York have spent thousands of dollars in trying to protect their birds from the onslaughts of Silz and his crowd.[6]

Hornaday did not want to see that money—or the birds—wasted.

The Audubonists had a valuable ally who the Silzites mistakenly claimed backed their quest: State Forest and Game Commissioner James S. Whipple. He based his

136 The Hat That Killed a Billion Birds

support on the decision of the court of appeals in the case of the State against Silz. The legislative defeat the Silzites occurred prompted them to petition the U.S. Supreme Court for a resolution to their case. The Supreme Court accepted it. That meant there would be no immediate resolution to the status of millinery sales.

The legalities of the standoff did not affect consumers, who continued to purchase feathered millinery. The milliners happily accepted the delay. They decided that until the court ruled they would continue to sell imported plumage, including the great bone of contention, the "White Badge of Cruelty."

Charles W. Farmer said, "This is simply the semi-annual scare of the Audubon Society, and we shall advise our readers to pay no attention to it." He was banking on a ruling from Judge John Cunneen, former New York State attorney general, who said that he knew of no law prohibiting the sale of imported aigrettes in the state. Farmer agreed. He overlooked the fact that the Supreme Court carried a little more weight in the legal world than did a former state attorney general. Farmer stated with a bit of bravado:

> The Silz case changes nothing, for that is still pending. Of course, if the decision of the Supreme Court goes against us, we shall have to submit, but I don't think it will. I don't think I am any less humane than the members of the Audubon Society. I am a church member and I live in the country and I love birds. But at the same time I don't believe in letting sentiment interfere with business. There is such a thing as carrying things too far.[7]

Farmer's words were encouraging to milliners. One large wholesale dealer in plumage said that even if the Supreme Court sustained the New York State court of appeals in the matter of the Silz case it would make no difference. "The point at issue there," he said, "is the right to sell imported game birds in the closed season of the state, and I don't see how the decision can be made to cover the case of the egret. Meantime we intend to go right on selling aigrettes."

The Audubon Society was equally sure that it would prevail at the U.S. Supreme Court. William Dutcher said, "We will make hot work for any milliner who attempts to sell aigrettes. The society is not made up of hysterical faddists. A large proportion of the members are hard-headed, conservative businessmen. We know what we are doing."

Dutcher got at the heart of the Audubon societies' long-term strategy and hope:

> We have waited until we had good legal ground to stand on, and now we intend to go ahead. We have not been able to touch the aigrette before, although we have prevented the use of other objectionable plumage, because it was impossible to tell in any given case whether the plumes were domestic or imported. But now this difficulty is removed, under the law, as interpreted by the Court of Appeals, which makes no discrimination between domestic and imported goods.[8]

Members of both parties eagerly anticipated the Supreme Court's decision. Finally, on November 2, 1909, the court ruled in the Audubonists' favor. The decision meant that successful evasion of the game law was no longer possible. The court ruled, in effect, that states may evolve their own game laws to meet their peculiar needs. That was a victory for the Audubonists and a blow for the milliners. The question was whether it would change anything.

Audubon groups in Oregon and California did not waste any time using the Supreme Court decision as a threat to milliners. California had just passed an amended law for the protection of birds and the state's Audubon president, David Starr Jordan, wanted to make sure milliners knew about its contents and the penalties attached.[9] Both

24. Silz Courts the Supremes

he and his counterpart in Oregon, William L. Finley, cited the Silz decision as the ultimate word as to whether or not the states had the right to regulate the possession and sale of feathers, plumage and other "birdstuff." Despite that, the court's decision did not put an end to murderous millinery.

U.S. Supreme Court decisions are not always absolute. This one was no different.

25

Welcome to Finley's World

"That the law empowers the [Audubon] Society or other interested persons to arrest women on the streets for wearing restricted feathers is not doubted by President Finley and his associates."[1]

The Oregon Audubon Society went on the offensive two months after the Supreme Court rendered the Silz decision, which became a catalyst for its president. Finley was an arch-typical representative of the ardent bird protectors whose zeal sometimes got the better of them. But they got the job done when it came to enforcing the laws against the sales and possession of forbidden feathers and bird parts, even to the point of threatening to rip feathered hats off women's heads.

Getting the job done was what mattered to Finley and his counterparts across the nation as they strove to resolve a national crisis by acting locally. Finley made that clear at the society's January 9, 1909, meeting in Portland, where he suggested that the Silz verdict was of absolute and imperative importance to Oregon. He explained to the attendees that the state's milliners and dealers in plumage had been trying to evade liability under an Oregon law passed in 1903 by contending that the plumes they dealt in came from other states or Europe. That had to stop. He acted immediately to make sure it would.

Finley declared that the Silz case outcome had closed every loophole in Oregon's law and made it entirely effective. He read the rough draft of a letter he was sending to every milliner and dealer in aigrettes and other plumage or skins or feathers of birds in the state.[2] In it he apprised them of the Silz decision, included an excerpt of the pertinent state law, and warned them to desist from any further sale or disposal of any such skins, plumage, aigrettes, etc., as prohibited by it. He promised immediate prosecution for a failure to abide by the Supreme Court's decision.

If Finley expected the milliners to accept his threat quietly, he was mistaken. The milliners had ignored the six-year-old law. They had not paid any penalties for engaging in what they considered a lucrative part of their business. There was no reason to assume they would take his letter seriously. The milliners did not know the tenacious William L. Finley.

Finley fired the opening shots in his campaign against the milliners even before he mailed his letter on January 15. That caused a lot of consternation throughout Oregon. The day after the January 9 meeting he effected the arrest of A. Reiner, a Portland furrier and hat seller. Reiner had placed an aigrette worth about $35 in his show window. Finley saw it, sought the help of deputy constable W.E. Kiernan, and ran Reiner in before Justice Olson, who was the first in a long line of Portland judges who would try local milliners for their indiscretions.

"I do not sell them; I make a sale, I drop them in," Reiner protested ingenuously.[3]

138

25. Welcome to Finley's World

Then he said that he had borrowed the aigrette from neighboring shopkeepers. Neither argument saved him from being arrested. Finley was not a forgiving man when it came to protecting the birds.

Finley stressed that the arrest was in line with his announced crusade undertaken against violators of the law forbidding the sale of bird plumage. "We do not intend to let up our watchfulness for violators of the law for a moment," he allowed. Many more milliners would find out firsthand how serious he was in his goal to end the market for aigrettes and other plumage in the northwest.

The next events took place in February, when Finley obtained warrants on behalf of the society for the arrest of representatives of the Baldwin Jewelry Company and milliners Bagnall & Boughton, Ethel and Caroline, respectively.[4] Finley charged that the Baldwin Company, specifically manager Charles Isaac, offered for sale two very valuable sets of plumage. He accused Bagnall & Boughton of offering for sale a hat trimmed with the forbidden aigrette.

That practice had been banned by Oregon's legislature the previous year, when it had passed a law prohibiting the killing of plumage birds in the state and making it an offense for merchants to offer the feathers for sale. The outcomes of the cases were not quite what Finley hoped for. At least he got a lesson about the vagaries of the law.

Bagnall appeared in Judge Conlan's department of the police court on February 16 to answer charges of having aigrettes in her possession and offering them for sale in violation of the state law. The session consisted chiefly in establishing the fact that Bagnall had aigrettes in her possession and for sale. Two hats were offered as evidence. The price of one was $95; the other had been marked $50. Finley had secured the evidence against the milliner by negotiating for the purchase of the hats.

To Finley's chagrin Conlan dropped the charges on a technicality. The assistant bond and warrant clerk mistakenly filled out the date on which the alleged offense was committed as February 14, 1909. It was a happy Valentine's Day for Bagnall—but her reprieve was short lived.

Finley did not let a legal technicality like a defective complaint stand in the way of justice. He swore out another complaint before Judge Deasy, who issued a new warrant that was served immediately to Miss Bagnall.[5] She was released on bail. Finley did not have the same luck in the Baldwin case.

The judge dropped the charge against Baldwin completely.[6] He ruled that the aigrettes in the tiara which had been on exhibition in the window of the Baldwin store were there solely to attract people's attention and were not for sale. The decision sidestepped the law, which stated explicitly that having aigrette's in one's possession was a violation. It was another lesson learned for Finley: he might lose a battle or two along the way, but his goal was to win the war.

"The purpose of the arrests is to break up the market," he explained. "Some time ago I made a report to the Audubon Society in Washington on the almost total disappearance of the heron from their former haunts around Klamath Lake. [President Theodore Roosevelt] created a bird reservation embracing Klamath Lake for the protection of herons and other birds which were being slain for their skins."[7]

Those were the types of victories Finley cherished. One lost court case would not sway him from his mission. There were more cases to win in the near future. They would be the ones that persuaded local dealers in the fur trade that fighting Finley and the law was a losing cause.

140   The Hat That Killed a Billion Birds

Finley left town for a short while. He returned on April 6 and found a pile of messages awaiting him from friends and members of the society. They reported that several stores were offering for sale aigrettes and other plumage that was banned. Finley immediately visited the district attorney's office. Deputy district attorney Fitzgerald granted him the authority to employ constable Wagner and deputy constable Kiernan to arrest the violators and signed the necessary legal papers. Finley gathered the rest of his gang and set off.

Armed with the necessary papers, Finley, his wife, Audubon secretary Bohlman, and the two constables rode by car with plans to visit nine stores on a whirlwind arrest tour. They hoped to reach all nine before word reached the last ones on the list that the posse was on the move. They started hurried visits to the stores on the list and caught some proprietors napping.

Finley's first targets were the Meier & Frank Company, Lipman, Wolfe & Company, and Allen & King. The posse arrested either the proprietors or employees at all three stores, using tactics that smacked of a sting.[8]

Mr. and Mrs. Finley posed as customers looking to buy aigrettes while the constables lurked in the background waiting for the right moment to pounce. Clerks seemed eager to produce the products and discuss prices. Once they were offered, Wagner and Kiernan made the arrests. In all fairness, Finley provided each store with a receipt for goods seized.

There were a large number of elaborate creations, ranging in price from $10 to $60 each, and trimmed with aigrettes on display at Lipman, Wolfe & Company. Finley wanted to confiscate the entire stock containing illegal goods but refrained when the proprietors agreed to remove from the display all the millinery to which he objected. He settled for 13 aigrettes valued at $50 as evidence, which Wagner and Kiernan took into custody, along with Will Lipman.

Lipman was released on his own recognizance and instructed to appear at the justice court for a trial that afternoon. He had an excuse for his transgression. He proved that the greater part of the responsibility for the infraction of the bird laws was due to the millinery department employee who either disregarded orders or did not take the matter seriously. Neither did any of the milliners on the list that day, despite the warnings that Finley had provided over the past three months.

The next stop was the Meier & Frank Company. They found aigrettes and other plumage on sale and arrested Ludwig Hirsch, who was in charge of this department. They seized one hat valued at $50 as evidence. Julius L. Meier ordered employees to remove the remainder of prohibited articles from view and told Finley that the sale would stop. So assured, Finley and the posse sped off to the next location, Allen & King's, where they added the proprietor, Mrs. Behm, to their list of arrested offenders.

Mrs. Behm resented being questioned when the Finleys asked about a hat on display in the store. She offered to sell it to them for $25. Mrs. Behm assured them that it was a good price and that she knew her business. He replied that he knew the law and that he would cause her arrest. She was astonished but agreed to appear in court. Three stores down, six to go.

There was one common thread among the employees and proprietors at each of the stores Finley and his group visited. They maintained initially that the aigrettes on display were not real; they were manufactured. When given evidence to the contrary, they realized that their attempts to deceive Finley would become public knowledge and

25. Welcome to Finley's World

affect adversely their business images, since customers might begin wondering whether they were paying for real aigrettes or imitations. They quickly dropped their claims that the aigrettes were manufactured and prepared to accept the consequences as the posse moved on.

Finley was afraid that if he didn't keep moving the other store owners on his list would be forewarned of his arrival and remove any incriminating evidence. The posse's movements had already attracted attention to something unusual going on in the district, and he could not afford any delays lest folks called ahead to his next targets. His worst fears were realized when he burst into Le Palais Royale, where the proprietor, Mrs. Becker, put up a fight.[9]

When the posse tried to seize some evidence, Mrs. Becker snapped, "I cannot let those feathers go. Show your authority. I don't believe you are officers. Anyway, I'll have to see my lawyer. No. I will not wrap them for you."

She instructed her employees to shut the door and lock it so "these people cannot get out until my lawyer gets here." Those were fighting words for Constable Kiernan, who was holding several aigrettes and a large black hat trimmed with forbidden feathers seized forcibly as evidence.

"If you lock that door I'll kick it down," he said.

Mrs. Becker responded by grabbing the feathers in his possession and engaging in a struggle. She damaged several of them, destroying about $50 worth of evidence. Kiernan saved the hat and arrested Mrs. Becker. But she was allowed to remain in the store until her court appearance.

Mrs. Becker's defiance provided a delaying action for some of her competitors. The posse visited two more stores and effected arrests, but that ended their profitable visits. They reached three more stores, but there was no evidence of any forbidden feathers in any of them.

Mrs. Becker had done some good even if she couldn't help herself. Nevertheless, it was a good day for Finley. He and his group had made nine arrests and confiscated copious amounts of evidence. The violators were facing heavy fines and, more important, the realization that the murderous millinery game was over for them. That was really Finley's crowning achievement.

Both Meier & Frank and Lipman, Wolfe & Company had been cited previously for trading in banned feathers. Interested parties believed they would incur heavy fines when arraigned in justice court. Deputy district attorney Fitzgerald had said he was in thorough sympathy with the action of the Audubon Society and would do everything in his power as prosecuting officer to help it. They took him at his word, for which they were disappointed.

The level of fines assessed was low in retrospect. There was a sliding scale established by Justice Olson in the justice court that guided the amounts levied. For selling forbidden feathers to women who had a penchant for wearing flocks of birds on their head the first offense cost $10 and the second three times that amount, or $30. For continued offenses a progressive rate of fines was assessed, the preceding fine being multiplied by three until the limit allowed by law was reached.

The anticipated heavy fines assessed on Meier & Frank and Lipman, Wolfe & Company were $30 each. Mrs. Becker, the only milliner who put up a fight, had to pay $10—the same as the miscreants who did not.[10] But the amounts were irrelevant. What mattered to Finley was that every dealer in the city had agreed to stop selling white

142   The Hat That Killed a Billion Birds

heron feathers altogether and would no longer try to defeat the law. That was a good business decision, and it meant that they would not have to pay any fines in the future. That did not placate Finley entirely, though. There was still the matter of Allen & King to deal with.[11]

Allen & King was the only firm to plead not guilty in court and escape punishment, contending that the hat seized by the officers belonged to a patron who had left it for alteration. Therefore, the company maintained, it was not responsible for the heron feathers. The officers of the Audubon Society did not believe the story, but they accepted it begrudgingly. They had won the battle—and the war was over in Portland.

There was more good news released after the raids. The city's milliners decided they were beaten and would make no further efforts to get around the law. Evidence supported that report. A salesman for an important eastern wholesale importing millinery house who had just arrived in Portland received word from different customers that they were obliged to cancel their orders.[12] He said he would lose fully $6,000 worth of orders for fall shipment.

Meier & Frank and Lipman, Wolfe & Company each canceled $1,000 orders. The wholesale firm of Lowengart & Company, which had been caught in Finley's web, rescinded orders for all its fall stock containing any of the prohibited birdstuffs. Many small dealers throughout the city followed suit. It had been a good day's work for Finley.

"This news was welcomed by us," Finley said in reference to the canceled orders. "We are in this fight in earnest and we propose to stop the sale of birdstuffs for feminine adornment in this state. We intend to see that the law is enforced. The things we seized will be confiscated and placed among the other exhibits in the City Hall."

Finley's actions did not go unnoticed outside Oregon. Editors elsewhere reported on it and urged their state authorities to emulate them. That was true in Montana:

> Over in Oregon there is a law making it a high misdemeanor to kill insectivorous birds either for food or for their plumage. Recently in Portland, officers acting under the direction of the state's attorney made a raid upon a number of millinery establishments where birds, plumes, and feathers, used to adorn hats, were seized to be used as evidence against the offending purveyors of woman's headgear.
>
> Oregon has done a great many things in the way of legislation worthy of emulation, but in this one particular it has set a most admirable example, and it is to be hoped that in Montana, and in every other commonwealth of the nation, the Oregon idea will find favor with the lawmakers, and the wanton slaughter of song birds shall be brought to an end.[13]

That was a wish expressed by a lot of people worldwide, and the idea was catching on, albeit slowly. Even if the slaughter did end, milliners such as Ethel Bagnall Rice could stay in business.[14]

She announced in June 1910 that she had purchased the interest of Caroline Bouton by mutual consent and carried on the business in Portland with its original name. She was liable for the firm as of June 1 that year—without white heron feathers in stock. But she was no Max Schlemmer, the poster boy for bird slaughter.

26

Meet Max Schlemmer

> "SCHLEMMER, Max. Formerly King of Laysan Island; dethroned by Frear, 1908; guano expert, with a few feathers on the side, using feathers for souvenir purposes only; claims jurisdiction of a few westward isles; Laysan Island consul to Japan for brief period."[1]

On February 3, 1909, President Theodore Roosevelt authorized the creation of a bird reservation comprising the small islands west of Honolulu that stretched for almost 1,000 miles. The federal government took seriously its responsibility for protecting the birds on the reservation and dispatched the U.S. Coast Guard revenue cutter *Thetis*, under the command of Captain W.V.E. Jacobs, to tour the islands in search of poachers.[2] The operation paid off, even though it created an international incident.

The fact that the U.S. Navy chose not to conduct the operation was significant. It wanted to save its vessels for war-related purposes. Thus, the Treasury Department, which was in charge of the Coast Guard, stepped in and assigned *Thetis* to the anti-smuggling and bird poaching mission. Captain Jacobs was the right man for the job.

Jacobs was thorough in his search. *Thetis* visited every island formation along the chain, from large rocks to reefs on which no land showed above water. That was difficult, in view of the thousands of miles the ship had to cover. Jacobs struck pay dirt on two of the larger islands, Laysan, the second largest single landmass in the northwestern Hawaiian Islands, and Lisianski, where he found and arrested a total of 23 Japanese poachers and seized tons of feathers and plumage. He returned most of the seized goods to Honolulu as evidence, which raised suspicion of international involvement in the Laysan feather trade.

The feathers and wings were packed in gunnysacks. Each bale was marked with Japanese characters, some of which allegedly spelled the name of a Paris importer of feathers. Once Jacobs invoked the name of a local businessman, Maximilian Joseph August Schlemmer, a German immigrant known better as just plain Max or "King Max" or "Captain Max," interest in the case heightened and the subsequent legal wrangling became a circus. But it did not seem as if anyone had any real interest in convicting the perpetrators of crimes, especially bird poaching.

U.S. officials kicked it off by empaneling a federal grand jury to ascertain whether anyone had broken American and/or international laws. The fact that there were 23 Japanese citizens involved in the case muddied the waters. No one, including them, was sure whether they worked for a Japanese or an American company—and nobody really cared.

The U.S. authorities were more interested in prosecuting Schlemmer and uncovering the identities of the unnamed—and unknown—"higher-ups" in a suspected bird

144 The Hat That Killed a Billion Birds

poaching ring than they were in prosecuting the laborers. Questions abounded, and the case became a test of just how serious the U.S. government was about protecting birds and prosecuting poachers. As it turned out, it had not been serious at all until President Roosevelt declared a bird reserve.

It had been evident to people in Honolulu in 1909 that some local Japanese were planning to gain control of Laysan and some of the other westward islands to conduct massive bird slaughter operations. U.S. officials were lukewarm on the idea of stopping them, until they realized it wasn't just a group of local Honolulans who were in on the plans. Some companies in Japan—and even the Japanese government—were involved as well. That put the U.S. government in an awkward position. The United States had annexed Hawaii. The Hawaiians expected their new government to protect their interests. That accounted for why President Roosevelt created the bird reservation. In doing so he disappointed a lot of Japanese leaders in Honolulu.

Bird protectionists in the United States and other countries were thrilled by the president's bold initiative. They believed the end of the bird slaughter was in sight. The Japanese were far from euphoric. They viewed Roosevelt's declaration as an obstacle to their plans of carrying out plumage poaching operations. They were particularly disappointed because they had planned to secure control of Laysan as a starting point for their Japanese countrymen, and many of them believed Schlemmer was prepared to help.

No one in Hawaii outside the suspected Japanese cabal had any definite information about the ploy. But there were many among them who were convinced that the ruthless slaughter of birds on the westward islands resulted in profits to some Honolulu people and the Japanese bird-hunters from Nippon. That was why Schlemmer imported 23 Japanese laborers to his Laysan and Lisianski fiefdoms. Some folks determined to find out if that was the case.

A Honolulu sea captain disseminated information about an understanding formulated in Japan between certain Honolulans and the bird hunters. Numerous stories circulated in the city about mysterious ventures of local Japanese and other people. Inquiring citizens in Honolulu sent letters to officials in Washington to find out if the story about the understanding was accurate or whether the rumors about strange doings were true. They didn't receive any definitive answers. But they learned that officials in Washington were going to address the Laysan matter.

Then, another startling piece of information surfaced. There had been a strike by Japanese sugar plantation laborers on Laysan during which many of them were arrested. During the strike an interesting document was discovered. It was a copy of a letter written by a Honolulu-based Japanese individual and addressed to a company of feather hunters of Japan. The writer assured his far-away countrymen that he would have no difficulty—for a consideration—in securing for them the use of Laysan Island for the ostensible purpose of handling guano. The real object was bird killing.

The offer did not seem relevant to the Schlemmer case, so it was not made public. Besides, there was a great deal of correspondence exchanged between the Japanese in Honolulu and Japan on the subject. And it wasn't restricted to the Japanese. There were other local business people interested in getting involved in the guano and bird slaughter business.

By 1909 interest in the business had grown to a point that alarmed the local officials. Honolulu and stateside newspapers began giving it a lot of coverage. That was when they suggested it was time for the United States to assign at least one naval vessel to patrol the islands to show the flag and warn prospective poachers to stay away from them if all they wanted to do was kill birds. Schlemmer, ready to stir dissension, added fuel to the fire.

He visited Japan, ostensibly to talk about the guano trade with government and business luminaries. Some of his associates in Japan reported to their contemporaries in Honolulu that companies there were trying to arrange island privileges with "King Max." Their goal was clear: they were trying to do an end run around the U.S. government and bargain with Schlemmer, who did not have the authority to make any deals regarding the islands. The discussions became so publicized in Honolulu social and business circles that the U.S. government was goaded into acting.

Rumors abounded about mysterious sampan fleets visiting the westward islands for some unknown reason. Locals recognized that they were visiting the islands for some nefarious purpose, such as transporting loads of filched feathers back to Japan. They appealed to the navy to step in. After all, those islands were now a part of the United States—and the feathers were too.

There was a U.S. Navy tug available at Honolulu, the *Iroquois*.[3] Unfortunately it was laid up because of boiler problems. The next likely candidate to play the role of revenue cutter was the lighthouse tender *Kukui*, pending the arrival of the Coast Guard's *Thetis*.

An order was received from Washington on November 12, 1909, for *Kukui* to sail to Laysan and the other western islands to stop any poachers from killing birds. That same day there arrived another order that canceled Schlemmer's lease for Laysan because the territory did not have the authority to grant it. The cancellation did not surprise many people.[4]

Many locals had never understood how he obtained a lease to begin with or grasp the fact that he in effect had a monopoly on such deals. Some old-time seafarers along the waterfront who had spent a lot of time at sea and knew conditions fairly well puzzled especially over how Schlemmer used the island with little or no accountability, even though many people suspected that there was evil afoot on his business grounds.

"Not a vessel has come from the Orient, nor a schooner from the westward islands, but has brought her share of stories, true or otherwise, in regard to the slaughter of birds, with always the question as to why did not the United States take a hand," one reporter wrote. He simply put into words what a lot of people were thinking.

"It is known that the Japanese fishermen and bird hunters feel that westward islands are theirs to do with as they please, irrespective of what he claims and, in addition, they are cocky enough to believe that the United States will not worry over these island specks," he concluded.

The order for *Kukui* to sail to the islands changed some people's perceptions of the U.S. government's commitment to stopping the poachers. It had taken a while, but the United States had finally acted and "a new order of things would most likely prevail to the end that birds will not much longer he slaughtered," the reporter speculated.[5]

That new order also meant that Laysan was no longer a part of the city and county of Oahu or of the Territory of Hawaii. Henceforth it was under the direct jurisdiction of the United States. There was a tradeoff. The Territory of Hawaii could no longer lease any westward island for guano deposits or anything else. But poachers had to stay off American preserves from that point on. That "somebody" meant Japan, which had to be convinced the United States was serious about enforcing anti-poaching laws. That was not going to be easy to do. But it was worth a try.

The Hat That Killed a Billion Birds

Shortly after *Kukui* began its patrol, *Thetis*, which was better equipped to deter poaching, arrived to relieve it. That instilled optimism in the Hawaiian locals. A reporter speculated, "It is likely that her presence in the waters to the west will have a wholesome effect."[6] It didn't, at least not immediately. *Thetis*'s presence, however, established the prelude to a new era in the United States' attempts to stop the rampant bird poaching occurring in the westward Hawaiian Islands. But its intercession was a stop-gap measure at best.

The Japanese did not stop their poaching activities near Hawaii. Instead, they moved their operations a little bit west. That news came on a postcard sent to Max Schlemmer from D.B. Grieg on Fanning (Tabuaeran) Island, which was administered by the British.[7]

Grieg told Schlemmer that the British warship *Algerine* had put into the virtually uninhabited Christmas Island, located off the country of Australia, where the crew found 13 Japanese bird poachers setting up for a long stay. The British sailors asked the Japanese politely to vacate the island, which they did—with an eye toward relocating on Fanning Island. Then Schlemmer received a letter from Emmanuel Rouger, a Frenchman who owned Fanning. Rouger asked Schlemmer what he thought about letting the Japanese settle there.

Shortly thereafter *Algerine* visited Honolulu. No one aboard mentioned the incident at Fanning Island. The Honolulans inferred that the British did not want to cause an international incident, so they told the Japanese it would be wise to leave. Their advice saved some birds from sure death, but that was not the way the Audubonists wanted to get the job done.

Schlemmer commented after hearing the news that "this news proves what I have always maintained, that there are Japanese hunters and fishermen all over the sea islands. It shows that they have landed on Christmas Island, and to me it seems certain that there are now Japanese around Laysan and the other islands in the group, while the revenue cutter *Thetis* lies idle in the harbor here."[8]

True, *Thetis* was not chasing poachers anywhere near Laysan or the other westward islands. It was being used more for ferry purposes than anything else. On May 13, 1911, *Thetis* set sail from Honolulu to Hawaii with officers' wives aboard. One of its scheduled stops was the volcano at Kilauea, where there were probably very few bird poachers.

In June *Thetis* departed Honolulu for Alaska.[9] The Treasury Department did not announce any immediate plans to replace it, although there was a vague promise of a faster, more up-to-date cutter to arrive sometime in the future. *Thetis* returned on November 15, 1912. No one was sure why.[10]

There was some conjecture about what *Thetis*'s duties would be, even though there were bird poaching activities reported at Bird Island, a large, isolated rock 107 miles west of Honolulu. Mail packets passing by had reported the activity. It seemed like bird poaching enforcement in the reservation had dropped in importance from rigid to sporadic if any at all.

On January 7, 1913, *Thetis* arrived from Midway with the governor's party aboard, which did not sound like an enforcement mission.[11] The Japanese, apparently, were welcome to slaughter birds for profit. The U.S. government had decided to combat poaching on a new front in 1913: through tariff laws. By that time all vestiges of bird poaching as a factor in Schlemmer's 1911 trial had been forgotten.

27

Looking at the Moon Without Rose-Colored Glasses

"There is no logical reason why wild birds should be slaughtered mainly for use as fancy millinery, especially when these creatures are of economic importance not only in the United States but in every country in the world."

—T. Gilbert Pearson[1]

There was no doubt that Schlemmer could be tried by a U.S. court. But, if the Japanese laborers, aka poachers, had in fact broken U.S. laws, could they be liable for punishment under them? Or would they be turned over to their own country for action? That was not likely to produce any results, since the Japanese government covertly supported feather poaching. The Japanese government showed no inclination to deal with the problem no matter who employed the laborers or whose laws were involved.

Did the United States actually want to convict Schlemmer? He was a well-known entrepreneur in Hawaii whose name was mentioned in connection with many business ventures. As one visitor to Laysan Island wrote, "Manager Max Schlemmer has braved the terrors of the solitude for the last four years, and does not seem to be any the worse for the wear. He is a typical island Governor, of whom we read, as he, in his 27 years of experience on the Hawaiian Islands, has turned his hand to almost every conceivable trade."[2]

That was reflected in a description of him as a "one-time monarch of all he surveyed on Laysan Isle, guano promoter, island acquirer, westward island promoter, and hero of many romantic ocean stories never published."[3] He had attempted to buy Laysan in 1907, albeit unsuccessfully.[4] Max Schlemmer was an enigmatic man.

He was often referred to as the "King of Laysan" because he managed a large guano collection operation on the island, which was home to millions of birds. His guano business was a front for bird poaching. Japanese companies had an interest in the operation, but for them it was more about collecting plumage and feathers than mining guano, which was hardly profitable. Anyone working on the islands was free to pursue either venture, since they were laxly regulated by U.S. authorities.

This was not the first time the words Schlemmer, Japanese, and feathers had been linked in a single report. Nine years earlier a ship named *Ceylon* arrived in Honolulu after a 22-day voyage from Laysan.[5] It had aboard Max Schlemmer, a load of guano, 13 Japanese who were alleged to be passengers, and miscellaneous cargo including the usual collection of Laysan warblers, eggs, and feathers. Nobody batted an eye at that news or connected the dots. The transportation of bird feathers was simply not a

The Hat That Killed a Billion Birds

problem in Hawaii, which was just emerging as a valuable geographical interest for the United States.

The United States' primary interest in Hawaii around the turn of the 20th century was its strategic location as a naval base. Of lesser importance were the many sugar plantations there owned primarily by Americans. The United States gave them generous terms to protect its interests in the world market and the isolated islands that were home to millions of birds that hunters targeted.

Government officials had realized Hawaii's geographical and military significance around the time of the Spanish-American War, when it needed a naval base between the mainland and Manila, where a good part of the Spanish fleet was based. So, in 1898, President William McKinley signed a joint resolution annexing the previously independent islands. Bird slaughter was rampant in the outer islands at the time, but the government did little to stop it until 1909. Then, Laysan took center stage.

The return on investment in guano mining was low at best and finding workers to do the job was difficult. For the most part the miners were Japanese laborers brought over from their native land. Their work history was dotted with violence. In August 1900, some of them rebelled against American management and refused to work. Their strike turned violent because of a language barrier. As a result, there were two deaths and two injuries.

Moreover, the guano output was low, despite the large number of birds available to produce it. Scientists who visited the islands after the annexation estimated that there were ten million seabirds on Laysan in 1903. By 1911 that number had dropped to a little more than a million, since the bird slaughter went relatively unchecked. Despite the number of birds, guano deposits mined did not produce a lot of product or profit.[6]

In the late 1800s the ships used to transport the guano from Laysan carried about 5,000 tons per trip. That amounted to one shipload every two months, which represented a lot of back-breaking work for little output. By 1904 the annual output from Laysan was 45,000 tons. Worse, guano mining adversely affected the island's ecosystem dramatically. The Pritchardia palms that were unique to Laysan and the island's sandalwood trees became extinct. Schlemmer did not help matters any.

Schlemmer arrived at Laysan in 1894 and made significant changes to its ecosystem in the interest of future business ventures. He released domestic rabbits, Belgian hares, English hares, and guinea pigs on the island. He expected them to multiply in large numbers and become the source of supplies for a future meat-canning business. That backfired.

The rabbits multiplied so rapidly they almost wiped out the vegetation. The Japanese laborers, looking for another source of income, continued to kill birds by the hundreds of thousands and export their plumage, feathers, and parts while Schlemmer looked the other way. Complaints about what was happening on the island reached the authorities in Honolulu, who terminated his lease and removed Schlemmer from Laysan. Too much damage had been done to the island by the time *Thetis* arrived.

The loss of vegetation had eliminated much of the island's plant cover. Consequently, the soil and sand became loose and blew about in devastating dust storms. By 1918, the rabbits had eaten so much that the remaining vegetation could only sustain 100 of them. Twenty-six plant species had been eradicated, and the Laysan Millerbird had become extinct. Two other endemic species, the Laysan duck and the Laysan finch, survived, but were listed as endangered. None of that was an issue as the 1910 grand jury began its deliberations. Curiously, the bird slaughter issue became a side show.

27. Looking at the Moon Without Rose-Colored Glasses

One of the first items on the jury's agenda was to establish who actually employed the arrested Japanese poachers.[7] The government maintained that it was Schlemmer, which was confirmed through the Japanese consulate in Honolulu by the Japanese company most people assumed employed them. The laborers had cabled the company in Japan to inquire about who their employer was. The company disavowed all knowledge of their status. The Japanese consul-general was not pleased that he was involved in the case, which the Japanese government thought was inconsequential. Schlemmer cleared everything up when he said he was responsible for them.

Another issue was what to do with the plumage *Thetis* had returned to Honolulu along with the prisoners. The government estimated the cargo's value at $112,000. Schlemmer said it wasn't worth more than $15,000. Regardless, since the goods had been seized on an American island, there was no need for condemnation proceedings. Marshal Hendry awaited instructions to sell the plumage at public auction. U.S. district attorney R.W. Breckons cabled authorities in Washington to determine what to do with it. Nobody there replied. The issue hung in the air, as did the matter of the charges under which Schlemmer and the laborers were to be tried.

Neither the grand jury nor the court wasted much time with the poachers. Schlemmer was the focus of their efforts. Federal judge Robertson sentenced the poachers to 24 hours in jail and costs remitted.[8] They had already served their time; they had been locked up since *Thetis* returned them to Hawaii. The judge explained that he let them off lightly because they were only "instruments" in the case. The sentence was tantamount to an acquittal in many people's eyes.

U.S. authorities ordered the poachers to stay in Honolulu to serve as witnesses against Schlemmer or any of the Japanese who might be prosecuted for alleged violations of the international law. They were ordered to be set free on bail of $250 each and given the freedom to roam the city.[9] Schlemmer was arraigned on charges of violation of U.S. immigration laws and released on $1,000 bail. Despite the bail order, the poachers remained incarcerated.

There was some question about how mere laborers were going to raise $250 each. The prosecution set bail that high for a reason. They hoped that affluent local Japanese would come to their rescue and pay it, which deepened the "higher-ups" theory. The prosecutors reasoned that if any local businessmen posted bail they might be among the mysterious "higher-ups" and be smoked out. There was no rush to the bondsman's office.

The poachers stayed in jail and were paid for the inconvenience. One local reporter commented, "But the Japanese don't care. They will get one dollar and a half a day for every day they are detained as witnesses, and they couldn't get one dollar and a half a day killing birds on Laysan and Lisianski, not to speak of not being able on those rocky islets to occupy such comfortable quarters as will be offered them by High Sheriff Henry."[10]

The government did not need 23 witnesses. In May 1910, U.S. commissioner Albert Judd ordered that 18 of them be deported; the other five should be detained as witnesses for Schlemmer's trial.[11] The grand jury turned its attention to Schlemmer, who offered some bizarre explanations for what happened on Laysan.

He and his attorneys introduced creative demurrers (assertions by the defendant that although the facts alleged by the plaintiff in the complaint may be true, they do not entitle the plaintiff to prevail in the lawsuit) that boggled the jurists' minds. In a blow to the prosecution, Judge Robertson upheld two demurrers on technical grounds.[12]

150   The Hat That Killed a Billion Birds

Robertson's rulings cast doubt on finding Schlemmer guilty of violating contract labor laws, poaching of the federal bird reservation, or any other charge the government could concoct. Up to that point in the proceedings, the government had lost every point in the case against Schlemmer. Worse, the indictments drawn by the district attorney all turned out to be faulty and the presentation of the cases to the court by assistant U.S. district attorney Rawlins was extremely weak. The prosecution was unable to present the facts in a way that would stand in court. The consensus in Honolulu was that Schlemmer would go free.

Schlemmer did not contest the fact that the arrested Japanese were acting under his direction and that they were engaged in taking out the guano deposits. They may have killed a few birds, he allowed. His "few" were actually numbered in the several hundreds of thousands, and all those birds were destroyed in just a couple years. But Schlemmer blamed everyone but himself and the Japanese poachers for that.

He accused Hawaii's governor, Walter Francis Frear, of being responsible for his difficulty.[13] Schlemmer alleged that the governor had kept him off Laysan until his lease was terminated. He claimed that if he had been allowed to go to the islands the present situation would not have arisen. The problem with that explanation, which Frear rejected, was that Schlemmer's connection with the bird-destroying operations had been well established. The truth was that the laborers were not on Laysan looking for guano. They were after the bird wings and feathers, which were much more profitable.

Governor Frear laughed at Schlemmer's charge. He explained that two years earlier Schlemmer wanted to renew his lease, which did not happen until the following year. That was just about the time that the governor learned that President Roosevelt had included Laysan Island in a bird reservation. He believed the formation of the reservation would invalidate Schlemmer's lease, which he told the "Captain."

Frear contacted the authorities in Washington for clarification. He did not get an answer. As he waited, Schlemmer asked the governor for permission to go to Laysan. The governor approved. But he made it clear to Schlemmer that if he went he would have to travel on his own responsibility. Frear surmised that Schlemmer's lease would be declared invalid, but he wanted to make sure. He contacted Washington again. This time he received a cablegram to the effect that Schlemmer's lease should be canceled.

"That's all I had to do with the matter," the governor said. "I didn't keep Schlemmer from going to Laysan, and I don't exactly see how I am responsible for the poaching."[14] That ended Schlemmer's attempt to blame Frear for his predicament.

Then Schlemmer and his attorneys argued that President Roosevelt illegally created the bird reservation.[15] He had no business or authority to set aside the islands to the west of Honolulu as a bird reservation, they argued. And he acted without his legal rights when he did, according to his attorney A.A. Wilder. He contended that only an act of Congress could create such a reservation, and it was lacking in this case. Judge Robertson took the claim under advisement.

Another of Schlemmer's ploys was to catch up on his rent.[16] He reasoned that since his lease had not been renewed he did not have to pay his rent. Ergo, since he had no claim to the islands anymore, he would have to vacate them. That was not in his plans. Shortly after the grand jury convened he tried to pay his rent anyway, as if he still had some claims over Laysan and Lisianski islands. He and Wilder visited the office of the territorial authorities and plunked down his payment of $12.50 in gold coin of the United States. The officials refused to accept it. That disappointed Schlemmer, who wanted to

27. Looking at the Moon Without Rose-Colored Glasses

maintain his legal hold on the two islands—and it foiled the scheme he and his attorneys had concocted.

Their thinking was simple: if Schlemmer was paying rent for the island he could not be accused of poaching on them, as he could do as he pleased since he was paying for the privilege. And he could not be prosecuted for the crime. The territorial authorities were one step ahead of him when they refused his money. That left Schlemmer in limbo, since he still did not know what the government planned to charge him with or what they planned to do about the Japanese poachers. Neither did the government officials, who were waiting for guidance from Washington that was slow in forthcoming.

The timeline in the case was telling. Schlemmer continued winning little steps after his indictment on March 22, 1910. On July 2, 1910, he was arraigned and charged with bringing aliens into the country, contrary to law. He pled not guilty. His trial was scheduled to begin in U.S. district court on July 29. That wasn't convenient for him. To accommodate Schlemmer the court continued his case until its October term on motion of counsel, with no objection being made, so he could travel to Laysan and return by the scheduled court date.[17] He appeared in court on the appointed date. The charges had no bearing on bird poaching.

They included importing Japanese into the territory and subleasing the island to the Japanese and giving them full permission to collect and dispose of all guano, etc. The "etc." was "birds." He was also charged with transferring his special constable privileges to the Japanese. As proof that he had done so, the prosecution introduced an agreement signed by Schlemmer and the Japanese, which was seized by Captain Jacobs of *Thetis* in January 1910. The agreement leased the island to the Japanese for 15 years at a rental of $150 a month.

George S. Curry, an inexperienced lawyer who had been admitted to the bar earlier that year, represented Schlemmer. Deputy district attorney Rawlins appeared for the prosecution.[18] Anyone betting on the outcome of the trial would not have cared about how much experience the defendant's lawyer had or if Schlemmer had been charged with something as specious as looking at the moon twice on a Monday without rose-colored sunglasses. The odds were that he would be acquitted. As expected, the jury, after a lengthy deliberation, delivered a verdict of not guilty.[19]

Schlemmer walked free. The issue of bird poaching was moot. The Audubonists had suffered a setback in their effort to protect the birds. The federal government had demonstrated that its commitment to eliminating bird poaching was not serious when its test case collapsed. But the setback was only temporary, although a lot of birds would die before they were awarded true protection. That was another three years off.

28

Delaware Thanks the Milliners

"Many of the birds of Delaware are protected by law, and railroads and other common carriers are liable to fines for transporting birds killed contrary to the laws of the state."[1]

The Schlemmer story attracted considerable nationwide attention to the need for laws to protect birds. Another, which occurred in Delaware a few years earlier, reflected negatively on the millinery trade and expanded interest in the Audubonists' activities. Bird protectors could only hope for more events of that type to generate free publicity.

The mantra of bird hunters around the turn of the 20th century seemed to be "We have to exterminate this bird [fill in the blank] species before it disappears altogether." Conservationists sought ways to stop that from happening. They concentrated on the legislative route, starting at the state level, in the belief that the passage of laws backed by strong public pressure would accomplish the task. It did not. The slaughter stopped because fashions changed and bird ornaments went out of style. Until then, fashion topped law.

Generally, where state laws to protect game birds were passed, the Audubon Society was mentioned as a catalyst. Newspaper editors were equally active in urging legislators to get involved in stopping the slaughter. One plea in particular stood out, as did the warning it included:

The problem therefore reduces itself to this form: Do the people of this country prefer to see women's hats adorned with dead birds, while the owners fight mosquitoes and the farmer and gardener fight insects, or do they prefer to see the hats decorated with ribbons and artificial flowers or ostrich plumes while the bird, in his natural state, ornaments the gardens and roadsides in the intervals of catching noxious insects?

Is the artistic object produced by shooting and stuffing a purple martin, and impaling him with a hat pin upside down, in the middle of a tangle of ribbons worth the trouble of fighting a million mosquitoes, more or less, in the course of the summer? If it is not it is about time that the legislatures of our several states looked into this matter and passed some laws against the destruction of insect-eating birds.

Otherwise, the copse where once the garden smiled is likely to be given to fragment of plants covered with bugs, and the porch entwined with honeysuckles, about which poets love to write, will be rendered uninhabitable to unprotected poet arms.[2]

Neither editors nor bird protection organizations were always successful in getting legislatures to take the need for bird protection laws seriously. Some states, such as Connecticut, didn't see it. Its legislature killed a bird protection bill in March 1899, which surprised, but did not discourage, the state's Audubon Society members.[3] True to their mission, they just pushed harder to educate Connecticut's representatives on the need for a bill.

28. Delaware Thanks the Milliners

Connecticut could have learned a lesson from Delaware, where conservationists were experiencing difficulty passing a specific bird protection law. They got around it by relying on an existing law against trespassing that suited their purpose, thanks to the ingenuity of president Witmer Stone of the American Ornithologist Union.[4]

Stone visited with Governor Ebe Tunnell to discuss the need for a bird protection law in Delaware. The governor vowed to enforce one if it were enacted. Tunnell promised that, until then, if he couldn't protect the birds through a specific law that prohibited killing them for plumage, he would apply an in-place trespassing act. Either way, he said, the birds were protected.

Tunnell and Stone had an advantage in enforcing a trespassing law as stand-in for an actual bird protection law. The state's farmers were solidly in favor of protecting birds from being killed for millinery purposes. "Such a sentiment against the killing of birds for adornment of bonnets has been stirred up among the farmers of the state that it will be practically impossible to hunt on the lands of southern Delaware," one reporter said.[5]

Just to make sure, Association for the Protection of Birds constables were located throughout the state to arrest immediately anyone violating the trespassing law. There was a rumor that a large millinery firm in New York had placed a significant order for 20,000 small birds to be killed in one county for its use in Easter bonnets. The saturation of constables made it very unlikely that the contract would be filled, even though the millinery trade tried to put the rumor to rest.

The *Millinery Trade Review* stated that there was no truth at all to the reports. No birds were wanted for Easter millinery trimming, it declared. In fact, there was no demand for birds. They were unsalable and of no value to the trade. "The dispatch is a canard of the worst type," the publication declared. "The name of the party given as having made the contract is unknown in the trade."[6]

Whether the story was true or not, the Audubon Society benefited from the publicity. The eponymously named Mrs. Edward Robins, secretary of the 6,000-member Pennsylvania Audubon Society, reported a gain of about 300 members from Delaware.[7] The increase was so large she believed it would lead to the formation of a separate Delaware society. Mrs. Robins was also happy to report that Miss Mary Gregg of western Pennsylvania had left her society a legacy of $1,000.[8] Neither the rumor nor the denial did much to help the milliners' image—especially after it came to light that the rumor was true.

The contract was public knowledge, although the details were incorrect. Newspapers across the country had published details about it. The terms called for the bodies of 12,000 birds, for which from 10 to 50 cents apiece was to be paid, and specified the species to be delivered. Details that specific made it difficult to believe that the story was just a rumor.

A.D. Poole, president of the Delaware Game Protective Association, chided the Milford *Chronicle* for writing that the story was a rumor and for not tracking down the facts.[9] Not only was the contract real, Poole said, but he named the two people who were responsible for it in a letter to a rival newspaper. Moreover, he said, they had admitted to witnesses having such a contract:

> I am entirely at a loss to understand the statement from the Milford *Chronicle* ... it being so entirely at variance with my own information.... I have been feeling around for information about the killing of birds, and find that one John Ward and John Bennett have agreed to furnish a large number for millinery purposes. The parties want crows, blackbirds and sea gulls.
> The people are up in arms and say they will prosecute any party they catch on their lands

for this purpose.... I can assure the public that this association will not be lulled into inactivity by it, but will redouble its efforts to prevent violations of the law, and would ask the hearty cooperation of the sportsmen and others to this end.[10]

Poole made it clear that laws alone were not sufficient to stop the bird slaughter. They had to be combined with strong public support and a willingness to see that laws were enforced.[11] That was shown time and time again as the efforts to protect birds accelerated, such as the action taken by the Pennsylvania Railroad Company to help in Delaware. The railroad issued instructions to its agents not to receive game birds for shipment. Such actions discouraged milliners' agents from carrying out their assignments and turned the public against them. In the long run, the Delaware situation was a turning point in the struggle to protect birds not only in the state but also nationally. An editorial in a state newspaper made that clear:

> The man who has been endeavoring to secure the skins of 20,000 black and other birds from Delaware, to be used as ornaments on ladies' hats, may prove to have been a greater friend of the birds than he intended. For years strong clubs and other organizations have existed having for their chief object the protection of song and insectivorous birds, and stringent laws with a similar purpose are on the statute books of many states.
>
> The organizations have done much towards awakening and strengthening popular sentiment against the use of birds or their wings in millinery work, but it is doubtful if all their efforts have aroused as much feeling as the man who contracted to have 20,000 feathered songsters killed in Delaware.
>
> The storm of righteous indignation which the announcement of the contract raised is unprecedented in its depth and extent, and it is undoubtedly increasing instead of diminishing. That there is a decided awakening to this fact and the desirability of taking this meritorious course is very evident, and, if it shall continue, as it should, the man who made a contract for the skins of 20,000 birds will not have wrought so badly, after all.[12]

There was truth in that editorial. The Audubonists needed all the help they could get to draw attention to their cause. Whether it came directly or inadvertently was unimportant. In the Delaware case it came because the milliners made a public relations faux pas. But the bird protectors benefited no matter what created the furor. They could only hope for more events of that type—and thank the milliners for shooting themselves in the foot.

29

The Law of Fashion Prevails

"Owing to the imperfections of human judgments our laws never attain to the perfection of positive law, therefore we must not hope for laws which will correctly adjust the rights of man. All legislation is imperfect for man is imperfect. This is the reason why so many laws are a dead letter."[1]

Witmer Stone's hands-on involvement typified how conservationists took matters into their own hands when necessary. They had to, since many states were slow to act to protect birds. That had been the case far too often, and it needed to change.

The first active steps toward game protection in this country were taken when the New York Association for the 1844 Protection of Game was formed. A group of notable sportsmen organized a society to advocate the passing and enforcement of appropriate game laws and promote a healthy public opinion in relation to game protection. The association laid important groundwork for future generations.

Game laws then were rare. Those that existed were lightly regarded. The founding members of the association discussed ways to stop the excess killing of wild birds—while shooting wild birds. The chief attractions at the annual conventions held by the association included shooting pigeons from a trap. Sometimes the birds used in these competitions were netted wild or passenger pigeons, a species that eventually became extinct because of overhunting.

In 1880 *Forest and Stream Magazine* condemned this practice.[2] That upset the hunters but the magazine stood adamantly by its opinion. As a result, the senseless shooting of released live pigeons as a test of skill ended. The magazine turned its attention to hunting seasons.

Until 1880 hunters shot woodcocks in the summer. The open season began on July 4, when the downy young were just able to fly. *Forest and Stream* attacked spring and summer shooting. Therefore, some states passed laws banning spring shooting. A few repealed them shortly after they were passed, which discouraged legislators in other states from enacting their own laws. Consequently, there were few permanent state laws extant forbidding spring and summer bird hunting for several years.

In 1884 and 1885 the growing use of native birds in millinery decoration, and their consequent wholesale destruction, was combatted by naturalists und sportsmen alike. There was a seminal bird prevention event in 1886. The American Ornithologists Union created a model law for non-game birds, which passed that year in the New York State legislature. Many other states followed New York's lead. A year later the Harris Game Bill became a reality in Pennsylvania. Those laws began an effort among bird protectors to get serious nationwide.

156 The Hat That Killed a Billion Birds

Even in the absence of laws some groups clamored for protection. In 1888 the Michigan Sportsmen's Association held its annual meeting and declared itself in favor of a non-exportation law and the protection of songbirds.[3] At the same time it condemned the use of the plumage of singing birds by milliners. Finally, the members appealed to the women of the state not to use the plumage of birds for millinery and ornamental purposes.

Individuals acted as well. Secretary Rice of the South Carolina Audubon Society obtained warrants through a magistrate against two Columbia dry goods and millinery businesses.[4] The warrants charged them with violating the laws against the protection of non-game birds. That was the second time Secretary Rice had used the law that way. It was effective: the milliners pleaded guilty and each paid fines of $2. That was unusual. The Audubonists not only pushed for state laws but in some states also actively helped enforce them.

Other states moved ahead with their own laws, but there was a lack of uniformity among them. Some states placed the onus for the slaughter on the hunters; some, such as Kansas, on the milliners; and some on the hat wearers.[5] Arkansas, one of the first states to pass legislation, opted to fine them all:

> Any person who shall have in possession or who shall sell or expose for sale any feathers or skins or parts of birds for use in millinery or similar purposes, or shall kill for such purposes any birds in this state, shall be deemed guilty of a misdemeanor, and upon conviction shall be fined not less than $25 nor more than $50 for each bird skin or part of skin or parcel of feathers so sold or offered for sale or killed for that purpose.[6]

That sweeping bill gave legislatures in other states a model on which to build. Better yet, they could follow the example of Wisconsin.[7] As early as 1887 the state legislature had made it a misdemeanor to kill birds for millinery purposes and set the fine for doing so at a maximum of $100.[8] And the only feathers women could wear on their hats were from hens.

Fourteen years later the state's legislature passed one of the toughest laws in the country to protect the birds. That brought a scolding from the Chicago *Tribune* to the Illinois legislature, one state away from Wisconsin, which had passed a law two years earlier similar to Arkansas' ordinance, with the same fines.[9]

"Through carelessness or something worse some of the Illinois game birds have been left without proper protection from the law," the *Tribune* confessed. "The Wisconsin legislature has put in force an act which, in its protective clauses, is far in advance of the game and song bird statutes of any other state."[10] That, the writer noted, happened despite the active and successful opposition from the dealers in millinery supplies.

Wisconsin's law gave game wardens the power to seize on sight any bird skins or parts of bird skins that were intended for decorative purposes. The pertinent section of the law read: "No person shall kill or catch or have in possession, living or dead, any wild bird other than a game bird. No part of the plumage, skin or body of any bird protected by this section shall be sold or had in possession for sale."

The penalty in Wisconsin for selling any part of a bird for millinery or other purposes was a fine of $5 for each such part of a bird or imprisonment for 10 days, or both, at the discretion of the court. The reporter concluded that "if fashion shall decree this fall that bird plumage must be worn, there will be an interesting time in Wisconsin." That would have applied to other states as well—if their laws had any meaningful impact, which was not always the case.

Legislators were usually late to the party when laws were needed. The bird slaughter

29. The Law of Fashion Prevails   157

had been in progress for almost 30 years by the time most states enacted laws to prevent it. Then, they were in a rush to enact them. Predictably, they were not particularly helpful.

Laws, no matter how well intentioned, are frequently ineffective as a deterrent over the long haul for a variety of reasons. They may be poorly worded to begin with and therefore hard to enforce. New York State's laws puzzled a lot of people because they were so complex the state had to issue a clarification so people could understand them.[11]

An editor took a jab at them by claiming that only an ornithologist could figure out what they meant:

> Is an ornithologist to be set up to regulate the fashion of women's hats? The new law for New York prohibiting the sale of the plumage of certain wild birds for use in millinery has been signed by Governor Roosevelt and the law is said to be so intricate that the services of an ornithologist will be required to determine, by an examination of the feathers, whether the law is being violated in each particular case that may come up.

The editor joked that "the wearing of the plumage of sparrows, crows, hawks, gulls, blackbirds, cranes, ravens, and kingfishers is not prohibited. But a woman would just as soon wear a frog's wing on her hat as a crow's feather. Go to it, O legislators!"[12]

The sometimes puzzling wording was demonstrated by a stock explanation from legislators who pointed to the failure of a law to accomplish what it is intended to do with a simple caveat: there's no such thing as a perfect law.

In some cases people ignore or circumvent a law, officials do not enforce it, it becomes outdated, technology supersedes it, the exemptions included weaken its effects, it is ruled unconstitutional in whole or part, or it is not publicized. A law has no value if no one knows it exists. That was highlighted in a peculiar case in New Jersey.

A game warden attempted to enforce a new law when he visited a millinery store in Union Hill. He seized 16 stuffed starlings that had been prepared to adorn women's hats. The warden was applying a law forbidding the sale or use of plumage birds for millinery. Unfortunately, he seemed to be the only person involved in the case who knew about the law.

Union Hill police officers summoned to the store were in the dark about it. They threatened to arrest the warden on a charge of larceny. Summarily, he had to appear in court to justify himself. The law was a mystery to the judge as well. He had to take a week off to study the new act.[13]

The case was amusing in retrospect, but the state legislature's neglect in providing public information about the laws it enacted led to the police officers' and judge's ignorance of this one in particular and all laws in general. That, a critic said, was common with all new statutes, but it explained why so many of them became dead-letter laws: the police, the public, and even judges, had no knowledge of them.

"This ignorance, which the State maintains by its neglect, is profitable to the lawyers and expensive to the public, which has to seek a lawyer to find out what the law is," one editor stressed. "It is bad for law enforcement."[14] It certainly didn't save any birds.

Another problem that arose with laws was the lack of insufficient penalties attached to them. Sometimes there were no penalties at all. That was just one more reason that played into the failure of legislators to end the murderous millinery era in jurisdiction after jurisdiction.

The only real hope that conservationists had for stopping the murderous millinery era was that fashion designers would lose interest in bird adornments and women would

Two examples of women's dress patterns and feathered hats (*American Dressmaker*, March 1911, p. 27).

see the folly of their ways and stop buying them. The women did not give up easily, though, and the laws did not stop them from patronizing the milliners' shops, especially in Missouri.

In 1905 Missouri enacted the Walmsley fish and game act that was supposed to be a strong deterrent to the unnecessary killing of birds for millinery use and the wearing of same.[15] It was so strict it prohibited anyone from passing through the state if they were wearing prohibited bird decorations. There was some fear among lawmakers that concerned citizens would appeal to the interstate commerce commission to repeal at least that provision of the law.[16] Nevertheless, the passage of the bill was a bold step forward for the state.

Missouri was a prime example of a state in which game laws were in place but ineffective. The destruction of the state's birds had gone on relentlessly, despite the enactment of laws that in some ways were commendable. Bird protectors theorized that if they had been rigidly enforced the state would have saved millions of dollars and large numbers of birds.

Significantly, there were no appropriations available for the prosecution of violators. Game wardens served voluntarily and without remuneration. Their work was one of love for the good of the community in both a material and aesthetic sense. Missouri was begging for Audubon Society intervention.

Around 1901 Letters of Incorporation were granted to the Audubon Society of Missouri.[17] The society's stated goals were to protect wild birds and game from extermination, prosecute violators of the bird and game laws, discourage the wearing of plumes, and educate the public to a point where citizens would encourage the General Assembly to enact protective statutes and make sufficient appropriations for their enforcement.

Audubonists and their supporters reckoned that if these ends were met Missouri would profit greatly. Newspaper editors encouraged farmers to support the organization in every way they could. Women especially, they said, could help by refraining from using dead birds on their millinery. Even diners could be useful if they would only stop eating the delicate "snow-birds" of elaborate menus.

The journalists were pushing the same message that people in so many other states were, albeit a bit later than some: everyone could help in the work of the Audubon Society. The birds had to be saved. That message didn't get through to members of the state's legislature for a few years.

Harry R. Walmsley, the author of the Missouri game law, knew the value of birds to the environment, especially that of the quail.[18] He would not kill and eat the flesh of one of these birds. He told a reporter that "a bird that is worth $50 to the farmers of the state to kill insects I would not think of sacrificing for a 15 cent meal."[19]

The act had been in effect for a year by the time that piece was published. Newspapers across the country had touted it as a major step forward in curtailing both killing and eating birds. The law failed to live up to its hype.

The new bill, effective as of June 16, 1905, drew praise from supporters. They claimed boldly that law, not fashion, would dictate what headgear the women from Missouri and elsewhere wore. According to the law, anyone who happened to be visiting or just passing through the state was subject to illegal headgear seizure after the state's new fish and game bill went into effect.

The restrictions may have upset some women, but they were not as bad as they seemed. The ladies would still be allowed a few birds with which to decorate their hats.

160 The Hat That Killed a Billion Birds

The news was worse for retailers. After June 16, thousands of dollars of forbidden feathers and bird bodies in wholesale and retail stores in Kansas City, St. Joseph and St. Louis would officially become contraband and no longer sold. There were exceptions.

Only the feathers of domestic birds such as ostriches, chickens, and ducks could be used, while the wild birds allowed milliners were confined to English sparrows, hawks, horned owls, and crows. Aigrettes were singled out as illegal. Section 2 of the Walmsley bill applied to birds used in millinery.[20] It provided that no person "shall catch or have in his possession, living or dead, any wild bird, or purchase, offer or expose for sale, transport, or ship in or without the state, any such wild bird after it has been killed or caught, except as permitted in the act." Violators were subject to fines.

Anyone who violated any of the provisions of the section would be held guilty of a misdemeanor and punished by a fine of $25 and an additional fine of $5 for each bird, living or dead, or part of a bird held in their possession. The bill also provided that none of the parts of birds prohibited by the act could be shipped into the state. There was a "work around" for talented women, however.[21]

Any woman who had paid attention to the fashion writers' "how to make your own hat" instructions was granted an exception. Women who were able to trim their own hats were allowed to wear birds during the summer of 1905, but the birds had be in their possession before June 16. How they could prove the accuracy of that date was not exactly clear.

The law ran into trouble immediately. Almost a year to the day after the law took effect the Missouri supreme court declared in the case of A. Weber of Jackson County that sections 64 and 66 of the Walmsley game and fish law were unconstitutional and void.[22] These sections provided that money collected from fines for violation of the fish and game law were to be paid into the state treasury and credited to the state game warden's fund. The state's constitution stipulated otherwise.

Weber had been convicted before a justice of the peace of violating the Walmsley law and fined $50, which he paid to A.C. Warner, treasurer of Jackson County. Warner credited the payment to the school fund. Game warden Rhodes initiated a mandamus proceeding (an order from a court to an inferior government official ordering the government official to properly fulfill their official duties or correct an abuse of discretion) to compel Warner to remit the money to the state treasury for the game warden's fund. That was required by the state's constitution, which mandated that such fines were to go into the public school fund of the county in which they were imposed. That put a temporary crimp in efforts to enforce the law.

There was a lull in enforcement for a while, but it was not forgotten entirely. H.W. Henshaw, chief of the federal Bureau of Biological Survey, noted in a report after the convention of state game commissioners held in New Orleans that the attention given to conservation laws in Missouri "is a distinct departure in game protection work."[23] Henshaw added that Missouri's game wardens had actively cooperated with other officials at every stage of the proceedings.

Encouraged by Henshaw's support, Missouri's game and fish commissioner made preparations to enforce the state's plumage law to the fullest and designated one of his deputies as "plumage expert."[24] The deputy was charged with inspecting and securing satisfactory identification of the goods displayed. That was a departure from three years earlier, just a year after the Missouri supreme court's ruling about the unconstitutionality of the law. Then, a newspaper reporter asked a salient question about the lack of enforcement.

29. The Law of Fashion Prevails

"How many years since you have seen a wild pigeon?" the reporter asked. "Millions of them used to fly over the country, but they have been killed off by the man with a gun. The other wild game in Missouri is going just as rapidly. Don't we need a game law, one that is rigidly enforced?"

That was a legitimate question not only in Missouri but also in other states that had passed laws to stop murderous millinery practices, so many of which were flawed. In fact, the "flawed law" syndrome dated back to 1897, when Massachusetts passed a meaningful law to protect its birds from milliners. Unfortunately, it became meaningless.[25]

30

From Missouri to Massachusetts

"Ladies will not be disturbed in their plumage, as the prohibition is against selling or having in possession for sale; and there are sufficient exemptions to satisfy the cravings of anyone for feathers."[1]

The Massachusetts legislature enacted what it considered to be a model law that made it an offense punishable by a fine to have in one's possession the body or feathers of any songbird or to wear such feathers for purpose of dress or adornment. The intent was to prevent the use of wild birds' feathers for millinery purposes. Detractors correctly said it would not have any serious impact. The law was too confusing and misinterpreted to be effective.

After it was passed a newspaper dispatched a reporter to get wholesalers' and retailers' opinions on it. They viewed it as ridiculous. They acknowledged, however, that the talk about the act affected their business immediately and would continue to do so until the initial excitement about it died away.

The interpretation of the statute seemed difficult even to the officials charged with enforcing it. Rufus R. Wade, longtime chief of the Boston district police, sent out notifications to the dealers that inspections of bird products would start soon. But who would do the inspecting? Naturalists and experienced dealers were the only ones capable of judging whether certain birds or feathers could be legally worn or sold. Almost anyone could recognize an owl, a parrot, or an English sparrow, but there were dozens of other millinery birds used for ornamentation that could be combinations of barnyard feathers, the like of which never walked or flew.

Pigeons, geese, ducks, turkeys, and other birds sold at markets for food contributed their plumage toward the milliners' stocks. The artisans of Europe arranged them so skillfully that the resulting ornaments could have been mistaken easily for songbirds. One of the largest wholesale dealers in New England interviewed said:

> I have thousands of dollars' worth of feathers in my possession. I paid the government a good price for the privilege of bringing them here from Europe: I pay the city taxes and am given the right to conduct my business. I should be glad if I might be arrested in order to have a test case of this absurd law. I haven't a feather in my stock that was not imported, and yet I can show many that might have been taken from birds killed here in Massachusetts.
>
> I shall proceed as before and buy what I think my customers will want. I understand that the ostrich is not included in the new law, when, as a matter of fact, the plucking of its feathers means actual cruelty.[2]

A buyer for one of the large retail houses cited instances of customers who had feathers removed from hats for fear of arrest. He added that he would not cancel the order he had placed in Europe for the following season, which included thousands of birds that constituted a large proportion of his millinery department's stock.

162

30. From Missouri to Massachusetts

A milliner with a large trade alleged that the law was the result of misdirected sentiment on the part of half a dozen persons who had nothing else to think about than making trouble for others. She said:

> I have always made it a point to have nothing in my stores that I knew to have been killed cruelly. Look around; you see no aigrettes. It is not in good taste to wear such things when there is a strong public sentiment against them; and my customers are quite willing to substitute a bit of lace, if only the delicate effect is desired. But all women cannot pay for thread lace and severely simple styles, and the dealers who supply the country trade are the ones who will feel the force of this interference with business.

She showed the reporter one of the most elegant and expensive hats in her stock.

> See this feather arrangement. It is the beauty of the trimming. An expert designer is paid a handsome salary to make just such novelties from what may be called refuse odds and ends, turkey wings, chicken wings, etc.
>
> The people who cry out against the wearing of birds' feathers would better stop and think of the women who work in the factories of Europe. If there is no demand for such goods their occupation is gone. I am not in the least afraid of the law, but I do think that by its enforcement, a large amount of business will be given to New York, for there will be no demand here; and then, I suppose, we shall be forbidden to sleep on feather beds.[3]

Chief Wade and General A.P. Martin, chairman of the board of police commissioners, were consulted by inquiring dealers regarding how the law would work. Even they were undecided as to what move they would make next. The Fish and Game Commission, on the other hand, determined to act at once. Its 60 deputies, stationed in various parts of the state, were ordered to enforce the law, which, strangely enough, made an exception of game birds, English sparrows, blackbirds, crows, jays, birds of prey, and wild geese.

Confusion reigned among law enforcement agencies as to who was going to do what. To make matters worse, the Massachusetts' attorney general interpreted the law a bit broadly. He said that it banned the women of the state from wearing on their bats only the feathers of birds taken within the state. In his opinion, they could legally wear the feathers of birds killed outside the state. One of the state's leading newspapers saw that as a good thing, as long as women paid attention to the spirit of the law, rather than the wording. A reporter who was commenting on the attorney general's decision said:

> But while little of the law remains for practical application to a crying evil, its enactment will not be in vain if such a recognition of decent and humane sentiment shall help in making the wearing of the plumage of birds unpopular and a matter for general condemnation. It would seem as if no self-respecting women could hereafter sin in this way, law or no law.
>
> Let the women take it up and give us an unwritten law more powerful than the attempted enactment of the general court, while men do their part in discouraging the slaughter of songbirds. An awakened public opinion can avail much.[4]

The writer was realistic, though. He, many of his colleagues, and conservationists in general knew that no single approach was going to deter women from buying their bird-adorned millinery. The only strategy that would work was multi-faceted, as he described:

> Already public sentiment is so much aroused that no woman can appear in public with adornment of birds' plumage without being the object of conscious observation and remark. But to complete the work and eradicate the evil must be a matter of time and education.

164   **The Hat That Killed a Billion Birds**

Teachers in the public schools from the primaries up should show their pupils what the bird slaughter means and the needless cruelty and wickedness of it. It is a subject which ought to engage the attention of the women's clubs, the King's Daughters, the Endeavor societies, the Alliance, and the women's guilds and societies of every kind.

The literature is abundant for many an evening's reading and study. As soon as women really begin to think on this subject they will stop wearing birds' plumage, and the milliners will gladly ply their deftest art to give them dainty adornment of ribbons, laces and flowers instead. No woman who, as child or adult, has made a study of the birds and become acquainted with individual members of the great family, will ever wear the body of a dead bird on her hat.[5]

Even that combined tactic approach had not been effective up until 1897, and it wasn't going to be immediately after. Therefore, forward-looking legislators forged ahead with the lawmaking strategy as a complement. State after state passed laws banning bird-bedecked hats in general, limiting where they could be worn, fining wearers, milliners, hunters ... the shotgun approach was welcomed by many people but ineffective. There was only the oft-quoted one way the fad was ever going to be stopped, as a journalist said tersely:

The purpose of the Massachusetts law was commendable and it had the approval of all right-minded men and women. As the event proves, however, its greatest effect will be in arousing public attention to a shameful evil. But the Republican is right in suggesting that the final and effective method of stopping the shameful slaughter and extermination of the wild birds must be through the aroused conscience and humane impulses of the women themselves.

The facts as to what this slaughter means have been so often and so fully stated that no intelligent woman is ignorant of them. Knowing these facts, no woman with a woman's heart in her can wish to give her aid to the evil. Let the women stop wearing birds' plumage and the milliners will stop providing it, and the slaughter of the birds will stop.[6]

That may have been the only solution some people believed would work, but legislators were not willing to wait for it to occur. Undeterred, states across the land took legislative action, often in conjunction with the Audubon Society. Their efforts did not always pay off as opposition was strong, especially from the milliners and women. To their credit, neither the Audubon societies nor state legislatures gave up despite occasional setbacks. They learned quickly that persistence was the key to successful legislation.

In New Jersey the state Audubon Society worked with the legislature to pass a bill for the protection of wild birds. It had a unique inclusion: if it was passed it would make wearing the plumage or any part of the skeleton or feathers of a bird on millinery unlawful and punishable by a fine or imprisonment. That didn't work.

Nine years later the society was back again to push an amendment to New Jersey's fish and game law known as the Radcliffe's bill, which provided that no person shall purchase, offer, or expose for sale any wild bird after it has been killed or caught and that no part of the plumage, skin, or body of any bird protected by this section shall be sold or had in possession for sale.[7] The bill did not apply to the birds of paradise, ostriches, domestic fowl, or domestic pigeons. The fine for violations of the law would be $20. It was not expected that the bill would pass.

The two biggest opponents were the millinery trade, which claimed that the bill threatened feather workers, and women, who resented the effort on the part of lawmakers to curtail their adornments. Despite their opposition the law passed and went into effect in August 1911. Persistence paid off in the Garden State, as it did in neighboring

New York. But women were not worried. They threatened to buy their hats in Philadelphia or Boston—or by mail order.

The milliners were worried, since the proposed laws would cut into their income. They were particularly concerned about the Francis amendment to New York's 1908 game law which, if passed, would likely close down the millinery trade in the state altogether. Members of the trade did not see what all the fuss was about, since the legislatures seemed to be more concerned about white heron feathers than anything else. They claimed that those feathers were actually from chickens and had been treated by a secret process.

The New York legislature finally passed a bill prohibiting the sale of feathers of native birds for women's hats in 1910, but it did not shut down the millinery trade in the state. It had a beneficial effect on the white heron population, though. The law helped bring the species back from the brink of extermination, which was important to the Audubon Society. Reports stated that white herons were seen for the first time in several years in New York State and Massachusetts.

T. Gilbert Pearson said that as quickly as the New York Legislature passed the new anti-plumage law the Audubon Society sent agents into the southern states to ascertain the whereabouts of the few remaining breeding colonies of these birds. In all 15 were found. These were situated chiefly in the Everglades and lake country of Florida and in the rice field section of South Carolina. Significantly, about 5,000 egrets lived safety in these colonies, and the society protected them from the agents of the millinery houses by hiring trusty guards.[8]

That was good news. Pearson noted, "It is freely stated that other species of plumage birds are being benefitted in a similar way by the passage of the law, which it was predicted would prove disastrous to many of the large millinery firms of this city."[9]

Some people did not care if certain species of birds were protected, since their interests overrode the protection afforded by the law. This tension between individual needs and bird protection often hindered the passage of state laws or their enforcement. A 1901 law in Oregon demonstrated that when wild geese, honkers and yellow legs started arriving on the 24,000-acre Sauvie's Island by the thousands on their way north.[10]

Some of the farmers there were unhappy with the law the state legislature had just passed, which forbid them to shoot these geese. They alleged that the geese were destroying their crops and devastating their pastures, and they demanded protection. One or two wild geese, hungry from a long flight, could play havoc with a grain field or a pasture. The farmers' problem was how to stop them from doing so.

One irate rancher was assured that he could not be harmed for protecting his crops and was told to take a club and kill as many of them as he could. He had no intention of undertaking any such "wild goose chase." He threatened to shoot them instead. That posed a conundrum for the farmer.

The law wasn't exactly clear on how many geese he could kill or how to dispose of them after he did. He could give them away, but if he tried to sell them the game warden would be after him. By contrast, in neighboring California the farmers could shoot the wild geese which took up residence on their farms by the wagonload.

The differences between individual states' laws was perplexing to farmers and hunters. The consensus was that the Oregon legislature overdid the matter of protecting game when it made it unlawful to shoot wild geese that interfered with the farming season. In retrospect, overdoing was better than not doing anything at all.

That message was sinking into more and more state legislators in the first decade of the 20th century. Finally, it was reaching federal authorities as well. All that they had to do was convince consumers that the laws were in place to help the birds survive. They had a more difficult time doing that than they did passing laws—and even that was not easy.

31

Milliners and Hats Are on Top

"Most of the states and territories have on their statute books laws for the protection of birds. A law of itself is of little avail. So long as women demand birds for their hats or sanction the use of birds by milliners, the supply will come."[1]

Prior to 1886 the milliners and high hat wearers had the playing field to themselves. Few people were speaking out about the numbers of birds being killed and becoming ornaments in part or in whole on ladies' hats. The milliners grew complacent about the lack of criticism. Even when the tide began to turn against them, they refused to read the signs that it was happening. Defense was not their strong point.

There were some people who thought the milliners did not have any defense for their trade to begin with, as a letter writer suggested:

Dead birds mean dollars to the feather dealer, and he would stifle the gush of song in the throat of the bobolink with as little compunction as he would crush a mosquito. It is not to be supposed that these men are going to volunteer any information that will injure their trade; on the contrary, it is their part to suppress all unpleasant facts, and to soothe and put to sleep the conscientious scruples of women on the subject of dead bird millinery.[2]

True, the milliners did not seem to be trying to prevent species from decimation. They preferred to let other individuals and organizations do the job, despite the cost in bird life, particularly to terns and sea swallows. The fad of wearing bird feathers on hats inflicted a terrible price on both species prior to the formation of the Audubon Society. They were numerous all along the eastern coast. Once women showed a predilection for them as hat decorations, their populations decreased steadily.

From Maine to Maryland their numbers dwindled to the point where there were only two or three colonies left, and they were in uninhabited places. One of them was on Little Gull Island, at the eastern end of Long Island, New York. By 1883 there were only 1,000 pairs of nesting birds there, and their lives were in danger.

The milliners' agents formed an expedition to visit Little Gull Island and hunt those few birds. That hunting party, in all likelihood, would have exterminated whatever birds lived there. A little known organization called the Linnaean Society, formed in New York in 1878, and several other entities came to their rescue.

The societies secured permission from the government to have the lightkeeper on the island double as a gamekeeper. They raised money and paid him a salary. Due to his protection efforts the number of birds tripled in two years. The turnaround was so successful that there was an overflow colony established on nearby Gardiner's Island.[3] A similar project was in progress in New Jersey a few years later.[4]

168   **The Hat That Killed a Billion Birds**

Terns and laughing gulls had once been as common along New Jersey's Atlantic coast as ants in its famous garden farms. By 1900 their breeding habitat had been limited to one spot along the coast. The New Jersey Audubon Society stepped in to provide breeding places for the birds. The increasingly interested public helped. Slowly the numbers of terns and laughing gulls increased. The success in New Jersey led optimists to hope that if the protection continued wherever the birds established a home the birds would rebound completely. That happened, and the project served as a model for stepped-up legislative efforts to save other species.

As a whole, milliners were not happy about the rising number of laws at the turn of the 20th century, even if enforcement was lax at times. The signs were clear. Pennsylvania and Massachusetts had laws for the protection of native birds, but they were not being enforced. Lawmakers in Wisconsin were mulling a bill, but skeptics there believed that if it became a law it would not protect birds a whit.[5]

The state had passed an abusive language law which no one enforced. Why would anyone think a bird protection law would be any different? The skeptics said it would be employed solely to gratify malice. That became an issue in New York State.

Skeptics suggested that it would make more sense to pass a law to prevent women from wearing high hats at theaters. That, they predicted, would get the backing of all the males in Wisconsin. The men would unite to punish any violation of such a law. The state passed such a law, which met with mixed success, as similar laws did in so many other states. That explained why milliners paid little heed to legislation designed to inhibit their operations.

Their first reaction when the formation of the Audubon Society was announced had been "who cares?" They were not concerned about the first New York State law passed in May 1886 that was designed to prevent the wholesale slaughter of native birds, other than game birds, for millinery purposes. Members of the trade believed that virtually no one in New York even knew it had been enacted and that one controversial component of the law would deter people from obeying it anyway. The law encouraged people to turn in violators of the law for financial gain.

The first sign that people were either blissfully unaware of the law or just didn't care about it was the large number of women around the state who continued to wear bird hats. The New York *Graphic* newspaper proved that with a survey.[6] A reporter rode on a horse car on Madison Avenue on a day when the sky was clear and the ladies were not afraid to wear their best bonnets and took notes about what he saw on the heads of 11 different ladies aboard. His findings were astounding.

One woman wore in her hat the heads and wings of three European starlings. Number two had an entire bird of foreign origin, but he could not identify the species. The count continued; number three, seven warblers, representing four species; number four, a large tern; number five, the heads and wings of three shore larks; number six, the wings of seven shore larks and grass finches; number seven, half of a gallinule; number eight, a small tern; number nine, a turtle dove; number 10, a vireo and a yellow-breasted chab; and number 11, ostrich plumes.

He allowed that ostrich plumes were not really included in the category of songbirds and their procurement did not result in the bird's demise. But even 10 women wearing bird hats was appalling. And, he noted, those results were typical of everyday habits. The reporter offered a suggestion that authorities should start looking into the matter. Said authorities didn't seem to have any appetite to follow his advice, and critics homed in on a "rat out your neighbor" inclusion in the law.

31. Milliners and Hats Are on Top

The law provided that no person "shall purchase or have in possession, or expose for sale any song or wild bird other than a game bird, or any part thereof, after the same has been killed." The next section riled people:

> Any person violating this provision of the act shall be deemed guilty of a misdemeanor, punishable by imprisonment in the county jail or penitentiary of not less than five or more than thirty days, or by a fine of not less than $10 or more than $50, or both at the discretion of the court. Moreover, one-half of the recovery shall belong to the plaintiff.

Critics suggested this part of the law, if enforced, offered a reward of between $5 and $25 for each successful complaint of a violation of the act and encouraged people to turn their neighbors in. The large number of bird hats a person could see any day on a fashionable street in this city demonstrated how large a fortune any snitch could earn by reporting them to the authorities. That could happen only if the law were enforced, however. The only place in the state where it was enforced with enthusiasm was Buffalo. That made it hard for would-be snitches to make money from the law.

The lack of enforcement intrigued reporters. One visited a member of the newly established Audubon Society, who said it was his impression that the milliners, taxidermists, and wholesale houses for the supply of feathers in this city were trying to create the impression that bird hats were becoming fashionable again. They were, he explained:

> They found their large stock rendered useless last year when the wave of indignation arose, and now that it has subsided they are trying to push their stock off. The law in question was passed through the efforts of the American Ornithologist Union. I don't think that all the milliners of this city are aware of this law. The Audubon Society was incorporated seven months ago for the protection of birds, but we propose to resort to moral suasion.[7]

That may have been their original intention, but they deviated from it as time passed. The society got actively involved in lobbying for legislation for the protection of birds and in some cases writing laws to be passed. But such legislation was new in 1886 and educating milliners, bird protectors, and consumers about it was difficult. The milliners in particular were perplexed about the existence and ramification of the new law in New York, as the intrepid reporter who had visited the Audubon Society learned.

He interviewed several prominent milliners and received a wide range of answers to his questions. One of them spoke about supplying bird hats as if it was his patriotic duty to do so: "If women want these bird-hats we have to furnish them. We are the public's servants, and that is the situation in a nutshell," he claimed.

"Have you heard of a law against selling birds for millinery purposes?" the reporter asked.

The milliner admitted he had, but apparently it did not concern him.

"Yes, and it was got up by a lot of cranks, who like to see their names in the papers. If these people want to be really charitable why don't they turn their attention to humanity? It is a preposterous law. It could never be enforced, for if any blackguard should inform against a lady he would be kicked out of court."

The reporter moved on. Another milliner said that he, too, had heard of the law. He was far more compassionate than the first interviewee, although he was adept at deflection:

> I am willing to co-operate with the Audubon Society to protect our native birds, but I don't see how this law could be carried out. To begin with the restriction is laid wholly on our native birds. Here, for example, is a beautiful red pheasant's breast. The bird was caught, shot,

or trapped, no one knows where. Then, too, the breast is a composite one, made up of hundreds of tiny feathers sewed or glued to a muslin foundation.

Now, suppose that I put that on a hat that I send to a fashionable customer. The lady goes out and a complaint is made against her. She is summoned and the bird is inspected. It is, of course, on the face of it, an imported article, but the lady has been subjected to an annoyance and nothing has come out of it.

Many of our native birds are sent to Paris and dyed there, and when they come back none but an expert can tell—and I doubt if he could in every instance—what the birds are. To employ experts as detectives in this business would be manifestly absurd.

In protecting song birds only the law is more sensible and likely to succeed, for as a general rule birds of song have dull plumage and are not so eagerly sought for decorations.

We also get a large supply of feathers, breasts and wings from the markets. Why don't these people protect kids and oblige women to wear cotton gloves? Why don't they protect the seals by prohibiting the sale of the sealskins? But, if you begin on that line there is no end.[8]

His claim about the birds sent to Paris for processing rang a bit hollow with some experts. One critic wrote that the birds born in millinery shops were miserable objects:

A gutter sparrow would not waste a second glance at the best of the lot. Parrots, which will be the bird of fashion for street wear, are built on the lines of a mocking bird in salad greens. The only natural feature is the blunt beak; the rest is a base imitation that poor Polly should get Olive Thorne to resent. Hand-made swallows are produced in turtle-dove plumage; they have a sad look in their glass eyes and abnormal length. Birds that show their feet have their feet pedicured.[9]

His comments may have been accurate, but there was still a market for manufactured birds. They cut costs and made bird hats more affordable for less-affluent purchasers in some cases. That was the attraction to milliners. Their job was to sell murderous millinery products. Quantity over quality ruled their world. When the flood of laws overseeing their business began, they did not appreciate either quantity or quality.

As the 19th century gave way to the 20th, the milliners were getting the feeling that they were losing ground on both the legislative and public sentiment fronts. Some members of the press may have been fooled by their change of heart due to the successes accrued by the Audubon Society.

"The passage by the American Milliners' Association of a resolution to the effect that no member of the association should use the plumage of song birds in the trimming of hats and bonnets is a gratifying evidence of the energy with which the Audubon societies of the country have carried on their commendable crusade against bird murder," a wishful-sounding journalist opined.

He noted, as had so many other stakeholders in the battle to save birds, that as long as the milliners did not join in the movement and the women refused to give up their hats, there was little hope for bird protection. He repeated, as had so many people before and after him, that the "only way to stop the use of the plumage of song birds in the millinery art was at the fountainhead; and since the arbiters of fashion are usually those who are pecuniarily interested in changing the styles as often as possible, much wisdom was shown in directing all efforts to convincing the Milliners' Association of the error of its ways."

His optimism was unbounded in his concluding remarks, filled with the prose that only a budding poet could concoct: "Inspired by the decision of that organization the morning lark of these beautiful June days should carol the rejoicings of the feathered tube from the highest point of the unfathomable blue, and give out the tidings that predatory man has given up an iota of his bloodthirstiness."[10]

31. Milliners and Hats Are on Top

Realists had a hard time believing that the American Milliners Association had seen the light and was moving away from murderous millinery. Rather, they suspected, the milliners had adopted an apparent "if you can't fight them, join them" attitude to enhance their image. They continued to fight for their businesses behind the scenes, though.

32

The Milliners Fight Back

"While we are talking about spring millinery, let us remember that a bird in the bush is worth two on a hat."[1]

Whereas bird lovers had missed the signs forecasting the extinction of species, the milliners did not. They had conducted their business practically interference free for 40 years before the specter of government regulations raised its head in the late 1800s. Once it did they had no choice but to fight for their economic survival.

Their strategies were questionable—and tasteless—at times, mainly because they were usually on the defensive side of the debate and they had a hard time getting their views disseminated. In fairness newspapers gave them space to clarify their positions for the public and trade members. Yet milliners were vexed by the Audubon Society's seemingly unlimited access to newspapers in New York, the hub of the trade in the United States.

Charles W. Farmer did not help the industry's cause when he lashed out at its critics. He sounded at times as if the trade's members were the victims of ignorant opponents who refused to recognize the value of its service, integrity, and honesty. There was reason at times to question its operations, especially when they used confusing terms.

Conservationists objected to the milliners' frequent and misleading reference to "osprey feathers." Witmer Stone made it clear that osprey feathers had no value to the trade and should be called what they really were. He said:

> Those who write their articles in favor of the milliners are wholly ignorant of the subject, or else they purposely mislead their readers. An evidence of this ignorance is further seen in the continual mention of the osprey as the plume bird, instead of the egret. The osprey is the common fish hawk of our coast and never bears any plumes or feathers of the slightest use to milliners.[2]

And they took exception to Farmer's claims that very few birds were harmed in the production of hats, as when he rejected the rumor of an order for 20,000 bird skins from Delaware, which, proved to be a fact.[3] The conservationists also did not appreciate the tone he used. Farmer said he could not help it if some people thought millinery merchants and manufacturers "go prowling about the streets of New York with guns on their shoulders killing off every bird they see."

Farmer added that he "thinks it a shame that milliners should be hounded as they are by some of the Audubon societies without anyone taking the trouble to inquire into the truth of the charges of wholesale bird slaughter." Such statements were unlikely to win many converts from the public as the trade tried to protect its image. Nor were some other of its promotions.

32. The Milliners Fight Back

173

A group of retail milliners highlighted the tasteless tactics under the adage "fine feathers make a fine bird." They initiated a "find the ugliest girl in New York" contest and offered the winner $100.[4] The thrust of their campaign was that even the ugliest girl could be made beautiful with the addition of the proper millinery aids. The winner was Miss Mary Dearby, who was featured in before (sans hat) and after (with hat) photos in national newspapers. The campaign demonstrated the milliners' desperation to maintain their trade.

There was a growing amount of opposition to the bird slaughter as more and more people learned about the source of the decorations on millinery items. Organizations, led primarily by the Audubon Society, lent their support to legislative actions and promoted effective public relations and education campaigns that put the millinery trade in a bad light. More and more—but not enough—women were refusing to buy products that were adorned with birds.

The fad began nearing its end as the public grew more enlightened. Convincing the members of the millinery trade that the end was near was not easy to do. Some stubborn bird-hat wearers did not help the milliners' cause—especially when one of them introduced live canaries in a cage on her head. That was a bit too much for the public and may have been the tipping point in the crusade to end the bird slaughter era.

New York actress Bess Ryan, aka "Toodles," shocked people along New York City's Fifth Avenue during a Sunday after-church parade when crowds observed her wearing a hat that was adorned with two live canaries in a cage.[5] It was a publicity stunt to advertise a play named *Experience* in which she was appearing. Nonetheless, bystanders were not amused.

A crowd approached Toodles in what she perceived as a threatening manner as she boldly said that she was the first person to wear such a hat—and would not be the last. She proclaimed that live birds on hats would be the new fashion style in the city's streets in the spring. That did not enthrall the crowd as it encircled her, so she jumped into a taxicab for safety and went home. Her stunt backfired and did nothing to help milliners advance their cause regarding the use of birds in their products. They just had to fight extra hard and make promises they had no intention of keeping. Few people outside their circle expected them to.

The Audubon Society of New York had announced that the woman who wore a bird on her hat would henceforth be anathema. A spokesperson said that the society had agreed with the Millinery Merchants' Protective Association to abstain from the importation or sale or use for decorative purposes of birds. That, the Audubonists naively believed, ended the era of birds on bonnets and "marked the beginning of the reign of the paint brush which rears itself so triumphantly on spring millinery." Not everybody believed that.

"It would seem to the unprejudiced observer that unless the women also promise to abstain from decorating a piece of toast with a cold, dead bird, that the Millinery Merchants' Protective Association will not do much for the cause," a skeptical editor wrote. "For what is the difference between a bird on a bonnet and on toast?"[6] The skepticism proved to be justified. The milliners kept on fighting.

Toodles had a male equivalent when it came to misjudging the public, A.L. Hamilton, vice president of the Illustrated Millinery Company.[7] He was a millinery expert from New York who pushed hard against the 1913 tariff. His arrogance shone through when he argued that there was no reason to ban the importation of feathers. After all, he said,

The Hat That Killed a Billion Birds

many game birds are killed for sport and food, and other birds are killed because they are pests. "Why do the Audubon Societies waste the feathers of all those birds?" he asked.

Hamilton intimated that the milliners had more of a right to kill birds than the Audubonists had to protect them after a bird devotee told him, "'I represent the birds, Mr. Hamilton. I speak for them. Whom do you represent, and what right have you to speak?"

Hamilton responded haughtily through the use of a parable.

"I represent the millinery trade," he said. "I speak for the thousands who will be thrown out of work if this foolish clause goes into effect. As to my right to speak, well, I think I'm rather in the position of the department store proprietor there."

And he launched into his lesson.

"A department store proprietor inaugurated in the basement a ten-cent, three-course luncheon for his workers. He thought one day he'd try the luncheon himself, and accordingly he hopped up on a peg and called for the soup. But the waiter, not knowing him, said 'Oh, no, mister! You ain't in on this. You don't belong to this store.'"

"I'm quite aware of that," the proprietor answered. "The store belongs to me."[8]

That type of attitude did not sit well with the public and it hurt the milliners' cause at a time when they could not afford to be hurt. Their backs were up against the wall, though, and they had to lash out. Their efforts met with occasional success, e.g., in the U.S. Congress and New York State in major political battles in 1913.

Bird protectors petitioning the U.S. Congress had a close call that year when their crusade was threatened by three senators who tried to change the direction of legislation in the milliners' favor: Hoke Smith (D–GA), William Hughes (D–NJ), and Charles F. Johnson (D–ME).[9] At the beginning of its legislative session, the House added an amendment to a proposed tariff bill that would prevent the importation of feathers, quills, heads, wings, tails, skins, or parts of skins, of wild birds, either raw or manufactured, which were not used either for educational or scientific purposes. The amendment did not apply to the feathers of domestic fowls of any kind.

Some people believed that curbing the importation of bird products would do nothing to solve the murderous millinery problem. That would not get to the root cause, as one newspaper editor averred.

> A number of eminent gentlemen representing the New York Zoological Society and the Audubon Society have urged the Ways and Means Committee of the House to impose in the new tariff bill such heavy duties on bird plumage for millinery purposes as to amount to an absolute inhibition of import.
>
> One of these gentlemen argued that the proposed exclusion would drive such plumage out of fashion in this country and thereby save money as well as check the killing of birds. This is one of the cases where zeal is liable to outrun discretion.
>
> It is not at all likely that any law enactable by Congress and enforceable by our courts and juries will ever prevent fashion from making use of fur and feathers in the dress and adornments of women. They are too beautiful, too becoming, and too costly for women ever willingly to abandon the use of them.

The editor concluded that "If then we turn out the foreign plumage there will be a premium on the home plumage. We have many pretty birds in our forests whose feathers will be in demand if the richer feathers of tropic birds are not to be had. Until we are sure we can protect out native bearers of fur and feathers let us not be too hasty to protect the foreigners."[10]

32. The Milliners Fight Back   175

His words went unheeded by Congress. The amendment passed the House of Representatives and would have passed the Senate easily had the milliners' lobbyists not stepped in. Wholesale milliners in various parts of the country hired two of the most formidable law firms in New York to represent their interests. The lawyers worked with Smith, Hughes, and Johnson to defeat the amendment, even though bird lovers all across the country were convinced that it would pass based on a humane standpoint alone.[11]

Hughes in particular came under fire from the bird protectors, who described him as a defender of the wild bird slaughterers. Hornaday and 20 or more prominent men issued a circular attacking all three senators. Hornaday was so deeply involved in the entire process that many people named the tariff bill after him, although Underwood ultimately got the most credit.

Hornaday wrote the section of the tariff bill which included the Schedule N that prohibited the importation into the United States of all foreign wild birds' plumage except for scientific or educational purposes.[12] Hornaday had signaled his intent in a November 1911 document he wrote in which he stated clearly, "Stop all killing of insectivorous birds for food, and of all birds for millinery purposes."

Ironically, New Jersey, Hughes's home state, had in place a law that forbid the sale of the plumage of any game birds. But, in one of those quirks in such laws, it did not forbid wild birds' plumage to be worn in the state. Its main effect had been to hurt the state's milliners' business. Rather than shop in New Jersey, women who wanted birds' plumage on their hats went out of state to buy it.

Hornaday and his fellow lobbyists of the Audubon societies tried to eliminate such quirks from the Underwood bill. They were influential in having it worded to forbid the importation of birds' plumage for millinery use, which the House's version would have done. More important, it would have put many large importing firms out of business. Those firms, and many others, had a strong lobby fighting against such prohibition. There was another factor to be considered: the prohibition as mandated by the House would have caused a loss to the government of about $90,000,000 obtained in tariff revenue from the importation of feathers. That wasn't going to fly in the Senate.

There were significant differences among the members of both bodies regarding the financial value of birds to the United States. They had debated during numerous hearings whether wild birds were useful members of society and needed protection. Some members denied that they had any value. Others said they did because of their service in destroying insects and vermin.

Some based their arguments for protection on sentiment alone, noting that their constituents favored it. There also arose the issue of "good" birds versus "bad" birds. Senator John Sharp Williams, a Mississippi cotton planter, represented the "good" side. He said that no birds were pests. He told his colleagues that even crows were useful and worth protecting.

Senator James Edward Martine of New Jersey declared just the opposite. He maintained that all birds were wholly pestiferous. Hornaday and his colleagues got involved in the debates by showing a movie to educate the congressmen that included illustrations of bird slaughter and bird usefulness. The debate was nothing more than political posturing. The bottom line for the Senate, as it always was, was the money.

When the tariff bill arrived at the Senate its Finance Committee did not factor in the sentimental and utilitarian arguments for the preservation of birds. Their main concern was the loss of revenue to the government if the importation of bird feathers was

176   The Hat That Killed a Billion Birds

banned. Committee members also emphasized that the House provision was so drastic that technically it would forbid the importation of birds allowed to be imported for food, unless they were first skinned. Anyone who expected the debate to be resolved quickly was disappointed, especially after Smith, Hughes, and Johnson tore into it.

When the bill reached the Senate caucus the exclusion clause against importation of wild bird plumage had entirely disappeared. The caucus approved the bill without it. Some senators justified its disappearance on the argument that if feathers were not imported there would be a greater slaughter of American birds to supply plumage. The Audubonists refuted that.

They said that as long as feathers were imported there could not be any real enforcement of laws to protect native birds. They argued that if the importation were banned, the wearing of feathers in millinery would stop. Neither side backed off its argument, but Hornaday and his friends seemed to be losing. Senator Smith signaled early that the amendment would fail and placed the blame for that on the lobbyists:

> Out of deference to the earnest entreaties of the women's clubs over the United States the House of Representatives adopted a provision in the tariff bill prohibiting the importation of "Aigrettes, egret plumes or the feathers, quills, heads, wings, tails, either raw or manufactured" of birds of plumage, with a view of their preservation throughout the world.
>
> The Committee on Finance of the Senate, however, in reporting the bill, have permitted the lobby maintained here by the feather importers to influence them to the extent of amending the provision so as to except from the operation of the proposed law "The feathers or plumage of birds commonly recognized as edible or pestiferous," which will admit into this country the feather or plumage of practically every species of bird in the world, as at present.
>
> Unless the women of the country and others interested in bird life acquaint their Senators with their wishes and public sentiment, in favor of the provision which passed the House the probabilities are that the proposed amendment will be adopted in the Senate and the protection which is desired to be given to bird life will be a failure.[13]

The three senators delivered a report favorable to the milliners, which was ratified in a caucus of Democrats. As a result, the amendment was defeated, which was a significant setback for the bird protectionists. Their only hope was that other influences could be brought to bear upon the three senators. They were—through the one way that causes politicians to change course and act in the best interests of the public, i.e., a massive outpouring of public support for a cause.[14] That is precisely what happened, even though dissenters in the Senate tried to ignore it. They failed.

An editorial writer said:

> It is a singular fact that practically the entire press of the country is opposed to the importation of feathers or plumes of birds for millinery as are practically women's clubs, associations organized for the purposes of the conservation of wild life, and state game commissioners. Notwithstanding this fact the provision in the tariff law has been so amended as to practicably annul the proposed legislation.[15]

Smith, Hughes, and Johnson ultimately could not ignore the overwhelming amount of public support on behalf of the birds, generated mostly by Hornaday and Pearson. The two conservationists inundated the country with detailed information and appeals for support. The senators in turn were flooded with letters from constituents who demanded the passage of the measure. The most active constituents in support of the measure were American women, who Hornaday and Pearson reached directly through their various clubs and societies.

32. The Milliners Fight Back

The New York Zoological Society and the National Association of Audubon Societies incited a variety of entities to inaugurate a campaign against the senators' opposition to the bird protection amendment. The coalition comprised a national and state federation of women's clubs, state Audubon societies, patriotic societies, the Women's League for Animals, and a host of other organizations and freelance leaders.

Significantly, the national press supported the campaign with vigor and enthusiasm. Some of the strongest editorials supporting the bird protectionists were published in cities and towns far from Washington, D.C. Letters in support of the protection amendment poured in from all points of the country. Experts estimated that the number of letters written to members of Congress exceeded 100,000.

Supporters could not overlook the fact that American women in large numbers saw the campaign as a golden opportunity to resolve the murderous millinery question in the birds' favor and put an end to a practice that so many of them had long abhorred. Finally, the importation traffic was swept out of the country on a tidal wave of indignant protest.

The Senate Democratic caucus voted to withdraw the amendment it had adopted to the bird protecting clause of the tariff hill and to restore that provision substantially as it was written into the tariff bill by the House Ways and Means Committee. The conference committee approved a few slight changes made to the amendment. That marked a significant setback for the milliner trade and spurred cries of "On to London, Paris, and Berlin" from the Audubon leaders. The signs were favorable for them, but the victory was not complete.

By 1913 fruit was replacing feathers on ladies. Yet a determined band of New York feather dealers succeeded in having bird butchery kept alive during the late stages of the state's assembly session, despite serious challenges from the National Association of Audubon Societies and the 83,000 farmers of the state grange. The bird protectionists declared that leaving the feathered crop guards as prey to the demand for women's hat trimmings for even one year more would deplete the already waning bird resources of the Empire State. That may have been hyperbole, which neither the milliners nor the protectionists were above resorting to on occasion.

Despite the setback, which the Audubonists believed was temporary, the societies assured their supporters that the fight for the birds' existence would not be dropped. Rather, it would be pursued more diligently by an alliance of farmers, orchardists, and ranchers not only from New York but from all across the United States. That fight would continue until the country's agricultural interests prevailed over the lobbyists representing a "few selfish dealers in bird scalps." Both sides dug in their heels deeper for the fight ahead as some fashion designers saw a change coming.

Two years earlier they had seen a need to replace birds as the focus of hats. They began to fixate on butterflies as a replacement in the millinery art:

> The law and sentiment have both combined to abolish the bird as a popular millinery decoration, wherefore it has been necessary to go into another department of zoology in search of hat adornment. Milliners say that if the butterfly hat becomes popular, the insect idea will be applied with variations by use of the grasshopper, the beetle, the spider, and, mayhap, the thousand-legger.[16]

Two years later a fashion writer noted that butterflies were still the vogue. But birds were by no means forgotten. The columnist stated that the fanciest hats were plume trimmed and, in a strange choice of words, declared that all kinds of bird plumage lend

178   The Hat That Killed a Billion Birds

their beauty to the autumn hats and advised women to wear their aigrettes with a difference, not the full bunch as of old.[17]

As Shakespeare's character Polonius said in *Hamlet*, "Neither a borrower nor a lender be." Birds did not want to lend their beauty to the autumn hats, especially when they knew it would be gone forever. Optimists might have taken comfort in the fact that a fashion writer was in effect telling women to cut back on the number of aigrettes they were using. The tariff talks ongoing cast some doubt on whether aigrettes would be available in the near future.

At last someone was reading the signs correctly.

33

Two Sides to the Story

"It was the best of times, it was the worst of times…"
—Charles Dickens, *A Tale of Two Cities*

As the noted British author and social critic Charles Dickens pointed out, a time period can be two things at once: good or bad. That was the case with the bird slaughter era. It was either good or bad, depending on individuals' viewpoints. No one could say with certainty what was right or wrong.

The preponderance of public opinion was on the side of the birds. Yet the people who profited from the use of birds in millinery presented their viewpoints rationally as well. And there were converts on both sides.

The real controversy did not begin until the Audubon Society and its allied groups drew a battle line starting in 1886. Perspicacious millinery trade activists realized immediately that they had a problem looming. They were no longer going to be able to slaughter birds with impunity. They reacted quickly by mounting a campaign based on hypocrisy. Public relations specialists for the *Millinery Trade Review* launched their first offensive for defensive purposes in an article titled "Spare the Birds and Beasts." The thrust of the article was that the folks who approved the use of birds' plumage on ladies' hats should take a close look at the rest of their accoutrements:

> Let them recollect the beautiful tortoise shell comb Miss Fashion wears in her hair was originally taken from a poor innocent creature who used this material for its only defense. The kid gloves she has on her hands were stripped from a babe whose parents had hoped that its maturity would be spent in the harmless amusement of bounding about on suburban rocks and foraging freely on fence board and circus posters. The satchel she carries on her arm but a short time ago formed part of an amphibious animal whose only crime consisted of basking in the sunshine on the mud flats of the St. John's River, Florida, occasionally frolicking in its waters or watching for an incautious [child] on whom to make a meal.…[1]

The writers used emotional arguments to point out that as many innocent creatures were slain needlessly for the sake of women's vanity as were birds. That was one facet of their arguments that seemed fallacious. No matter how many people the writers tried to convince that the effects of the bird slaughter was overblown, they had one major obstacle to overcome: the world noticed the disappearance of birds but not the number of tortoises, alligators, goats, or elephants. Yet the millinery trade publicists continued to present what they believed were cogent arguments on the industry's behalf. They gained some allies as the era progressed, including women and the U.S. government.

A female editor became upset with the constant criticism from men who pointed their fingers at women for the overuse of birds in millinery and set in motion a

The Hat That Killed a Billion Birds

newspaper and gender war of words.[2] She was especially irritated at an editorial penned by one of her male peers in Wilton, South Dakota, who wrote: "A woman will yank up the guy ropes until she almost squeezes her immortal soul out of place, put on a hat that is ornamented with the dead body of a song bird, and go strutting around town, selling tickets to a missionaries' entertainment to raise money to send to our missionaries to reform the heathen Chinese and prevent the women from binding their feet."[3]

That was a call to arms for the female editor, especially after her colleagues at other newspapers reprinted her counterpart's piece ostensibly to join in the journalistic battle—which also sold newspapers. Their action incurred her wrath. She laid into men in general in her rebuttal that focused on hypocrisy among them:

> And a man will saturate himself with filthy tobacco, soak himself with wicked whisky, and spit all over the office floor while he writes about the depravity of women who wear stuffed birds in their hats and trail their garments over filthy pavements—made filthy by men themselves.
>
> This manner of man writes barrels of nonsense about matters which do not concern him, and the millinery bird has a special leverage on his sympathies. It may be remembered that woods and waters are full of—not women, but men armed with guns, knives, traps, harpoons and nets, and these men kill and slaughter the innocents on sight—they kill for pure love of "sport," or, worse still, to tempt woman's love of beauty with fun and feathers and deep sea pearls.
>
> These be the same stripe of man who talks loudest and writes hardest about feminine follies. The chap who will chase a poor rabbit to death with dogs and call it fun is just the sort of a chap who berates women for wearing the dear little birds and things which died by his cupidity and which were gathered, cured and shoved on the market by himself.
>
> Try something else.[4]

One editor in another community could not resist chiming in:

> Now it would be unfair to presume that the talk about the "guy ropes" or the dead bird or the tickets to the missionary entertainments aroused any personal resentment in the bosom of the Republican Editor. It is more likely that the Wilton man's fling reached this bright woman as a sort of last straw added to an already large load of similar slams at her sex…. Does the Wilton man realize that something in the paprika line has been handed to him?[5]

The exchanges were fairly local and little more than a tempest in a teapot. But they highlighted the passions involved in the bird slaughter debates from people on both sides. The fact that there were two distinctly developing sides was one of the reasons the era lasted so long. Neither side convinced the other of the seriousness of the situation. The arguments amounted to little more than a public relations battle in which participants went back and forth.

An eponymously named writer, Dorothy Quill, published a newspaper piece in which she explained how she was won over to the milliners' point of view. Her epiphany began after a friend lambasted her for buying a hat adorned with birds. The incident prompted Quill to do some investigative journalism.

"You have not cared that the most joyous of God's creatures was slain while twittering in the sunlight in which it had a divine right to live unmolested; that perhaps its tiny throat was stilled in the very act of pouring forth a flood of melody to make glad the hearts of those who listened?" her friend asked. "Think of it, and ask yourself if you have any right to assist in the wholesale butchery of these feathered innocents."

Quill thought about it and agreed with her friend. After all, she said, "I am not

33. Two Sides to the Story

wholly devoid of conscience, and I do not relish the idea of blood being spilled in the cause of personal vanity." She went home, hid her hat, and went to bed. The birds haunted her dreams. She replied:

> The voice of conscience dinned itself in to my ears all day, and in my dreams, when night came, that birdlet hopped painfully out of its bandbox grave, perched itself upon the foot of my bed, and turned its glassy eyes upon me with a reproachful and immovable stare that entered like iron into my soul. If you have never been haunted by a bird ghost, of course you cannot fully appreciate my feelings.

The next day she started a crusade to confront people in the millinery trade to ask them why they supported the slaughter of birds. She was surprised at what she found.

On her first stop she entered the shop of a wholesale dealer who deigned to make a nefarious living by selling dead birds, grabbed a bird carcass, and asked, "Do you think that it is right to kill these beautiful creatures in order that you make money?"

His response puzzled her.

"Do you think," he answered, "that it is right to kill a chicken in order that you may make a meal?"

He explained that it was the markets of a city that practically supply the millinery trade—the markets and the farmers who protect their crops by slaughtering pests such as the English sparrow, the starling, and the parrot in the southern countries. He told her that such birds annually destroyed millions of bushels of corn and other products of the field despite farmers' efforts to keep them from doing so.

"Shall these birds eat and man starve?" he asked. "Which is better, to kill them or let the farmers go hungry?"

Those were the birds that were utilized by countless thousands for the millinery trade, he said. "It is a great mistake to suppose that every bird worn upon a hat represents a life sacrificed for mere vanity's sake. About 1 per cent of the birds seen are really slaughtered for that purpose, and they are not singers, for it is a well-known fact that birds of brilliant plumage have no singing voice. Like the peacock, they are for show, not to make melody."

Then he gave her a lesson in economics. Since real birds of paradise are very expensive, the wholesalers supplied the bulk of trade with cheap articles in the bird and feather line. They weren't even real birds. They were manufactured out of common waste material thrown aside in the markets, gathered in bags, and sold to the factories at so much per pound. He asked:

> What would you reformers who have so much to say about cruelty do with the thousands of women, men and girls in the United States, to say nothing of those in other countries, who would be thrown out of employment if women were to cease the wearing of feathers and birds upon their hats? In New York City alone there are 50,000 women engaged in the feather industry. Will the people who cry down the feather trade provide for them in some other way?

Quill was taken aback once more. She could not answer the question, so she switched topics by bringing up the subject of egrets. That struck a chord of sympathy with the wholesaler.

"It is true that the egret is killed wantonly," he admitted. But, he added, a large proportion of the so-called egrets were not egrets at all. The aigrets used were actually peacock feathers with the "eyes" removed or other feathers altered to simulate the egret. Technology played a role in that ruse.

182   The Hat That Killed a Billion Birds

He explained that feathers could be made pliable by steam and various treatments at the factory and bent or curved into any shape. In fact, he observed, almost any kind of bird could be manufactured so skillfully that someone would have to tear it to pieces to discover the deception. In short, he declared, the millinery bird was an important part of industrial life that gave the means of subsistence to a small army of wage earners.

He invited her to see for herself. Quill poked the small body, spread the stiff wings, and pulled apart the beak that "never more could open in song—nay, never had opened in song." All she found were shiny strips of leather stamped into the shape of made of wire, tissue paper, and paste surrounded by cotton from beak to tail. She was still not satisfied.

"How about the plumage?" she asked.

"Chicken feathers dyed," he answered. "As a rule the beaks are genuine, being picked up in the markets along with the feathers. And by the way, do you know that turkey feathers are very largely used in hat garniture?"

That, he added, was another economic boon. It was a branch of the industry that gave employment to artists who painted the feathers. And as simple a thing as eating a traditional Thanksgiving dinner helped the industry as well.

"For quills there is nothing so desirable as turkey feathers. Just remember that, when you are eating your Thanksgiving dinner," he advised. "Remember, too, that there are at least half a hundred girls in San Francisco making a living by working in feathers. Go and watch them, and you will find that every bird in stock at the factory has been made by hand."

Quill visited a facility at which the owners led a tour through a room she described almost as a feather-making utopia in which 50 to 100 young ladies were steadily employed. It was

> filled with rosy-cheeked girls and gaudy feathers, the rings of the pretty workers sitting around two iron tables deftly manipulating feathers of every conceivable shade and size, some curling them over a short, blunt knife, some steaming them, others bending them into shape and wiring them, and others packing them into boxes.

"Just now they were filling some large orders for California ostrich feathers, but certainly I should see a bird made if I wished."

Quill had an epiphany:

> As the wire, cotton and feathers flew, as it were, into shape beneath nimble fingers, the bird seemed oddly familiar to me. Then I knew that its twin was at home in my bandbox. The happy conviction was borne in upon me—my bird, too, was a fake. It had not been sacrificed to pander to my contemptible vanity. It had never twittered in the sunlight. It wasn't God's little bird at all. I was not accessary to a crime. In the fullness of my joy I went out and bought an ice cream soda.[6]

The millinery trade had won a convert. Several years later the U.S. government backed up some of the claims that the members of the millinery mob had made when it admitted that not all aigrettes came from egrets. That did not come as a shock to some people, especially those in the millinery trade.

If nothing else, the trade was guilty of deception which may have bilked untold numbers of women out of their money for years when they had been paying for aigrets and getting rooster feathers and turkey quills. Even that may not have been intentional. Fashion writers acknowledged that milliners were using artificial products. One supported: "Most in Demand: Artificial feathers have, I understand, been substituted for

33. Two Sides to the Story 183

real ones on some of the transatlantic millinery. Bird of paradise, impeyan and logophore feathers are those most in demand for hat trimming."[7]

Such admissions still didn't explain why so many aigret-producing birds had disappeared in the second half of the 19th century, despite the millinery industry's sometimes clumsy attempts to convince doubters that the birds walked up to the milliners and handed them their feathers voluntarily. That was the implication in a *Millinery Trade Review* article in which the writers demanded that their critics tell the truth about murderous millinery rather than use scare tactics to put milliners in a bad light:

> Several articles have recently appeared in New York newspapers with the old time "scarehead" entitled "A Plea Against Murderous Millinery," written by "La Reine Helen Baker," and which have been extensively copied by other newspapers. It is the same old untruth with a little different dressing.
>
> These "penny-a-liners" borrow from one another year in and year out; it makes no difference to them whether the story is truth or mere fiction, as long as it serves their purpose. Like Hamlet's ghost "It will not down," as long as the fanatics have the center of the stage, or as the politicians say, it is "a good enough story until after election."
>
> In other words, it is a good enough story to influence votes in a legislature in passing an anti-bird plumage bill. The story, as far as the bird plumage paragraph is concerned, is a misstatement of facts and does the milliner, as well as the vast majority of the women of our country an injustice, inasmuch as it attributes to them a lack of humanitarianism.

Truthfully, the *Review* invited such attacks when it printed stories that tried to convince consumers that aigrette collecting was a game that even the herons loved to play and that governments monitored religiously. That was evident later in the article, when the writers attacked the messenger and said in modern-day terms that no birds were harmed:

> The writer of the article states that she "even preaches." It is to be hoped that she confines herself to the truth when she speaks from the pulpit, the place where the "gospel truth" only is supposed to be uttered, and does not draw upon her imagination or make statements that, while pleasing for her audience to hear, are not absolutely true. No one objects to the writer of the article being a vegetarian, or anything else that she wants to be, including a "suffragette," but we want her to be truthful in all that she says regarding the wearing of bird plumage on women's hats.[8]

Ironically, the word suffragette was anathema to people on both sides of the murderous millinery debate. Technically, a suffragette was a woman who worked to get voting rights for women at a time when women were not allowed to vote. But suffragettes did not confine themselves to voting rights, which made some crusaders shudder. They zealously injected themselves into all arguments involving the real or perceived deprivation of human and/or animal rights and their crusades often turned off people on both sides—although not always.

They played valuable roles at the time. "I never saw a suffragette wearing a fashionable hat, says a milliner," one gagster wrote. "At this season such a statement gives us increased respect for the suffragettes."[9]

Simply put, the *Review* objected to Helen Baker's statement which it did not consider true. But that was her view. The writer concluded that "it is such statements as these that have created a strong sentiment against wearing bird plumage in millinery and which have influenced legislatures to enact laws that are a miscarriage of justice, and deal an injury of no little extent to a great body of people engaged in commerce as well as to women who are not one of her kind."

184 The Hat That Killed a Billion Birds

In defense of the industry the *Review*'s writer pointed to a report from Venezuela that proved the fallacy of the murderous millinery crowd. It echoed the testimony of Mayene Gzisol, a naturalist and explorer who had resided for 20 years or more in Venezuela, from which much of the plumage used by U.S. milliners was imported. Gzisol stated with authority that the egret there was protected by the government and its plumage was gathered, not plucked, and sold as an article of commerce.

He said that they left their feathers everywhere on the ground as well as on the tree branches and on the bushes and thickets. Workers gathered the feathers from September to November. Gzisol suggested the "delightful birds" were happy "to leave us of such incomparable ornaments" in great numbers. "There are some Garzeros, where daily from three to four kilos of these magnificent feathers may be gathered," he declared.

"Gathered" was the operative word. He insisted that heron feathers were gathered or picked from the ground and from branches of bushes and that other birds helped in the process. Gzisol explained that some species of birds constructed the interior of their nests with white heron feathers which they gathered abundantly. It was not unusual that these nests contained from five to 10 grams of feathers that always maintained their value, even if the birds twisted them in order to form a soft down on which to rest their eggs and their little ones. He knew of a place in the city of Guarico in which 125 to 130 pounds of feathers were gathered or picked up frequently.

In summary, Gzisol said:

> The feathers exported from Venezuela for our markets are for the greatest part gathered feathers, and the exception being those coming from birds killed, the meat of which serves as food to the natives living in these regions.... I know certain owners who successfully began the raising of white herons ... and I also affirm that every year more than 1,000 kilos of white heron feathers are exported from Venezuela, gathered and picked up as I stated. The harvest is considerable, and is increasing precisely because they protect the birds which furnish their feathers, one of the most appreciable revenues of these rich countries.

Most important, he averred, Venezuela had strict laws regulating the gathering of aigrets. The development of the heron feather industry was subject to strict state control. Gzisol stressed that the hunting of herons with firearms or in any other way causing the extermination of these birds was absolutely prohibited. In the opinion of the milliners, that settled the issue of whether any birds were being slaughtered for their feathers:

> As the greater portion of the aigrettes used in America and imported from Paris or London direct from South America are a Venezuelan product, this statement should silence forever the American cranks making use of the term, "murderous millinery," when referring to the wearing of the plumage of the egret or white heron.... All that the trade is doing is seeking to protect its rights and be permitted to conduct its business legally and righteously.[10]

Maybe there was some truth to the millinery trade's defense after all. The U.S. government acknowledged that herons were not being used by the trade as widely as some people believed.[11] The government's report stated large numbers of Americans were under the mistaken supposition that they were wearing "fancy feathers" on their hats when they were indisputably sporting the feathers of ordinary barnyard fowl.

The report did not exonerate the millinery trade completely. Government authorities stated without reservation that herons were threatened and needed protection, in spite of the *Millinery Trade Review*'s claims.

The extermination of the egret was imminent in the United States, the report

33. Two Sides to the Story

warned. Government agencies were doing what they could to protect egrets, especially since efforts to raise them on a commercial scale for their plumage had been unsuccessful, as were attempts to manufacture imitation aigrettes. Meanwhile, the report acknowledged, true aigrettes retained a significant position in the "fancy feathers" industry. Most aigrettes used in the United States came from foreign countries, and enormous quantities of them were fashioned from the feathers of barnyard fowls, as the milliners suggested.

But, the government cautioned, no official data regarding their production in the United States were available. Amazingly, the report revealed, statistics relating to the manufacture of fancy feathers were included in census returns with those of artificial flowers. In any case, protection of herons and other threatened birds was necessary.

The report explained that the threatened extermination of egrets in the United States had led to remedial legislation wherever the birds existed. The protection was paying off. The number of egrets was increasing slowly, and trade in its feathers had been restricted, in part because several foreign nations had enacted laws that prohibited the exportation of egret plumage. The U.S. government and several states had done the same, especially with the implementation of bird sanctuaries.

The report gave credit to the federal government in particular for its protection programs for egrets and other plumage birds through its supervision of interstate commerce. Setting apart national bird reservations had prevented the complete extermination of the egret and other native wild birds by affording them protected areas for breeding and refuge during migration. There were at least 56 reservations in place. With few exceptions they were either small rocky islands or tracts of marshland of no agricultural value. That was encouraging for bird protectors.

The upshot of the debates was that both sides had some valid arguments regarding the effects of the relationship between bird slaughter and the millinery trade. They might not have been as bad as the opponents made them out to be and the people involved in the trade had some justifications for their operations. Nevertheless, the debate raged. But the one result that mattered at the turn of the 20th century was that the birds were being afforded badly needed protection and their extermination had been forestalled. That had a significant effect on the business of birds.

34

The Business of Business

> America, cruelty is run riot, in order that designers of madame's bonnet may have feathers to stick on it. Talk of "protecting wool," let the feminine world "protect" birds by refusing to admire, and much less buy, the feather-trimmed headgear set before it as the "latest fashion."[1]

There is always an economic impact to crises like the bird slaughter. This was evident from the onset of the era to the end. Economics affected everyone in the business chain in a variety of ways. The "follow the money" adage had a significant impact on why the era lasted so long. But why did Americans sacrifice their songbirds for the sake of profit—especially when that profit was enjoyed by foreigners?

One reporter asked that question to raise readers' awareness of the oncoming bird slaughter crisis.

> A feature of it that is doubly exasperating is the sale of the plumage gathered at the expense of American groves and fields, to foreign manufacturers. It is bad enough to rob our country of one of its chief natural attractions for the benefit of our domestic trade, but far more unpleasant is the idea that the bodies of our little feathered friends are going to enrich a people so careful of their own birds as to protect them by the most stringent laws. If the French decorators want bright plumage, let them raise it themselves.
>
> But, after all, a large share of the work of devastation is done for our people. If all American women would cease to buy bird ornaments simply because some foreigner has made them "the fashion," the market would receive so little support that there would be no profit in it, and an end would presently be put to the slaughter. Our women have headed so many reforms in behalf of good morals that it is not too much to expect that they will be ready to set one in motion in behalf of good taste and against this brutalizing business of bird murder.[2]

Unfortunately, bird murder was profitable for some people. American women spent about $10,000,000 a year on the flowers and feathers used in trimming for their headgear at the turn of the 20th century. The center of the industry in the United States was New York, where 10,000 women were employed. In November 1899 the women were working day and night to fill the demand for trimming material.

Since June 1 this little army had been working exclusively on fancy feathers, yet it experienced difficulty keeping up with the orders. Manufacturers could have employed many hundreds more, but there was a shortage of skilled labor in this line. The heavy work was expected to end briefly around December 1.

By the end of the following May the stock for the next summer and autumn was ready for the inspection of purchasers, who flocked into New York City then. The same women who fashioned the feather trimmings from June to December were also skilled in the art of flower making. As a consequence they were guaranteed continuous employment throughout the year.

34. The Business of Business

The women who were adept at working with roses commanded the highest salaries, from $20 to $25 a week.[3] "To transform the dyed, starched cotton, the sateen, silk, velvet and the other materials employed into a queen of the garden which will not look like an imitation, but as natural as the growing rose, is what every woman in the workroom aspires to do some time, because to do that successfully insures a comfortable income," an observer noted. They had to start their apprenticeship with something simpler, like the violet.

The violet was easier to create because it had very few petals and was simple to construct. But the position provided limited opportunities. The artificial foliage was fashioned almost entirely by machinery, being stamped and cut by special mechanical devices. But rose makers had to start somewhere—if they could find one of the few jobs available.

The wages paid to feather and flower workers ran from $6 to $15 a week. Women who became experts in either skill earned from $95 to $120 a week. Some of the dyers who had a secret successful process of their own in coloring commanded their own salaries. There were not enough of them to fill the demand in the United States, so American manufacturers had to import French dyers.

That meant the French took $5,000,000 of the $10,000,000 which American women spent annually for hat trimming, but the system didn't always work. Some of the best dyers employed in French establishments when brought over to this country found it impossible to produce the same colors that they had success with at home, and they attributed the difficulty chiefly to the water in the United States.

Whether foreign countries protected their own bird populations in order to take advantage of the Americans' feathered creatures was debatable. At the business session of the annual meeting of the American Ornithologists Union several years later the committee on bird protection expressed a bit of optimism, stating that in 1898 there was a greater use of birds' wings in millinery. At the same time, the level of protest against their use was never greater.

The committee reported that investigations showed that many of the birds used for millinery purposes were imported from foreign countries where there were no laws against the killing of all birds.[4] In either case the answer to questions about the growth of the millinery trade despite increasing protests could be found in the numbers, which are the basis of any business.

Dr. L.O. Howard, a pioneer American entomologist who worked in the U.S. Department of Agriculture, estimated that the United States paid "$300,000,000 tribute to the bug annually."[5] He concluded that if the year's wheat crop sold at 50 cents a bushel, an average price received by the Western farmer, it would bring in only a little more than that enormous sum.

Worse, he stated, the monetary amount had grown greater each year due to a 46 percent decrease in the number of birds in America over a 15-year period. That factor led to a significant increase in harmful insects and bugs that affected crops adversely. That was not surprising. Every average insectivorous bird destroyed at least 2,400 insects every year of its life.[6] Significantly, since the great majority of birds were insectivorous, the 46 percent decrease was bound to be felt. Howard calculated that the United States was annually sacrificing the equivalent of an entire wheat crop for the privilege of killing the song and game birds. People didn't always make the connection between the loss of the birds and the economy.

188 The Hat That Killed a Billion Birds

The millinery trade's appetite for birds was insatiable in the early years of the 20th century. The importation numbers for the first five years alone as more and more species entered the country showed that.[7] On average, one consignment of foreign birds arrived in the country nearly every day each year. In busy seasons as many as 10,000 birds reached New York City on a single steamer. In one year more than 200,000 canaries and 40,000 miscellaneous birds reached American shores.

Between January 1, 1900, and June 30, 1905, 1,563 permits were issued, covering the entry of 2,841 mammals, 819,970 canaries, and 185,765 miscellaneous birds, of which 30,837 were game birds. In addition, 19 permits were issued for the importation of 7,128 game bird eggs for propagation—and eventual slaughter. That explained why the milliners fought so hard to perpetuate their businesses and protect jobs. Whenever the millinery industry was threatened, it reverted to the classic argument about the number of jobs that would be affected. Changing styles were always a threat, as were tariffs.

In July 1886 there was an economic report revealing that within the past 12 or 15 months bird skins had almost totally disappeared from the hats and bonnets of women. Worse, the treasury department had decided to levy a 25 percent ad valorem duty fee on imported birds mounted for millinery purposes.[8] There had been no duty fees previously. Those two factors posed a double threat to the millinery trade.

Trade representatives resorted to the familiar argument that the new duty fee would raise the prices of their products, cause increased warfare on American birds, and lead to job losses due to decreased sales. Opponents countered that the return of ribbons to replace birds would provide employment to thousands of ribbon weavers and increased vigilance over the killing of American birds would reduce the predicted warfare on them. Similar arguments obtained every time fashion styles changed in the era, which was often.

Census figures for 1900 created a picture of how much birds save farmers.[9] That year there were in the United States 5,739,675 farms comprising 841,201,546 acres valued at $20,614,001,838. The revenue for farmers' and fruit growers' crops was $7,733,118,752. Experts estimated that insects and rodents destroyed about $200,000,000 worth of crops each year, even with the birds protecting them. There was no telling how much that figure would rise if the birds disappeared, partially or entirely.

The ubiquitous National Association of Audubon Societies put the figure in a different perspective in a letter to all New York State granges advocating for a revision of the bird laws in this country for the protection of the birds and the benefit of the farmers. It included some startling statistics and a sop to the recipients in its opening: "If the bird laws are to be improved, it can only be done through the powerful influence of the grangers...."

The letter also contained a warning that the millinery trades did not want the bird laws changed; it fought every attempt to improve them. The industry was trying to protect the livelihoods of the people who depended on the bird slaughter for a living.

"Have you ever contrasted the relative size of the two interests of millinery and agriculture?" the letter writer asked. "If not, carefully examine the following figures taken from the last United States census report (1900)":

Capital invested in the millinery (wholesale and retail) business in New York State, $11,805,903.

Capital invested in agriculture in New York State: Land, $551,174,220; Farm buildings, $337,000,000. Total, $838,174,220.

34. The Business of Business

There are 228,720 farmers in the state. Almost 250,000 farmers and their families depend on the products of these farms.

There are 22,648,109 acres in these farms; every acre harbors swarms of insect and rodent pests that destroy crops, entailing enormous losses annually.

Birds are the means supplied by the Creator to keep in check insect and rodent pests.

Farmers, are you willing to have your best friends destroyed? In 1900 you spent $27,102,130 for labor. The birds work for you without pay. Can you do less for them than to see that they have the fullest legal protection?[10]

The figures the society presented were eye-opening. Yet the economics of such magnitude puzzled some people. In 1903 the boll weevil caused a loss to cotton growers of $50,000,000. Conversely, the value of the birds slaughtered for millinery in the same period was estimated at half a million dollars. Some folks speculated that if the birds had been left alone they would have destroyed the weevils. As one commentator noted, "It is a queer economy we practice sometimes."[11]

The numbers were not only puzzling, but they were meaningless if people continued to buy murderous millinery. The pressure to make sure ladies in particular learned about the dangers inherent in bird slaughter increased after the Audubon Society formed.

There was another side to the business aspect: the sometimes strange impact of legislation on business owners, as in the case of Robert Jacobs, who operated a small egg farm in East Hampden, Maine.[12] He made a meager living supplying local hotels with eggs. The doves in the area were eating him out of his profits.

Every time he strewed grain for his hens around the farm the doves swooped in and devoured almost every bit of it. They took more than two bushels of grain and meal every day for weeks. Jacobs did what he could to stop them. He built wire enclosures to keep his chickens in pens and the doves out, but that didn't work. He thought of installing fine netting to divert the pests, but he couldn't afford it. So he started shooting the doves.

Shooting doves was not wise in Maine, since they were protected under the state's game laws. The state imposed a fine of $5 with costs for every dove slain. That did not deter Jacobs, who began blasting away. The local authorities arrested him on the charge of having killed and converted to his own use 146 doves.

Everyone expected Jacobs to enter a plea of not guilty and contest the suit rather than pay the fine of $730 plus costs. Instead, he confessed to killing not only the 146 doves mentioned in the warrant but more than 1,000 in the last year. Jacobs was not apologetic. He told the judge that shooting the doves was the only way he could save his operation and make a living.

He made no bones about his situation. "Now, I can't pay a fine and do not propose to do so," he told the judge. "If you send me to jail you will have to feed me, and the town will be obliged to care for my family. Go ahead and do your worst."

The judge consulted with the town selectmen, then put the case on file and advised Jacobs to go and sin no more. In his typically honest fashion, Jacobs said he could not do that.

"I shall shoot every dove that comes to my hen pens," he replied. "Doves have no more right to live than I have."

His was a perfect example of how games laws could help and hurt legitimate business owners, egg farmers and milliners alike.

190　　The Hat That Killed a Billion Birds

Similarly, laws in one state might hurt its own business owners and help those in a neighboring state. That was made clear when Arkansas passed its 1899 bird protection law.[13] As one astute editor noted, the law would hit the millinery business in Arkansas pretty hard. But, he said, it wouldn't prevent any woman who really wanted to adorn her head with parts of birds from doing so, even if she had to risk paying a fine for just wearing such a hat. The editor predicted she would procure her hats from neighboring Missouri or Texas. The mail order business was booming and travel to and from other states was fairly easy.

Conversely, since travel was easier, hunters moved about more than they had in previous times. That created a new opportunity for them and destinations that promoted travel for hunters looking for new adventures, such as California.[14] Their arrival had an adverse impact on California's native hunters due to the bird slaughter epidemic.

The state's hunting industry was centered in its northern counties, where fish, ducks, geese, and deer abounded and game supervision was lax. Many out-of-state hunters visited the area for long stays to take advantage of the abundance of game. Local recreational and subsistence hunters who did not use all the meat, parts, feathers, and plumes they gathered sent what they didn't need to San Francisco for processing and to collect payments for their efforts.

For the most part the native hunters had the area to themselves. What they killed did not have an adverse impact on the game population. But as the 19th century closed that began to change. Market and pot hunters gathered en masse in the northern counties and began taking game in large numbers and shipping it to San Francisco for profit. Supervision remained lax until authorities suddenly realized what was happening and started calling for strict enforcement of game rules.

The market and pot hunters began pushing the local hunters out of their own territory. Visiting hunters stopped traveling to the northern counties. Farmers who collected fees for letting hunters on their land, hotel keepers, restaurant owners, and other business owners who catered to the visiting hunters lost revenues. "Now it is the market hunter who gets the cream, and the local men only get the skim milk of hinting," a journalist observed.[15]

Authorities started calling for strict enforcement of game laws and higher financial fees for the market and pot hunters. The lost business was one more indication that murderous millinery impacted the economy more deeply than some experts had anticipated. That was not news to businesspeople whose livelihoods were affected adversely by its tentacles.

35

Calling All Ladies

> "Fashions," said a blackbird, solemnly, "are made by men. What law is there, among birds or knooks, that requires us to be the slaves of fashion?"[1]

Society decided that if the problem of murderous millinery was going to be solved the solution had to appeal to—and be supported by—women. They were the primary purchasers and wearers of the hats and assorted items of apparel that were the birds' final resting places. The question was how to do both by inviting them into the coalition without making them think they were being coerced to bow to legislation.

Some people thought there should be laws regulating what the women wore and punishing them with fines and possible imprisonment for violating them. Others agreed that there should be laws, but they should protect the birds and punish the people who engaged in the millinery trade. A third group advocated regulating the milliners themselves. A final faction maintained that there were no laws required; the fad would disappear over time. The problem with that approach was that the birds might disappear as well.

"Why not just appeal to women's natural empathy and sympathy and common sense to resolve the problem," some people asked. "All it takes is a public relations campaign to educate them about what they are doing to their fine feathered friends. They will then stop buying the hats and accessories."

One of the notable figures who backed that resolution was Edward Bok, a writer for the influential *Ladies' Home Journal*. He posited that the last thing anyone wanted to do was insult the ladies by passing laws that were clearly aimed at them:

> The agitation of this subject is both timely and wise, and the support of every man and woman having a spark of humanity can be relied upon so long as radical measures are not resorted to as an end. The common sense and human feeling of women must be appealed to and reached. The tenderness of a woman is unfailing, and once the American women fully realize the barbaric tortures which the wearing of bird plumage on their hats mean to the birds they will of their own free will and accord, and by the use of their own common sense, and a community which never fails the normal woman, stamp out the outrages which are committed so that their headgear may receive ornamentation.

His next observation was cogent: "But to insult a woman's intelligence and freedom of action by passing laws prohibiting them from wearing bird-millinery cannot be otherwise than ineffective." In fact, he suggested, any laws would be ineffective due to Americans' general antipathy to them.

> The American woman cannot be told by law what she will wear on her hat, any more than can the American man be told by law, with any degree of effectiveness, what kind of beverages he

192   **The Hat That Killed a Billion Birds**

shall put into his mouth. In effecting reforms it is always well not to trample upon the freedom of people, and of all people the American public is the last upon which to practice such measures. The common sense of the American public can be trusted if the right means are employed to win its attention. But the means must be tempered with moderation. Something must be left for people to supply themselves.[2]

Bok was correct. There were individuals and groups who made efforts to end the buying of bird-related clothing. The problem was that there weren't enough of them to make a difference in the initial stages of the crusade against bird slaughter. That changed as the problem became more acute and women joined forces to combat it.

"Fifty-one national societies were represented at the meetings of the National Council of Women held in Boston on Dec. 3 and 4, 1897," a headline in the *Record-Union* of Sacramento, California, declared on January 3, 1897. "Happily, with few exceptions, the organizations' reports showed gratifying progress in work undertaken." Actually, the report revealed mixed messages.

One of the exceptions appeared in a report delivered by Mrs. M.A. Lovell of Philadelphia on the work of the Antivivisection Society, which was involved in inhibiting the slaughter of birds for millinery purposes. She denounced the practice and begged every woman present who wore an aigret in her hat to tear it out before she left the building.

"I have had only occasional glimpses of the speakers here today through a grove of the plumes plucked from the breasts of mother birds, while hovering over their young," she said. Then she offered some bad news. Mrs. Lovell told the audience that almost no progress had been made toward getting women to stop the encouragement of these cruel practices. In fact, she said, the demand for bird plumage is practically no less than it has been for a number of years.[3]

That was not encouraging. Nevertheless, some influential women around the world took up the fight. Many of them were society women, rather than the "plain folks" who were less affluent and more likely to be protective of their hats, which were status symbols to them.

The leading women's club of New York City, based in Brooklyn, initiated a movement to encourage women to remove bird paraphernalia from their hats and refuse to buy new millinery so adorned.[4] They adopted a tactic that was to become popular among similar organizations. They made and exhibited birdless hats at the clubroom to encourage visitors to follow their lead. The members reported that their exhibit was having a favorable impact on their visitors. How that affected sales of murderous millinery was not reported, however.

Similar reports surfaced elsewhere. The purpose was to prove to the devotees of style that beauty could be attained in millinery without cruelty to birds. The Philadelphia Audubon Society made an exception by including ostrich plumes in its decorations.[5] Its members also sponsored an exhibition at which flowers, airy choux and chiffon, ribbons, and ostrich plumes were used in the decorations. A millinery display in which bird decorations were absent entirely was presented at the Audubon exhibition in St. Louis under the auspices of the Humane Society.[6]

Women across the country were becoming more enthused about conquering murderous millinery. Two hundred leading members of Chicago's female population started a statewide drive in Illinois to protect the bird population.[7] That encouraged newspaper editors to join the crusade. Why, they asked, could not the city's women's and girls' clubs, the Endeavor Society, the King's Daughters, and similar organizations do the same?

35. Calling All Ladies

There were public awareness programs galore available to keep women and their families informed. The program at the Baraboo, Wisconsin, woman's club was "one in harmony with the spring time, as the quotations were concerning birds and bird-life, and there was a discussion of the Audubon Society, which is believed to have been the beginning of the strong and growing sentiment against the use of birds for millinery purposes."[8]

The General Federation of Woman's Clubs, meeting in Denver in 1899, telegraphed to U.S. Speaker of the House Thomas Hackett Reed a recommendation that Senator Hoar's bill, protecting birds and forbidding the wearing of them, be passed.[9] Some people believed that if the delegates—who were mainly society women—said that bird millinery must go, it would go.

What's more, they declared, the "builders of bonnets" should make up their minds to "dispense with the incongruous and inartistic decorations which have caused such havoc among the song birds." Their rhetoric soared as they suggested that "in order to emancipate herself from the thraldom of Dame Fashion, to refuse submission to her capricious and arbitrary decrees, is one of the prerogatives of the oncoming woman who is to live an applied Christianity in the marts of trade, in the home, the school, the world."

American society leader and social reformer Mrs. Herotin labeled the "oncoming woman" the "colossal woman." Regardless of what she was called, if the society women could not convince their less affluent sisters to join them, their cause was less likely to succeed.[10]

News came from France that Mme. Mathilda Georgina Roberty of Rouen had started a campaign against the destruction of bird life for millinery purposes.[11] She formed a Ladies Bird Protective Association, whose members promised to defy the Parisian fashions. Mme. Roberty appealed to Americans interested in the same movement to send her statistics dealing with this "movement humain."

British royalty joined the effort, although some of the Audubon Society's strongest supporters were not sure the bird slaughter could be stopped. Winifred Anna Cavendish-Bentinck, the Duchess of Portland, a British turn-of-the-twentieth-century advocate for bird protection, said in 1903 that "it is useless to protest yet once more against the reckless slaughter of bird life. This barbarous fashion, which entails the vulgar personal vanity, which sacrifices not life only, but the very race of birds, created for beautifying the world, is unworthy of the civilization of the twentieth century."[12]

That was a strange choice of words for someone who was a devoted fan of birds. In 1891, she became the first (and longest serving) president of the Royal Society for the Protection of Birds and was vice-president of the Royal Society for the Prevention of Cruelty to Animals. She was also president of the ladies committee of the RSPCA.

Even a suggestion of doubt was not exactly the type of support the society was looking for, especially when her conversion elicited "no small offense from her enemies and sneers at her superiority in smart circles." The leaders of the opposition wanted more positive support that was likely to expand, especially when celebrities and members of royalty such as the Queen of England threw in their support.

The British parliament introduced a bill in 1906 prepared under the auspices of the Selborne Society, a group of naturalists and bird lovers that threatened women's hat adornments. The proposed new law would ban the importation of bird skins. That would have serious implications in London, which was one of the global hubs for the milliner trade. It was also a center of opposition to bird hats.

The Audubonists got a tremendous boost when Queen Alexandra of the United Kingdom and the British Dominions and Empress of India from 1901 to 1910 refused to wear "ospreys" in her hats and to forego their use in general.[13] Her opposition was born largely out of a bad experience in the late 1880s, when a wounded bird fluttered into her lap at a gun club match.[14] From that point on she was hostile to wanton bird shooting and bird millinery. That added a little more support to the new law that sought to restrict the importation of egrets, birds of paradise, and other rare kinds of plumage into England.

The hope among America bird protectionists was that the English would enforce their laws stringently and their results would transfer to the United States. Their fear was that American women did not care what the Queen of England thought. It was going to take more than the actions of a member of the British royalty to wean them off bird hats. It was an uphill climb for female leaders to convince their peers that supporting the milliners was not helpful.

American women were not sitting on their hands as their British "sisters" acted. There were sporadic attempts among them to promote anti–bird millinery pledges and half-hearted boycotts of milliners who sold such items. Often the attempts were made in conjunction with groups like the Audubon Society. One group pledge by 71 members of the Woman's Club in Denver, Colorado, in 1898 typifies the actions.

The ladies, hoping to start a state-wide effort, signed an Audubon pledge and vowed they would not wear any hats or bonnets adorned with plumage or feathers, except for ostrich plumes and quills. Their goal was avoid bird destruction in Colorado. They were particularly opposed to the use of aigrettes, since it took six dead birds to fill out one hat.

Their meeting was bird themed. The junior choir sang a "little bird song," one member sang "The Bird That Came in Spring," and another presented a research paper on the story of birds. Then Mrs. James H. Ecob presented the Audubon action plan.

She read the statistics of the great wholesale houses, showing the enormous slaughter of bird life to satisfy the demand for birds for millinery purposes. Next, she read a letter from the Audubon Society urging the ladies to ask Colorado's senators and representatives to support legislation against the killing of birds. The members' excitement about the issue was palpable throughout the room, especially when Mrs. Platt took the floor.

The good lady told the audience that she had just ordered a new hat but demanded that a bird be removed from its border before she would accept it. The milliner asked her why. Mrs. Platt answered that it was against her principles to wear such ornaments and that she never wore them. She got the audience's attention when she offered the milliner's response: "For Mercy's sake, is the woman's club going to take that stand? If it does, it will injure our business."

That was precisely the message the 71 signees wanted to spread far and wide: milliners cared more about their revenues than birds. There was a headlong rush to sign pledges, which had an added bonus. Anyone who signed a card would automatically be enrolled in the Denver Audubon Society, which would be formed the following fall in conjunction with the Woman's Club. The meeting did not end there, however.

The members appointed a committee to urge Denver school administrators to integrate bird day exercises with the traditional Arbor Day programs normally held on the last Friday in April in the United States. They realized that their timing was a tad off, since most birds were safe in the spring. The majority of them were destroyed in the fall, just before the new line of winter hats were released. They covered that, too, and concocted a plan to help the milliners recoup any losses they might incur from diminished bird hat sales.

Members made plans to arrange a millinery exhibit at the Woman's Club in the fall, just before the Colorado winter set in. They would invite all the local milliners to display their hats and bonnets then, as long as none of their wares featured the forbidden bird plumage. That would provide free advertising for the milliners, and the women would be asked to buy as many hats as possible.

The overall plan was filled with potential. Unfortunately, it and others like it were not sufficient to stop sales on a wide basis. It was a good start, though. It proved that women cared about ending the wanton destruction of birds. Moreover, some of them were not shy about attacking other women for not participating in their Audubon campaigns.[15]

The year before the Denver group spoke out, 15 women in Lincoln, Nebraska, sent a letter to a local newspaper to encourage local ladies to join them in a campaign to save the birds.

> It is trite to speak of women as the gentler sex, if by her merciless vanity the most beautiful part of the natural world is destroyed, the other sex can laugh admonition to scorn, get other mentors, and put and keep women in the state of subjection which their wanton cruelty deserves. The only superiority worth having is that of the heart and the head.
>
> When women show that they have neither by refusing an appeal to both, at the same time they resign, consciously or unconsciously, any claims to superior moral instincts. However women have never yet refused to aid a righteous cause.[16]

Their message was clear: sign the pledge they had started in Lincoln, which read, "I will not wear upon my hat or dress the plumage of any bird except that of the ostrich and domestic or game birds, and I will do my best to influence others to take this pledge." Their goal was admirable. The problem was the lack of unanimity among women in making such pledges, which led to pessimism among some anti–bird slaughter supporters.

"It is hopeless, good people. Do what you will, a few enthusiastic crusaders can never crush out fashion," an editorial writer noted. "You may scotch the snake, but you can never kill the varmint consuming the bright-plumaged denizens of the air. Birdless hats and bonnets indeed! Would that it were possible to make it a criminal act to destroy even one bird."[17]

The writer labeled anyone who supported the wearing of bird hats as inhuman, but they would not be stopped from plying their lucrative trade. He pointed out that when every new fashion season rolled around the anti–bird millinery factions begged, prayed, and entreated for mercy for the birds, to no avail. After all, he explained, the slaughter of birds was a business, and it must not be interfered with.

The women in the large cities, where most of the major milliner supply companies and designers were located, were cognizant of the bird slaughter problem. But their counterparts in smaller communities seemed to be more enthralled with the products than the problem. The changing styles gave fashion columnists in small towns a chance to display their knowledge of big city styles—even when they noted, at least subconsciously, that there was something unsavory about the trends, as columnist Lucy Carter did.

She pointed to a changing trend before she began her description of the new hats. "Millinery birds and plumage are used to an unusual extent. Crowns are sometimes completely encircled by narrow, darting wings. They form a chosen completion to full garniture of flowers."

She followed that with words that amounted to a paean to plumage. Her description alone could have killed six birds:

Single quill feathers rise saucily as ever; birds breasts are used to some extent; entire birds embedded in flowers are placed on turbans or may form the sole trimming, a typical turban in rough red straw having a red bird with partly outstretched wings, seated on the indented crown. A unique yellow straw has two long white ostrich plumes laid underneath the brim. Ostrich tips are everywhere, and fancifully, shaped straws often have ostrich tips as the sole trimming. Sometimes also wide brimmed hats have a number of rich nodding plumes as the only garniture.[18]

The ladies of Denver and Lincoln would have been aghast at Lucy Carter's fascination with bird hats, no matter the cost to birds everywhere. Therein lay the crux of the women's problem. For every enlightened group that opposed the slaughter of birds there were one or two that extolled the virtues of the millinery they adorned. The question was which side was going to win the public relations battle. It was a long time before any answer came as the extinction of birds progressed.

36

White Herons and Birds of Paradise

"Just as the aigrette reigns supreme on French and English millinery, so likewise does the bird of paradise in its natural coloring wave above Roman brows and noses. So lavish are they with these gorgeous yellow feathers that two and even three birds in their entirety are used on a single small hat. Hence the most that can be said of the typical hat of Roman fashion is that it's a bird."[1]

The high-hat craze just would not die, so birds died instead. The two species that best represented the wanton destruction of birds for gaudy plumage and feathers were the white heron and bird of paradise. Both species narrowly escaped extinction. They were more fortunate than some of their avian relatives.

The decimation of the birds of paradise began in earnest around 1882. Ten years later nature writer Jules Forest deplored the destruction which had been going on since.[2] He stressed that it was no longer possible to procure the same type of perfect specimens that had been common. The birds had been so overhunted that none of them were allowed to live long enough to reach full maturity, and it required several years for the development of the full plumage of the male bird.

The birds of paradise that were flooding the Paris market were mostly young ones still clothed in their first plumage, which lacked the brilliancy displayed in the older birds. Consequently, they were of lesser commercial value. That did not lessen the demand. As a result, on January 1, 1892, strict regulations for the preservation of the bird of paradise went into force in German New Guinea. Forest appealed to the English and Dutch governments to follow the Germans' good example.

A second component of the push to protect the birds of paradise included public relations programs to urge women to exercise common sense. They had to be made aware that tropical bird species such as the bird of paradise could not withstand the strains being placed on them. "The ruthless destruction, merely to pander to the caprice of a passing fashion, will soon place one of the most beautiful denizens of our earth in the same category as the great auk and the dodo," a journalist predicted.[3] The birds did not have to die.

An unnamed New York dealer said they did not have to be killed for their feathers.[4] "It isn't necessary to kill the birds in order to get their feathers, but it is usually more convenient," he said while calling for protection for the birds. "Lately, since they have been growing so scarce, they are frequently trapped and released after the feathers have been cut, so that a new spread can be grown."

The Hat That Killed a Billion Birds

He explained the process. Only the grown male bird had the gorgeous spread of feathers coveted by commerce, he revealed. The feathers were at their best during the courting season, when the birds held their annual dancing exhibits for the benefit of the less gorgeous but highly prized females. Unfortunately, that was when the birds let their guards down.

"Except at their dancing parties, the birds of paradise are naturally cautious and well able to protect themselves," he said. "They have but few natural enemies, but their families are small, being limited usually to two offspring a season, so that they increase but slowly. This is all the more reason why they should be protected from human depredations."

That was long after the high hat era had ended allegedly. Forty years had passed, and authorities were still asking for protection for certain birds. The only good thing that could be said in that respect was that the demand for bird of paradise feathers had diminished.

As early as 1896 the outlook for the reestablishment of the snowy heron, from which the aigrette was obtained, was not encouraging. In 20 years snowy herons in the south had gone from abundant to rare. Women seemed to be fonder of decorating not only their hats but their hair with aigrettes more than anything else.

Part of the reason herons were hunted so vigorously was misinformation about their habits. Some folks pushed the narrative that sea cranes and herons were responsible for the disappearance of fish from parts of the Florida coast, so it was okay to hunt them to the brink of extinction. That myth was eventually disproved and scientists showed that water birds were valuable as scavengers, sort of seagoing sanitary officers.[5] They emphasized that the birds should be protected for that service alone. As usual, that suggestion came too late to help untold numbers of sea birds, especially herons.

In 1876 travelers in Florida would see these birds resting in the Mangrove Islands on the coast in such large numbers that they looked like a white sheet or a blanket of snow over the island. In the intervening 20 years they had been hunted almost to extinction. In fact, by 1896 hunting egrets was not worth the effort for people looking to profit off aigrette sales.

A correspondent of *The Audubon Magazine* wrote in the July 1887 issue what he had seen in Pinecastle, Florida:

Through my meanderings I watched closely for birds and deer. I saw but a few hundred birds, where formerly I had seen from 10,000 to 20,000. I met plenty of hunters with buggies and wagons loaded with bird plumes. The birds are killed at a season of the year when they are rearing their young.

On passing the rookeries where the hunters had been a few days previous, the screams and calls of the starving young birds were pitiful to hear. Some were just fledged, while others were so young that they could make but little noise. But all must inevitably starve to death. I cannot describe the horror it gave me to hear the pitiful screams of the dying little birds.[6]

By that time there were very few market hunters left in the state. They had decimated not only Florida's heron population but that of many southern states and left for other parts of the world. Milliners finally admitted to the damage they had done.

Charles Farmer had complained that milliners had been accused unjustly of killing songbirds for trade purposes. B.S. Bowdish responded with comments about their after-the-fact virtue signaling and hypocrisy:

Mr. Farmer has some justification for his complaint inasmuch as very few birds like robins are shot for millinery purposes in this day. But he makes a number of statements that are not as accurate as might be desired, and the general tenor of his communication is somewhat misleading.

The millinery trade acknowledges that its traffic has robbed Florida of its plume birds. These birds were not songbirds and were of much less economic value than many other species, but they were of some use. And they made such an attractive feature to the swamps, the rivers, and the lakes of Florida as to prove a very strong source of interest to tourists and others visiting the state.

Today the places that were made brilliant by the wonderful abundance of this bird life a few years ago are barren and unattractive as a result of this extermination. The milliners are making a virtue of a necessity in that they are not killing or handling the birds native to the state and protected under its laws.[7]

But hunters were still killing the birds south of the United States. First they exterminated the heron population along the coast of the Yucatan in Mexico. Then they set out to do the same in the Orinoco and the Amazon in South America. Their rationalization was simple: herons didn't serve any useful purpose for mankind. As usual, the rationalizations were irrational.

It was difficult to teach the wearers of herons' plumes that they were helping hunters wipe out species of birds. So the egret, once an abundant bird in Florida, became one of its rarest inhabitants. The hunt switched to South America. The number of egrets killed in Venezuela alone in 1898, according to the official reports of the British Consul, was 1,500,003.[8] That did not represent the entire slaughter, since there was no way to count the bodies of the young herons left helpless in their nests. Then there was the human cost.

A doctor in Yucatan explained what had happened there after the herons were killed.[9] There had been a significant increase in human mortality. What the hunters overlooked, ignored, or did not care about was that herons fed on decayed animal matter thrown up by the sea. Once they were gone there was nothing to eliminate that matter, which carried diseases with it. More local residents got sick; more died. That was the problem with rationalizations about birds. They led to higher numbers of deaths: the birds and humans!

Humans had to be convinced that the deaths of mature herons mattered. Each bird was a producer of an average of 40 to 50 aigrettes, which grew between their shoulders from the center of the back of the heron. The aigrettes were of two varieties: one was straight and the other curled. These "wedding dresses" worn by both sexes during the nesting season were what attracted the hunters. Usually, the death of one mature bird meant the loss of an egg and ultimately led to starvations of the young birds who couldn't fend for themselves after the parents' deaths.

Math-wise those numbers added up for market hunters. The herons nested in large colonies. The hunters, using noiseless rifles, hid themselves until their target neared its nest. Usually the bird landed near, but not at, the nest. That was when the hunter shot it. The bird never got home and the young heron was not harmed. It was left to die while the hunter stripped its parent.

One plume hunter in Florida recounted to a reporter that he had killed 300 herons in one afternoon that way. That would be between 15,000 and 18,000 aigrettes for a single afternoon's work. Another said that he and his partner had killed 130,000 in one season—around 7,000,000 aigrettes.[10] That number of birds was twice as many as there were in the Museum of Natural history at the time, and the birds exhibited there arrived from all over the world.

200 The Hat That Killed a Billion Birds

"There wasn't one bird killed in the interest of science where 1,000 were killed to satisfy the demand of vain or unthinking women," a writer commented. At the rate hunters reported killing herons there was no way the birds could sustain their population. Aigrettes continued to flood the market, despite efforts to protect the herons. Milliners still claimed that the herons of the world weren't threatened. That elicited a strong letter of commendation from Witmer Stone, who also took the opportunity to lambaste the millinery trade:

> In your issue of January 14 there appeared a very misleading and erroneous statement regarding the extermination of plume birds for the millinery. The article was based upon the statement of a wholesale milliner, who says that because the supply of egrets is not diminished the birds are not being exterminated, and that all the talk about killing the birds on their nests is a mistake and no hunter would be so foolish.
>
> Statements like the above have found their way into a number of our papers, written in the interest of the millinery trade to counteract the prejudice against the use of wild birds for ornamentation which is being aroused by the Audubon societies.
>
> There is not one grain of truth in these statements. We have the unquestioned testimony of ornithologists and travelers of the highest authority as to the annihilation of the birds in Florida and elsewhere, where the plume traffic has been carried on for any length of time.
>
> The only reason that the supply continues undiminished is that there are still wild coasts in less frequented parts of the world where the birds can still be procured. As to killing the birds on their nesting-grounds, the matter has been proved beyond question. This is the only time of year when the plumes are worn, and anyone who has made any attempt to inquire into the question will find abundant confirmation of the shooting of the birds on their nests.[11]

Ample proof existed that heron feathers were in great demand. In April and May 1909 customs officers at New York seized $1,000 worth of aigrettes from herons. Normally, they would have been offered at auction but the National Audubon Society asked that they be destroyed instead.[12] The leaders did not want any aigrettes made available to milliners and consumers.

Collector Loeb submitted the request to the solicitor of the treasury, who answered it in a Solomonesque manner. He stated that the tariff laws in effect could not be affected or controlled by a protest from the Audubon Society or the statutes of New York State, but.... He ruled that the act of Congress allowed the destruction by assigning the plumage in question the same status as if the herons been taken and produced in New York. Under this interpretation, the solicitor decreed, the customs collector could destroy the aigrettes. The Audubon Society had gained one more ally and tool.

There was another bit of good news the following year. Herons, along with terns and laughing gulls, were on the rebound thanks to Louisiana.[13] There was a group of islands off the state's east coast where government protection provided the birds a safe home. The result of this protection was extraordinary.

Herbert K. Job wrote an article in *Harper's Magazine* to describe what he saw there.[14] Herons covered every inch of the ground. More important, many of them left the islands and started repopulating the surrounding coast. Hopefully, they would fare better than they had before with more protection.

Just when it seemed like the assault on white herons was over, there was another scare years later. In 1933 Pennsylvania's secretary of the state game commission, Ernest E. Harwood, ordered game wardens to increase their vigilance over the areas of the state inhabited by the American egret.[15] Two of the birds had been found with their wings crushed by shot.

36. White Herons and Birds of Paradise

Harwood issued a warning to hunters that anyone convicted of shooting egrets would be given maximum penalties. The crisis passed quickly. If the original crisis three decades had passed as quickly, the bird world would have been better off. It still wasn't out of the woods, though.

A fashion writer advised ladies in 1955 that "a bird perched on the side of your head for late day won't seem strange these days. An adaptation of a Paris design, a pale satin headband with a brightly feathered bird, with head pointing downward and wings spread, alighting on one side, is currently being seen."[16]

That may have caused a shudder among anti–bird slaughter crusaders. Fortunately, the passage was not a harbinger of things to come. The passage of birds on a large scale had come and finally gone. It had taken a long time, but people no longer had to worry about a world with no birds. Hopefully, they will never have to again.

37

The Ostrich

"He behaved like an ostrich and put his head in the sand, thereby exposing his thinking parts."

—George Carman

The downfall of ostriches, which had been a somewhat unappreciated mainstay of the millinery industry for decades, was hastened by nature and a war. They were excluded from most laws against bird slaughter because they did not have to die to sacrifice their feathers. So, as species after species was protected by law and their feathers, plumes, and parts were removed from the supply line, ostrich feathers became more important to milliners.

Consumers probably never gave much thought or thanks to the ostriches for their contributions to the millinery world. Neither did fashion designers, whose main concern was the supply line. They believed the supply was inexhaustible, since the ostriches did not have to die to give up their feathers. That made the bird unique in the avian and fashion worlds—and puzzling to some critics, who raised significant ethical arguments or rationalized about the killing of animals in general for humans' comfort. The ethicists argued:

> It is interesting to know that the Audubon ladies do not object to ostrich feather trimmings because they reason that to obtain ostrich feathers it is not necessary to kill the birds. But isn't it really carrying the idea of preserving life a little too far when one goes so far as to object to the killing of birds for ornament. Think if this idea were consistently carried out how inconvenient it would be. There would be no more kid gloves because it would be wicked to kill kids and kid gloves are not really necessary you know.
> There would be no heads or tails for fur trimmings and indeed if one were to be perfectly consistent one would be unwilling to wear fur at all unless it were made up in the plain style of wrap so that on no account could it be laid open to the indictment of being used for other purposes than warmth and warmth only.[1]

However, ethical arguments did not apply to ostriches. The one thing most people agreed on regarding ostriches was that they did not have to be killed for their feathers, so the ethical arguments were moot. Beyond that they did not know if ostriches were songbirds, leftover vestiges of dinosaurs, able to feel pain … it didn't matter as long as they provided plumes or feathers or whatever highlighted the displays on hats.

Rationalizers claimed that humans were actually doing ostriches a favor by removing their feathers.[2] The process gave them some relief in the warm weather in summer and caused them no further inconvenience than the growing of more feathers. So ostrich feathers were a perfectly legitimate millinery appendage. Nevertheless, people still had trouble justifying the use of ostrich feathers when so many other birds were dying to give up theirs.

37. The Ostrich
203

The confusion was manifested by a meeting at the aforementioned W.C.T.U. convention in Minneapolis, which engendered some curious conversations and votes.[3]

There was discussion of birds' feathers for millinery that was paused for a vote as a result of which one of the members who addressed the chair with ostrich feathers in her hat was ordered to remove them.

The delegates wrestled with the conundrum and settled it to their satisfaction. One of their conclusions was that ostriches were songbirds, according to a reporter who noted that it was the first time on record that ostriches were ever classified as such. But the attendees accepted the decision without question.

They also agreed that possessing attractive feathers tended to shorten the lives of the unfortunate birds that were killed to acquire them. Since they did, it was beneficial to pluck the deceased avians' feathers and to sell them to milliners to decorate women's bonnets. Some of the delegates intimated that the birds might need some form of legislative protection. That generated a passionate debate.

Mrs. Lovell, superintendent of the department of anti-vivisection, brought the subject before the convention in this resolution:

> In view of the wholesale destruction and threatened extinction of whole species of beautiful and useful song birds for millinery purposes, and the consequent rapid multiplication of insect pests and serious menace to the agricultural interests of our country and the world, and in view of the manifest inadequacy of moral suasion and aesthetic motives to prevent the wearing of birds and parts of birds on women's bonnets, that we earnestly pray that congress will pass a law prohibiting the sale, by hunters or milliners, of any bird plumage except ostrich feathers.
>
> I have observed that since our last convention women have gone back to the style of wearing birds' feathers in their bonnets, and I think it ought to be prevented.

"It is wicked to shoot birds," the influential delegate Anna Shaw stated. She was one of the most accomplished women and suffragettes of her time. She was a physician and one of the first ordained female Methodist ministers in the United States. "But I am opposed to women appealing to men to pass laws to regulate their wearing apparel." She specified men because there were no female senators or congressional representatives at the time.

"We should not be obliged to have any law passed and would not if we acted in accordance with the dictates of our conscience," Shaw concluded. "Such a request is not dignified. I am opposed to asking Congress to act."

Mrs. Upham moved an amendment to accept the recommendation for congressional action.

"We have game laws to protect birds," said Mrs. J.H. Lawton of Idaho.

"I did not understand that the meaning was to protect birds," said Mrs. Shaw, "but I say we should not appeal to Congress."

Then the delegates veered off in another direction.

"Is it a fact," asked Mrs. Walker of Nebraska, "that ostriches are hurt when their feathers are plucked?"

"The chair would rule that it is," replied Mrs. Stevens.

"But ostriches would become extinct if their feathers were not regularly plucked," a delegate in the rear of the church interjected.

This information surprised the delegates. A vote on the amendment was taken and it was lost.

That signaled a new topic once again.

The eclectic Anna Shaw (left), a leader of the U.S. women's suffrage movement, a physician, and one of the country's first ordained female Methodist ministers, hard at work with unidentified companion (Bain News Service, undated).

"Why is it wrong to wear songbird feathers?" asked Mrs. Loye of Pennsylvania, "and not to wear turkey feathers?"

No one had an answer to that question apparently, so they voted on Mrs. Lovell's resolution, which was carried by a vote of 106 to 27, and Congress would be asked to design women's bonnets in the future.[4]

But, the reporter advised, "the ostrich had better hide his head. He will soon be in demand." He may have written that in jest, but he was prescient.

Male ostriches had one thing in their favor when it came to having their feathers plucked. The females' feathers were more in demand because of their splendor, although the males' feathers were more durable. And no self-respecting woman would wear the Cadillac of the high hat, the Gainsborough, if it contained male ostrich feathers. And it had to be the big affair with sweeping plumes made famous and familiar by the pictures of the beautiful Duchess of Devonshire, not the modified version. The thought of anything less drove fashion writers to distraction.

Designers predicted that the Gainsborough hat would reign supreme in 1901's midsummer millinery. They promised that the Gainsborough carried out all in white would be most fashionable and dressy in the extreme. What woman could resist one based on the description, they asked?

> Rich sweeping white plumes on a hat lacelike and fine in texture is the acme of millinery beauty. But such hats are only appropriate with costumes equally rich and dressy

and for fashionable functions. It is to be hoped the public will not be treated to the sight of dust-covered and dingy-white Gainsboroughs with bedraggled, uncurled feathers, on street cars and afternoon shopping expeditions. The black Gainsborough will undoubtedly be the favorite with the majority of women. It is stylish, suitable for all occasions and quietly elegant.

There were drawbacks. Gainsboroughs weren't the best hats for beachgoers. It was every woman's ambition to own one, but "though she loudly proclaims its style and beauty, deep down in her heart are many misgivings as to what the plumes will look like after a few days at the shore. With straight draggled looking feathers, a Gainsborough is a parody."[5] That's where the new-fashioned ostrich entered the picture.

The fashion writers had some salient advice to Gainsborough wearers. When they bought their hats, they had to give careful scrutiny to the plumes. It was within their power as buyers to choose the plumes that would not lose their curl, which they could maintain at home if necessary. The choices were limited to the two kinds of ostrich plumes that were used by milliners: those from the male bird and those from the female.

The female ostriches' plumes were prettier and showier looking than the males.' The females' feathers were rather dull in appearance, had a fluffy look, and the fiber of each barb was much broader than that of the male. The thick, soft, fluffy-looking plumes were those of the female bird, but they lost all their prettiness in damp surroundings.

On the other hand, the writers noted, the feathers of the male bird at first glance had a cheap look, but they were shiny. Milliners were diplomatic when describing them: "they have a high luster."[6] Sadly, the barbs were thinner and narrower and there was none of that fuzz on them that gave the desired fluffy appearance. But the male feathers weren't all bad: they compensated for their lack of good looks through their durability. No amount of dampness or sudden thunderstorms could disturb their curliness.

If women were going to buy Gainsboroughs, they could pin their faith to the feathers of the male ostrich if they wanted tranquility and peace of mind. It was a good thing ostriches could not read or get offended by fashion writers' comments. It was their job to produce feathers and plumes.[7] That was all the women cared about. The lives of the birds were inconsequential. That was the story of the bird slaughter era.

If the women who bought the Gainsboroughs and other high hats had a prayer, it was this: "Lord, don't let the ostriches disappear. They are in our service and we need their feathers." To the supplicants' dismay, their prayers almost went unanswered. There was a temporary panic during World War I, when the supply of ostrich feathers was threatened. The concern among milliners was less about the supply than it was about the trend that fashion was going to take in the ostrich line.

Common sense dictated that the trend was irrelevant if the supply was inhibited. Designers never seemed to think about inhibited supplies, however. They were more inclined to think that if they designed millinery with a certain bird in mind the supply would be there to satisfy the fashion. That line of thinking was to blame in large part for the extinction or near disappearance of several species of birds. Nature did not follow the dictates of fashion. Nor did war makers.

Designers modified their plans when the war began secure in the knowledge that any shortages would be temporary. They recognized that there would be a spirited scramble for the diminishing supply of ostrich feathers among foreign buyers as soon as the belligerents resumed peaceful relations and reopened their closed markets. They anticipated better times in the European and American markets since European and American buyers of ostrich feathers would engage in the old competition and drive

206   The Hat That Killed a Billion Birds

prices up. That did not happen. Nature got revenge on the ostrich farmers and the millinery trade.

Ostriches were native to Africa, which was where many of the feathers were produced. Unfortunately, South Africa in particular was in the grips of a long drought that showed no signs of easing as World War I progressed. Farmers could not afford to feed their birds due to the drought. As a result they lost an estimated two-thirds of all the ostriches in the country. Experts suggested that even that estimate was too low.[8]

One South African farmer lost 900 out of 1,300 birds; another lost 693 out of a 700-bird flock. The loss of feathers dealt a severe blow to the millinery industry, which no longer had access to many of their reliable sources due to the war and increasing government regulations on bird slaughter. The future of murderous millinery was growing gloomier.

Transforming the ostrich feather from a crude to a beautiful form required the skills of a specialist rather than a less talented feather maker. There was not an abundance to work with. Ostrich feather production did not increase appreciably over the years. Significantly, although style had much to do with the demand, the supply was not found much in excess of the demand any year.

The entire crude production of Africa, which was exported from the Cape of Good Hope, was valued at $3,000,000 a year.[9] Egypt produced $1,000,000 worth, which constituted virtually the entire ostrich crop of the world. Other places where the ostrich was raised for its feathers could not be counted on because of the insignificance of the total results.

Mrs. L.S. Hertzberg established a breeding facility at Huntington, New York, for ostriches and other plumage birds. Her goal was to collect their feathers. She envisioned "doing with the ostrich work that has been done with the chrysanthemum."

She was at a loss as to how her plans became known. Mrs. Hertzberg did not want to build a conglomerate immediately. Rather, she intended to start on a small scale and work up quietly. Her true goal was to develop a technologically advanced plume made by stitching several ostrich feathers together.

"It should be possible to get ostrich plumes far heavier than they are today," she explained. "Several smaller birds used in millinery will be raised on the place. It seems to me that birds carefully raised for their plumage should produce feathers of a higher commercial value than can birds not so favored."[10]

Her goal was admirable, but there was some question regarding her plan for a small operation. If profit were a motive the return on investment might not have been worth the effort. She might as well have tried to obtain feathers from a chrysanthemum as an ostrich if she were trying to operate a money-making venture. There was money to be made in the business but not with a small scale operation.

Ostrich feathers in their crude state imported into the United States amounted to $1,250,000. They cost from $3 to $100 a pound. The job of dressing them was done mostly in New York City. Philadelphia was the only other place any dressing was done, and that was on a small scale.

There were 30 ostrich feather importers in New York, which combined employed about 2,000 women, each of whom made from $10 to $13 a week. Their wages varied with their skill levels, and they performed entirely on a "piece-work" basis. They worked from 8 a.m. to 5:30 p.m., just as the fancy feather makers did. Many of them put in several hours a night at home or in the factory. They earned an additional $3 to $5 a week.

The manager of the one large establishment claimed that it was almost impossible for her business to make a feather in excess of $7. That was the price at which the most beautifully made feathers were sold to the wholesale and commission salesmen, who in turn sold them to the retailers. At the end of the chain, by the time all the mark-ups were added in, ostrich plumes sold for as much as $30 apiece in some parts of the United States. Yet some women continued to buy millinery even at that price. The ostriches did not earn a penny from any of it, although they paid a terrible price for their contribution.

38

Game Wardens

"McLeod's death broke the logjam of opposition to prosecution of plume hunters. Laws in all states were given teeth and stiff fines levied against wholesale milliners."[1]

A great deal of the work people, mostly hunters, did on behalf of the millinery trade was illegitimate or, at best, shady. Pot hunters in particular were driven underground by mounting public opinion and laws against bird slaughter. That didn't stop them from operating. Among the key players in the battle to ferret out the illegal activities were game wardens. They did their job well, often at great risk to themselves.

Their work ranged from routine business checks to patrols in areas where hunters were likely to be involved in illegal activities. They performed detective services that resulted in surprises on occasion. In a New York case wardens were checking an Arctic freezing company's warehouse when they uncovered a cache of game birds that on closer inspection contained thousands of songbirds the company was passing off as something else.[2]

The collection contained birds that the wardens knew weren't supposed to be killed at any time of the year. The warehouse owner tried to convince them that they were left over from the previous open season and were being held in storage until the next season. That did not fool the wardens, who transported a few of the dead birds to an ornithologist for a species identification. The expert identified them as "fledgling high-holes," which were common to the area. The dealers had been palming them off to unsuspecting customers as snipes or squab pigeons. That was a violation of game laws as well as a gustatory affront to the public.

States varied in their hiring practices. In Arkansas all sheriffs, deputies, constables and their deputies were ex officio game wardens.[3] It was their job to arrest all violators of the state's game laws. As a bonus, they got to keep all the fines collected from violators. That incentive worked against violators, whose pocketbooks provided open invitations to the "wardens" to enforce the law.

Virginia's system was a hodgepodge.[4] In 1904 there were 61 counties without game wardens. The following year the number was down to 36. The number of wardens jumped from 61 to 96 between 1904 and 1905. Some were paid, some were not. Some were hired by the county, some by the state. Some were regulars, some were special. There was one commonality. There weren't enough of them.

The lack of wardens prevented any consistent enforcement of game protection in the state, which did not bode well for the birds. The state wardens in particular weren't sure about their sphere of authority.[5] They were dubious about their power to enforce both county and Virginia game laws.

It wasn't until 1917 that state game commissioner John S. Parsons clarified that they could. He sent a letter to attorney general John Garland Pollard asking if state game wardens could enforce both. Pollard ruled that the wardens had a duty to do so. That didn't increase the number of wardens in Virginia.

Some states, such as Minnesota, didn't have the money to hire game wardens.[6] There, game laws had to be enforced by gun clubs working with wardens who were paid on a fee basis. Early in 1914 the state fish and game commission had only $6,000 available to fund its expenses. That didn't leave any money to hire game wardens. In an all too familiar scenario, the state had collected $38,000 in hunting licenses that year, but the money went into Minnesota's general fund. That gave pot hunters a license to kill birds with impunity, with or without a license.

Maine was ahead of its time. One of the state's wardens had a dog named Scip, whose unerring ability to uncover poachers was legendary.[7] One of his best-known apprehensions occurred when he sniffed a barrel marked fish and "pointed" it out to his partner.

The warden did not believe that Scip was correct in suggesting that the barrel contained anything other than finny creatures. But he trusted the dog. The barrel contained some fresh caught cod—and a couple dozen plump partridges hunters were trying to smuggle outside the state in violation of Maine's hunting laws.

That was an important find, but it was just one small arrest among a large number of illegal hunting activities. It proved that game wardens played a vital role in stemming bird hunting violations, but they could not stop the slaughter by themselves. That could only be done by a coordinated effort among law enforcement authorities backed by comprehensive legislation and a judicial system that backed them up. Such coordination was lacking in the United States in the first decade of the 1900s, but the wardens did they best they could.

Sometimes people expected a little more from game wardens than they could deliver or gave them too much credit. When the bird slaughter crisis reached a point of no return status in Texas in 1910, Pennsylvania newspaper editors hinted that all the Lone Star State's officials needed to do was employ a few game wardens. After all, they had all but saved Pennsylvania from losing all its birds.

The Texas Audubon Society issued an appeal to the people of the state to insist upon effective enforcement of the laws for the protection of the birds and wild animals. The society intimated that if they didn't there wouldn't be any birds or wild animals left to protect. The spokespeople asserted that at the present rate of destruction, unless something effective was done within five years, all of them would be gone.

The society stressed the necessity of enforcement of existing laws rather than the passing of new ones. The dire plea was based on a unique circumstance: the rapid increase of immigrants in Texas who were allegedly disposed to kill every bird that flew, either through ignorance of the law or disregard of its penalties. That was what the Pennsylvania editors inferred, which prompted them to offer unsolicited advice based on their state's experience.

They stated that the Texas warning was a timely one and was in line with the experience of Pennsylvania and other states in their attempts to protect the birds and game. They explained that in Pennsylvania the law against the indiscriminate slaughter of songbirds was usually and rigidly enforced through a "hit 'em in the pocketbook" process.

"The newly arrived foreigner with his gun is quite as prone in Pennsylvania to killing robins and flickers as in Texas, but our game wardens have made this a very costly form of law breaking by rigorous infliction of fines," the editors observed. "The man who has paid $10 apiece for slaughtering a half a dozen robins is not likely to do it again."

The claim was accurate as the game wardens in other states had proved. And there was no reason that approach couldn't work elsewhere, they averred. It had saved Pennsylvania's bird population from disappearing, thanks to the game wardens. The result of the strict enforcement was a perceptible increase of state's robins, thrushes, and other songbirds.

"Indiscriminate bird slaughter can be halted in any commonwealth altogether whenever public sentiment demands it," the editors concluded. "Game laws will not enforce themselves anywhere, but game wardens that make it costly to shoot the birds can put an end to their slaughter in a very brief period."[8]

If the solution were that easy, every state would have employed scores of game wardens immediately. Some would have had to hire guards to protect the wardens, since game wardens, particularly in the southern states, were putting themselves at risk of death in doing their jobs, for which they were paid a mere pittance. Since many states did not employ their own wardens, the Audubon Society did it for them.

The society got six wardens deputized to police violations in the south. They were authorized to serve warrants and arrest illegal hunters. The society paid them $35 a month (about $1,040 in today's values) and equipped each of them with a boat to conduct their operations. The money wasn't an issue for the wardens. Essentially, they were volunteers. They performed their jobs because they believed in a need for their services.

Two wardens were appointed in Florida. Guy M. Bradley was assigned to Flamingo to patrol the Florida Keys and the Everglades. Columbus G. (George) McLeod was posted to police the rookeries in northern Charlotte Harbor. Both sacrificed their lives in the line of duty.

Three wardens were brutally murdered between 1905 and 1908 in southern states during the performance of their duties.[9] Bradley was the first. A notorious plume hunter named Walter Smith shot and killed him on July 8, 1905. Smith encountered Bradley trying to arrest his son on the family's schooner for killing birds illegally. Bradley's body was found floating in his aptly named boat *Audubon* two days later.

Smith was apprehended but not indicted. He pleaded self-defense and was not charged. He did not escape justice completely. His enraged neighbors burned down the Smith family house and set out to lynch Walter and his sons. They got away safely.

The next warden murdered was L.P. Reeves, near Branchville, South Carolina. His murderer was not convicted either. Nor was that of McLeod, the third warden murdered. He was slain on November 30, 1908. His body was never found, and there was no proof that his murder was connected to his work as a warden, although anecdotal evidence suggested strongly that it was.

Authorities located his boat at the bottom of the harbor, weighed down by two heavy sandbags. In it they found his hat, which had two long gashes apparently cut with an ax. The cuts contained bits of hair and a considerable amount of blood. They theorized that McLeod's body had been in the boat, broken loose, floated out to sea, and was eaten by flesh-eating fish.

McLeod's gruesome death highlighted how determined bird killers were to preserve their illegal activities rather than save the avians. They also succeeded in forcing the Audubon Society to stop appointing game wardens in western Florida. The sad fact was that there were fewer plume birds in Florida at the time of the wardens' murders than there were when Bradley was assigned. That was a step back for the society and game wardens but it was not a game changer.

Even though the wardens' collective vigilance had virtually eliminated every large plume and feather operation in the south, they were not particularly effective against the private individuals who were determined to make a living trading plumes, feathers, and bird parts. Their deaths had some meaning, though; they heightened citizens' awareness of the need for legislation to protect the birds. There were no more murders of wardens after McLeod died, but the memories of the three wardens who had given their all were enough to push additional legislation regarding hunting regulations. Significantly, most of it was endorsed by legitimate hunters.

The new laws, specious as they were at times, combined with the introduction of bird sanctuaries, provided hope that the ongoing extinction of American water fowl and songbirds would decline. It was a start. But the depredations of the previous decade had been so severe that it would take many years of protection to replace the lost birds. There was no question in the minds of scientists that despite all the measures being taken in the first decade of the 1900s that there were some species whose numbers had been so depleted that they would never again be seen in large numbers. That was thanks in no small part to the hunters who were killing and selling birds.

39

The Hunters

"Those who kill the bird cannot be rightly attacked. They simply supply a demand. The reform in this matter lies with the women who have adopted this fashion."[1]

Killing birds for plumage, feathers, and parts was a lucrative business for hunters, who fell into several categories. Some were legitimate, some were not. Some were ethical, some were not. Some hunted in the country, some hunted in the city. Most of them were driven by the dollar to kill birds by whatever method.

The work paid well—so well, in fact—that some people left their regular jobs to hunt birds. The pleasure boatmen at Barnegat and Beach Haven, New Jersey, stopped boating to earn $50 a week killing terns at 10 cents apiece, together with crow blackbirds, red-winged blackbirds and snow buntings.[2] In a New York wholesale hat store 20,000 skins of those birds were offered for sale at one time.

Aigrettes were worth their weight in gold. Spoonbills, ibises, breeding plovers, sandpipers, terns, boat tailed blackbirds, gray ring-birds, owls and hawks brought from 10 cents to $1 a carcass and from 20 cents to 12.50 a skin. Other prices included gulls, 10 cents; egrets (back feathers), 40 cents; snowy herons (back, breast, head), 40 cents; Ardea rufa, a reddish egret (back), 40 cents; Ardea ruficolli, a red-breasted egret (back), 10 to 15 cents; Ward's herons (head and back), 75 cents; and roseate spoonbills (whole skin), $2.00 to $2.50.

Birds were at such a premium for hunters that they didn't have to leave the comfort of their city homes to earn significant pay. A professional bird catcher in Burlington, Iowa, in one week captured and killed a large number of beautiful songsters.[3] He claimed to be under contract to furnish Eastern wholesale millinery houses with red birds, which were his favorite prey. He revealed that he had made as much as $2,800 in one year trapping birds.

A hunter didn't have to be a professional—or even hunt. An amateur could get paid for feathers even in small amounts. Arthur Tate of Brattleboro, Vermont, owned a pet peacock that was not only an attraction to the village for two or three summers but also a "working pet."[4] His feathers were in great demand and brought him a good price at the local millinery stores. Sadly, the bird died. Tate gave him a fitting send-off. He had the bird mounted. Ironically, his plumage was at its best at the time. No wonder Tate lamented his loss—as did the local milliners.

Milliners who were sometimes willing to turn a blind eye to where their material came from paid hunters well for the products they delivered. Their returns on investment were guaranteed as long as consumers were willing to pay high prices for the millinery they sold. The whole business was based on money.

39. The Hunters

A good hunting day at Black Dog Lake, ca. 1890 (T.W. Ingersoll, photographer).

The millinery industry could not have thrived without hunters. The most necessary for milliners were the market hunters, the commercial professionals who killed birds by the thousands in single operations, sometimes outside the parameters of whatever laws existed, just to trade their flesh, parts, feathers, and plumes. The numbers told the tale.

In 1896 the plumage of 3,000,000 birds arrived in New York City.[5] A year later a single New York milliner employed 40–60 hunters to kill herons and egrets off the coast of Florida. It was not uncommon for a single hunter to kill 100 birds a day for days at a time. Multiply the number for each hunter by 40, 50, or 60, and it is easy to see why herons and egrets in North America all but disappeared as a species. The record for one hunter was purportedly 141,000 birds in a season.[6] The numbers may have been in the millions, not thousands, as some members of the millinery industry claimed they were.

"Any person who notices these aigrette plumes waving not singly, but often in clusters, on the heads of so many women, must know that the slaughter has not been by thousands, but by millions," one editor commented.[7] All evidence backed up that claim.

It was not uncommon for plumage hunters in Oregon to earn from $400 to $500 a day when white herons were plentiful in the state. The plumes sold wholesale at $32 to

The Hat That Killed a Billion Birds

$50 an ounce.[8] It took the plumes from four birds to make an ounce. The hunters became victims of their own success. They slaughtered the sources of their income, but it was good while it lasted. The last white heron was seen in Oregon around Lake Klamath in June of 1909, a lonesome symbol of a disappearing species.[9]

The market hunters' brethren, recreational or subsistence hunters, aka sportsmen, killed birds to provide food for themselves and their families. Occasionally they sold their kills to earn a few dollars. They did not pose much of a threat to the bird population.

Pot hunters, who did not care about game laws, operated in the shadows. They killed birds for the money and nothing else. It took a while before government officials recognized that they were a problem group who gave other hunters a bad name. Pennsylvania was one of the first states to attempt to rein them in.[10]

The state passed a new game law in 1897 that affected pot hunters at least tangentially. One important clause of the bill prohibited the shipping of game from the state limits and put a stop to the selling of game killed in Pennsylvania at any market or by any dealer. That was the feature of the bill that the framers hoped would prevent pot hunters from devastating the forests of mammals and birds.

Statistics showed that during the last few years prior to 1897 certain hunters in various portions of the state had slaughtered thousands of dollars' worth of game. That woke up the state's sportsmen, who realized that pot hunting would have to be stopped or there would be no opportunity for them to hunt occasionally. Consequently, the Pennsylvania Sportsman's Association endorsed the new bill.

Pot hunters were not only harmful to the entire hunting industry, but they were at times dangerous to anyone who tried to stop them. A Connecticut lighthouse keeper, "Captain" Oliver N. Brooks, demonstrated how devastating their operations could be to the bird population.[11] More important, he proved that individuals could make a difference in the struggle to protect and restore the bird population.

Brooks, a lighthouse keeper at Faulkner Island off the coast of Connecticut, was a bird lover. He bought a small uninhabited island resort for wild birds named Goose Island, situated near Faulkner, when he learned that pot hunters were overrunning it and decimating the bird population there. He banished the pot hunters and the bird population recovered in numbers so great that their collective noisemaking was loud enough in rough weather to warn passing boats they were too near land.

There were gamekeepers, young boys, and farmers who killed birds because they considered them vermin, pests, or targets. Collectively they wreaked havoc on the bird population across the globe. The young boys in particular were a menace. They were one of two primary reasons the ladies of Winona, Minnesota, organized an Audubon Society.[12] One was to prevent the wanton destruction of birds by boys; the other was to discourage the use by ladies in their millinery of birds, birds' wings, aigrettes and the like.[13]

The boys were not much of a threat to game birds with their slingshots and peashooters. Besides, the game birds were protected to some extent by law because their destruction during nesting seasons would profoundly affect food markets and sportsmen. Boys were more likely to kill robins, meadowlarks, thrushes, and other field birds, and what laws existed to protect them were not enforced. Therefore, "the murderous small boy who is only happy when he is killing or torturing something can kill as many birds as his skill, which, providentially, is as undeveloped as his sympathy, will permit," a journalist said.[14] That was a serious indictment on the damage caused by boys on the bird world.

39. The Hunters

Not all the hunters had nefarious goals. Some were sportsmen who shot birds legitimately for their meat. Scientists killed a limited number of them for research purposes. There was no cap on the number of birds killed for the sake of murderous millinery, but millions of birds ended up in their entirety or in parts on caps, despite crusaders' efforts to protect them. Sometimes they couldn't protect their own birds.

Fruit grower L.J. Johnson of Vancouver, Washington, shot birds just to protect his crops.[15] Technically, he wasn't a hunter. He made it clear that despite laws against it to the contrary, he was going to shoot Chinese pheasants that threatened his strawberries. Johnson was of the opinion that laws protecting the bird had become so numerous that they favored the birds over his valuable crops. So he served notice on deputy game warden Elmer Barbeau that he would shoot the next birds he saw in his strawberry patch. He explained that he had found numerous berries pecked into by the festive game bird with the millinery plumage, and it made him mad. Other hunters empathized with him.

At the annual meeting of the Society for the Protection of Birds held in 1903 at the Westminster Palace Hotel in London, the Duke of Bedford said he hoped that a recently passed education bill might have a beneficial effect on the efforts of the society to protect birds.[16] The duke revealed that he had lost an Amherst pheasant, shot by a boy with a catapult, and that a flamingo and two Manchurian cranes which had left his park were "collected" in Yorkshire and Lincolnshire.

He was not happy about the needless loss of his birds and he admitted the murderous propensities of a boy with a catapult were difficult to repress. The "collector," who operated in both scientific and commercial capacities, was a great terror. Other speakers echoed his sentiments.

The Duchess of Somerset called attention to the murderous millinery which had for many years been deprecated by the society. Canon Lyttelton and Mr. Bosworth Smith spoke long and eloquently, amid frequent applause, about the protection of birds. They also touched on the ruthless destruction of birds of prey by gamekeepers, by whom they were classed as vermin. They were also desirable targets for hunters, since milliners valued their feathers and parts and accepted their deaths as the price of doing business.

40

Birds Don't Have to Die When They Can Be Dyed

"The egret, the bird of paradise, the red, yellow, green and blue parrots, and the hundreds of other brilliantly colored aristocrats of the feathered world cannot contribute a bit more beauty to milady's bonnet than the barnyard hen, duck, goose, pigeon or pheasant, once they have passed through the dye vats of the chemist."

—F.L. Lewton[1]

Winston Churchill advised people to never let a good crisis go to waste. That applied to the murderous millinery crisis. One of the ways people of the time tried to deal with it was to seek alternatives to killing birds. Americans have never been short of ideas in the middle of a crisis. The bird slaughter era was no exception.

One solution was the use of artificial animal eyes, which were available for a variety of uses.[2] Both bird and animal eyes were used in mounting birds for millinery trimming, for the heads in fur rugs, in cane and umbrella beads made in imitation of animals, and for many kinds of toys. Artificial eyes were also made for living animals. It was not uncommon for horses and dogs to have glass eyes, and in at least one case a calf had been supplied with one. For the most part, they were used in mounting natural specimens.

The eyes were created in imitation of nature, and many of them were beautiful. Manufacturers and milliners kept stocks on hand in a wide variety. There was no artificial eye that could not be supplied. There were hummingbirds' eyes, alligators' eyes, swans' eyes, and eyes for owls, eagles ... for birds of all kinds and species.

The artificial eyes for birds and animals were sold primarily to milliners and furriers. They were usually sold in pairs, and sales were huge. The busiest seasons were fall and winter. Artificial eyes couldn't replace birds' feathers, plumes, and parts, but they were useful in the creative process. At least hunters didn't have to kill birds just for their eyes.

Audubon Society representatives were apt to visit fancy feather factories to talk to the workers and examine the material used in constructing the birds, parts, feathers, and other decorations that appeared on hats. One of their primary interest was the feathers. They gained some interesting information, not all of which could be verified or trusted.

An Audubonist asked the forewoman of a large factory about the origin of several large boxes of peculiar-looking feathers awaiting processing. The woman explained that they were all chicken feathers from which, after they had been dyed, the workers made breasts, blackbirds, cock feathers, and ostrich plumes. She picked up a sweeping fold

40. Birds Don't Have to Die When They Can Be Dyed

of what appeared to be the breast of some white and brown bird of rich plumage, a tiny blackbird, a smart tuft of shining cock feathers and a plume which would vie with the handsomest an ostrich would grow to demonstrate the process.

They are first assorted and then dyed, she explained, while she directed the placing of two little legs in a very small blackbird, which a novice was battling with:

> The feathers which compose this breast were originally a drab brown from a very common type of chicken and are those which grow, as you will see by their shape, under the wings and around the breast and back.
>
> The feathers in the blackbird are generally pigeon feathers, but they grow small enough on some parts of the chicken for the coat of a blackbird. The long, fine feathers from the tail of the chicken compose the cock feathers. This year we are producing a feather designed as a substitute for an ostrich plume. Here is a specimen.

She held up a long, rich, lustrous plume with curled edges. The visitor had a hard time believing that the plume was constructed from the neck feathers of roosters. She noted that there was scarcely any difference in the thousands of layers composing the plume, and each one was put in place by skilled fingers.

As the Audubonist continued her tour she saw workers in various parts of the workroom painting wings and quills with bright splashes of color. They were shaping sea gull, pheasant, and grebe breasts as quickly as nimble fingers could maneuver their needles. Other young girls were assorting eagle feathers by length and color. They were popular trimmings on street hats at the time.

The forewoman said proudly that very few American birds were used in that factory. According to her, the crude material used in the manufacture of fancy feathers came almost exclusively from abroad, although some came from Chicago. Her breakdown was illuminating:

> China contributes the largest amount, and next, perhaps, Germany.
>
> The duty is 15 per cent.
>
> Goose, chicken, duck, turkey and pigeon feathers constitute the variety utilized from barnyard fowls, domestic and foreign. The great bulk comes from Germany, France and Italy.
>
> Texas contributes large numbers of gulls, whose breasts will adorn many handsome hats this winter, and Japan and China contribute pelican and turkey quills.
>
> The South American grebe are also imported in immense quantities from Russia and California.
>
> Tropical countries export birds of bright plumage in great quantities, and their feathers undergo no change of color.[3]

Those facts seemed like a red herring as she declared that no songbirds were used in her factory. That may have been true in her facility but not elsewhere. A catalogue of one auction sale in London included thousands of small birds and wings dyed every color of the rainbow to satisfy the demand of domestics, factory operatives, and the less wealthy generally. That provided a faint idea of the slaughter of birds necessary to fill millinery demands, including dyed songbirds from around the globe.

The list of birds that were included and the countries from which they came were revealing. There were a lot of birds being killed somewhere and ending up as millinery adornments. That was the heart of the matter.

"The song bird is really not bright and pretty enough to employ as an ornament, and his feathers are too few to make his killing worthwhile without the coloring," the forewoman explained. "The skins and wings of game birds, plover, partridge, grouse, woodcock and other edible varieties which are killed in season we find little occasion to change, as their natural color is most desirable for walking hats. These are used in great quantities."

Finally, she implied that as long as barnyard feathers were available and dyed, no songbirds were used, and the raw products used to make millinery adornments were imported, there was no bird slaughter crisis. Chickens, turkeys, ducks, and barnyard fowl in general were the answer to the problem if only milliners would capitalize on their feathers, which could be dyed and processed to suit everyone's needs. She concluded:

> So, you see, out of waste material birds of gay plumage of every variety are made. Chicken feathers and coloring stuff are remarkable materials when you place them in the hands of a skilled workman. No bird is impossible to the worker.
>
> She has a sample before her, and that is all that is necessary. If there were a systematic business in crude feathers of domestic poultry and game done in this country as there is abroad, there would be found money in it. Some little attention is given this business in Chicago, but when we want great quantities we must send abroad to procure them.[4]

There may have been an element of truth in what she said, but consumers still preferred genuine feathers, so the slaughter went on apace.

41

Those Who Refuse to See
the Birds for the Trees

"The Fur Company may be called the exterminating medium of these wild and almost uninhabitable regions, which cupidity or the love of money alone would induce man to venture into. Where can I now go and find nature undisturbed?"

—John James Audubon[1]

Rationalization ran rampant in the minds of many people involved in the millinery trade regarding the fates of birds destined to spend their premature afterlives atop hats. There were people who swore that no birds were harmed in the production of those hats. Others claimed that the birds would have died whether or not they eventually became hat ornaments. The only people they had to convince with such arguments were themselves.

One journalist scolded the bird slaughter rationalizers:

It is of no avail for any intelligent woman to excuse herself for wearing bird plumage on the plea that most, or many of the milliners' birds are manufactured, for such is not the case. And there are few credulous to believe that there are a "horsehair kind of aigrettes that look exactly like real ones," or that the birds' plumage offered them consists only of such feathers as have been dropped by birds in flight. [2]

Yet those were the types of ideas milliners wanted women to believe and perpetuate. Denial that birds were slaughtered was a common ploy among milliners. They swore that birds were safe from milliners. Their arguments were disingenuous as defenders of the industry insisted that birds were not threatened just because a few dead ones ended up decorating hats. Some could be saved.

"Not ten percent of the birds or parts of birds used in millinery are song birds or parts of song birds," the *Millinery Trade Review* declared in 1898. "But 75 percent are imported from China and Japan and are killed for their destructiveness, and the balance are feather of birds used for food."[3]

"The idea that the wearing of wings, breasts and other feather ornaments on women's millinery necessitates the wholesale slaughter of birds is all bosh," one manufacturer of feather goods declared loudly in 1906.

He admitted that

once in a while a fashion comes in that calls for a particular feather or quill that only one bird produces, but wings, breasts and even the whole birds are made from the feathers plucked from poultry dressed for table use. We take bales of feathers, sort them, dye them, brush them, curl them, and work them up into whatever is wanted, and not a bird's life is sacrificed.[4]

Physician William W. Arnold, better known as an ornithologist, with two bird patients at his hospital for disabled wild birds (ca. June 16, 1919).

He did not define "once in a while," nor did he explain how the particular feathers or quills were obtained. Those details might have been of interest to people trying to protect birds. The statement also hinted at the constantly changing fashion styles, which placed stress on different species of birds as designers changed their preferences. Denial was an effective tool, and it was used over and over again as the decades passed.

41. Those Who Refuse to See the Birds for the Trees

William Wilson of Wantagh, New York, claimed to be the largest dealer in the United States for stuffed birds for hats in this country—and that was after a major fire destroyed his factory in November 1899. The timing was not good for Wilson.

The news account was terse:

> A factory at this place, where the skins and plumage of birds were prepared for the purpose of ornamenting women's hats, was destroyed. The establishment was the largest of its kind in the United States, and had agents in the South and at numerous other places engaged in shooting or trapping birds for millinery purposes.... The immediate loss occasioned by the fire is placed at $5,000, but the damage to Mr. Wilson's business just at this time when the busy season had begun will be very much larger. He will rebuild the plant at once. The factory was 100×50 feet, one story high, and built of wood.[5]

The underlying question was why the fire had occurred when it did. Only a few weeks earlier his stock of birds and wings had been very low, but he had just received some big shipments of valuable bird skins preparatory to beginning the active season of preparation for the spring demands and especially on the Easter hat trade. Thousands of these skins were destroyed, but the setback was only temporary.

Normally, Wilson employed 50 people, and he would have increased his force before the Christmas holidays. The stock on hand at the time of the fire included 10,000 stuffed sea gulls, 20,000 wings of various other birds, and 10,000 heads of birds, representing many varieties from the beautiful plumed birds of the south to the plain Long Island crow. The resources of the establishment had been severely taxed during the past year to provide long wings and single feathers, and numerous special hunters were sent out to provide a supply of those birds that would meet that demand.

Wilson's business found a use for every kind of bird. Even guinea hens were used. Sometimes special styles of trimmings were made by combining the head and body of one bird with the wings and tail feathers of others. Luckily for him, some of his stock escaped the fire. He had live birds in the factory in a small apartment. Workers set out cages and caught several of them, including several fancy pigeons that were used in the preparation of a line of high-class hat ornaments. Wilson's business would survive, even if the birds didn't.

"I probably handle more birds than any other three men in the business," he boasted. And he made no bones about the fact that he was providing an important service both by employing people and supplying birds for a variety of uses. Wilson claimed that he employed 20 men to skin and stuff birds for the millinery market. But, he said, nearly all of his birds were purchased in the market, skinned, their wings cut off, and resold to restaurateurs and hotel keepers.

He explained proudly:

> During the past year I have handled about twenty thousand wild ducks, mostly teal, broadbills, mallards and shell drakes, which were purchased in the markets of Washington, Baltimore and New York. All of these birds were killed for the market and would have been killed just the same, even though it were not fashionable for the ladies to wear feathers on their hats.
>
> I might add that all of these were resold after being skinned, for table purposes. The same is true of the thousands of snipe and other game birds which are handled in the millinery line; the birds are killed for the market, and will continue to be killed, whether or not fashion calls for the use of feathers in the millinery art.
>
> The pigeons, which are used quite extensively, are purchased at the markets and from the sporting clubs, but the principal trade commodity is the wings of ducks and other game birds,

which are chopped off by the marketmen and sold to me in large quantities. No song birds are killed for millinery.[6]

Ornithologists employed to identify birds on the thousands of hats for sale in New York disagreed. They reported that larks, robins, blackbirds, bluebirds, swallows, wrens, hummingbirds, terns, and gulls were used. Moreover, they attested, there was evidence that the songbirds of New England had been appreciably diminished, as many sources had pointed out correctly. They refuted Wilson's claim about no songbirds being killed for millinery purposes by using a simple method: look at the hats.

The ornithologists said the argument could be settled entirely by examining the wings and birds that decorate the hats. They were real. That did not impress Wilson or other dealers and taxidermists whose business had been affected adversely by the increasing outcry from the public for the protection of songbirds. Wilson was not backing down, however.

Newspaper reporters exposed Wilson by publishing his address in Wantagh, Nassau County, New York, which did not seem to faze him. He invited anyone who had questions about his business to contact him. They knew where he lived, thanks to the media.

Wilson said he kept a record of all the birds his business handled and he offered to furnish to anyone interested in songbirds and their preservation any further information about them. He was convinced he wasn't do anything wrong, and he was willing to try to convince everyone else as well, even if some of his arguments were based on rationalization. He was by no means alone in employing that strategy. But people across the globe were catching on.

42

The Campaign Goes International

"Only by putting a stop to the export and import of birds butchered for commercial purposes can the nations of the earth hope to retain their valuable bird resources. It remains for the American people to take the first step in this very vital movement for the international protection of our birds."

—William Dutcher[1]

People hardly noticed when the insidious bird slaughter era began. There was little or no recognition from country to country that the loss of birds was global. Communications were limited between countries and it took a while before government officials, business owners, milliners, and other stakeholders discovered that there was a problem brewing. It took almost a quarter-century before international cooperation, instigated by the Audubon Society, to address the slaughter became paramount.[2]

In July 1910 William Dutcher presented recommendations for the prohibition of feather traffic by non-export and non-import laws to U.S. Secretary of State Henry Knox. Dutcher's goal was to bring together 14 nations to address the murderous millinery problem. In addition to the United States they included Great Britain, Germany, France, Italy, Russia, Norway, Sweden, Belgium, Denmark, Holland, Hungary, Austria, and Bavaria.

Dutcher had just represented the United States at the International Ornithological Congress in Berlin, Germany, where delegates from every part of the world had framed and unanimously endorsed the recommendation. The initiative itself was not new. The international cooperation was novel. England and several other foreign nations were already considering this urgent call of the world's ornithologists. The representatives expected that the United States would take the lead in the effort to preserve the wild birds that saved the crops and health of people across the globe.

The mutual effort marked the first time that ornithological experts united in a simple course of action to check the wanton slaying of wild birds. They didn't act out of sympathy for the birds necessarily. Their goal was a byproduct of the "follow the money" theory behind every serious attempt to address a problem affecting numerous countries' economies.

Government officials had realized that the loss of wild land and water birds led to an increase in the numbers of pests attacking crops and the resulting economic costs. There were ample studies available detailing those costs. One pointed out in 1912— long after experts thought they had a handle on saving the birds—that one-fourth of all

223

224   **The Hat That Killed a Billion Birds**

cultivated crops were destroyed by insect pests, which meant that farmers and consumers paid 25 percent more for them than they would but for their depredations.

This condition increased in direct proportion to the decrease in the bird population, which people were still slaughtering for food, for millinery, or for fun. "The great bird army was one of this nation's greatest resources, but, like our forests and our fauna, it has been wasted for 'fun,'" a critic noted. "And we 'pay the fiddler' by giving up, each year, one-fourth of the greatest farm crop produced by any nation. Such fun comes high."[3]

The fewer the birds to control the pests, the more damage the crops and the economies suffered. The losses amounted to billions of dollars each year. It was a "chicken vs. the egg" conundrum. If the "chickens" died and there were fewer eggs available to reproduce avian species, the insects would prevail and humanity would suffer. The alliance between government and ornithology was born out of exigency, then.

It was generally conceded by both groups that bird slaughter and sale for millinery purposes was the chief cause for the threatened extinction of valuable bird life. That was Dutcher's primary argument at the Berlin conclave and to Knox. He stressed that local and national programs like rational shooting laws and acquainting the public with the value of birds that the U.S. Congress had been advocating were a start, but they were not helpful globally. What was needed were coordinated efforts with world powers for the prohibition of export, import, purchase or sale of the plumes of wild birds for millinery purposes.

The first step was the inevitable committee to study the problem. About 20 well-known ornithological experts formed the "International Committee for the Protection of Birds." Dutcher and Dr. Palmer represented the United States. The members, selected from the aforementioned 14 nations, submitted to their individual governments the proposition of cooperation to break up the destruction of bird life by the worldwide traffic in feathers. It was a start.

The committee members pressed their governments with a simple argument: although they had programs in place to extend reasonable protection to their birds, their bird life would continue to decline as long as other nations offered markets for their native feathers, plumes, parts, etc. That was particularly true in the United States, which had a patchwork of bird protection laws in place along state lines. As Dutcher observed eloquently, domestic and international patchwork approaches were not going to resolve the bird slaughter crisis:

> Americans need the help of the great world powers, as every other people need our help to check the destruction of the birds who work for our common prosperity and health. On the other hand, thousands of the valuable insectivorous wild birds and game birds of Europe are shipped here as cage birds and to make choice tidbits in our restaurants.
>
> Only by putting a stop to the export and import of birds butchered for commercial purposes can the nations of the earth hope to retain their valuable bird resources. It remains for the American people to take the first step in this very vital movement for the international protection of our birds.[4]

The American people did, and they were joined by their counterparts in other countries. In 1922 T. Gilbert Pearson founded an organization known today as BirdLife International, a worldwide alliance of nongovernmental organizations to promote the conservation of birds and their habitats. Over the years similar organizations and treaties have been implemented, such as the International Convention on the Protection of

Birds (1950), Partners in Flight (1990), and the Agreement on the Conservation of Albatrosses and Petrels (2001). Bird species are more protected than ever, and the murderous millinery era has faded into history.

There is no longer a threat of a world without birds—but civilization came perilously close to one a little over a century ago. Hopefully, that was a one-time thing.

Epilogue: One Good "Tern" Deserves Another

"A society known as the Dublin Society for the Protection of Birds has just been formed with the object of directing public attention to the destruction of wild birds as well as to protest against the wearing of egret plumes and other forms of bird decoration in millinery."[1]

There were some species of birds that made it through the slaughter era due mainly to last-minute intercessions by conservationists and government agencies. They included terns, white herons, and the bird of paradise. Sadly, it was too late for other species like the passenger pigeon and the great auk, which exist today only in natural history museums and bird anthologies. The fact that more did not disappear was nothing short of a miracle.

Technology had a lot to do with the preservation of some species, as F.L. Lewton, the curator of textiles of the National Museum in Washington, D.C., pointed out.[2] He arranged a special exhibit designed to teach the American public that egrets, birds of paradise, parrots, and other brilliantly colored birds used during the murderous millinery era could not contribute more beauty to women's hats than did the feathers of the common barnyard fowl once they had passed through dye vats.

His message was simple: the art of camouflaging features had made remarkable advances during the past few years, so that the difference between a bird of paradise plume and one plucked from a tame bird without injury to the creature could be distinguished only by an expert.

The exhibit was of significant historical value, but it was too little, too late for the millions of birds that had been slaughtered before the value of dye to the millinery trade was discovered. And part of that history was still alive since some women were still wearing bird-adorned millinery that did not contain dyed fowl feathers. For the most part, however, the murderous millinery era had passed.

The presentation was as brilliant as some of the feathers displayed. The feathers of the most attractive jungle birds were placed side by side with those of farm fowls. The feathers were real. Dr. H.C. Oberholser of the Biological Survey had donated to the museum about $20,000 worth of feathers confiscated by the federal government. That was just a small part of the survey's collection, which was valued at more than $100,000, equivalent to the feathers of 1,000 birds. The feathers of a single bird were often worth more than $100.

The larger part of the material displayed consisted of whole birds, plumes of the bird of paradise and of the American and snowy egret, and parts of birds consisting of the wing feathers and head. Other birds represented were the goura, roseate

228 **Epilogue: One Good "Tern" Deserves Another**

spoonbill, wood ibis, ring-necked pheasant, whistling swan, gull, Mallard duck, Canada goose, pied-billed grebe, American eared grebe, Holboell grebe, western grebe, loon, red-throated loon, penguin, great blue heron, and the European and Japanese heron.

The collection included dyed feathers and partly finished millinery trimmings made from bird plumage banned by law. The curator solicited the dyed feathers from the leading manufacturers that used artificial feathers or feathers obtained from the barnyard fowls. The display presented visitors with an insightful look back at the worst days of the era and the effort by assorted government agencies, private and public associations, and individuals to protect birds, their successes, and their failures. For once, the successes were outpacing the failures.

One of the first birds rescued from extinction was the white heron.[3] The U.S. government established the Key West National Wildlife Refuge in Florida in 1908 as a preserve and breeding ground for native birds and other wildlife. Wisely, it and similar refuges were designed to limit human use and influence in order to preserve the quality, character, and integrity of these protected wilderness lands.

In 1938, years after the crisis passed, the government established a national wildlife refuge to protect great white herons from extinction. The refuge also became a haven for migratory birds and other wildlife. The facility did what it was supposed to do. The white heron population rebounded not only in Florida, but elsewhere, and it flourishes today.

The tern, a small migratory marine bird, began its rebound shortly after World War I.[4] By 1921 there were about 100 pairs of them nesting on Collins Island in Biscayne Bay in Miami, Florida. Another colony of terns had established a home on some filled land along the city's waterfront. Their survival was attributed to federal protection.

The species had a narrow escape. Terns had become almost extinct by 1891. Their numbers started rebounding nicely and they were becoming more plentiful as the 20th century progressed. Bird protectors doffed their feather-free hats to the federal government for its protection.

Similarly, the bird of paradise narrowly averted extinction due to the unprecedented international cooperation on conservation issues in the early 1900s that continued well into the 20th century. It even became an international symbol of conservation. That was a small consolation for its predecessors that had died by the multitudes in the distant past, as did its relatives of so many other species.

The legislation passed during that time curtailed the global trade in bird feathers and ended the proliferation of high hats decorated with flora and fauna of all forms. By the mid–twentieth-century bird hats had for the most part become outdated. They were consigned to museums as showpieces of an American era gone by. There were still occasional references to birds on millinery, such as a hat described in 1921 through the words of a gifted fashion writer who carried on the long tradition of effusive prose employed to glorify the needless deaths of birds for the sake of sales: "It's a wise bird that lights on the smart woman this fall season, the Owl—Minerva's bird—gives the latest 'hoot' in fall millinery. This smart Joseph model bears the bird of wisdom as if it were on Minerva's helmet. The beak forms the peak of the turban and the bright eyes shine out from their natural colored feathers as though their knowledge of fashion's decree."[5]

Cherie Nicholas harked back to the bird slaughter era:

> If there is one place more than another that daytime fashions show off in a panorama of surpassing style interest, it is at the races. The influence of the French races and Ascot was very evident at the openings of our own American tracks this season.

Epilogue: One Good "Tern" Deserves Another

Women hunters pose with their dogs and dead birds between 1918 and 1920 (Otto M. Jones, photographer).

> Although there were no trailing skirts there were the reminiscent cartwheels, the tiny elaborate "doll" hats which smart Frenchmen love so well with flower, vegetable and bird trimming—millinery fantasies such as are almost amusing in their eccentricities, yet quite worthwhile in that they are adding such zest to the current mode.[6]

It was only 16 years after the unofficial end of the bird slaughter era and the fad was already something of the past. One thing was certain, though. Americans were still taking their fashion cues from France and England, which were only three years away from World War II. The war would occupy the minds of fashion writers and designers for six years. That guaranteed that the only birds slaughtered on the continent—and most places across the globe—would die combat deaths unrelated to millinery.

But the people who remembered the bird slaughter era may not have thought about it as "almost amusing in [its] eccentricities." It certainly wasn't for the birds—or for civilization in general. Rather, it was an era that showed the worst side of humans and that almost wiped out avian life in its entirety. Fortunately, it did not. A world without birds is unimaginable. Civilization came perilously close to finding out just how unimaginable it could be only a century ago. Lesson learned—and may it never have to be learned again.

Appendix A: Confusing Bird Protection Laws[1]

Exempt Species

Twenty-seven states, the District of Columbia and four Canadian provinces exempt from protection certain species which are commonly considered injurious. These species include the English sparrow, birds which destroy poultry and game, as black birds, crows and rice birds, and birds which destroy fish, as loons, fish-eating ducks, herons and kingfishers. Of these thirty-two states and provinces, twenty-eight specifically mention the English sparrow, and South Dakota and Quebec virtually include it with other sparrows, thus leaving only two, Nevada and South Carolina, which do not include it in the list of injurious species.

An examination of the various state laws shows that definitions of non-game birds afforded protection are in most cases very loose. The matter of definition is a difficult one in view of the fact that the number of bird species now recognized in North America is over 1,110, and that the list of even so small a state as Rhode Island, with an area of only 1,100 square miles, contains no less than 201 species, while 374 species are known to occur in Colorado and 410 in Nebraska.

The general term "plume birds" is used by the Agricultural Department to include not only herons, which are killed for their nuptial plumes, but a number of water birds, which are used for decorative purposes, such as pelicans, terns, gulls and grebes. The snowy heron furnishes the well-known aigrettes, pelicans supply quills and breasts, gulls and terns are worn in great numbers on hats, while grebes' breasts, besides being used for trimming hats, are also made into muffs, collarets, and capes.

There is an enormous demand for plume birds by the millinery trade in years when they are in fashion and the localities where the birds breed are scoured by hunters, who find a ready market for the skins at prices varying from 10 to 50 cents apiece. As these birds all nest in colonies, it is a simple matter to destroy large numbers on the breeding grounds; and so thoroughly is the work done that some of the species, particularly the egrets and terns, have been almost exterminated along the southern and eastern coasts of the United States.

Valuable Species

The value of herons, terns, and grebes is not generally appreciated. And even the services of the gulls as scavengers are recognized in comparatively few places. As a result birds of plume being neither game, song nor insectivorous, are not protected by ordinary game laws, unless by chance they happen to be mentioned in the list of protected species. Thus, by a curious perversity of circumstances, the species which are killed most mercilessly and in the greatest numbers are the very ones which are afforded the least protection.

Plume birds as well as insectivorous birds are protected in states which have comprehensive laws prohibiting the killing of all birds except game birds and certain designated species commonly considered injurious. But these states are few in number, and include only Arkansas, Illinois, Indiana, Massachusetts, New York, Rhode Island, and Vermont, and also the provinces of Manitoba and Ontario.

232   Appendix A: Confusing Bird Protection Laws

The only states that have special legislation for plume birds are Florida and Texas. In a law enacted in 1877 Florida prohibited the destruction of nests, eggs or young of any sea bird or bird of plume under a fine not exceeding $20; two years later it made the killing of any birds for the purpose of obtaining plumes by persons who were not citizens of the United States a crime punishable by a fine of not more than $100. Later, in 1891, the killing of cranes, egrets, ibises, curlews or herons for purposes of sale, or the purchasing or trading in such birds was made a misdemeanor punishable by a fine not exceeding $300.

The plume bird law of Texas declares the killing of sea gulls, terns, shearwaters, egrets, herons and pelicans a misdemeanor, punishable by a fine of from $5 to $25.

Appendix B: Expansion of the Migratory Bird Treaty Act of 1918

Since 1918, similar conventions between the United States and four other nations were incorporated into the Migratory Bird Treaty Act of 1918: Mexico (1936), Japan (1972)[1] and the Soviet Union (1976). Some of the conventions stipulated protections not only for the birds themselves, but also for habitats and environs necessary for the birds' survival.

The statute made it unlawful without a waiver to pursue, hunt, take, capture, kill, or sell nearly 1,100 species of birds listed as migratory birds. It did not discriminate between live or dead birds, and it granted full protection to any bird parts, including feathers, eggs, and nests. A March 2020 update of the list increased the number of species to 1,093.

There were the usual exceptions in the act, including the current eagle feather law, which regulates the taking, possession, and transportation of bald eagles, golden eagles, and their "parts, nests, and eggs" for "scientific, educational, and depredation control purposes; for the religious purposes of American Indian tribes; and to protect other interests in a particular locality." The U.S. Fish and Wildlife Service issues permits for otherwise prohibited activities under the act. These include permits for taxidermy, falconry, propagation, scientific and educational use, and depredation, an example of the last being the killing of geese near an airport, where they pose a danger to aircraft.

Constitutionally, this law is of interest as it is a use of the federal treaty-making power to override the provisions of state law, a factor that contributed to the controversy over Weeks-McLean. The principle that the federal government may do this was upheld in the case Missouri v. Holland. In a defense of the treaty, Federal Judge Valerie Caproni, on August 11, 2020, wrote in a decision, "It is not only a sin to kill a mockingbird, it is also a crime." That was just as true in 1880 as it was in 2020.

The American Game Protective Association decreed that the new treaty enacted in 1918 was bigger and better than its predecessor, with exactly the same object. But it provided what the former law lacked, an efficient machinery for its enforcement. Significantly, the governments involved were united in the protection of all the birds of North America above the Rio Grande River, the border between Texas and Mexico.

Notes

Introduction

1. "The tyranny of fashion," Bridgeton, NJ, *Pioneer*, Nov. 23, 1899, p. 4.

2. "Spare the birds," Erie, PA, *The Erie Times*, p. 8.

3. "Murderous millinery," Barre, VT, *Daily Times*, Dec. 2, 1905, p. 3.

4. Audubon, IA, *Republican*, July 26, 1894.

5. https://www.bbc.com/news/world-us-canada-58740362.

6. "A new fad," Kansas City, MO, *Daily Journal*, Oct. 18, 1896, p. 4.

7. "There is an enormous demand...," Atlanta, GA, *Semi-Weekly Journal*, May 1, 1902, p. 6.

8. "Birds on hats," Manning, SC, *Times*, Apr. 26, 1905, p. 6.

9. "Game laws and millinery," Washington, D.C., *Evening Times*, Aug. 22, 1898, p. 4.

10. https://naldc.nal.usda.gov/download/IND43647023/PDF.

11. "Birds on hats," Seattle, WA, *The Seattle Star*, Mar. 22, 1905, Night Edition, p. 4.

Chapter 1

1. "A new fad," Kansas City, KS, *Daily Journal*, Oct. 18, 1896, p. 5.

2. "The passing of the birds," Portland, ME, *Daily Press*, Jan. 1, 1894, p. 4.

3. "Census of our birds," Bismarck, ND, *Daily Tribune*, Jan. 29, 1908, p. 8.

4. "Peril of the birds," Wheeling, WV, *Daily Intelligencer*, Dec. 21, 1896, p. 6.

5. Florence A. Merriam, *How Birds Affect the Farm and Garden* (New York: Forest and Stream, 1896).

6. "Census of our birds," Coeur d'Alene, ID, *Evening Press*, Feb. 1, 1908, p. 3.

7. "The Passing of the Birds," Salt Lake, UT, *The Herald*, Jan. 28, 1894, p. 3.

8. "Some could be spared," Salt Lake, UT, *Herald-Republican*, Apr. 21, 1910, p. 4,

9. *Ibid.*

10. "The tyranny of fashion," Bridgeton, NJ, *Pioneer*, Nov. 23, 1899, p. 4.

11. "The tyranny of fashion," Decorah, IA, *Public Opinion*, Dec. 13, 1899, p. 2.

12. *Ibid.*

13. *Ibid.*

Chapter 2

1. "Great decrease of the bird life," Birmingham, AL, *Age-Herald*, May 9, 1898, p. 4.

2. *Ibid.*

3. *Ibid.*

4. *Ibid.*

Chapter 3

1. "Birds killed for plumage," Bennington, VT, *Evening Banner*, May 13, 1909, p. 3.

2. "Birds in fall hats," New York, NY, *Tribune*, Aug. 29, 1902, p. 7.

3. "Pleading for the birds," New York, NY, *Tribune*, June 27, 1886, p. 11.

4. Olive Thorne Miller, *True Bird Stories* (Boston: Houghton Mifflin, 1903), p. 24.

5. *Ibid.*

6. "Cobb's Island shooting," Washington, D.C., *Evening Star*, July 28, 1884, p. 4.

7. "Points on the fashion." Washington, D.C., *Evening Star*, Nov. 6, 1886, p. 7.

Chapter 4

1. "Bird murder and women's hats," Kendallville, IN, *Daily Sun*, Aug. 18, 1898, p. 3.

2. "Millinery ad," Washington, D.C., *Times*, Sept. 29, 1898, p. 10.

3. "New York fashions," Staunton, VA, *Spectator and Vindicator*, Oct. 21, 1897, p. 1.

4. "An Ohio girl...," Savannah, GA, *Morning News*, Dec. 17, 1884, p. 2.

5. "Bird murder and women's hats," Nebraska City, NE, *Conservative*, Aug. 18, 1898, p. 14.

6. "Murderous millinery," Griggs County, ND, *Courier*, Sept. 8, 1898, p. 3.

7. "Bird murder and women's hats," loc. Cit.

8. "Fashion robs the farmers," Lincoln County, OR, *Leader*, Oct. 15, 1909, p. 2.

9. "Birds useful in the war against cotton boll weevil," Deland, FL, *The Florida Agriculturist*, May 29, 1907, p. 1.

236   Notes—Chapters 5, 6 and 7

10. "Massacre of birds," Trenton, NJ, *Times*, Mar. 24, 1888, p. 1.

Chapter 5

1. https://en.wikipedia.org/wiki/15_minutes_of_fame.

2. "A high-hat symposium," Sacramento, CA, *Daily Record-Union*, Feb. 12, 1887, p. 6.

3. "Fall fashions," Washington, D.C., *National Tribune*, Nov. 11, 1886, p. 7.

4. "The winged wheel," New Haven, CT, *Morning Journal and Courier*, Sept. 28, 1882, p. 1.

5. "Fashion's fancies," Watertown, WI, *Republican*, Jan. 21, 1880, p. 3.

6. "Fashion wrinkles," Washington, D.C., *Evening Star*, Oct. 7, 1882, p. 7.

7. "Fashion notes," Abbeville, SC, *Press and Banner*, Oct. 25, 1882, p. 1.

8. "Fashion notes," Washington, D.C., *Bee*, Feb. 13, 1892, p. 2.

9. *Ibid.*

10. "For the fair sex," Opelousas, LA, *Courier*, Apr. 28, 1894, p. 6.

11. "Dainty millinery," Milan, TN, *Exchange*, June 12, 1886, p. 2.

12. "Millinery," Martinsburg, WV, *Independent*, Aug. 14, 1886, p. 4.

13. "In woman's world," Jersey City, NJ, *The Jersey City News*, July 13, 1899, p. 3.

14. "Forecast of fashions," Minneapolis, MN, *Journal*, Sept. 5, 1903, p. 12.

15. "The Audubon Society and the Milliners," Bennington, VT, *The Evening Banner*, Aug. 14, 1909, p. 2.

16. "Chanticleer's Day," Massillon, OH, *Evening Independent*, Apr. 1, 1910, p. 10.

17. "Ask World Powers to Protect Birds ," Trenton, NJ, *Evening Times*, July 25, 1910, p. 12.

18. "Fashion will not be crushed," Washington, D.C., *Evening Star*, May 1, 1897, p. 20.

19. "The end of fine feathers," Wilmington, DE, *Daily Commercial*, April 27, 1922, p. 4.

20. "Rare birds, Ancient gluttons," Grenada, MS, *Sentinel*, June 12, 1886, p. 3.

21. "Owls new in favor," East Carroll Parish, LA, *Banner-Democrat*, Feb. 12, 1898, p. 4.

22. "News and notes for women," Freeland, PA, *Tribune*, Jan. 10, 1898, p. 2.

23. "Velvet to be popular again this season," Little Falls, MN, *Herald*, Sept. 20, 1901, p. 7.

24. "Flowers in fancy colors and shapes," Salt Lake, UT, *Tribune*, Mar. 7, 1905, p. 11.

25. "Unique autumn outing hats," San Francisco, CA, *Call*, Sept. 28, 1902, p. 7.

26. Advertisement, Washington, D.C., *Evening Star*, Nov. 28, 1885, p. 3.

Chapter 6

1. "An Audubon Society," Savannah, GA, *The Savannah Morning News*, Mar. 11, 1903, p. 12.

2. "Audubon Society," Mesa, AZ, *Free Press*, Feb. 11, 1898, p. 2.

3. "Iowa opinions and notes," Marshalltown, IA, *Evening Times-Republican*, May 8, 1902, p. 4.

4. "Peril of the birds," Wheeling, WV, *Daily Intelligencer*, Dec. 21, 1896, p. 6.

5. "Women and birds," Baton Rouge, LA, *Banner-Democrat*, Sept. 28, 1901, p. 1.

6. "Slaughter of the birds," Holbrook, AZ, *Argus*, Nov. 17, 1906, p. 7.

7. "Eaglets," Chicago, IL, *Eagle*, May 12, 1900, p. 4.

8. "On rights of birds," El Paso, TX, *Herald*, Apr. 11, 1912, p. 10.

9. "The work of a lover of birds," Morrisville, VT, *News and Citizen*, Apr. 16, 1902, p. 2.

10. "At a recent meeting…," Deland, FL, *The Florida Agriculturist*, Aug. 11, 1897, p. 509.

11. "Smaller hats will obtain," Los Angeles, CA, *Herald*, Apr. 4, 1909, p. 6.

12. "Kilbourn events," Wausau, WI, *Pilot*, Nov. 5, 1907, p. 5.

13. "Songs without words; birds without song," New Haven, CT, *Daily Morning Journal and Courier*, Jan. 1, 1897, p. 7.

14. "After the women," Wausau, WI, *Pilot*, Dec. 9, 1902, p. 8.

15. "Woman's realm," Highland County, VA, *Recorder*, July 25, 1902, p. 4.

16. "Robbing the birds," Waterbury, CT, *Democrat*, Aug. 4, 1897, p. 1.

17. "Farm matters," McConnellsburg, PA, *The Fulton County News*, July 24, 1902, p. 7.

Chapter 7

1. Mark Twain, "Jim Baker's Blue Jay Yarn," https://americanliterature.com/author/mark-twain/short-story/jim-bakers-blue-jay-yarn.

2. "The birds," Brattleboro, VT, *Phoenix*, May 28, 1897, p. 1.

3. "Saving the birds," Washington, D.C., *Evening Star*, Dec. 29, 1909, p. 9.

4. "Farm notes," Watertown, WI, *Republican*, Jan. 21, 1880, p. 3.

5. "The relation of birds to crops," Deland, FL, *The Florida Agriculturist*, May 6, 1896, p. 301.

6. "Protect the birds," Oxford, MS, *Eagle*, June 26, 1902, p. 4.

7. "Farmer's best friend," Billings, MT, *Gazette*, Apr. 6, 1909, p. 4.

8. "The Audubon Societies and the milliners," Bennington, VT, *Evening Banner*, Aug. 14, 1909, p. 2.

9. "Address Delivered by G.O. Shields Before the High School," Caldwell, ID, *Gem State Rural*, Apr. 1, 1909, p. 3.

10. "The birds on the hats," Wichita, KS, *Eagle*, Jan. 4, 1890, p. 7.

11. "For Easter morning," New York, NY, *Sun*, Mar. 22, 1891, p. 24.

Chapter 8

1. Sample newspaper headlines of the time.
2. "A society which is laboring…," Hickman, KY, *Courier*, May 17, 1895, p. 1.
3. "Slaughter of birds," Wheeling, WV, *Daily Intelligencer*, Dec. 11, 1897, p. 4.
4. "Bird destroyers," Rock Island, IL, *Argus*, June 24, 1886, p. 2.
5. "Pretty gown models of Paris," Richmond, VA, *Planet*, Nov. 21, 1903, p. 7.
6. "Peril of the birds," Wheeling, WV, *The Wheeling Daily Intelligencer*, Dec. 21, 1896, p. 6.
7. "Songs without birds, birds without song," New Haven, CT, *Daily Morning Journal and Courier*, Jan. 1, 1897, p. 7.
8. "An eminent scientist…," Idaho Territory, *Semi-Weekly World*, Apr. 2, 1886, p. 1.
9. "For women only," WaKeeney, KS, *Western Kansas World*, June 5, 1886, p. 10.
10. "Songs without birds, birds without song."
11. "Peril of the birds," Wheeling, WV, *Daily Intelligencer*, Dec. 21, 1896, p. 6.
12. "Of lovely woman and the fashions," San Francisco, CA, *Call*, Mar. 16, 1909, p. 6.

Chapter 9

1. "Karl Lagerfeld's Wittiest, Most Iconic, and Most Outrageous Quotes of All Time," https://www.harpersbazaar.com/fashion/designers/a26405187/karl-lagerfeld-quotes/.
2. "Home hints," San Saba County, TX, *News*, July 21, 1893, p. 3.
3. "Fashion letter," Lafayette, LA, *Advertiser*, Oct. 13, 1894, p. 8.
4. "The era of individuality," Bridgeport, CT, *Evening Farmer*, Apr. 23, 1910, p. 8.
5. "The question box," Newark, NJ, *Evening Star and Advertiser*, Jan. 16, 1908, p. 4.
6. "The era of individuality," Guthrie, OK, *The Daily Leader*, June 11, 1910, p. 6.
7. "On the crime of wearing an aigrette," El Paso, TX, *Herald*, Apr. 17, 1911, 3d Extra, p. 6.
8. "Novelties in trimming," St. Louis, MO, *Republic*, Oct. 27, 1901, Magazine Section, p. 48.
9. "Fall hats depend on fine feathers for 'chic-ness,'" South Bend, IN, *News-Times*, Aug. 7, 1921, p. 21.
10. "New ideas in toilettes," Fulton County, PA, *News*, Oct. 24, 1901, p. 6.
11. "In the style," Mitchell, SD, *Capital*, Oct. 22, 1886, p. 3.
12. "The last heron," Eagle River, WI, *Review*, July 30, 1909, p. 6.
13. *Ibid.*
14. "The ostrich plume supply is very limited," Fargo, ND, *Forum and Daily Republican*, Mar. 25, 1916, p. 36.
15. *Ibid.*
16. *Ibid.*
17. "Bird hats popular," Ardmore, OK, *Daily Ardmoreite*, Feb. 24, 1922, p. 3.

Chapter 10

1. "Dress reformers," Wilmington, DE, *Evening Journal*, Nov. 1, 1911, p. 4.
2. "Fair sex scored," San Francisco, CA, *Morning Call*, Nov. 15, 1894, p. 4.
3. "Dress reformers."
4. "Dress reformers," Wilmington, DE, *Evening Journal*, Nov. 1, 1911, p. 4.
5. "A society which is laboring…," Hickman, KY, *Courier*, May 17, 1895, p. 1.
6. "A despicable device," Omaha, NE, *Daily Bee*, Jan. 1, 1905, p. 10.
7. "A despicable device," Omaha, NE, *Daily Bee*, Jan. 1, 1905, Editorial Section, p. 10.
8. "Bird destroyers," Stanford, KY, *Semi-Weekly Interior Journal*, June 25, 1886, p. 4.
9. "Prof. Scott relieves the women," Marble Hill, MO, *Press*, June 5, 1901, p. 2.
10. "Spare the birds," Salt Lake City, UT, *Tribune*, Dec. 7, 1909, p. 5.

Chapter 11

1. https://www.goodreads.com/author/quotes/426038.Joseph_Pulitzer#:~:text=~%20Joseph%20Pulitzer%20%22What%20a%20newspaper%20needs%20in,condensation%20and%20accuracy%.
2. "A woman's cause that should win," Americus, GA, *Times-Recorder*, June 28, 1913, p. 4.
3. "The animosity of the Rev. Ann," Kansas City, MO, *Journal*, Nov. 20, 1898, p. 4.
4. "More work for Audubons," New Haven, CT, *Daily Morning Journal and Courier*, Sept. 29, 1902, p. 6.
5. "Woman's League and ornithology," Los Angeles, CA, *Herald*, Feb. 28, 1897, p. 15.
6. "Kate Jordan's chat," Gloucester County, NJ, *Democrat*, Sept. 6, 1894, p. 1.
7. "A society has been organized…," Harrison, NE, *The Sioux County Journal*, Apr. 4, 1895, p. 2.
8. "Woman's realm," Highland County, VA, *Recorder*, July 25, 1902, p. 4.
9. "Bloody Easter bonnets," Washington, D.C., *Herald*, Apr. 10, 1911, p. 4.
10. "A society has been organized," Harrison, NE, *Sioux County Journal*, Apr. 4, 1895, p. 2.
11. "Cruelty to be checked," Birmingham, AL, *Age-Herald*, May 11, 1903, p. 4.

Chapter 12

1. "Peril of the birds," Wheeling, WV, *Daily Intelligencer*, Dec. 21, 1896, p. 6.
2. "No pity for the birds," Portland, ME, *Daily Press*, Apr. 14, 1898, p. 4.
3. "Not worth the price," Topeka, KS, *State Journal*, Apr. 17, 1897, p. 6.
4. "The week in society," San Antonio, TX, *The Daily Express*, Sept. 21, 1902, p. 22.

238   Notes—Chapters 13, 14, 15 and 16

5. "Pitiful sight," Reynoldsville, PA, *The Star*, June 26, 1907, p. 2.

6. "Late summer millinery," Washington, D.C., *Evening Journal*, July 23, 1903, p. 3.

7. "Murderous millinery," Coalville, UT, *Times*, Apr. 17, 1903, p. 3.

8. "Murderous millinery," Prescott, AZ, *Daily News*, Mar. 10, 1908, p. 2.

9. "Fashion the foe of song birds," Mineral Point, WI, *Tribune*, Dec. 28, 1899, p. 7.

10. "The week in society."

11. "Saturday Globe glances," Saint Paul, MN, *Globe*, Mar. 23, 1901, p. 4.

12. "Move to stop bird slaughter," Salem, OR, *Daily Capital Journal*, Feb. 14, 1913, p. 5.

13. "Ostrich farms," The Birmingham, AL, *Age-Herald*, Nov. 29, 1908, p. 16.

Chapter 13

1. https://www.si.edu/spotlight/passenger-pigeon.

2. Barry Yeoman, "Why the Passenger Pigeon Went Extinct," *Audubon Magazine*, May–June 2014, https://www.audubon.org/magazine/may-june-2014/why-passenger-pigeon-went-extinct.

3. "Little laughs," Austin, TX, *The Weekly Statesman*, Feb. 24, 1887, p. 6.

4. "A lady told me…," Annapolis, MD, *Evening Capital*, June 21, 1887, p. 1.

5. https://scottishwildlifetrust.org.uk/scotlands-wildlife/osprey-fact-file/.

6. "Protecting birds," San Francisco, CA, *Call*, Oct. 16, 1913, p. 6.

7. "Magazines and notes," Washington, D.C., *The National Tribune*, Oct. 16, 1902, p. 2.

8. "Craze of women for feathered hats makes American water fowl scarce," El Paso, TX, *Herald*, Dec. 30, 1910, p. 6.

9. "The water fowl club," Detroit, MI, *The Detroit Times*, Dec. 29, 1910, p. 10.

10. "Powerful lobby for slaughter of birds," Norwich, CT, *Bulletin*, Mar. 17, 1911, p. 1.

11. "A state game bird farm," Franklin Parish, LA, *The St. Mary Banner*, Dec. 18, 1909, p. 9.

12. "Saving the birds," Washington, D.C., *Evening Star*, Dec. 29, 1909, p. 9.

13. "Save the birds," Washington, D.C., *Evening Star*, Sept. 13, 1912, p. 6.

Chapter 14

1. "The saddest cat in Maine…," Augusta, ME, *Daily Kennebec Journal*, May 15, 1900, p. 4.

2. "No law against wearing feathers," Morris County, NJ, *Chronicle*, June 5, 1906, p. 6.

3. "Destruction of birds," Salt Lake City, UT, *The Evening Telegram*, Nov. 26, 1906, p. 7.

4. "The dove is the most popular bird…," Richmond, KY, *The Climax*, June 21, 1899, p. 4.

5. "The application of the interstate…," Omaha, NE, *Daily Bee*, Feb. 19, 1903, p. 6.

6. "The birds are here," Hocking, OH, *Sentinel*, Mar. 28, 1901, p. 1.

7. "'Audubon' Protecting Florida for 100 years," Daytona, Beach, FL, *The News-Journal*, Apr. 3, 2000, p. 4.

8. "A new bird book," Washington, D.C., *Times*, July 5, 1903, Editorial Society Section, p. 5.

9. "After bird trappers," Wood County, WI, *Reporter*, June 23, 1898, p. 3.

10. "Renewal of war against milliners," Defiance, OH, *Crescent News*, Jan. 30, 1903, p. 6.

11. "Every milliner in town to be arrested," Spokane, WA, *Press*, Sept. 20, 1904, p. 1.

12. "Milliners aren't worried," Stark County, OH, *Democrat*, Jan. 23, 1903, Weekly Edition, p. 7.

13. "Still hope for the ladies," Canton, OH, *Stark County Democrat*, Jan. 27, 1903, p. 6.

14. "Crusade against stuffed birds," Richwood, OH, *Gazette*, Jan. 22, 1903, p. 4.

Chapter 15

1. "The habit of using the heads…," Manchester, IA, *Democrat*, June 7, 1899, p. 6.

2. "Social gossip," Indianapolis, IN, *State Sentinel*, Apr. 7, 1886, p. 3.

3. "The game is not for us alone," New York, NY, *Sun*, Nov. 12, 1919, p. 20.

4. "In defense of the birds," Seattle, WA, *Post-Intelligencer*, Sept. 29, 1895, p. 6.

5. "Dead birds and nose rings," Brattleboro, VT, *Vermont Phoenix*, Sept. 24, 1886, p. 2.

6. "Birds on hats," Manning, SC, *Times*, Apr. 26, 1905, p. 6.

7. "Birds on hats," Spokane, WA, *The Spokane Press*, Mar. 24, 1905, p. 2.

8. "The birds are here," Hocking, OH, *Sentinel*, Mar. 28, 1901, p. 1.

9. "The birds on the hats," Wichita, KS, *Eagle*, Jan. 4, 1890, p. 7.

10. "Peril of the birds," Wheeling, WV, *Daily Intelligencer*, Dec. 21, 1896, p. 6.

Chapter 16

1. "Audubon Society has made the District bird sanctuary," Washington, D.C., *Evening Star*, Apr. 1, 1923, p. 72.

2. "Clubs to study birds," Red Lodge, MT, *Picket*, Sept. 20, 1901, p. 2.

3. Jonathan Alderfer, *National Geographic Kids Bird Guide of North America, Second Edition* (Washington, D.C.: National Geographic, 2018).

4. "Peril of the birds," Wheeling, WV, *Daily Intelligencer*, Dec. 21, 1896, p. 6.

5. "Magazines and notes," Washington, D.C., *National Tribune*, Oct. 16, 1902, p. 2.

6. "Why not ornithology?" Tazewell, VA, *Republican*, June 14, 1900, p. 2.

7. "The birds are here," Hocking, OH, *Sentinel*, Mar. 28, 1901, p. 1.

8. *Ibid.*

Notes—Chapters 17, 18, 19 and 20

9. "No pity for the birds," New York, NY, *Sun*, Jan. 16, 1898, p. 5.

10. "Bird protection," Saint Paul, MN, *Daily Globe*, June 4, 1894, p. 4.

11. *Ibid.*

12. "News from the schools," Minneapolis, MN, *Journal*, Mar. 11, 1906, p. 5.

13. "A country without song birds," Washington, D.C., *Evening Star*, Nov. 27, 1885, p. 3.

14. "Bird Protectors," Danville, PA, *Montour-American*, May 28, 1908, p. 3.

15. "Wear feathers? Never," Annapolis, MD, *Evening Capital and Maryland Gazette*, Apr. 13, 1916, p. 4.

16. "A bird day suggested," Chicago, IL, *Universalist*, Aug. 8, 1896, p. 3.

17. *Ibid.*

18. "Moline mention," Rock Island, IL, *Argus*, Mar. 28, 1903, last edition, p. 2.

19. "For protection of birds," Salisbury, CT, *Connecticut Western News*, Mar. 10, 1898, p. 3.

20. "Bird day in the schools," Nebraska City, NE, *Conservative*, Feb. 16, 1899, p. 5.

21. "Birds and trees," Nebraska City, NE, *Conservative*, Apr. 24, 1902, p. 9.

22. "Craze of women for feathered hats makes American water fowl scarce," El Paso, TX, *Herald*, Dec. 30, 1910, p. 6.

23. "The great economic importance of sea gulls," Ottumwa, IA, *Tri-weekly Courier*, Dec. 23, 1915, p. 6.

24. "Will not hold school fair," Richmond, VA, *Times Dispatch*, Feb. 4, 1911, p. 8.

25. "Arbor Day," Point Pleasant, WV, *Register*, Mar. 23, 1910, p. 9.

26. "Arbor and bird day," Mt. Sterling, KY, *Advocate*, Oct. 25, 1911, p. 6.

27. "Special school days," Marshalltown, IA, *Evening Times-Republican*, Feb. 8, 1901, p. 3.

Chapter 17

1. "Ladies spare the birds," New York, NY, *Sun*, Dec. 1, 1897, p. 7.

2. "Bird millinery," Marietta, OH, *Daily Leader*, Jan. 6, 1900, p. 2.

3. "Birds as millinery ornaments," New York, NY, *Tribune*, July 19, 1897, p. 2.

4. "After the milliners," Brownsville, TX, *Daily Herald*, Oct. 21, 1902, p. 2.

5. "About the fashions," Salt Lake, UT, *Herald*, Jan. 24, 1892, p. 15.

6. *Ibid.*

7. "Game wardens indorse Audubon Society," Savannah, GA, *Morning News*, Mar. 12, 1903, p. 12.

8. *Ibid.*

9. *Ibid.*

Chapter 18

1. "Songs without birds, birds without song,"

New Haven, CT, *Daily Morning Journal and Courier*, Jan. 1, 1897, p. 7.

2. "Uncle Sam puts up bars against odd variety of importations," Washington, D.C., *Herald*, Nov. 17, 1912, Magazine Section, p. 9.

3. "Milliners and plumage birds," New York, NY, *Tribune*, March 14, 1909, p. 13.

4. "Two sides of the bird questions," Washington, D.C., *Evening Times*, Apr. 15, 1898, p. 4.

5. "Legal status of birds," Atlanta, GA, *Semi-Weekly Journal*, May 1, 1902, p. 6.

6. "Say that birds belong to all," Fargo, ND, *Forum and Daily Republican*, Nov. 2, 1915, p. 18.

7. "Man who sent up costs of feathers for hats," Fargo, ND, *Forum and Daily Republican*, Apr. 19, 1913, p. 1.

8. "Migratory bird law said still effective," Klamath Falls, OR, *The Evening Herald*, Jan. 17, 1919, p. 4.

9. "On the crime of wearing an aigrette," El Paso, TX, *Herald*, Apr. 17, 1911, 3d Extra, p. 6.

Chapter 19

1. https://en.wikipedia.org/wiki/Weeks%E2%80%93McLean_Act.

2. "Why they are there," Heppner, OR, *The Gazette-Times*, Sept. 11, p. 2.

3. "Protection of American birds," St. Louis, MO, *Sea Coast Echo*, September 6, 1913, p. 5.

4. "Dr. Hornaday asks Senate to stop bird slaughter," Honolulu, HI, *Star-Bulletin*, June 6, 1913, p. 3.

5. "Protect the birds," Las Vegas, NM, *Optic*, Apr. 4, 1913, p. 7.

6. "Tariff worries fishermen," New York, NY, *Sun*, July 13, 1913, Sixth Section, p. 7.

7. "Fear feather frame-up," Ellsworth, ME, *American*, Jan. 14, 1914, p. 4.

8. "Fear feather frame-up," Butler, MO, *Weekly Times*, Jan. 15, 1914, p. 4.

9. "Fear feather frame-up," Belfast, ME, *Republican Journal*, Jan. 29, 1914, p. 2.

10. *Ibid.*

11. "Two senators who saved birds," Portland, OR, *Morning Oregonian*, Sept. 11, 1913, p. 8.

Chapter 20

1. "What the government is doing," Washington, D.C., *Evening Star*, Jan. 11, 1914, p. 4.

2. "French milliners foresee billion dollar trade year," Washington, D.C., *Evening Star*, Apr. 4, 1920, p. 47.

3. *Ibid.*

4. "Paradise plumes in last stand," Colfax, IN, *Clinton County Review*, May 25, 1922, p. 7.

5. "Aigrettes," Fargo, ND, *Forum and Daily Republican*, Oct. 10, 1913, p. 4.

6. "What the government is doing," Washington, D.C., *Evening Star*, Jan. 11, 1914, p. 4.

Chapter 21

1. "Birds killed for plumage," Bennington, VT, *Evening Banner*, May 13, 1909, p. 2.
2. "Black belt of cruelty," Bamberg, SC, *Herald*, Jan. 12, 1911, p. 7.
3. "Robin most numerous of birds," Shepherdstown, WV, *Register*, Feb. 25, 1915, p. 1.
4. "Louisiana game laws hold good," Birmingham, AL, *Age-Herald*, Mar. 18, 1907, p. 5.
5. *Ibid.*
6. "Saving the birds," Washington, D.C., *Evening Star*, Dec. 29, 1909, p. 9.
7. "Slaughter of songbirds for food is awful," Clarksburg, WV, *Daily Telegram*, Nov. 22, 1915, p. 10.
8. "Saving the birds," Washington, D.C., *Evening Star*, Dec. 29, 1909, p. 9.
9. "Oklahoma has joined the states," Fulton County, PA, *News*, Nov. 15, 1917, p. 8.
10. "Sell the birds," Topeka, KS, *The Topeka State Journal*, Oct. 7, 1897, p. 8.
11. *Ibid.*
12. "The destruction of our wild birds," Newark, NJ, *Star and Newark Advertiser*, Feb. 11, 1908, p. 8.
13. "Birds and millinery," Honolulu, HI, *Pacific Commercial Advertiser*, Aug. 9, 1909, p. 4.
14. "No more feathers on Iowa women's hats," Leon, IA, *Reporter*, May 3, 1906, p. 1.

Chapter 22

1. "The era of individuality," Bridgeport, CT, *Evening Farmer*, Apr. 23, 1910, p. 8.
2. "Merchants and Audubonites agree," Jersey City, NJ, *Evening Journal*, May 11, 1903, p. 14.
3. "Milliners promise to protect birds," St. Louis, MO, *Republic*, May 10, 1903, p. 49.
4. *Ibid.*
5. "The Audubon Society and the Milliners," Bennington, VT, *Evening Banner*, Aug. 14, 1909, p. 2.

Chapter 23

1. "Fall bonnets," Canton, MS, *American Citizen*, Sept. 12, 1874, p. 1.
2. "Birds killed for plumage," Bennington, VT, *Evening Banner*, May 13, 1909, p. 2.
3. "Destruction of our birds," Newberry, SC, *Herald and News*, Oct. 27, 1886 , p. 3.
4. https://en.wikipedia.org/wiki/Great_auk.
5. "Hummingbird export," Trenton, NJ, *Evening Times*, July 1, 1943, p. 2.
6. "Automobile coats made of Hummingbird skins," Washington, D.C., *Herald*, Apr. 27, 1913, Magazine Section, p. 6.
7. *Ibid.*
8. "Life and doom of the hummingbird," Washington, D.C., *Evening Star*, Apr. 4, 1909, p. 36.
9. "Automobile coats made of Hummingbird skins," Washington, D.C., *Herald*, Apr. 27, 1913, Magazine Section, p. 6.

10. "Scarcity of birds," Nashville, TN, *Union and American*, Oct. 22, 1871, p. 4.
11. "The blackbird of commerce," Wichita, KS, *Eagle*, Nov. 14, 1889, p. 2.
12. "Shooting the wild turkeys," New Haven, CT, *Morning Journal and Courier*, Oct. 6, 1892, p. 1.
13. "Some of the details," Wessington Springs, Dakota, *Herald*, Apr. 23, 1886, p. 6.

Chapter 24

1. "The egret again," New York, NY, *Tribune*, May 26, 1906, p. 4.
2. "Foreign game possession," New Haven, CT, *Daily Morning Journal and Courier*, Aug. 25, 1905, p. 8.
3. *Ibid.*
4. "Against foreign game," New York, NY, *Tribune*, Feb. 28, 1906, p. 2.
5. *Ibid.*
6. "The game dealers' new bill," New York, NY, *Daily Tribune*, Mar. 19, 1906, p. 6.
7. "The egret again," New York, NY, *Tribune*, May 26, 1906, p. 4.
8. *Ibid.*
9. "Audubon Society to start campaign," Los Angeles, CA, *Daily Herald*, Apr. 29, 1909, p. 11.

Chapter 25

1. "Aigrettes cause trouble," Portland, OR, *Oregonian*, Apr. 3, 1909, p. 10.
2. *Ibid.*
3. "Reiner," Portland, OR, *Oregon Journal*, Jan. 11, 1909, p. 2.
4. "Forbidden aigrettes offered for sale," San Francisco, CA, *Call Bulletin*, Feb. 15, 1910, p. 1.
5. "New complaint made against milliner," San Francisco, CA, *Call Bulletin*, Feb. 18, 1910, p. 16.
6. "Case against jeweler dropped," San Francisco, CA, *Call Bulletin*, Feb 17, 1910, p. 3.
7. *Ibid.*
8. "Pounces on the milliners," Astoria, OR, *Morning Astorian*, Apr. 3, 1909, p. 1.
9. *Ibid.*
10. "Scale of Feather Fines...," Portland, OR, *Oregonian*, Apr. 14, 1909, p. 16.
11. *Ibid.*
12. "More birds found," Portland, OR, *Morning Oregonian*, p. 12.
13. "Farmer's best friend," Billings, MT, *Gazette*, Apr. 6, 1909, p. 4.
14. "Notice of dissolution of copartnership," San Francisco, CA, *Call Bulletin*, July 3, 1910, p. 58.

Chapter 26

1. "Schlemmer, Max," Honolulu, HI, *Hawaiian Star*, Feb. 5, 1910, 2nd Edition, p. 12.
2. Arthur G. Sharp, *The Bear and the Northland: Legendary Coast Guard Cutters in the Alaskan Ice* (Jefferson, NC: McFarland, 2023).

Notes—Chapters 27, 28 and 29

3. https://en.wikipedia.org/wiki/USS_
Iroquois_(1859).

4. "King Max of Laysan is deposed," Honolulu, HI, *The Hawaiian Gazette*, Nov. 12, 1909, p. 5.

5. "Local Japanese had planned to secure control of Laysan," Honolulu, HI, *Hawaiian Star*, Nov. 11, 1909, 2nd Edition, p. 1.

6. *Ibid.*

7. "Japanese bird pirates busy," Honolulu, HI, *Evening Bulletin*, March 28, 1911, p. 1.

8. "U.S.S. *Thetis* departs for Hawaii," Honolulu, HI, *Evening Bulletin*, May 13, 1911, p. 15.

9. "Report *Thetis* away for good," Honolulu, HI, *Evening Bulletin*, Aug. 26, 1911, p. 1.

10. "*Thetis* to visit Hawaii," Honolulu, HI, *Star-Bulletin*, Nov. 15, 1912, p. 2.

11. "Telegraphic news," Wailuku, HI, *Wailuku-Maui News*, Jan 11, 1913, p. 2.

Chapter 27

1. "Wholesale milliners defeat bird lovers," Salem, OR, *Daily Capital Journal*, Aug. 12, 1913, p. 3.

2. "Laysan Island," Honolulu, HI, *Pacific Commercial Advertiser*, Oct. 19, 1897, p. 2.

3. "Schlemmer accusers jailed," Honolulu, HI, *Hawaiian Star*, Mar. 16, 1910, p. 2.

4. "Fruit shipment proves successful," Wailuku, Hi, *Wailuku-Maui News*, Oct. 12, 1907, p. 1.

5. "Ceylon's rough trip," Honolulu, HI, *Evening Bulletin*, July 17, 1901, p. 1.

6. "Is king of the Laysan Island," Honolulu, HI, *Hawaiian Star*, Nov. 16, 1904, p. 7.

7. "Schlemmer faces an indictment," Honolulu, HI, *Hawaiian Star*, Feb. 7, 1910, p. 1.

8. "Poachers are free," Honolulu, HI, *Hawaiian Star*, Mar. 15, 1910, p. 1.

9. "Bird poachers get off easy," Honolulu, HI, *The Hawaiian Gazette*, Mar. 18, 1910, p. 8.

10. "But the Japanese don't care," Honolulu, HI, *The Hawaiian Gazette*, Mar. 18, 1910, p. 8.

11. "Bird poachers get off easy," Honolulu, HI, *Hawaiian Star*, May 31, 1910, 2nd Edition, p. 2.

12. "Judge sustains Max Schlemmer," Honolulu, HI, *The Hawaiian Gazette*, Apr. 22, 1910, p. 3.

13. "Killing birds on the side," Honolulu, HI, *Pacific Commercial Advertiser*, Feb. 4, 1910, pp. 1 and 4.

14. *Ibid.*

15. "Roosevelt had no authority," Honolulu, HI, *Pacific Commercial Advertiser*, Apr. 9, 1910, p. 1.

16. "Cheaper to pay rent than move," Honolulu, HI, *The Hawaiian Gazette*, Feb. 15, 1910, p. 2.

17. "Federal court in session," Honolulu, HI, *Evening Bulletin*, July 2, 1910, p. 1.

18. "King of Laysan is on trial," Honolulu, HI, *Hawaiian Star*, Oct. 27, 1910, 2nd Edition, p. 8.

19. "Schlemmer not guilty," Honolulu, HI, *Evening Bulletin*, Oct. 28, 1910, p. 1.

Chapter 28

1. "To prevent killing of birds," Wilmington, DE, *Evening Journal*, Mar. 13, 1900, p. 1.

2. "Mosquitoes and whip-poor-wills," Kingwood, WV, *Argus*, Sept. 12, 1901, p. 1.

3. "The Audubon Society...," Salisbury, CT, *Connecticut Western News*, Mar. 23, 1899, p. 2.

4. "Crusade upon bird killers," Wilmington, DE, *Gazette and State Journal*, Mar. 22, 1900, p. 3.

5. *Ibid.*

6. "Those Delaware birds," Wilmington, DE, *Evening Journal*, Mar. 23, 1900, p. 1.

7. *Ibid.*

8. *Ibid.*

9. "Bird story is a fake," Wilmington, DE, *The Daily Republican*, Mar. 17, 1900, p. 2.

10. "The work will go on," Wilmington, DE, *Gazette and State Journal*, Mar. 22, 1900, p. 3.

11. "Contemporary opinion," Wilmington, DE, *Evening Journal*, Apr. 4, 1900, p. 2.

12. *Ibid.*

Chapter 29

1. "Dairy legislation," North Yakima, WA, *Ranche and Range*, Jan. 1, 1898, p. 11.

2. "The game is not for us alone," New York, NY, *Sun*, Nov. 12, 1919, p. 20.

3. "No feathers' on their wives' bonnets," Mahaska County, IA, *Oskaloosa Herald*, Feb. 2, 1888, p. 3.

4. "Fines for birds on hats," Fredericksburg, VA, *Freelance*, Nov. 3, 1908, p. 2.

5. "The Arkansas legislature...," Missouri Valley, IA, *Times*, May 4, 1899, p. 8.

6. "Stuffed birds on hats," Philadelphia, PA, *Inquirer*, June 7, 1899, p. 16.

7. "Fine the city sportsmen," St. Paul, MN, *Daily Globe*, Apr. 8, 1887, p. 4.

8. "It is now a misdemeanor...," Manitowoc, WI, *Pilot*, Apr. 14, 1887, p. 2.

9. "The legislature of Illinois...," Opelousas, LA, *Courier*, Apr. 29, 1899, p. 1.

10. "To protect birds," Washington, D.C., *Evening Star*, July 5, 1901, p. 9.

11. "No law against wearing feathers," New York, NY, *Sun*, June 1, 1906, p. 8.

12. "Is an ornithologist...," El Paso, TX, *Daily Herald*, May 9, 1900, Last Edition, p. 2.

13. "A game warden...," Mount Holly, NJ, *News*, August 8, 1911, p. 2.

14. "Public kept in ignorance of new laws," Newark, NJ, *Evening Star and Newark Advertiser*, Aug. 4, 1911, Last Edition, p. 6.

15. "The new game law," Lexington, MO, *The Lexington Intelligencer*, May 6, 1905, p. 2.

16. "Missouri bars birds upon hats of women," Washington, D.C., *Times*, Apr. 2, 1905, Metropolitan Section, p. 12.

17. "Save the birds," St. Louis, MO, *Republic*, Sept. 1, 1901, Part I, p. 6.

242 Notes—Chapters 30, 31, 32 and 33

18. "Walmsley, the author...," Mexico, MO, *Message*, Feb. 7, 1907, p. 4.

19. *Ibid.*

20. "Law knocks out fashion in Missouri," Jasper, IN, *Weekly Courier*, Mar. 31, 1905, p. 5.

21. "Missouri hats go democratic," Minneapolis, MN, *Journal*, Mar. 29, 1905, p. 2.

22. "Walmsley fines to schools," Potosi, MO, *Journal*, June 27, 1906, p. 3.

23. "Saving the birds from fashion's murderous banditti," Honolulu, HI, *Hawaiian Star*, Jan. 4, 1911, 2nd Edition, p. 6.

24. "Walmsley, the author...," Mexico, MO, *Message*, Feb. 7, 1907, p. 4.

25. "The Bay state's bird law," New Haven, CT, *Daily Morning Journal and Courier*, Aug. 12, 1897, p. 6.

Chapter 30

1. "Birds protected," Trenton, NJ, *Evening Times*, Apr. 18, 1911, p. 6.

2. "The Bay state's bird law," New Haven, CT, *Daily Morning Journal and Courier*, Aug. 12, 1897, p. 6.

3. *Ibid.*

4. "The birds," Brattleboro, VT, *Vermont Phoenix*, Aug. 20, 1897, p. 1.

5. *Ibid.*

6. "The birds," Bennington, VT, *Phœnix*, Aug. 20, 1897, p. 1.

7. "Hat bill of bachelor raises ire of fair sex," Washington, D.C., *The Washington Times,* Mar. 25, 1910, Last Edition, p. 15.

8. "Rare birds saved through new laws," Trenton, NJ, *Evening Times*, Aug. 21, 1912, p. 14.

9. "White egrets increasing," Bridgeport, CT, *Evening Farmer*, Aug. 20, 1912, p. 12.

10. "Thousands of wild geese," Lake Providence, LA, *The Banner-Democrat*, Sept. 28, 1901, p. 2.

Chapter 31

1. "Peril of the birds," Wheeling, WV, *Daily Intelligencer*, Dec. 21, 1896, p. 6.

2. "The birds on the hats," Wichita, KS, *Eagle*, Jan. 4, 1890, p. 7.

3. "Peril of the birds," Wheeling, WV, *Daily Intelligencer*, Dec. 21, 1896, p. 6.

4. "Craze of Women for Feathered Hats Makes American Water Fowl Scarce," El Paso, TX, *Herald*, Dec. 30, 1910, p. 6.

5. "A bill has been introduced...," Manitowoc, WI, *Pilot*, Feb. 28, 1889, p. 3.

6. "The New York Graphic," Salisbury, CT, *Connecticut Western News*, May 5, 1886, p. 1.

7. "Wearing song birds," Jamestown, ND, *Weekly Alert*, Dec. 16, 1886, p. 6.

8. "Wearing songbirds," Richland County, ND, *The Wahpeton Times*, Dec. 9, 1886, p. 2.

9. "Birds of millinery," New York, NY, *Evening World*, Sept. 17, 1894, Extra 2 O'Clock, p. 2.

10. "Protecting the birds," Tazewell, VA, *Republican*, June 14, 1900, p. 2.

Chapter 32

1. "While we are talking," Missoula, MT, Daily *Missoulian*, Mar. 16, 1913, Morning, p. 4.

2. "The osprey and the egret," New York, NY, *Tribune*, Jan. 31, 1897, p. 3.

3. "Charles W. Farmer...," New Haven, CT, *Daily Morning Journal and Courier*, Mar. 22, 1900, p. 4.

4. "Ugliest Girl in New York before and after milliners tried their arts on her," Pendleton, OR, *East Oregonian*, Feb. 21, 1920, Daily Evening Edition, Sec. 2, p. 11.

5. "Canary cage hat sets avenue agape," New York, NY, *Tribune*, Apr. 19, 1915, p. 3.

6. "The woman who wears a bird....," Saint Paul, MN, *Globe*, May 13, 1903, p. 4.

7. "Feathers of game birds," New York, NY, *The New York Times*, May 5, 1913, p. 8.

8. "Anecdotes concerning well known people," Washington, D.C., *Evening Star*, June 22, 1913, p. 5.

9. "Wholesale milliners defeat bird lovers," Salem, OR, *Daily Capital Journal*, Aug. 12, 1913, p. 3.

10. "A law that may react badly," New York, NY, *Evening World*, Feb. 6, 1913, Final Edition, p. 18.

11. "Audubon Society criticizes Hughes," Newark, NJ, *Evening Star and Newark Advertiser*, Aug. 23, 1913, p. 4.

12. "Protecting birds from millinery trade," Forest City, SD, *Press*, Feb. 27, 1914, p. 3.

13. "Smith afraid tariff bill will kill legislation for protection of bird life," Oakley, ID, *Herald*, Aug. 1, 1913, p. 6.

14. "A victory for the birds," New York, NY, *Sun*, Sept. 18, 1913, p. 8.

15. "Smith afraid tariff bill will kill legislation for protection of bird life," Oakley, ID, *Herald*, Aug. 1, 1913, p. 6.

16. "The butterfly hat," Ardmore, OK, *Daily Ardmoreite*, Mar. 2, 1911, p. 3.

17. "Fashions and fads," Wilmington, DE, *Evening Journal*, Oct. 20, 1913, p. 10.

Chapter 33

1. "Spare the birds and beasts," Wilmington, DE, *Daily Republican*, June 9, 1886, p. 1.

2. "The woman ahead," Canton, SD, *Dakota Farmers' Leader*, Jan. 3, 1902, p. 5.

3. "A woman will yank...," McRory, AR, *Woodruff County News*, Nov. 9, 1901, p. 8.

4. "The woman ahead," Canton, SD, *Dakota Farmers' Leader*, Jan. 3, 1902, p. 5.

5. *Ibid.*

6. "The birds on my lady's hat," San Francisco, CA, *Call*, Nov. 21, 1897, p. 22.

7. "Most in demand," Washington, D.C., *Evening Star*, Oct. 13, 1900, p. 17.

Notes—Chapters 34, 35, 36 and 37 **243**

8. "Asked to tell the truth about bird plumage in millinery," Bridgeport, CT, *Evening Farmer*, Feb. 23, 1911, p. 3.

9. "Freaks of fashion," Mt. Sterling, KY, *Advocate*, May 26, 1909, p. 1.

10. *Ibid.*

11. "Fancy feathers worn by women come from rooster," Washington, D.C., *Times*, Nov. 29, 1912, Last Edition, p. 13.

Chapter 34

1. "Fashion will not be crushed," Washington, D.C., *Evening Star*, May 1, 1897, p. 20.

2. "A correspondent of THE STAR…," Washington, D.C., *Evening Star*, Oct. 2, 1886, p. 4.

3. "No song birds," Indianapolis, IN, *Journal*, Nov. 5, 1899, Part One, p. 4.

4. "Must have birds' wings," Salt Lake, UT, *Herald*, November 15, 1899, p. 7.

5. "Save the birds," St. Louis, MO, *Republic*, Sept. 1, 1901, Part I, p. 6.

6. "Spare the birds," Fairfield, SC, *News and Herald*, April 27, 1898, p. 4.

7. https://naldc.nal.usda.gov/download/IND43647023/PDF (importation statistics).

8. "Honey for the ladies," Omaha, NE, *Daily Bee*, July 24, 1887, p. 11.

9. "Bird protection," Montgomery, AL, *Advertiser*, May 3, 1903, p. 11.

10. "Want grange's help in revising bird laws," Eugene, OR, *East Oregonian*, Nov. 16, 1909, Evening Edition, p. 3.

11. "Timely topics," Marshalltown, IA, *Evening Times-Republican*, May 26, 1904, p. 3.

12. "Maine's wicked doves," New Haven, CT, *Daily Morning Journal and Courier*, Dec. 17, 1903, Part 2, p. 11.

13. "The women of Arkansas," New Haven, CT, *Daily Morning Journal and Courier*, Apr. 25, 1899, p. 4.

14. "Rail slaughter near Belmont," San Francisco, CA, *Call*, Oct. 30, 1897, p. 10.

15. *Ibid.*

Chapter 35

1. "The enchanted types," St. Louis, MO, *The St. Louis Republic*, Apr. 21, 1901, p. 54.

2. "Use of birds in millinery," Milwaukee, WI, *Weekly Advocate*, Oct. 21, 1898, p. 7.

3. "The aigret," Pine Bluff, AR, *Daily Graphic*, Jan. 7, 1897, p. 3.

4. "A reform begun in Brooklyn," Brattleboro, VT, *Phoenix*, May 28, 1897, p. 2.

5. "Busy women," St. Paul, MN, *The Saint Paul Globe*, June 2, 1898, p. 4.

6. "Brief bits of news," Kansas City, MO, *Journal*, Jan. 27, 1898, p. 1.

7. "A reform begun in Brooklyn," Brattleboro, VT, *Phoenix*, May 28, 1897, p. 2.

8. "Clubs," Baraboo, WI, *News*, Apr. 5, 1905, p. 8

9. "The colossal woman," Ellsworth, ME, *American*, Jan. 25, 1899, p. 5.

10. *Ibid.*

11. "Of interest to women," Paris, KY, *Bourbon News*, Oct. 30, 1903, p. 3.

12. "Protect the birds," Omaha, NE, *Daily Bee*, Nov. 1, 1903, p. 1.

13. "A recent London dispatch…," Colfax, WA, *Gazette*, Apr. 24, 1908, p. 4.

14. "Since a wounded bird…," Morris County, NJ, *Chronicle*, Apr. 24, 1906, p. 2.

15. "Pledged to defy Dame Fashion," Denver, CO, *Rocky Mountain News*, May 8, 1898, p. 13.

16. "Observations," Lincoln, NE, *Courier*, Apr. 17, 1897, p. 2.

17. "Fashion will not be crushed," Washington, D.C., *Evening Star*, May 1, 1897, p. 20.

18. "New York fashions," Oskaloosa, IA, *Evening Herald*, May 11, 1897, p. 4.

Chapter 36

1. "Fads and fancies in realm of fashion," Chickasha, OK, *The Chickasha Daily Express.*, May 14, 1915, Second Section, p. 7.

2. "Few birds of paradise," Marietta, OH, *Daily Leader*, Jan. 24, 1896, p. 4.

3. "Few birds of paradise," Silver City, NM, *The Eagle*, Feb. 12, 1896, p. 14.

4. "Paradise plumes in last stand," Worcester, MA, *Democrat and the Ledger-Enterprise*, Aug. 12, 1922, p. 8.

5. "Craze of women for feathered hats makes American water fowl scarce," El Paso, TX, *Herald*, Dec. 30, 1910, p. 6.

6. "The birds on the hats," Wichita, KS, *Eagle*, Jan. 4, 1890, p. 7.

7. "Milliners and plumage birds," New York, NY, *Tribune*, March 14, 1909, p. 13.

8. "Women's realm," Highland County, VA *Recorder*, July 25, 1902, p. 4.

9. "Spare the birds," Omaha, NE, *Daily Bee*, Dec. 12, 1897, Part III, p. 18.

10. "Peril of the birds," Wheeling, WV, *Daily Intelligencer*, Dec. 21, 1896, p. 6.

11. "The osprey and the egret," New York, NY, *Tribune*, Jan. 31, 1897, p. 3.

12. "The last heron," Eagle River, WI, *Review*, July 30, 1909, p. 6.

13. "Where birds are safe from guns," Fergus County, MT, *Democrat*, Mar. 8, 1910, p. 4.

14. *Ibid.*

15. "Protect white egrets," Indianapolis, IN, *Times*, Aug. 10, 1933, p. 1.

16. "Millinery bird," Washington, D.C., *Evening Star*, Apr. 24, 1955, p. D-22.

Chapter 37

1. "About the fashions," Salt Lake, UT, *Herald*, Jan. 24, 1892, p. 15.

244   Notes—Chapters 38, 39, 40, 41, 42 and Epilogue

2. "Ostrich farming paying," Aberdeen, SD, *The Aberdeen Democrat*, Nov. 25, 1904, p. 7.

3. "Turn a deaf ear," Saint Paul, MN, *The Saint Paul Globe*, Nov. 16, 1898, pp. 1 & 2.

4. *Ibid.*

5. "Women's page," Topeka, KS, *State Journal*, Aug. 3, 1901, Last Edition, Editorial Section, p. 13.

6. "To put the curl back in feathers," Washington, D.C., *The Washington Herald*, May 20, 1915, p. 7.

7. "Feather vs Plume—What's the difference? | WikiDiff." There is a difference between a feather and a plume for millinery purposes. A feather is a branching, hair-like structure that grows on the bodies of birds. It is used for flight, swimming, protection and display. A plume is a feather of a bird, especially a large or showy one.

8. "The ostrich plume supply very limited," Fargo, ND, *Forum and Daily Republican*, Mar. 25, 1916, p. 3.

9. "No song birds," Indianapolis, IN, *Journal*, Nov. 5, 1899, Part One, p. 4.

10. "Bird breeding for plumes," Danville, PA, *Montour American*, Dec. 10, 1908, p. 3.

Chapter 38

1. "Pioneers for conservation murdered for bird feathers," Englewood, FL, *Sun*, July 9, 2000, "Our Town," p. 4.

2. "Ruthless bird slaughter," Kalamazoo, MI, *Gazette*, June 2, 1901, p. 6.

3. "Arkansas game laws," Mena, AR, *Weekly Star*, Oct. 15, 1908, p. 5.

4. "Game wardens: What they do," Richmond, VA, *Times Dispatch*, July 30, 1905, p. 16.

5. "Local officers, too," Richmond, VA, *Times Dispatch*, Jan. 4, 1917, p. 10.

6. "Wood's funeral is not mine...," Virginia, MN, *Enterprise*, Apr. 10, 1914, p. 2.

7. "Maine's canine game warden," Washington, D.C., *Evening Star*, Dec. 29, 1900, p. 15.

8. "Saving the birds," Salt Lake, UT, *Telegram*, Jan. 15, 1910, p. 17.

9. "Pioneers for conservation murdered for bird feathers," Englewood, FL, *Sun*, July 9, 2000, "Our Town," p. 4.

Chapter 39

1. "The birds," Brattleboro, VT, *Phoenix*, May 28, 1897, p. 1.

2. "Fashion the foe of songbirds," Mineral Point, WI, *Tribune*, Dec. 28, 1899, p. 7.

3. "Word comes from Burlington...," Pittsburgh, PA, *Dispatch*, Mar. 23, 1890, p. 4.

4. "The peacock owned...," Brattleboro, VT, *Phœnix*, Jan. 18, 1907, p. 9.

5. "The birds," Brattleboro, VT, *Phoenix*, May 28, 1897, p. 1.

6. "Many bird skins burned," Wilmington, DE, *Evening Journal*, Nov. 27, 1899, p. 3.

7. "Something for women to think of," Brattleboro, VT, *Phoenix*, Apr. 17, 1896, p. 4.

8. "Deadly work of plumage hunters," San Francisco, CA, *Call-Bulletin*, Feb. 17, 1910, p. 4.

9. "The last heron," Eagle River, WI, *Review*, July 30, 1909, p. 6.

10. "Pennsylvania's game law," Philadelphia, PA, *Inquirer*, Feb. 4, 1897, p. 6.

11. "Brooks the bird slayer," New Haven, CT, *Morning Journal and Courier*, Jan. 19, 1898, p. 7.

12. "The ladies of Winona...," Little Falls, MN, *Herald*, Dec. 9, 1898, p. 4.

13. "Observations," Lincoln, NE, *Capital City Courier*, Apr. 24, 1897, p. 1.

14. *Ibid.*

15. "Millinery birds harmful," Portland, OR, *Morning Oregonian*, June 1, 1912, p. 5.

16. "Society for Protection...," London, England, *St. James Gazette*, Feb. 11, 1903, p. 8.

Chapter 40

1. "Barnyard 'Biddy' with a Bit of Dye Becomes Swanky Bird of Paradise," Washington, D.C., *Evening Star*, July 2, 1925, p. 20.

2. "Artificial animal eyes," Bryan, TX, *Daily Eagle*, Sept. 26, 1896, p. 3.

3. "A woman's occupation," Indianapolis, IN, *Journal*, Nov. 5, 1899, Part One, p. 4.

4. "Peril of the birds," Wheeling, WV, *Daily Intelligencer*, Dec. 21, 1896, p. 6.

Chapter 41

1. https://www.brainyquote.com/authors/john-james-audubon-quotes.

2. "The birds," Brattleboro, VT, *Phoenix*, May 28, 1897, p. 2.

3. "Birds in millinery," Jackson, MI, *Citizen Patriot*, May 25, 1898, p. 4.

4. "Our woman's world," Middletown, DE, *Transcript*, Apr. 14, 1906, p. 1

5. "Many bird skins burned," Wilmington, DE, *Evening Journal*, Nov. 27, 1899, p. 3.

6. "Millinery birds," Lincoln, NE, *Courier*, May 5, 1900, p. 2.

Chapter 42

1. "Ask World Powers to Protest Birds Fourteen Nations to Be Arrayed Against Cruelty of Millinery," Trenton, NJ, *Evening Times*, July 26, 1910, p. 12.

2. *Ibid.*

3. "Insect pests," Des Moines, IA, *Iowa State Bystander*, July 12, 1912.

4. "Nations to shield birds," Falls City, NE, *The Falls City Tribune*, July 29, 1910, p. 6.

Epilogue

1. "A society known...," Salt Lake City, UT, *The Intermountain Catholic*, June 25, 1904, p. 2.

Notes—Appendix A and B

2. "Barnyard 'Biddy' with a Bit of Dye Becomes Swanky Bird of Paradise," Washington, D.C., *Evening Star*, July 2, 1925, p. 20.

3. https://www.fws.gov/southeast/pubs/key-west-great-white-heron-tearsheet.pdf.

4. "Collins Island resting place for marine bird," Lakeland, FL, *Evening Telegram*, July 25, 1921, p. 2.

5. "Owl perches on fall hat," Ottawa, IL, *Free Trader-Journal and Fair Dealer*, July 25, 1921, p. 3.

6. "Smart Silks for Spectator Sports," Holt County, NE, *Frontier*, June 25, 1936, p. 7.

Appendix A

1. "Enforcing Lacey law," Washington D.C. *Evening Star*, Oct. 15, 1900, p. 15

Appendix B

1. In Japan birds are regarded as sacred, and for this reason the agriculturist gladly shares with them the fruit of his toil.

Bibliography

Books

Alderfer, Jonathan. *National Geographic Kids Bird Guide of North America*. 2nd ed. Washington, D.C.: National Geographic, 2018.

Merriam, Florence A. *How Birds Affect the Farm and Garden*. New York: Forest and Stream, 1896.

Miller, Olive Thorne. *True Bird Stories*. Boston: Houghton Mifflin, 1903.

Sharp, Arthur G. *The Bear and the Northland: Legendary Coast Guard Cutters in the Alaskan Ice*. Jefferson, NC: McFarland, 2023.

Walker, Margaret Coulson. *Bird Legend and Life*. New York: Baker and Taylor, 1908.

Online Sources

Key West and Great White Heron National Wildlife Refuges. U.S. Fish and Wildlife Service. https://www.fws.gov/sites/default/files/documents/key-west-great-white-heron-tearsheet.pdf.

Palmer, T.S. "Federal Game Protection—A Five Years' Retrospect." *Yearbook of the Department of Agriculture*. Accessible at the National Agricultural Library Digital Collections. https://naldc.nal.usda.gov/download/IND43647023/PDF.

"US declares 23 bird, fish and other species extinct." BBC.com, September 29, 2021. https://www.bbc.com/news/world-us-canada-58740362.

Yeoman, Barry. "Why the Passenger Pigeon Went Extinct." *Audubon* online. https://www.audubon.org/magazine/may-june-2014/why-passenger-pigeon-went-extinct.

Newspapers

"About the fashions," Salt Lake, UT, *Herald*, Jan. 24, 1892, p. 15.

"Address Delivered by G.O. Shields Before the High School," Caldwell, ID, *Gem State Rural*, Apr. 1, 1909, p. 3.

"Advertisement," Washington, D.C., *Evening Star*, Nov. 28, 1885, p. 3.

"After bird trappers," Wood County, WI, *Reporter*, June 23, 1898, p. 3.

"After the milliners," Brownsville, TX, *Daily Herald*, Oct. 21, 1902, p. 2.

"After the women," Wausau, WI, *Pilot*, Dec. 9, 1902, p. 8.

"Against foreign game," New York, NY, *Tribune*, Feb. 28, 1906, p. 2.

"The aigret," Pine Bluff, AR, *Daily Graphic*, Jan. 7, 1897, p. 3.

"Aigrettes," Fargo, ND, *The Forum and Daily Republican*, Oct. 10, 1913, p. 4.

"Aigrettes cause trouble," Portland, OR, *Oregonian*, Apr. 3, 1909, p. 10.

"Anecdotes concerning well known people," Washington, D.C., *Evening Star*, June 22, 1913, p. 5.

"The animosity of the Rev. Ann," Kansas City, MO, *Journal*, Nov. 20, 1898, p. 4.

"The application of the interstate...," Omaha, NE, *Daily Bee*, Feb. 19, 1903, p. 6.

"Arbor and bird day," Mt. Sterling, KY, *Advocate*, Oct. 25, 1911, p. 6.

"Arbor Day," Point Pleasant, WV, *Register*, Mar. 23, 1910, p. 9.

"Arkansas game laws," Mena, AR, *Weekly Star*, Oct. 15, 1908, p. 5.

"The Arkansas legislature...," Missouri Valley, IA, *Times*, May 4, 1899, p. 8.

"Artificial animal eyes," Bryan, TX, *Daily Eagle*, Sept. 26, 1896, p. 3.

"Ask World Powers to Protect Birds," Trenton, NJ, *Evening Times*, July 25, 1910, p. 9.

"Asked to tell the truth about bird plumage in millinery," Bridgeport, CT, *Evening Farmer*, Feb. 23, 1911, p. 3.

"At a recent meeting...," Deland, FL, *The Florida Agriculturist*, Aug. 11, 1897, p. 509.

"Audubon Protecting Florida for 100 years," Daytona, Beach, FL, *The News-Journal*, Apr. 3, 2000, p. 4.

"Audubon Society," Mesa, AZ, *Free Press*, Feb. 11, 1898, p. 2.

"The Audubon Society...," Salisbury, CT, *Connecticut Western News*, Mar. 23, 1899, p. 2.

"An Audubon Society," Savannah, GA, *The Savannah Morning News*, Mar. 11, 1903, p. 12.

"The Audubon Society and the milliners," Bennington, VT, *Evening Banner*, Aug. 14, 1909, p. 2.

"Audubon Society criticizes Hughes," Newark, NJ, *Evening Star and Newark Advertiser*, Aug. 23, 1913, p. 4.

"Audubon Society has made the District bird

248 Bibliography

sanctuary," Washington, D.C., *Evening Star*, Apr. 1, 1923, p. 72.

"Audubon Society to start campaign," Los Angeles, CA, *Daily Herald*, Apr. 29, 1909, p. 11.

"Automobile coats made of Hummingbird skins," Washington, D.C., *Herald*, Apr. 27, 1913, Magazine Section, p. 6.

"Barnyard Biddy with a Bit of Dye Becomes Swanky Bird of Paradise," Washington, D.C., *Evening Star*, July 2, 1925, p. 20.

"The Bay state's bird law," New Haven, CT, *Daily Morning Journal and Courier*, Aug. 12, 1897, p. 6.

"A bill has been introduced...," Manitowoc, WI, *Pilot*, Feb. 28, 1889, p. 3.

"Bird breeding for plumes," Danville, PA, *Montour American*, Dec. 10, 1908, p. 3.

"Bird day in the schools," Nebraska City, NE, *Conservative*, Feb. 16, 1899, p. 5.

"A bird day suggested," Chicago, IL, *Universalist*, Aug. 8, 1896, p. 3.

"Bird destroyers," Rock Island, IL, *Argus*, June 24, 1886, p. 2.

"Bird destroyers," Stanford, KY, *Semi-Weekly Interior Journal*, June 25, 1886, p. 4.

"Bird hats popular," Ardmore, OK, *Daily Ardmoreite*, Feb. 24, 1922, p. 3.

"Bird millinery," Marietta, OH, *Daily Leader*, Jan. 6, 1900, p. 2.

"Bird murder and women's hats," Kendallville, IN, *Daily Sun*, Aug. 18, 1898, p. 3.

"Bird pluming on spring millinery," Salt Lake, UT, *Tribune*, Mar. 7, 1905, p. 7.

"Bird poachers get off easy," Honolulu, HI, *The Hawaiian Gazette*, March 18, 1910, p. 8.

"Bird poachers get off easy," Honolulu, HI, *Hawaiian Star*, May 31, 1910, 2nd Edition, p. 2.

"Bird protection," Montgomery, AL, *Advertiser*, May 3, 1903, p. 11.

"Bird protection," Saint Paul, MN *Daily Globe*, June 4, 1894, p. 4.

"Bird protectors," Danville, PA, *Montour-American*, May 28, 1908, p. 3.

"Bird story is a fake," Wilmington, DE, *The Daily Republican*, Mar. 17, 1900, p. 2.

"The birds," Bennington, VT, *Phœnix*, Aug. 20, 1897, p. 1.

"The birds," Brattleboro, VT, *Phoenix*, May 28, 1897, p. 1.

"Birds and millinery," Honolulu, HI, *Pacific Commercial Advertiser*, Aug. 9, 1909, p. 4.

"Birds and trees," Nebraska City, NE, *Conservative*, Apr. 24, 1902, p. 9.

"The birds are here," Hocking, OH, *Sentinel*, Mar. 28, 1901, p. 1.

"Birds as millinery ornaments," New York, NY, *Tribune*, July 19, 1897, p. 2.

"Birds in millinery," Jackson, MI, *Citizen Patriot*, May 25, 1898, p. 4.

"Birds killed for plumage," Bennington, VT, *Evening Banner*, May 13, 1909, p. 2.

"Birds of millinery," New York, NY, *Evening World*, Sept. 17, 1894, Extra 2 O'Clock, p. 2.

"Birds on fall hats," New York, NY, *Tribune*, Aug. 29, 1902, p. 7.

"Birds on hats," Manning, SC, *Times*, Apr. 26, 1905, p. 6.

"Birds on hats," Seattle, WA, *The Seattle Star*, Mar. 22, 1905, Night Edition, p. 4.

"The birds on my lady's hat," San Francisco, CA, *Call*, Nov. 21, 1897, p. 22.

"The birds on the hats," Wichita, KS, *Eagle*, Jan. 4, 1890, p. 7.

"Birds protected," Trenton, NJ, *Evening Times*, Apr. 18, 1911, p. 6.

"Birds useful in the war against cotton boll weevil," Deland, FL, *The Florida Agriculturist*, May 29, 1907, p. 1.

"Black belt of cruelty," Bamberg, SC, *Herald*, Jan. 12, 1911, p. 7.

"The blackbird of commerce," Wichita, KS, *Eagle*, Nov. 14, 1889, p. 2.

"Bloody Easter bonnets," Washington, D.C., *Herald*, Apr. 10, 1911, p. 4.

"Brief bits of news," Kansas City, MO, *Journal*, Jan. 27, 1898, p. 1.

"Brooks the bird slayer," New Haven, CT, *Morning Journal and Courier*, Jan. 19, 1898, p. 7.

"Busy women," St. Paul, MN, *The Saint Paul Globe*, June 2, 1898, p. 4.

"But the Japanese don't care," Honolulu, HI, *The Hawaiian Gazette*, Mar. 18, 1910, p. 8.

"Canary cage hat sets avenue agape," New York, NY, *Tribune*, Apr. 19, 1915, p. 3.

"Case against jeweler dropped," San Francisco, CA, *Call Bulletin*, Feb 17, 1910, p. 3.

"Census of our birds," Bismarck, ND, *Daily Tribune*, Jan. 29, 1908, p. 8.

"Census of our birds," Coeur d'Alene, ID, *Evening Press*, Feb. 1, 1908, p. 3.

"Ceylon's rough trip," Honolulu, HI, *Evening Bulletin*, July 17, 1901, p. 1.

"Chanticleer's Day," Massillon, OH, *Evening Independent*, Apr. 1, 1910, p. 10.

"Charles W. Farmer...," New Haven, CT, *Daily Morning Journal and Courier*, Mar. 22, 1900, p. 4.

"Cheaper to pay rent than move," Honolulu, HI, *The Hawaiian Gazette*, Feb. 15, 1910, p. 2.

"Clubs," Baraboo, WI, *News*, Apr. 5, 1905, p. 8.

"Clubs to study birds," Red Lodge, MT, *Picket*, Sept. 20, 1901, p. 2.

"Cobb's Island shooting," Washington, D.C., *Evening Star*, July 28, 1884, p. 4.

"Collins Island resting place for marine bird," Lakeland, FL, *Evening Telegram*, July 25, 1921, p. 2.

"The colossal woman," Ellsworth, ME, *American*, Jan. 25, 1899, p. 5.

"Contemporary opinion," Wilmington, DE, *Evening Journal*, Apr. 4, 1900, p. 2.

"A correspondent of THE STAR...," Washington, D.C.. *Evening Star*, Oct. 2, 1886, p. 4.

"A country without song birds," Washington, D.C., *Evening Star*, Nov. 27, 1885, p. 3.

"Craze of women for feathered hats makes

Bibliography

American water fowl scarce," El Paso, TX, *Herald*, Dec. 30, 1910, p. 6.

"Cruelty to be checked," Birmingham, AL, *Age-Herald*, May 11, 1903, p. 4.

"Crusade against stuffed birds," Richwood, OH, *Gazette*, Jan. 22, 1903, p. 4.

"Crusade upon bird killers," Wilmington, DE, *Gazette and State Journal*, Mar. 22, 1900, p. 3.

"Dainty millinery," Milan, TN, *Exchange*, June 12, 1886, p. 2.

"Dairy legislation," North Yakima, WA, *Ranche and Range*, Jan. 1, 1898, p. 11.

"Dead birds and nose rings," Brattleboro, VT, *Vermont Phoenix*, Sept. 24, 1886, p. 2.

"Deadly work of plumage hunters," San Francisco, CA, *Call-Bulletin*, Feb. 17, 1910, p. 4.

"A despicable device," Omaha, NE, *Daily Bee*, Jan. 1, 1905, p. 10.

"Destruction of birds," Salt Lake City, UT, *The Evening Telegram*, Nov. 26, 1906, p. 7.

"Destruction of our birds," Newberry, SC, *Herald and News*, Oct. 27, 1886, p. 3.

"The destruction of our wild birds," Newark, NJ, *Newark Star and Newark Advertiser*, Feb. 11, 1908, p. 8.

"Dr. Hornaday asks Senate to stop bird slaughter," Honolulu, HI, *Star-Bulletin*, June 6, 1913, p. 3.

"The dove is the most popular bird...," Richmond, KY, *The Climax*, June 21, 1899, p. 4.

"Dress reformers," Wilmington, DE, *Evening Journal*, p. 4.

"Eaglets," Chicago, IL, *Eagle*, May 12, 1900, p. 4.

"The egret again," New York, NY, *Tribune*, May 26, 1906, p. 4.

"An eminent scientist...," Idaho Territory *Semi-Weekly World*, Apr. 2, 1886, p. 1.

"The enchanted types," St. Louis, MO, *The St. Louis Republic*, Apr. 21, 1901, p. 54.

"The end of fine feathers," Wilmington, DE, *Daily Commercial*, April 27, 1922, p. 4.

"The era of individuality," Bridgeport, CT, *Evening Farmer*, Apr. 23, 1910, p. 8.

"The era of individuality," The Guthrie, OK, *Daily Leader*, June 11, 1910, p. 6.

"Every milliner in town to be arrested," Spokane, WA, *Press*, Sept. 20, 1904, p. 1.

"Fads and fancies in realm of fashion," Chickasha, OK, *The Chickasha Daily Express*, May 14, 1915, Second Section, p. 7.

"Fair sex scored," San Francisco, CA, *Morning Call*, Nov. 15, 1894, p. 4.

"Fall bonnets," Canton, MS, *American Citizen*, Sept. 12, 1874, p. 1.

"Fall fashions," Washington, D.C., *National Tribune*, Nov. 11, 1886, p. 7.

"Fall hats depend on fine feathers for 'chic-ness,'" South Bend, IN, *News-Times*, Aug. 7, 1921, p. 21.

"Fancy feathers worn by women come from rooster," Washington, D.C., *Times*, Nov. 29, 1912, Last Edition, p. 13.

"Farm notes," Watertown, WI, *Republican*, Jan. 21, 1880, p. 3.

"Farmer's best friend," Billings, MT, *Gazette*, Apr. 6, 1909, p. 4.

"Fashion letter," Lafayette, LA, *Advertiser*, Oct. 13, 1894, p. 8.

"Fashion notes," Abbeville, SC, *Press and Banner*, Oct. 25, 1882, p. 1.

"Fashion notes," Washington, D.C., *Bee*, Feb. 13, 1892, p. 2.

"Fashion robs the farmers," Lincoln County, OR, *Leader*, Oct. 15, 1909, p. 2.

"Fashion the foe of song birds," Mineral Point, WI, *Tribune*, Dec. 28, 1899, p. 7.

"Fashion will not be crushed," Washington, D.C., *Evening Star*, May 1, 1897, p. 20.

"Fashion wrinkles," Washington, D.C., *Evening Star*, Oct. 7, 1882, p. 7.

"Fashion's fancies," Watertown, WI, *Republican*, Jan. 21, 1880, p. 3.

"Fear feather frame-up," Belfast, ME, *Republican Journal*, Jan. 29, 1914, p. 2.

"Fear feather frame-up," Butler, MO, *Weekly Times*, Jan. 15, 1914, p. 4.

"Fear feather frame-up," Ellsworth, ME, *American*, Jan. 14, 1914, p. 4.

"Feathers of game birds," New York, NY, *The New York Times*, May 5, 1913, p. 8.

"Federal court in session," Honolulu, HI, *Evening Bulletin*, July 2, 1910, p. 1.

"Few birds of paradise," Marietta, OH, *Daily Leader*, Jan. 24, 1896, p. 4.

"Few birds of paradise," Silver City, NM, *The Eagle*, Feb. 12, 1896, p. 14.

"Fine the city sportsmen," St. Paul, MN, *Daily Globe*, Apr. 8, 1887, p. 4.

"Fines for birds on hats," Fredericksburg, VA, *Free-lance*, Nov. 3, 1908, p. 2.

"Flowers in fancy colors and shapes," Salt Lake, UT, *Tribune*, Mar. 7, 1905, p. 11.

"For Easter morning," New York, NY, *Sun*, Mar. 22, 1891, p. 24.

"For protection of birds," Salisbury, CT, *Connecticut Western News*, Mar. 10, 1898, p. 3.

"For the fair sex," Opelousas, LA, *Courier*, Apr. 28, 1894, p. 6.

"For women only," WaKeeney, KS, *Western Kansas World*, June 5, 1886, p. 10.

"Forbidden aigrettes offered for sale," San Francisco, CA, *Call Bulletin*, Feb 15, 1910, p. 1.

"Forecast of fashions," Minneapolis, MN, *Journal*, Sept. 5, 1903, p. 12.

"Foreign game possession," New Haven, CT, *Daily Morning Journal and Courier*, Aug. 25, 1905, p. 8.

"Freaks of fashion," Mt. Sterling, KY, *Advocate*, May 26, 1909, p. 1.

"French milliners foresee billion dollar trade year," Washington, D.C. *Evening Star*, Apr. 4, 1920, p. 47.

"Fruit shipment proves successful," Wailuku *Maui News*, Oct. 12, 1907, p. 1.

"The game dealers' new bill," New York, NY, *Tribune*, Mar 19, 1906, p. 6.

"The game is not for us alone," New York, NY, *Sun*, Nov. 12, 1919, p. 20.

250   **Bibliography**

"Game laws and millinery," Washington, D.C. *Evening Times*, Aug. 22, 1898, p. 4.

"A game warden…," Mount Holly, NJ, *News*, August 8, 1911, p. 2.

"Game wardens indorse Audubon Society," Savannah, GA, *Morning News*, Mar. 12, 1903, p. 12.

"Game wardens: what they do," Richmond, VA, *Times Dispatch*, July 30, 1905, p. 16.

"Great decrease of the bird life," Birmingham, AL, *Age-Herald*, May 9, 1898, p. 4.

"The great economic importance of sea gulls," Ottumwa, IA, *Tri-Weekly Courier*, Dec. 23, 1915, p. 6.

"The habit of using the heads…," Manchester, IA, *Democrat*, June 7, 1899, p. 6.

"Hat bill of bachelor raises ire of fair sex," Washington, D.C., *The Washington Times*, Mar. 25, 1910, Last Edition, p. 15.

"A high-hat symposium," Sacramento, CA, *Daily Record-Union*, Feb. 12, 1887, p. 6.

"Home hints," San Saba County, TX, *News*, July 21, 1893, p. 3.

"Honey for the ladies," Omaha, NE, *Daily Bee*, July 24, 1887, p. 11.

"Hummingbird export," Trenton, NJ, *Evening Times*, July 1, 1943, p. 2.

"Importance of bird protection," Washington, D.C., *Evening Star*, Oct. 15, 1900, p. 15.

"In defense of the birds," Seattle, WA, *Post-Intelligencer*, Sept. 29, 1895, p. 6.

"In the style," Mitchell, SD, *Capital*, Oct. 22, 1886, p. 3.

"In woman's world," Jersey City, NJ, *The Jersey City News*, July 13, 1899, p. 3.

"Insect pests," Des Moines, IA, *Iowa State Bystander*, July 12, 1912.

"Iowa opinions and notes," Marshalltown, IA, *Evening Times-Republican*, May 8, 1902, p. 4.

"Is an ornithologist…," El Paso, TX, *Daily Herald*, May 9, 1900, Last Edition, p. 2.

"Is king of the Laysan Island," Honolulu, HI, *Hawaiian Star*, Nov. 16, 1904, p. 7.

"It is now a misdemeanor…," Manitowoc, WI, *Pilot*, Apr. 14, 1887, p. 2.

"Japanese bird pirates busy," Honolulu, HI, *Evening Bulletin*, March 28, 1911, p. 1.

"Judge sustains Max Schlemmer," Honolulu, HI, *The Hawaiian Gazette*, Apr. 22, 1910, p. 3.

"Kate Jordan's chat," Gloucester County, NJ, *Democrat*, Sept. 6, 1894, p. 1.

"Kilbourn events," Wausau, WI, *Pilot*, Nov. 5, 1907, p. 5.

"Killing birds on the side," Honolulu, HI, *Pacific Commercial Advertiser*, Feb. 4, 1910, pp. 1 & 4.

"King Max of Laysan is deposed," Honolulu, HI, *The Hawaiian Gazette*, Nov. 12, 1909, p. 5 "Ladies spare the birds," New York, NY, *Sun*, Dec. 1, 1897, p. 7.

"King of Laysan is on trial," Honolulu, HI, *Hawaiian Star*, Oct. 27, 1910, 2nd Edition, p. 8.

"The ladies of Winona…," Little Falls, MN, *Herald*, Dec. 9, 1898, p. 4.

"The last heron," Eagle River, WI, *Review*, July 30, 1909, p. 6.

"Late summer millinery," Washington, D.C., *Evening Journal*, July 23, 1903, p. 3.

"Law knocks out fashion in Missouri," Jasper, IN, *Weekly Courier*, Mar. 31, 1905, p. 5.

"A law that may react badly," New York, NY, *Evening World*, Feb. 6, 1913, Final Edition, p. 18.

"Laysan Island," Honolulu, HI, *Pacific Commercial Advertiser*, Oct. 19, 1897, p. 2.

"Legal status of birds," Atlanta, GA, *Semi-Weekly Journal*, May 1, 1902, p. 6.

"The legislature of Illinois…," Opelousas, LA, *Courier*, Apr. 29, 1899, p. 1.

"Life and doom of the hummingbird," Washington, D.C., *Evening Star*, Apr. 4, 1909, p. 36.

"Local Japanese had planned to secure control of Laysan," Honolulu, HI, *Hawaiian Star*, Nov. 11, 1909, 2nd Edition, p. 1.

"Local officers, too," Richmond, VA, *Times Dispatch*, Jan. 4, 1917, p. 10.

"Louisiana game laws hold good," Birmingham, AL, *Age-Herald*, Mar. 18, 1907, p. 5.

"Magazines and notes," Washington, D.C., *National Tribune*, Oct. 16, 1902, p. 2.

"Maine's canine game warden," Washington, D.C., *Evening Star*, Dec. 29, 1900, p. 15.

"Maine's wicked doves," New Haven, CT, *Daily Morning Journal and Courier*, Dec. 17, 1903, Part 2, p. 11.

"Man who sent up costs of feathers for hats," Fargo, ND, *Forum and Daily Republican*, Apr. 19, 1913, p. 1.

"Many bird skins burned," Wilmington, DE, *Evening Journal*, Nov. 27, 1899, p. 3.

"Massacre of birds," Trenton, NJ, *Times*, Mar. 24, 1888, p. 1.

"Merchants and Audubonites agree," Jersey City, NJ, *Evening Journal*, May 11, 1903, p. 14.

"Migratory bird law said still effective," Klamath Falls, OR, *The Evening Herald*, Jan. 17, 1919, p. 4.

"Milliners and plumage birds," New York, NY, *Tribune*, March 14, 1909, p. 13.

"Milliners aren't worried," Stark County, OH, *Democrat*, Jan. 23, 1903, Weekly Edition, p. 7.

"Milliners promise to protect birds," St. Louis, MO, *Republic*, May 10, 1903, p. 49.

"Millinery," Martinsburg, WV, *Independent*, Aug. 14, 1886, p. 4.

"Millinery ad," Washington, D.C., *Times*, Sept. 29, 1898, p. 10.

"Millinery bird," Washington, D.C., *Evening Star*, Apr. 24, 1955, p. D-22.

"Millinery birds," Lincoln, NE, *Courier*, May 5, 1900, p. 2.

"Millinery birds harmful," Portland, OR, *Morning Oregonian*, June 1, 1912, p. 5.

"Missouri bars birds upon hats of women," Washington, D.C., *Times*, Apr. 2, 1905, Metropolitan Section, p. 12.

"Missouri hats go democratic," Minneapolis, MN, *Journal*, Mar. 29, 1905, p. 2.

Bibliography

"Moline mention," Rock Island, IL, *Argus*, Mar. 28, 1903, last edition, p. 2.

"More birds found," Portland, OR, *Morning Oregonian*, p. 12.

"More work for Audubons," New Haven, CT, *Daily Morning Journal and Courier*, Sept. 29, 1902, p. 6.

"Mosquitoes and whip-poor-wills," Kingwood, WV, *Argus*, Sept. 12, 1901, p. 1.

"Most in demand," Washington, D.C., *Evening Star*, Oct. 13, 1900, p. 17.

"Move to stop bird slaughter," Salem, OR, *Daily Capital Journal*, Feb. 14, 1913, p. 5.

"Murderous millinery," Barre, VT, *Daily Times*, Dec. 2, 1905, p. 3.

"Murderous millinery," Coalville, UT, *Times*, Apr. 17, 1903, p. 3.

"Murderous millinery," Griggs County, ND, *Courier*, Sept. 8, 1898, p. 3.

"Murderous millinery," Prescott, AZ, *Daily News*, Mar. 10, 1908, p. 2.

"Must have birds' wings," Salt Lake, UT, *Herald*, November 15, 1899, p. 7.

"Nations to shield birds," Falls City, NE, *The Falls City Tribune*, July 29, 1910, p. 6.

"A new bird book," Washington, D.C., *Times*, July 5, 1903, Editorial Society Fiction, p. 5.

"New complaint made against milliner," San Francisco, CA, *Call Bulletin*, Feb. 18, 1910, p. 16 "New ideas in toilettes," Fulton County, PA, *News*, Oct. 24, 1901, p. 6.

"A new fad," Kansas City, KS, *Daily Journal*, Oct. 18, 1896, p. 5.

"The new game law," Lexington, MO, *The Lexington Intelligencer*, May 6, 1905, p. 2.

"New York fashions," Oskaloosa, IA, *Evening Herald*, May 11, 1897, p. 4.

"New York fashions," Staunton, VA, *Spectator and Vindicator*, Oct. 21, 1897, p. 1.

"The New York Graphic," Salisbury, CT, *Connecticut Western News*, May 5, 1886, p. 1.

"News and notes for women," Freeland, PA, *Tribune*, Jan. 10, 1898, p. 2.

"News from the schools," Minneapolis, MN, *Journal*, Mar. 11, 1906, p. 5.

"No feathers' on their wives' bonnets," Mahaska County, IA, *Oskaloosa Herald*, Feb. 2, 1888, p. 3.

"No law against wearing feathers," Morris County, NJ, *Chronicle*, June 5, 1906, p. 6.

"No law against wearing feathers," New York, NY, *Sun*, June 1, 1906, p. 8.

"No more feathers on Iowa women's hats," Leon, IA, *Reporter*, May 3, 1906, p. 1.

"No pity for the birds," New York, NY, *Sun*, Jan. 16, 1898, p. 5.

"No pity for the birds," Portland, ME, *Daily Press*, Apr. 14, 1898, p. 4.

"No song birds," Indianapolis, IN, *Journal*, Nov. 5, 1899, Part One, p. 4.

"Not worth the price," Topeka, KS, *The Topeka State Journal*, Apr. 17, 1897, p. 6.

"Notice of dissolution of copartnership," San Francisco, CA, *Call Bulletin*, Jul 3, 1910, p. 58.

"Novelties in trimming," St. Louis, MO, *Republic*, Oct. 27, 1901, Magazine Section, p. 48.

"Observations," Lincoln, NE, *Capital City Courier*, Apr. 17, 1897, p. 2.

"Observations," Lincoln, NE, *Capital City Courier*, Apr. 24, 1897, p. 1.

"Of interest to women," Paris, KY, *Bourbon News*, Oct. 30, 1903, p. 3.

"Of lovely woman and the fashions," San Francisco, CA, *Call*, Mar. 16, 1909, p. 6.

"An Ohio girl...," Savannah, GA, *Morning News*, Dec. 17, 1884, p. 2.

"Oklahoma has joined the states," Fulton County, PA, *News*, Nov. 15, 1917, p. 8.

"On rights of birds," El Paso, TX, *Herald*, Apr. 11, 1912, p. 10.

"On the crime of wearing an aigrette," El Paso, TX, *Herald*, Apr. 17, 1911, 3d Extra, p. 6.

"The osprey and the egret," New York, NY, *Tribune*, Jan. 31, 1897, p. 3.

"Ostrich farming paying," Aberdeen, SD, *The Aberdeen Democrat*, Nov. 25, 1904, p. 7.

"Ostrich farms," Birmingham, AL, *Age-Herald*, Nov. 29, 1908, p. 16.

"The ostrich plume supply is very limited," Fargo, ND, *Forum and Daily Republican*, Mar. 25, 1916, p. 36.

"Our woman's world," Middletown, DE, *Transcript*, Apr. 14, 1906, p. 1.

"Owl perches on fall hat," Ottawa, IL, *Free Trader-Journal and Fair Dealer*, July 25, 1921, p. 3.

"Owls new in favor," East Carroll Parish, LA, *Banner-Democrat*, Feb. 12, 1898, p. 4.

"Paradise plumes in last stand," Colfax, IN, *Clinton County Review*, May 25, 1922, p. 7.

"Paradise plumes in last stand," Worcester, MA, *Democrat and the Ledger-Enterprise*, Aug. 12, 1922, p. 8.

"The passing of the birds," Portland, ME, *Daily Press*, Jan. 1, 1894, p. 4.

"The passing of the birds," Salt Lake, UT, *The Herald*, Jan. 28, 1894, p. 3.

"The peacock owned...," Brattleboro, VT, *Phoenix*, Jan. 18, 1907, p. 9.

"Pennsylvania's game law," Philadelphia, PA, *Inquirer*, Feb. 4, 1897, p. 6.

"Peril of the birds," Wheeling, WV, *Daily Intelligencer*, Dec. 21, 1896, p. 6.

"Pioneers for conservation murdered for bird feathers," Englewood, FL, *Sun*, July 9, 2000.

"Pitiful sight," Reynoldsville, PA, *The Star*, June 26, 1907, p. 2.

"Pleading for the birds," New York, NY, *Tribune*, June 27, 1886, p. 11.

"Pledged to defy Dame Fashion," Denver, CO, *Rocky Mountain News*, May 8, 1898, p. 13.

"Poachers are free," Honolulu, HI, *Hawaiian Star*, Mar. 15, 1910, p. 1.

"Points on the fashion," Washington, D.C., *Evening Star*, Nov. 6, 1886, p. 7.

"Pounces on the milliners," Astoria, OR, *Morning Astorian*, Apr. 3, 1909, p. 1.

Bibliography

"Pretty gown models of Paris," Richmond, VA, *Planet*, Nov. 21, 1903, p. 7.

"Prof. Scott relieves the women," Marble Hill, MO, *Press*, June 5, 1901, p. 2.

"Protect the birds," Las Vegas, NM, *Optic*, Apr. 4, 1913, p. 7.

"Protect the birds," Omaha, NE, *Daily Bee*, Nov. 1, 1903, p. 1.

"Protect the birds," Oxford, MS, *Eagle*, June 26, 1902, p. 4.

"Protect white egrets," Indianapolis, IN, *Times*, Aug. 10, 1933, p. 1.

"Protecting birds from millinery trade," Forest City, SD, *Press*, Feb. 27, 1914, p. 3.

"Protecting the birds," Tazewell, VA, *Republican*, June 14, 1900, p. 2.

"Protection of American birds," St. Louis, MS, *Sea Coast Echo*, September 6, 1913, p. 5.

"Public kept in ignorance of new laws," Newark, NJ, *Evening Star and Newark Advertiser*, Aug. 4, 1911, Last Edition, p. 6.

"The question box," Newark, NJ, *Evening Star and Advertiser*, Jan. 16, 1908, p. 4.

"Rail slaughter near Belmont," San Francisco, CA, *Call*, Oct. 30, 1897, p. 10.

"Rare birds, ancient gluttons," Grenada, MS, *Sentinel*, June 12, 1886, p. 3.

"Rare birds saved through new laws," Trenton, NJ, *Evening Times*, Aug. 21, 1912, p. 14.

"A recent London dispatch...," Colfax, WA, *Gazette*, Apr. 24, 1908, p. 4.

"A reform begun in Brooklyn," Brattleboro, VT, *Phoenix*, May 28, 1897, p. 2.

"Reiner," Portland, OR, *Oregon Journal*, Jan 11, 1909, p. 2.

"The relation of birds to crops," Deland, FL, *Florida Agriculturist*, May 6, 1896, p. 301.

"Renewal of war against milliners," Defiance, OH, *Crescent News*, Jan. 30, 1903, p. 6.

"Report *Thetis* away for good," Honolulu, HI, *Evening Bulletin*, Aug. 26, 1911, p. 1.

"Robbing the birds," Waterbury, CT, *Democrat*, Aug. 4, 1897, p. 1.

"Robin most numerous of birds," Shepherdstown, WV, *Register*, Feb. 25, 1915, p. 1.

"Roosevelt had no authority," Honolulu, HI, *Pacific Commercial Advertiser*, Apr. 9, 1910, p. 1.

"Ruthless bird slaughter," Kalamazoo, MI, *Gazette*, June 2, 1901, p. 6.

"The saddest cat in Maine...," Augusta, ME, *Daily Kennebec Journal*, May 15, 1900, p. 4.

"Saturday Globe glances," Saint Paul, MN, *Globe*, Mar. 23, 1901, p. 4.

"Saving the birds," Salt Lake, UT, *Telegram*, Jan. 15, 1910, p. 17.

"Save the birds," St. Louis, MO, *Republic*, Sept. 1, 1901, Part I, p. 6.

"Saving the birds," Washington, D.C., *Evening Star*, Dec. 29, 1909, p. 9.

"Saving the birds from fashion's murderous banditti," Honolulu, HI, *The Hawaiian Star*, Jan. 4, 1911, 2nd Edition, p. 6.

"Say that birds belong to all," Fargo, ND, *The Forum and Daily Republican*, Nov. 2, 1915, p. 18.

"Scale of Feather Fines...," Portland, OR, *Oregonian*, Apr. 14, 1909, p. 16.

"Scarcity of birds," Nashville, TN, *Union and American*, Oct. 22, 1871, p. 4.

"Schlemmer accusers jailed," Honolulu, HI, *Hawaiian Star*, Mar. 16, 1910, p. 2.

"Schlemmer faces an indictment," Honolulu, HI, *Hawaiian Star*, Feb. 7, 1910, p. 1.

"Schlemmer, Max," Honolulu, HI, *Hawaiian Star*, Feb. 5, 1910, 2nd Edition, p. 12.

"Schlemmer not guilty," Honolulu, HI, *Evening Bulletin*, Oct. 28, 1910, p. 1.

"Sell the birds," Topeka, KS, *The Topeka State Journal*, Oct. 7, 1897, p. 8.

"Shooting the wild turkeys," New Haven, CT, *Morning Journal and Courier*, Oct. 6, 1892, p. 1.

"Since a wounded bird...," Morris County, NJ, *Chronicle*, Apr. 24, 1906, p. 2.

"Slaughter of birds," Wheeling, WV, *Daily Intelligencer*, Dec. 11, 1897, p. 4.

"Slaughter of song birds," Wilmington, DE, *Gazette and State Journal*, March 29, 1900, p. 1.

"Slaughter of songbirds for food is awful," Clarksburg, WV, *Daily Telegram*, Nov. 22, 1915, p. 10.

"Slaughter of the birds," Holbrook, AZ, *Argus*, Nov. 17, 1906, p. 7.

"Smaller hats will obtain," Los Angeles, CA, *Herald*, Apr. 4, 1909, p. 6.

"Smart Silks for Spectator Sports," Holt County, NE, *Frontier*, June 25, 1936, p. 7.

"Smith afraid tariff bill will kill legislation for protection of bird life," Oakley, ID, *Herald*, Aug. 1, 1913, p. 6.

"Social gossip," Indianapolis, IN, *State Sentinel*, Apr. 7, 1886, p. 3.

"Society for Protection...," London, England, *St. James Gazette*, Feb. 11, 1903, p. 8.

"A society has been organized," Harrison, NE, *Sioux County Journal*, Apr. 4, 1895, p. 2.

"A society known...," Salt Lake City, UT, *The Intermountain Catholic*, June 25, 1904, p. 2.

"A society which is laboring...," Hickman, KY, *Courier*, May 17, 1895, p. 1.

"Some could be spared," Salt Lake, UT, *Herald-Republican*, Apr. 21, 1910, p. 4.

"Some of the details," Wessington Springs, Dakota, *Herald*, Apr. 23, 1886, p. 6.

"Something for women to think of," Brattleboro, VT, *Phoenix*, Apr. 17, 1896, p. 4.

"Songs without words; birds without song," New Haven, CT, *Daily Morning Journal and Courier*, Jan. 1, 1897, p. 7.

"Spare the birds," Fairfield, SC, *News and Herald*, April 27, 1898, p. 4.

"Spare the birds," Omaha, NE, *Daily Bee*, Dec. 12, 1897, Part III, p. 18.

"Spare the birds," Salt Lake City, UT, *Tribune*, Dec. 7, 1909, p. 5.

"Spare the birds and beasts," Wilmington, DE, *Daily Republican*, June 9, 1886, p. 1.

Bibliography

"Special school days," Marshalltown, IA, *Evening Times-Republican*, Feb. 8, 1901, p. 3.

"Still hope for the ladies," Canton, OH, *Stark County Democrat*, Jan. 27, 1903, p. 6.

"Stuffed birds on hats," Philadelphia, PA, *Inquirer*, June 7, 1899, p. 16.

"Tariff worries fishermen," New York, NY, *Sun*, July 13, 1913, Sixth Section, p. 7.

"Telegraphic news," Wailuku-Maui, HI, *News*, Jan 11, 1913, p. 2.

"There is an enormous demand...," Atlanta, GA, *Semi-Weekly Journal*, May 1, 1902, p. 6.

"*Thetis* to visit Hawaii," Honolulu, HI, *Star-Bulletin*, Nov. 15, 1912, p. 2.

"Those Delaware birds," Wilmington, DE, *Evening Journal*, Mar. 23, 1900, p. 1.

"Thousands of wild geese," Lake Providence, LA, *The Banner-Democrat*, Sept. 28, 1901, p. 2.

"Timely topics," Marshalltown, IA, *Evening Times-Republican*, May 26, 1904, p. 3.

"To prevent killing of birds," Wilmington, DE, *Evening Journal*, Mar. 13, 1900, p. 1.

"To protect birds," Washington, D.C., *Evening Star*, July 5, 1901, p. 9.

"To put the curl back in feathers," Washington, D.C., *The Washington Herald*, May 20, 1915, p. 7.

"Turn a deaf ear," Saint Paul, MN, *The Saint Paul Globe*, Nov. 16, 1898, pp. 1 & 2.

"Two senators who saved birds," Portland, OR, *Morning Oregonian*, Sept. 11, 1913, p. 8.

"Two sides of the bird questions," Washington, D.C.. *Evening Times*, Apr. 15, 1898, p. 4.

"The tyranny of fashion," Bridgeton, NJ, *Pioneer*, Nov. 23, 1899, p. 4.

"The tyranny of fashion," Decorah, IA, *Public Opinion*, Dec. 13, 1899, p. 2.

"Ugliest Girl in New York before and after milliners tried their arts on her," Pendleton, OR, *East Oregonian*, Feb. 21, 1920, Daily Evening Edition, Sec. 2, p. 11.

"Uncle Sam puts up bars against odd variety of importations," Washington, D.C., *Herald*, Nov. 17, 1912, Magazine Section, p. 9.

"Unique autumn outing hats," San Francisco, CA, *Call*, Sept. 28, 1902, p. 7.

"Use of birds in millinery," Milwaukee, WI, *Weekly Advocate*, Oct. 21, 1898, p. 7.

"U.S.S. *Thetis* departs for Hawaii," Honolulu, HI, *Evening Bulletin*, May 13, 1911, p. 15.

"Value of birds to the farmers," The Rockford, IL, *Morning Star*, Jan. 17, 1907, p. 10.

"Velvet to be popular again this season," Little Falls, MN, *Herald*, Sept. 20, 1901, p. 7.

"A victory for the birds," New York, NY, *Sun*, Sept. 18, 1913, p. 8.

"Walmsley fines to schools," Potosi, MO, *Journal*, June 27, 1906, p. 3.

"Walmsley, the author...," Mexico, MO, *Message*, Feb. 7, 1907, p. 4.

"Want grange's help in revising bird laws," Eugene, OR, *East Oregonian*, Nov. 16, 1909, Evening Edition, p. 3.

"Wear feathers? Never," Annapolis, MD, *Evening Capital and Maryland Gazette*, Apr. 13, 1916, p. 4.

"Wearing song birds," Jamestown, ND, *Weekly Alert*, Dec. 16, 1886, p. 6.

"Wearing songbirds," Richland County, ND, *The Wahpeton Times*, Dec. 9, 1886, p. 2.

"The week in society," San Antonio, TX, *The Daily Express*, Sept. 21, 1902, p. 22.

"What the government is doing," Washington, D.C., *Evening Star*, Jan. 11, 1914, p. 4.

"Where birds are safe from guns," Fergus County, MT, *Democrat*, Mar. 8, 1910, p. 4.

"While we are talking," Missoula, MT, *Daily Missoulian*, Mar. 16, 1913, Morning, p. 4.

"White egrets increasing," Bridgeport, CT, *Evening Farmer*, Aug. 20, 1912, p. 12.

"Wholesale milliners defeat bird lovers," Salem, OR, *Daily Capital Journal*, Aug. 12, 1913, p. 3.

"Why not ornithology?" Tazewell, VA, *Republican*, June 14, 1900, p. 2.

"Why they are there," Heppner, OR, *The Gazette-Times*, Sept. 11, p. 2.

"Will not hold school fair," Richmond, VA, *Times Dispatch*, Feb. 4, 1911, p. 8.

"The winged wheel," New Haven, CT, *Morning Journal and Courier*, Sept. 28, 1882, p. 1.

"The woman ahead," Canton, SD, *Dakota Farmers' Leader*, Jan. 3, 1902, p. 5.

"The woman who wears a bird....," Saint Paul, MN, *Globe*, May 13, 1903, p. 4.

"A woman's cause that should win," Americus, GA, *Times-Recorder*, June 28, 1913, p. 4.

"Woman's League and ornithology," Los Angeles, CA, *Herald*, Feb. 28, 1897, p. 15.

"A woman's occupation," Indianapolis, IN, *Journal*, Nov. 5, 1899, Part One, p. 4.

"Woman's realm," Highland County, VA, *Recorder*, July 25, 1902, p. 4.

"Women and birds," Baton Rouge, LA, *Banner-Democrat*, Sept. 28, 1901, p. 1.

"The women of Arkansas," New Haven, CT, *Daily Morning Journal and Courier*, Apr. 25, 1899, p. 4.

"Women's page," Topeka, KS, *The Topeka State Journal*, Aug. 3, 1901, Last Edition, Editorial Section, p. 13.

"Wood's funeral is not mine...," Virginia, MN, *Enterprise*, Apr. 10, 1914, p. 2.

"Woodward & Lothrop ad," Washington, D.C., *Evening Star*, Sept. 20, 1902, p. 7.

"Word comes from Burlington...," Pittsburgh, PA, *Dispatch*, Mar. 23, 1890, p. 4.

"The work of a lover of birds," Morrisville, VT, *News and Citizen*, Apr. 16, 1902, p. 2.

"The work will go on," Wilmington, DE, *Gazette and State Journal*, Mar. 22, 1900, p. 3.

Index

Numbers in **bold italics** indicate pages with illustrations

Abell, Representative 99
Agreement on the Conservation of Albatrosses and Petrels 224
Alabama 120–121
Alaska 13, 102
albatross 32, 76, 225
Algerine 146
Allen & King 140
American Game Protective Association 109, 233
American Milliners Association 170–171
American Ornithologists Union 86, 88–89, 106, 125, 153, 155, 169, 187
American Society for Prevention of Cruelty to Animals 119
Anti-Audubon Society 98
Antivivisection Society 192
Arbird Day 90, 92
Arbor Day 92, 95–97, 194
Arkansas 156, 190, 208, 231
Armstrong, William H. 4
Arnold, William W. **220**
Association for the Protection of Birds 153
Astley, Hubert D. 71
Atlanta *Journal* 88
Audubon, John James 219
Audubon Magazine 198
Audubon Society 10, 17, 20, 24, 31, 35–36, 49, 56, 59, 62, 65, 67, 77–79, 80–86, 88–91, 95–100, 105–106, 112–114, 116–118, 120, 122–123, 125–128, 132–133, 136, 141, 146, 151–154, 156, 159, 164–165, 167–170, 172–177, 179, 188–189, 192–194, 200, 209–211, 214, 216–217, 223
auk 56, 130, 197, 227
Australia 31, 66, 71
Austria 223

Babcock, C.H. 93
Bache, Rene 130–131

Bachman's warbler 1
Bagnall and Boughton 139
Baker, Helen 183
Baldwin Jewelry Company 139
Baltimore, Maryland 19, 94, 221
Bangor, Maine 44
Barbaroo, Wisconsin 193
Barbeau, Elmer 215
Barnegat, New Jersey 212
Battledore Islands 108
Bavaria 223
Beach Haven, New Jersey 212
Beautiful Joe 49
Becker, Mrs. 141
Bedford City, Virginia 96
Beeman, Henry 81, 88, 92
Behm, Mrs. 140
Belgium 223
Belhaven, North Carolina **14**
Bennett, John 153
Berlin, Germany 46, 88, 177, 223–224
Bird Day 92–93, 95–97, 194
Bird Island 146
Bird Life International 224
Bird Lore 88, 90
bird of paradise 2, 20, 31–33, 69, 70, 111, 115, 121, 164, 181, 183, 194, 197–198, 227–228
black skimmer 19
blackbird 9, 29, 36, 44, 86, 100, 123, 129, 131, 153, 157, 163, 191, 212, 216–217, 222, 231
blue jay 8, 26–27, 42, 45, 163
bluebird 15, 57, 129, 222
bobolink 48, 87, 167
bobwhite 34
Bok, Edward 191–192
Bortree, M.R. 82
Boston, Massachusetts 40, 49, 81, 126–127, 131, 165
Bowdish, B.S. 105, 198
Bradley, Guy M. 210–211
brahma 26
Branchville, South Carolina 210
brant 123

Brattleboro, Vermont 212
Brazil 131
Breckons, R.W. 149
Bridgehampton, New York 94
Brockport, New York 15
Brooks, Oliver N. 214
Brown, J. Hamilton 95
Brown, Julius I. (Mrs.) 38
Bruner, Lawrence 95
Bryn Mawr, Pennsylvania 93
Buffalo, New York 169
Burlington, Iowa 212
buzzard 70

California 14–15, 82, 103, 121, 136, 165, 190, 217
Canada 89, 102, 117, 134, 231
canary 28, 46–47, 104, 123, 173, 188
Cape Cod 1
Caproni, Valerie 233
Carnegie Institution 106
Carter, Lucy 195–196
Cavendish-Bentinck, Winifred Anna 193
cedar bird 129
Central America 14
chab 168
Chamberlain, George E. 111, 113–114, 117
chanticleer 31
Chapman, Frank. M. 88, 92, 98–99
Charlotte Harbor, Florida 210
Chicago, Illinois 9–10, **72**, 81–84, **103**, 192, 217–218
Chicago *Tribune* 156
chicken 26, 29, 121, 160, 165, 181–182, 216–218, 224
China 105, 217, 219
Christmas Island 146
Churchill, Winston 216
Cincinnati, Ohio 82, 84
Clark, Edward B. 82–83
Cobb's Island, Maryland 19
Coco Chanel **7**
Colombia 131

256 **Index**

Colorado 194–195, 231
Columbia, South Carolina 156
Columbus, Ohio 83
Conlan, Judge 139
Connecticut 14, 95, 97, 135, 152–153, 214
Constantinople 57
Convention for the Protection of Birds Related to Agriculture 84
Convention on Nature Protection and Wildlife Preservation in the Western Hemisphere 85
Cooper Ornithological Club of California 58
coot 123
crane 15, 157, 198, 215, 232
crow 10, 26, 44–45, 123, 153, 157, 160, 163, 175, 221, 231
Cuba 1
Cullen, Judge 134
Cunneen, John 136
curlew 123, 232
Curry, George S. 151
Cuvier Press Club 84

Dearby, Mary 173
Deasy, Judge 139
Delaware 152–154, 172
Delaware Game Protective Association 153
Denmark 223
Denver, Colorado 193–194–196
DeVoe, Helen 86–87
Dickens, Charles 98, 179
dove 14–15, 80, 106, 119, 168, 189
Dublin Society for the Protection of Birds 227
Duchess of Fife 100
Duchess of Somerset 215
duck 15, *28*, 29, 76–78, 87, 101, 103–194, 121, 123, 126, 160, 162, 190, 217–218, 221, 228, 231
Duke of Bedford 215
Dutcher, Adam 99
Dutcher, William 24, 67, 94, 99, 136, 223–224

eagle 26–27, 29, 35 76, 216–217, 233
East Hampden, Maine 189
East Indies 1
East Indian 29
Eastern Female High School 94
Ecuador 131
egg collecting) 14, 75, 123; *see also* egg collectors
egg collectors 13, 15, 59
egret 31, 58, 67, 69–70, 74–75, 94, 112, 115, 117, 123, 125, 127, 172, 176, 181–182, 185, 194, 199–201, 212–213, 227, 231–232
Egypt 25, 69, 75, 133, 206

England 1, 31, 43, 59, 71, 75, 80, 87, 113, 133, 223, 229
Engle, J. 127, 128
Enosburg, Vermont 14

Fanning Island, Hawaii 146
Farmer, Charles W. 98–99, 133, 136, 172, 198
Faulkner Island, Connecticut 214
Field and Stream 20, 50
finch 20, 74, 168
Finley, Mrs. 140
Finley, William L. 137–142
Fitzgerald, Asst. District Attorney 140–141
flamingo 15, 112, 215
Flamingo, Florida 210
flicker 210
Florida 14, 74, 81, 94, 106, 108, 112, 119, 121, 165, 179, 198–200, 210–211, 213, 228, 232
Fond du Lac, Wisconsin 31
Forbes, S.A. 8
Forbush, Edward Howe 17, 119, 126–129
Forest, Jules 197
Forest and Stream 155
France 80, 217, 223, 229
Francis Amendment 165
Frear, Walter Francis 150

Gainsborough hat 204–205
gallinule 123, 168
Gardiner's Island, New York 167
geese 15, 76–77, 103–104, 121, 123, 162–163, 165, 190, 217, 228
Georgetown, South Carolina 76
Georgia 44, 101, 119
Germany 36, 57, 80, 88, 126, 217, 223
Givry, Annette 49
goura 127
Grand, Sarah 62
Great Britain 74, 84, 109, 223; *see also* England
Grebasch, Louis 82
grebe 67, 123, 125, 217, 228, 231
Greenbaum, Samuel (Justice) 134
Gregg, Mary 153
Grieg, D.B. 146
Grinnell, George Bird 20–*21*
Griswold, Hattie Tyng 59–60, 62
grouse 15, 123, 127, 217
guano 144–145, 147–148, 150
Guatemala 111
guinea hen 221
gull 15, 17, 19, 26–27, 29–30, 33, 35, 67, 70, 76, 78, 96, 100, 119, 121, 123, 125, 127, 153, 157,

168, 200, 212, 217, 221–222, 228, 231
Gzisol, Mayene 184

Hackett, Thomas Reed 193
Hamilton, A.L. 173–174
Hamilton, Ohio 84
Harper's Bazaar 129
Harper's Weekly 87, 129, 200
Harris Game Bill 155
Harwood, Ernest E. 200–201
Hawaii 108, 144–148
hawk 10, 15, 24, 44, 46, 123, 157, 160, 172, 212
heath hen 15, 106
Hendry, Marshal 149
Henshaw, H.W. 160
heron 2, 15, 22, 30–32, 34–35, 53–54, 56, 67, 69, *72*, 76, 94, 101, *107*, 117, 119, 123, 125, 127, 139, 142, 165, 183–185, 197–200, 212–214, 227–228, 231–232
Herotin, Mrs. 193
Hertzberg, L.S. (Mrs.) 206
Hill, John 133–135
Hoar, George Frisbie *102*, 105, 193
Holland 223
Honolulu, Hawaii 143–146, 148–149
Hornaday, William T. *12*, 67, 111–114, 117, 135, 175–176
Hotchkiss, Ella Antoinette 39–40, 49, 50–51, 102
Howard, L.O. 187
Hughes, Governor 76
Hughes, William 174–176
hummingbird 20, 32, 36, 46–47, 67, 70, 80, 123, 126, 129–131, 216, 222
Hungary 223
Huntington, New York 206

ibis 15, 69, 112, 123, 212, 228, 232
Idaho 103
Illinois 82–83, 95, 156, 231
impeyan 183
India 70, 75, 80
Indiana 8, 231
International Committee for the Protection of Birds 224
International Convention on the Protection of Birds 224
International Ornithological Congress 223
Iowa 97, 123
Iroquois 145
Isaac, Charles 139
Italians 13–14, 121
Italy 71, 75, 217, 223

Jacobs, Robert 189
Jacobs, W.V.E. 143, 151

Index

257

Japan 2, 71, 143–151, 219, 233
Jefferson, Ohio 93
Jessup, Morris K. 99
Job, Herbert 200
Johnson, Charles 174–176
Johnson, L.J. 215
Johonot, Marion 62
Jordan, David Starr 71, 136
Judd, Albert 149

Kansas 15, 156
Kansas City, Missouri 2, 160
Kauai O'o 1
Kentucky 96–97
Kenwood, Illinois 10
Kerouac, Jack 129
Key West National Wildlife
  Refuge 228
Kiernan, W.E. 138, 140–141
kingbird 45
kingfisher 36, 43–43, 80, 157,
  231
Klamath Lake, Oregon 139; see
  also Lake Klamath
Knox, Henry 223–224
Kukui 145–146
Kurzman, Charles 116

LaBranche, G.M.I. 113
Lacey, John F. 81, 102
Lacey Act 80–82, 84, 105, 107,
  111, 134
Ladies Home Journal 191
Lake Klamath, Oregon 214
Lane, Harry 111, 113–114, 117
Lange, Professor 94
lark 14, 24, 44, 60, 87, 168, 170,
  214, 222
Laysan duck 148
Laysan finch 148
Laysan Island 143–150
Laysan Millerbird 148
League of American Sportsmen
  81
Le Palais Royale 141
Levy Bill 77
Lewton, F.L. 216, 227
Lincoln, Nebraska 195–196
Linnaean Society 167
Lipman, Wolfe & Company
  140–142
Lisianski Island 143–144,
  149–151
Little Bird Hunter 60–*61*
Little Gull Island, New York
  167
London, England 1, 23, 30, 36,
  51, 57. 67, 80, 114, 130–131, 177,
  184, 193, 215, 217
London Saturday Review 23
Long Island 1
Long-Sheide Bill 77
loon 228, 231
lophophore 129, 181

Los Angeles, California 39
Louisiana 42–43, 96, 108,
  119–121, 130, 200
Loveday, H.W. 82
Lovell, M.A. (Mrs.) 192, 203
Lowengart & Company 142
Lyttleton, Cameron 215

Macmillan Publishers 90
Maddox, Thomas (Judge) 133
Maine 167, 209
Manitoba 231
marabou 31, 33
March Island, New Jersey 96
market hunter 13, 190, 198–199,
  213–214
Martin, A.P. 163
Martine, James Edward 175
Maryland 95, 167
Maryland Wildlife Protection
  Association 95
Massachusetts 14, 24, 40–41,
  161–163, 168, 231
McCracken, Josephine Clifford
  52
McKinley, William 39, 81, 148
McLean, George P. 108–*109*
McLeod, Columbus P. (George)
  208, 210–211
Meier & Frank Company
  140–142
Merriam, C. Hart (Dr.) 44–45
Mexico 14, 47, 82, 117, 127, 199,
  233
Miami, Florida 228
Michigan Sportsmen's
  Association 156
Migratory Bird Treaty 84,
  109–110, 232
Milford Chronicle 153
Millinery Jobbers Association
  126
Millinery Merchants Protective
  Association 173
Millinery Trade Review 33, 69,
  98, 105, 125, 153, 179, 183–184,
  219
Milwaukee, Wisconsin 126
Minneapolis, Minnesota 203
Minnesota 209
Mississippi 42–43
Missouri 159–162, 190
mockingbird 22, 170, 233
Moline, Illinois 95
Montana 92, 103, 142
mud hen 123

Nashville, Tennessee 131–132
National Association of Game
  Commissioners 78
Nebraska 14, 231
Nevada 231
New Castle, Pennsylvania 93
New Guinea 31, 70–71, 197

New Jersey 29, 96, 122, 135, 157,
  164, 167, 175
New Mexico 112
New Orleans, Louisiana 121,
  160
New York Association for the
  1844 Protection of Game 155
New York City 2, 19, 30, 51, 56–
  57, 81, 88, 105–106, 121–122,
  126, 134, 153, 165, 169, 172–173,
  186, 188, 192, 200, 206, 208,
  213, 221
New York Graphic 168
New York Millinery Merchants
  Protective Association
  125–126
New York Poultry and Game
  Trade Association 135
New York State 1, 14, 76–77,
  79, 86, 92, 99, 106, 109, 128,
  133–134, 155, 157, 165, 168, 174,
  188, 200, 231
New York Zoological Society
  12, 112, 174, 177
Nicholas, Cheryl 228
nightingale 71
Norfolk, Virginia 48, 60
North Carolina 15, 44
Norway 223

Oahu County, Hawaii 145
Oberholser, H.C. 227
O'Connor, Warden 100
Ohio 82, 84, 121
Oil City, Pennsylvania 93
Oklahoma 121
Olson, Justice 138, 141
Ontario 231
Oregon 15, 56, 103, 136, 138, 142,
  165, 213–214
oriole 8–9, 24, 129–130
Orpheus Sailing Club 19
osprey 75, 115, 172, 194
ostrich 26, 30, 32–33, 50, 55–57,
  65, 71, 89, 152, 160, 162, 164,
  168, 182, 192, 195–196, 202–
  203, 205–206, 216–217
Ostrich Feather Manufacturers
  Association 56–57
Ouida 66; see also Rame, Maria
  Louis
owl 15, 17, 25–27, 33, 44, 46, 65,
  119, 123, 160, 162, 212, 216, 228

Palmer, T.S. 4, 106, 224
parakeet 15, 36, 74, 80, 112
Paris, France 2, 4, 19, 23, 27,
  30, 32, 39, 46, 50–51, 56, 75,
  115, 126, 130, 143, 170, 177, 184,
  197, 201
parrot 15, 20, 28–29, 65, 94, 123,
  162, 181, 227
Parsons, Jon S. 209
Partners in Flight 224

Index

partridge 15, 78, 104, 106, 121, 123, 135, 209, 217
passenger pigeon 2, 15, 22, 74, 155, 227
peacock 31, 54, 181, 212
Pearson, T. Gilbert 67, 108, 112, 114, 117, 121–122, 147, 165, 176, 224
peashooter 49–50, 59–60, 94, 214
pelican 26, 60, 67, 123, 125, 217, 231
Pelican Island, Florida 108
Pelican Island, Texas 60
penguin 228
Pennsylvania 14, 44, 98–99, 135, 155, 168, 200, 209–210, 214
Pennsylvania Railroad Company 154
Pennsylvania Sportsman's Association 214
pheasant 15, 78, 104, 123, 127, 169, 215, 217, 228
Philadelphia, Pennsylvania 1, 50, 81, 165, 192, 206
pigeon 15, 27, 33, 121, 126, 155, 161–162, 164, 208, 217, 221
Pinecastle, Florida 198
Pittsburgh, Pennsylvania 126
plover 123, 212, 217
poachers 143–147, 149–151
Poland fowl 26
Pollard, John Garland 209
Poole, A.D. 153–154
Porterfield, J.C. 83
Portland, Oregon 118, 138, 142
pothunter 19, 81, 190, 208–209, 214
prairie chicken 123
Princess Louise 100
Princess of Wales 100
Puck 3
purple martin 24, 152

quail 15, 106, 121. 123, 159
Quebec 231
Queen Alexandra 194
quetzal 111
Quill, Dorothy 180–182

Radcliffe's Bill 164
rail 15, 123
Rame, Maria Louise 66
ravens 157
Rawlins, District Attorney 150–151
recreational hunter 214
Reed, Ethel *32*
reed birds 48, 81
Reeves, L.P. 210
Reiner, A. 138
Rhode Island 231
Rhodes, Warden 160
Rice, Secretary 156

rice bird 231
Roberts, W.H. 62
Robertson, Judge 149–150
Roberty, Mathilda Georgina 193
robin 8, 45, 60, 81, 94, 119, 198, 210, 214, 222
Robins, Mrs. Edward 153
Roosevelt, Theodore 100, 108, 139, 143–144, 150, 157
rooster 25–27, 31, 126, 182, 217
roseate spoonbill 112, 212, 227
Rouger, Emmanuel 146
Royal Society for the Protection of Birds 193
Russell, Lillian *2*
Russell, Kansas 93
Russia 29, 133, 217, 223, 233; *see also* Soviet Union
Russian cock 26
Ryan, Bess 173
Ryan, Charles I. 83–84

Sacramento *Record-Union* 192
Saint Joseph, Missouri 160
Saint Louis, Missouri 160, 192
Saint Paul, Minnesota 94
San Francisco, California 190
sandpiper 15, 123, 212
Savannah, Georgia 100
Schlemmer 142–150, 152
Schorger, A.W. 74
Scientific American 129
Scip (dog) 209
Scotland 75, 133
Scott, William Earl Dodge 62
Seattle, Washington 86
Selborne Society 193
Shakespeare, William 178
Shaw, Anna (Rev.) 65, 203–*204*
Shawkey, M.P. 96
Shea Law 54
Shields, George O. 36, 46
Shiras, George III 107
Silz, August 133–135, 138
Skinner, Charles R. 92
Slotkin, N. 82
Smith, Bothsworth 215
Smith, Hoke 174–176
Smith, Walter 210
smuggling 115–118
snipe 15, 123, 208
snow bunting 212
Society for Protection of Birds 67, 74, 215
South Africa 57, 71, 206
South America 27, 29, 31, 66, 75, 80, 130–131, 184, 199, 217
South Carolina 101, 132, 165, 231
South Dakota *12*, 231
Soviet Union 233
sparrow 8, 10, 22, 24, 30, 40, 80, 119, 123, 131, 157, 160, 162–163, 181, 231

Spenser, Edmund 55
Starbuck, Alex 84
starling 129, 157, 168, 181
Stone, Witmer 153, 155, 172, 200
Stuart, Katharine H. 96
Supreme Court, Missouri 160
swallow 8, 13, 19, 24, 60, 89, 167, 170, 222
swan 104, 123, 216, 228
Sweden 223

Talmage, DeWitt (Dr.) 25
tanager 9, 129–130
Tate, Arthur 212
tattler 123
Tennessee 44
tern 15, 17, 19, 25, 35, 67, 76, 89, 96, 108, 119–120, 123, 125, 127, 132, 167–168, 200, 212, 222, 227–228, 231
Texas 80, 190, 209–210, 217, 232–233
Thetis 143, 145–146, 148–149, 151
thrush 10, 129, 210, 214
Titusville, Pennsylvania 93
Tonkin 80
Truelock, Charles 84
Tulare, Nevada 79
Tunnell, Ebe 153
turkey 15, 121, 123, 132, 162, 182, 204, 217, 218

ugliest girl 173
Underwood, George W. 82, 175
Underwood Tariff Bill 110–112, 115, 117, 175
Union City, New Jersey 157
U.S. Department of Agriculture 8, 44–45, 77, 81, 95, 104, 187
U.S. Fish and Wildlife Service 233
U.S. Supreme Court 5, 132–138
Urner, Mabel Herbert 53–55
Utah 15

Vancouver, Washington 215
Venezuela 184, 199
Vermont 42, 231
Vescott, A. 101
vireole 168
Virginia 208–209
vulture 76

Wade, Joseph M. 129
Wade, Rufus R. 162–163
Wagner, Constable 140
Walmsley, Harry R. 159
Walmsley Fish and Game Act 159–160
Wantagh, New York 221–222
warbler 9, 168
Ward, John 153
Warner, A.C. 160
Warner, Charles Dudley 50

Index

Warner, Tennessee 106
Washington County, Maryland 4
Washington D.C. 10, *91*, 105–106, 144, 151, 177, 221, 231
Washington State 15, 103, 123
Water Fowl Club of America 76
Webb, Edwin Y. 113–114
Weber, A. 160
Weed, Clarence 81
Weeks, John W. 108–*109*
Weeks-Mclean Law 108–111, 117, 233

West Virginia 96–97
Whipple, James S. 135
White Badge of Cruelty 54, 136
Wilcox, Edna Wheeler 36, 39, 75
Wilder, A.A. 150
Williams, John Sharp 175
Wilson, William 221–222
Wilton, South Dakota 180
Winona, Minnesota 214
Wisconsin 14, 74, 156, 168
Women's Christian Temperance Union (W.C.T.U.) 65, 203

Women's League for Animals 177
woodcock 106, 123, 155, 218
Woodhouse, Samuel Washington *23*
woodpecker 1, 9–10, 15, 24, 40, 45, 48, 60, 106
wren 222
Wyoming 15, 92

Yellowstone National Park 92

Milton Keynes UK
Ingram Content Group UK Ltd.
UKHW010756280724
446142UK00008B/145